Surviving Dictatorship

Written as a book for undergraduate students, *Surviving Dictatorship* is also both a visual sociology and a case study that communicates the lived experience of poverty and powerlessness in an authoritarian society: Pinochet's Chile. So powerful a shaper of the poor's experience is a dictatorship, that one might add "degree of authoritarianism" (conceived by Patricia Hill Collins) as an additional dimension to the idea. This book is ideal for courses in social inequalities, poverty, and race/class/gender.

Jacqueline Adams is the author of articles and a book on the making of dissident art under dictatorship, shantytown women's reactions to the end of dictatorship, exile, and decision-making about migration. She has won a Pacific Sociological Association award and had an article selected as a "benchmark" by SAGE. She has worked as an assistant professor of sociology in Hong Kong, senior researcher at the University of Coimbra, and research fellow and visiting scholar at the University of California at Berkeley, where she is currently based.

Contemporary Sociological Perspectives
Edited by **Valerie Jenness**, University of California, Irvine and **Jodi O'Brien**, Seattle University

This innovative series is for all readers interested in books that provide frameworks for making sense of the complexities of contemporary social life. Each of the books in this series uses a sociological lens to provide current critical and analytical perspectives on significant social issues, patterns and trends. The series consists of books that integrate the best ideas in sociological thought with an aim toward public education and engagement. These books are designed for use in the classroom as well as for scholars and socially curious general readers.

Published:

Political Justice and Religious Values by Charles F. Andrain

GIS and Spatial Analysis for the Social Sciences by Robert Nash Parker and Emily K. Asencio

Hoop Dreams on Wheels: Disability and the Competitive Wheelchair Athlete by Ronald J. Berger

The Internet and Social Inequalities by James C. Witte and Susan E. Mannon

Media and Middle Class Mom: Images and Realities of Work and Family by Lara Descartes and Conrad Kottak

Watching T.V. Is Not Required: Thinking about Media and Thinking about Thinking by Bernard McGrane and John Gunderson

Violence Against Women: Vulnerable Populations by Douglas Brownridge

State of Sex: Tourism, Sex and Sin in the New American Heartland by Barbara G. Brents, Crystal A. Jackson and Kate Hausbeck

Social Statistics: The Basics and Beyond by Thomas J. Linneman

Sociologists Backstage: Answers to 10 Questions About What They Do by Sarah Fenstermaker and Nikki Jones

Gender Circuits by Eve Shapiro

Transform Yourself, Transform the World: A Practical Guide to Women's and Gender Studies by Michelle Berger and Cheryl Radeloff

Stargazing: Celebrity, Fame, and Social Interaction by Kerry Ferris and Scott Harris

The Senses of Self, Culture and Society by James Tyner

Who Lives, Who Dies, Who Decides? by Sheldon Ekland-Olson

The Womanist Idea by Layli Maparyan

Forthcoming:

Families Worldwide by Agnes Riedmann

Issues, Implications, and Practices in Mixed Method Designs by Jodi O'Brien

Law in Action by Ryken Grattet

Surviving Dictatorship

A Work of Visual Sociology

Jacqueline Adams
University of California, Berkeley

Routledge
Taylor & Francis Group

NEW YORK AND LONDON

Please visit the companion website at www.routledge.com/cw/adams

First published 2012
by Routledge
711 Third Avenue, New York, NY 10017

Simultaneously published in the UK
by Routledge
2 Park Square, Milton Park, Abingdon, Oxon OX14 4RN

Routledge is an imprint of the Taylor & Francis Group, an informa business

© 2012 Taylor & Francis

Library of Congress Cataloging in Publication Data
Adams, Jacqueline.
  Surviving dictatorship: a work of visual sociology/Jacqueline Adams.
  p. cm.—(Contemporary sociological perspectives)
  Includes bibliographical references and index.
  1. Poor women—Chile—Social conditions—20th century. 2. Poor women—Political activity—Chile—History—20th century. 3. Squatter settlements—Chile—History—20th century. 4. Dictatorship—Chile—History—20th century. 5. Chile—Social conditions—1970– 6. Chile—Politics and government—1973–1988. 7. Chile—History—1973–1988. 8. Visual sociology. I. Title.
  HQ1547.A33 2011
  983.06'4—dc23
  2011039699

ISBN: 978-0-415-99803-1 (hbk)
ISBN: 978-0-415-99804-8 (pbk)
ISBN: 978-0-203-13739-0 (ebk)

Typeset in Times New Roman and Helvetica Neue
by Florence Production Ltd, Stoodleigh, Devon

Printed and bound in the United States of America by Sheridan Books, Inc.(a Sheridan Group company)

To my parents, Paul Henry Adams and
María Angélica Adams

Contents

About This Book

This book possesses unique features: a novel conceptualization of resistance, extensive inclusion of visual and archival data that bring the text to life, and the examination of a little-studied but numerically important group: female shantytown inhabitants under dictatorship. Its multiple annotated web links point students towards carefully selected websites that will broaden their knowledge about human rights, the arts in resistance, women's struggles for democracy, economic survival, and gender emancipation. Instructors will find it useful for courses on resistance, authoritarian regimes, human rights, women's history, poverty in industrializing countries, urban history, qualitative methods, and oral history, within the academic programs of sociology, history, political science, anthropology, geography, women and gender studies, human rights, peace and conflict studies, development studies, and Latin American studies. Its benefits as a teaching tool include the following:

- It offers a theory of shantytown women's resistance to dictatorship and puts forward the concepts of incidental resistance, reluctant resistance, solidarity resistance, endemic fear, specific fears, generalized repression, and targeted repression, which instructors can use as a basis for discussion and debate among students.
- With its combination of photographs, lively interview excerpts, and flyers, bulletins, and art by shantytown women, it provides students with a vivid picture of shantytown women's survival strategies and resistance under dictatorship.
- This book is based on mixed methods: oral history interviews, photo elicitation, the analysis of visual data and shantytown documents, archival research, and participant observation. Professors teaching courses on qualitative methodology and oral history will find it useful for helping students understand these methods.
- Professors of gender and women's studies courses will find that this book enables them to broaden students' understanding of the lives, resistance, and history of a relatively little-studied group of women: the inhabitants of shantytowns under dictatorship.

How instructors can use this book:

- As a case study that will broaden students' understanding of dictatorship, repression, resistance, urban poverty, and survival strategies.
- As a means of developing students' critical thinking about the nature of resistance.
- As a starting point for discussion and debate about the resistance and survival strategies of women and the poor.

- As a point of comparison with other struggles for democracy or emancipation.
- As a means of clarifying for students the ways in which human rights are violated under dictatorship.
- As an example of how to use various qualitative methods and oral history interviews.

Series Foreword

In *Surviving Dictatorship* Jacqueline Adams humanizes and interrogates the lives of women in shantytowns in Pinochet's Chile. As an exemplar of visual sociology and classic case study sociology, the empirical analysis takes seriously the context in which these women's lives are shaped and unfold and, at the same time, reveals the nuanced ways in which women resist external forces. Although poverty and repression loom large in this authoritarian society, the women who live in these shantytowns reveal creative and effective ways of resisting the regimes that contextualize their lives and determine their life chances. Adams draws on a wealth of data—from photos and participant observation to interviews and archival work—to, quite literally, show these women's lives through provocative images and to offer a compelling analysis of their lives through multiple sociological lenses. The result is a moving sociological presentation of the multiple venues through which women in Chile's shantytowns survive dictatorship, advance their own cause, and reconstitute the conditions of their lives. For example, the book reveals how the women skillfully organize themselves into small groups to share information and raise consciousness, artistically express the realities of Pinochet's repressive regime through "arpilleras" (hand-made sewn pictures that are as beautiful as they are telling), and effectively create and sustain money-making enterprises, health awareness programs, and educational programs. Through these and other activities, the women in shantytowns survive extreme poverty and act as a force for self-determination and social–political change. This is an inspiring story that, on the one hand, does not downplay or glorify the damage done by poverty and authoritarianism; on the other hand, it presents the myriad ways resistance can unfold in even the most oppressive conditions. For this reason, it is a valuable contribution to larger efforts to understand the ways in which poverty, state structures, gender, and social change intersect. Likewise, it is an enticing springboard from which to engage students in discussions of survival strategies and resistance.

Valerie Jenness
Jodi O'Brien
Series Editors

Preface

This book examines the ways in which women in shantytowns experience and resist dictatorship. Its focus is the regime of General Pinochet in Chile, and the shantytown women of Santiago, Chile's capital. I became interested in this subject matter while conducting research on dissident art that shantytown women, relatives of the disappeared, and political prisoners had produced under Pinochet and subsequently. My being half Chilean but having grown up in Europe, eager to learn more about Chile, and interested in gender and art were influences in the decision to study the "arpilleras," as these dissident art forms were called. In a Ph.D. dissertation I explored the process whereby the arpillera-makers became radicalized as a result of joining arpillera workshops, and in subsequent articles and a book I examined their sense of loss once the dictatorship had ended, the forces that shape dissident art, the change in the arpilleras from sharply denunciatory to bucolic and decorative, the international network that develops around the export, distribution, and buying of "solidarity art," and the meanings that art from home holds for exiles.

During the year's ethnographic fieldwork that I carried out for this earlier research, conducting participant observation, interviews, and archival work, and creating a large visual database of arpilleras, the women from Santiago's shantytowns told me about the many other forms of resistance in which they engaged, and about the repression and poverty they had endured. I did not want this information to be lost. At the same time, I wanted to offer a testimony of sorts of what the dictatorship had been like in the shantytowns, and I wished to draw attention to women's energetic and creative efforts to survive their impoverishment and chip away at the regime's power. With the idea of writing a book that would meet these goals, first in English and then in Spanish, I embarked on a new phase of data collection that saw me conducting further interviews and archival research, and creating a visual database of photographs of shantytown life under Pinochet, and digitized copies of the flyers, bulletins, and public declarations that shantytown women had produced, and which the Princeton University's Department of Rare Books and Special Collections had had the foresight to collect. In parallel, I expanded the arpillera database by photographing further private collections, and reproductions of arpilleras in books. It was from the analysis of both these data and the data gathered for my earlier research that the conceptualization of shantytown women's resistance as self-protection, community affirmation, and mounting an offensive derives. Also emerging from this analysis is my theory about how shantytown women's resistance arises, and the concepts of incidental resistance, reluctant resistance, solidarity resistance, endemic fear, specific fears, generalized repression, and targeted repression.

The ingenious means used by the women to feed their families in the face of severe poverty and unemployment, when previously they had been discouraged from joining groups and working outside the home, and the wealth of resistance activities in which they coura-geously engaged, cannot be studied without a feeling of tremendous admiration. It has been a great privilege to have been able to get to know these women and hear their stories.

Acknowledgments

My greatest debt is to the women of Chile's shantytowns who allowed me to interview them and join them in their group activities. They shared their experiences with me and patiently answered my questions: many thanks. Ada, Juanita, Sara, Estrella, and Toya showed me much "cariño," for which I remain grateful and touched, and I remember the warmth of many more. I am grateful to the staff members of the Vicaría de la Solidaridad, feminist organizations, and NGOs who allowed me to interview them; it was a privilege to meet so many courageous, determined, and caring people. I thank the staff of the archives of the Vicaría de la Solidaridad, who allowed me to plough through their materials, and Boris Hau, who brought the Vicaría photo albums to my attention. I am grateful to the Princeton University Libraries, thanks to which I was able to access an outstanding collection of documents produced by shantytown women during the regime, which the University's Department of Rare Books and Special Collections had had the foresight to collect. I would like to express my gratitude, as well, to Liisa Flora Voionmaa Tanner, who allowed me to use some of her photographs of an arpillera group in northern Santiago, and to Isabel Morel, Verónica Salas, Andy McEntee, André Jacques, Geneviève Camus, David Kunzle, Riet Delsing, Paulina Waugh, the Association of Relatives of the Detained and Disappeared, the Fundación Salvador Allende/Museo de la Solidaridad, the Fundación Solidaridad, and Magasins du Monde, Switzerland, all of whom allowed me to photograph their arpillera collections. I am grateful to the photographers whose work I have used for their precious records of life under Pinochet, in particular Miguel Budnik and Carlos Alvarez Morales, and to the researchers/photographers Clarisa Hardy and Mariana Schkolnik, whose work I have drawn on heavily. I also thank Paulo Slachevsky, who helped track down some of the photographers. During the periods of data gathering in Chile, Anita Morandé, Pilar Moreno, and Irene Moreno were the best possible aunties.

I am indebted to the University of California at Berkeley, where my congenial and lively colleagues made for a stimulating academic home during periods of data gathering for this book. When the manuscript was completed, Ellen Fernandez Sacco and Michèle Pridmore-Brown read and commented on parts of it, and Katherine Poethig generously gave me feedback on all its chapters. The work of the staff of the Interlibrary Loan Service at Berkeley's Doe Library was invaluable. They found the many obscure Chilean and exile documents and publications that I requested, even offering me a space in their offices so that I could check which of the multiple publications that came in at the same time contained relevant photographs and which did not, and thus be able to carry a less heavy and more manageable pile back to the office. Their work and the excellent holdings of the Doe Library at Berkeley made the research much easier than it would have been otherwise. The Data Lab in the same library was where I did most of the scanning, and I am grateful for its staff's amiable professionalism. Beatrice Lau, Tamara Wattnem, Bram Draper, Brittany Gabel, and Trilce Santana, all of whom I taught within UC Berkeley's Undergraduate Research Apprentice Scheme, assisted me in my scouring of sources for visual data and in my literature search, historical background section, and the initial phases of website design, and I am grateful to them for their diligent efforts. I continued the work at the Center for Social Studies at the University of Coimbra thanks to funding from the Fundação para a Ciência e a Tecnologia of Portugal, and during this period Maria José Carvalho proved a most collegial and helpful chief librarian. I am very grateful indeed to Howard Saul Becker and Colin Samson, who taught me how to collect, analyze, and write up data, and have since become mentors and greatly appreciated colleagues.

My father, Paul Henry Adams, allowed himself to be roped in at the editing stage and used his expertise as a United Nations translator focused on human rights to offer feedback on my translations of the interview excerpts, and writing, and I much appreciate his efforts. My mother, María Angélica Adams, provided enthusiastic support throughout, often telling me about yet another friend who had just said that she wanted to read the book so I must hurry up and finish it. The book would probably not have been written at all if it were not for her being Chilean. I am grateful to my husband for his reading and constructive criticism of each of the chapters, for his cropping of many of the figures, and for his support throughout. I would also like to thank the peer reviewers of the book: Doug Harper of Duquesne University, Cynthia Pope of Central Connecticut State University, and Ananya Roy of University of California, Berkeley. Last and by no means least, I wish to express my thanks to Steve Rutter and Leah Babb-Rosenfeld at Routledge, and to Val Jenness, the editor of the series, for their enthusiasm about the project, and suggestions.

1.1–1.4

These women from the shantytown of La Victoria in southern Santiago would have lived lives of hardship that did not begin with the dictatorship. They may not have had a home of their own in their first years of married life, lodging instead with relatives, which was sometimes a source of anguish and frustration. They might then have participated in the 1957 land seizure that gave birth to La Victoria, living in a tent for several months, and this tent would gradually have become a wooden hut and then a brick home, cold and damp in winter, and hot in summer. For at least some of their lives, they would have worried about the cost of food and other essentials. Years of childbearing and child rearing while not being sure they would be able to give their children what they needed would have added to the strain. The group picture suggests that, between some women neighbors in the shantytown, there was affection and friendship. These four women of La Victoria gather for a chat at what is probably a shop that one of them has set up in the front room of her house.

1.6

An inhabitant of La Victoria, in front of one of the shantytown's many murals.

1.5

A woman bakes bread, which was cheaper than buying. A fire made with sticks sits on top of a metal drum. The numerous buckets in the background suggest a lack of room in the house, and were perhaps used to fetch water at the communal faucet, while the metal receptacle was probably used for clothes washing or catching drips from the roof. The houses are close together, suggesting an overcrowded shantytown.

1.7

The wall of wood against which the woman with the baby leans is most likely part of her home, the number on it her house number.

1.8

This family stands on the baked earth that surrounds their home and the mother sits on a rough wooden stool.

One

Shantytown Women and Dictatorship

On September 11 1973, Chile's armed forces bombed Santiago's presidential palace and overthrew the leftist government of President Salvador Allende. At ten minutes to eight that morning, Catarina,[1] who lived in a "población" [Chile's version of the *favela*, or shantytown] in southern Santiago, turned on the radio and learned that people were being arrested. She then heard that there were soldiers in the wide road that bordered her neighborhood, shooting into her población to prevent people from moving. She had been working in the local clinic for years, and someone came to fetch her so that she might help a woman who had been shot while running after her child who had gone to the street corner to see the convoy of military vehicles. Because soldiers were shooting everything that moved, as she put it, she had to squat down to get there, keeping to the edge of the street. She took out the woman's bullet, and treated a child whose throat had been grazed by another bullet while he was looking out from the second floor of his home. However, there was little she could do for some of the injured, who died. The relatives kept the bodies in their homes for five days, and some dug holes in which to bury them. Helicopters would shoot down on the población from above, and there was a night-time curfew. Before long, Catarina's house was raided. "They would raid our homes," she told me. "They took all the men out into the street at midnight, to an open space that had not yet been built on. They would even take out adolescents, and boys, even. They'd leave the women in the house, and the police and members of the armed forces and soldiers would come in and examine everything. You'd get very scared . . . You'd feel invaded in your privacy. It was the first invasion you felt; strangers' eyes, strangers' hands touching your things."

This book explores how women like Catarina, living in Santiago's poblaciones [favelas], experienced and resisted the ensuing Pinochet dictatorship. As repression and exacerbated poverty were arguably the two aspects of the Pinochet years most prominent in their minds, it begins by examining these, before turning to the women's struggles against poverty, and their resistance. In the course of this journey it explores the consequences of the women's resistance, both for the dictatorship and for the women themselves. The poblaciones in which these experiences and resistance took place were impoverished urban areas that formed a ring around Santiago's center except for on its north-eastern side.[2] They had poor-quality housing, under-funded schools and clinics, partially paved or unpaved roads, and variable access to water, electricity, and a sewerage system.[3] Some poblaciones were only a few months old at the beginning of the dictatorship; others had existed for two decades. I will use the word "shantytowns" when referring to them, although this is a poor substitute, suggesting as it does expanses of wooden shacks with corrugated iron roofs. Chile's shantytowns in the 1970s and 1980s included such expanses, but also orderly rows of very small brick houses, normally divided into two homes, the tidy façades belying the economic difficulties within.

A central theme of the book is resistance to dictatorship. Shantytown women's resistance, I propose, consisted of self-protection, community affirmation, and the mounting of an offensive against the regime. Women became involved in resistance activities primarily because the regime's economic policies and national security doctrine led their husbands or partners to become unemployed. This unemployment worsened their poverty, and distressed the women because it meant that they were unable to feed their families adequately, send their children to school, or have running water and electricity in their homes. Mainly but not exclusively because they wanted to acquire money and food, they joined local income-generating and food-procuring groups that were mushrooming in the shantytowns. Once they had become group members, they were drawn into resistance because the groups occasionally engaged in resistance activities "on the side." Group leaders encouraged their involvement and even put pressure on them to participate at times when they were not eager to do so. The women, then, did not set out to resist the dictatorship, but rather their resistance was an outcome of their joining groups in order to solve an immediate problem; it was *incidental resistance*. Some of the women's resistance was also *reluctant resistance*. For example, when group leaders encouraged them to participate in marches, the women did so reluctantly, afraid of violence by the armed forces and worried about what would happen to their children if they themselves were arrested. Much of the women's resistance can also be described as *solidarity resistance*; resistance that their group engaged in not so as to express its own needs and wishes, but rather so as to show its solidarity[4] with another group. It took the

1.9   Emergence of Shantytown Women's Resistance

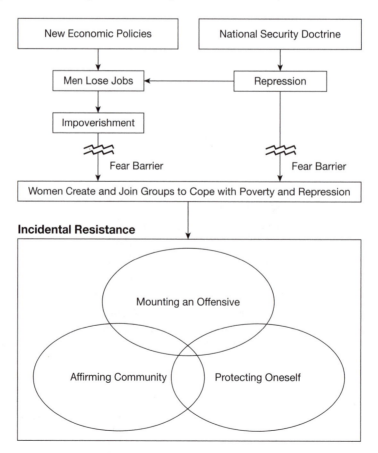

Website Link 1.1:
The recent protests that have rocked Tunisia, Egypt and other countries in the Middle East are discussed by several members of the Duke faculty interviewed by the Duke News and Communications. The videos of these interviews are featured on this website. "Spotlight on the Middle East. Duke Faculty Offer Insights into Recent Events." www.jhfc.duke.edu/disc/events/SpotlightonMiddle East.htm

form of lending concrete support or expressing sympathy with the other group's cause or troubles, and encouraging others to do the same.

Some shantytown women came to resistance via an alternative route. Their husband, partner, son, daughter, father, or other close relative disappeared or was executed, thrown in jail, or exiled, pushing the women to begin searching for them, in prisons, morgues, and government offices. In the process, seeking moral support, they formed or joined a group of "relatives of" the disappeared, political prisoners, executed, internally exiled, or exiled, as the case may be, and through such groups became involved in resistance activities. Raising public awareness, demanding information, and denouncing the particular form of repression they had endured were central to these groups' activities. As most shantytown women did not experience the forms of persecution that were the motivation for such groups, I do not focus on these groups in this book. I focus, rather, on the more common situation of shantytown women joining groups so as to survive poverty, and the trajectory towards political resistance of these women. Of course, while most resistance by shantytown women occurred in the context of a group, it was not limited to this. Of the three main categories of resistance activity in which shantytown women engaged, namely affirming community, mounting an offensive, and self-protection, the first two usually took place in a group and the third did in some cases but not in others.[5]

The women's resistance and the hundreds of groups in which they carried it out had consequences for the regime. Tarrow's (2008: 10) words about China were also true of Chile, when he stated,

> China's authoritarian system will not be transformed by . . . capillary changes alone, and modern authoritarianism has more robust tools to suppress dissent than England's eighteenth-century polity had. But such incremental changes and the unintended responses to them can often be more effective in bringing about regime change than more open challenges that question the bases of political legitimacy.

Each new group of shantytown women and each new resistance activity was an incremental change that eventually contributed to the anti-Pinochet community's winning the plebiscite that ended the dictatorship, and paved the way for a democratic transition.

Besides helping us understand resistance to dictatorship, this book contributes to several other areas of scholarly interest. A second theme is the experiences that shantytown women have of poverty under dictatorship. The book explores what their poverty meant to shantytown women, and how they coped with it. The Pinochet government developed neoliberal economic policies that, for most of the first two-thirds of the dictatorship, produced high rates of unemployment, particularly for shantytown inhabitants. At the same time, a national security doctrine caused leftists[6] to be fired from their jobs in both the public and private sectors. These phenomena caused exacerbated poverty, which shanty-town women experienced and understood in gendered ways, as shantytown women and mothers. The practices that they adopted to survive this impoverishment were also influenced by their gender, and in particular by their being mothers; in addition, they were shaped by the repression.

A third theme is how shantytown women experience repression and national security doctrines. Most shantytown men and women did not experience disappearances, torture, arrest, executions, and exile; at least not directly. Such forms of state violence are examples of *targeted repression*, that is, repression expressly directed at a particular individual. Instead, the repression that most shantytown women experienced was *generalized repression*, that is, repression meted out on the shantytown as a whole, or on an area of the shantytown. This included soldiers shooting people who were out after

1.10

An arpillera depicting two facets of life that greatly troubled shantytown women, unemployment and repression. The factory on the left has an employee standing in the doorway, which signifies that there was employment, and the date May 1973, that is, a few months before the military coup. The one on the right, on the other hand, has a red cross over the door, signifying that it was not offering work, and bears the date of May 1 1983. This was a time of economic crisis, protests, and intense repression. Two soldiers in green beat up some civilians, while a water cannon sprays others. Blood comes out of the head of the civilian on the right.

curfew, members of the armed forces patrolling the streets, police and soldiers raiding all the homes in a neighborhood, helicopters flying overhead, and military vehicles being stationed in the shantytown for short periods of time. Both generalized and targeted repression are forms of *direct physical repression*. Shantytown women also experienced *non-violent repression*, that is, repression not immediately backed by violence, including restrictions on their freedom to organize, vote, and produce, own, or disseminate leftist or anti-regime messages. Together, the direct physical repression and non-violent repression made fear a central part of shantytown women's experience of the dictatorship.

The experiences that shantytown women have of repression is a theme closely related to a fourth topic that this study allows us to explore: the interconnectedness of repression and poverty. The repression impacted shantytown women's experiences of poverty and their efforts to survive it. The Pinochet dictatorship's national security doctrine identified leftists as dangerous enemies, and the persecution that ensued caused some of the women's husbands to become unable to work because they were fired, arrested, or disabled by police violence. Hence the repression contributed to furthering their family's impoverishment. When the women sought to cope with their impoverishment by joining food-procuring or income-generating groups, the repression affected this too, in that it made them nervous to be in groups that might be thought leftist, fearful about engaging in certain group activities, and careful to take measures to protect their group, such as the use of secrecy and disguise. In these and other ways, the repression affected the poverty that shantytown women endured and the ways they worked to survive it.

Conversely, being poor and living in a shantytown shaped the repression women experienced. The armed forces meted out harsher repression on the shantytowns than on middle-class neighborhoods, where soldiers did not conduct raids on all homes in a particular neighborhood, shoot at citizens after curfew, or throw stones at their windows.[7] Meanwhile the women's poverty affected their struggles against the repression. When they made flyers in which they expressed that they wanted the repression to stop, for example, these flyers were often hand-written and produced simply with the aid of a photocopying machine, because the women could not afford anything better. When they made dissident art (*arpilleras*) in which they denounced incidents of repression, they used cheap materials, including their own recycled clothes and sometimes sacking, and their tools were simply needles, scissors, and threaders. Poverty shaped both their experiences of and struggles against repression.

A fifth, related theme in the book is the impact that being a woman and mother has on one's experience of dictatorship. Shantytown gender expectations were central to the ways in which shantytown women experienced the poverty and repression that the dictatorship inflicted upon them. To them the dictatorship meant having to keep their children indoors after curfew, worrying about the effects of the violence on them, and being unable to feed or school them. Children and home are at the forefront of these meanings, because they are the spheres for which shantytown gender expectations held women responsible. These same gender expectations affected their experiences of resistance; some of the self-protection in which they engaged was aimed at protecting their children, for example.

Shantytown women's joining groups in reaction to impoverishment and repression caused a change in the gender regime within families, albeit a temporary one. For instance, when husbands ceased to be the providers they were supposed to be, it became more acceptable for the women to participate in groups and take up paid work, where previously the gender regime had dictated that they spend nearly all their time at home looking after house and children, while men worked for wages. Husbands were forced to accept these changes where previously they would not have done so, although some were recalcitrant.[8] Hence, ironically, a repressive military regime's policies ultimately resulted in women's occupying powerful roles within the family, and experiencing fewer restrictions on the scope of their activities than previously. These same policies caused shantytown women to develop into a force that undermined the dictatorship.

A sixth and final theme of this study is the Pinochet regime. The book's analysis of shantytown women's experiences sheds light on aspects of the dictatorship previously examined through other lenses. We learn how its national security policy played itself out in the lives of the urban poor. We come to understand more about how the regime's abrupt introduction of neoliberal economic policies affected shantytown inhabitants.[9] Since this study uses visual data, we are able to "see" the consequences of the dictatorship for the women of the shantytowns.

With its exploration of these six themes, the book aims to fill certain lacunae in the literature. Shantytown women's resistance to dictatorship has been little studied. There exist analyses of the struggles of women in other classes or categories[10], and there are studies of multi-class women's movements[11] that include shantytown women, of shantytown men and women's joint resistance,[12] of shantytown men's resistance[13], and of other categories of urban poor,[14] but almost no studies focusing just on shantytown women. Even Scott (1985), who brings to us now classic analyses of resistance, which apply to the underdog in many different oppressive situations, does not focus on dictatorship, although his analysis informs our understanding of authoritarian contexts. Some scholars dismiss men and women shantytown inhabitants' efforts to organize altogether, seeing them as a mass of unorganized individuals and a few isolated, weak organizations,[15] or viewing them as conformist and reluctant to act.

There have been few analyses of repression in shantytowns.[16] Studies of repression under dictatorship tend to focus on targeted as opposed to generalized repression, and neglect shantytown inhabitants. The relatives of the disappeared, most of whom were drawn from the urban poor in Chile, have inspired a number of works,[17] but they are a special group in the way that they were targeted. Shantytown women who did not endure targeted repression have been largely ignored by scholars. Poverty under repressive regimes has fared better; there being many studies of the urban poor's experiences of poverty and efforts to survive it, both internationally and in Chile.[18] However, few analyze the ways in which repression and shantytown poverty are connected.

There are a number of ways in which shantytown resistance and experiences of poverty and repression under Pinochet are relevant today. First, as the multiple uprisings in the Middle East and North Africa remind us, surviving and resisting dictatorships is part of what a great many people do. Authoritarian regimes have been very common historically, and still make up about half of the world's countries.[19] There are many comparable cases of resistance to authoritarian regimes, ranging from the recent revolutions in Egypt, Tunisia, and Libya, to the resistance in Yemen, Syria, Bahrain, China, Myanmar, Zimbabwe, and historically in Latin America. Where appropriate, studies on these are referenced throughout the text as endnotes.

Second, shantytown inhabitants make up a substantial proportion of the population of authoritarian regimes. Authoritarian regimes are concentrated in developing countries, which are experiencing urbanization; the rapid growth of their cities means that many of their poor, and even of their population as a whole, are the "urban poor." Shantytown inhabitants also represent a significant proportion of the world's population. Based on United Nations data, Davis (2006: 23) states, "Residents of slums, while only 6 percent of the city population of the developed countries, constitute a staggering 78.2 percent of urbanites in the least-developed countries; this equals fully a third of the global urban population."[20] There are probably more than 200,000 slums on earth, ranging in population from a few hundred to more than a million people, notes Davis (2006: 26).[21] Research on shantytown inhabitants, then, is research on a significant fraction of humanity.

With continued migration from the countryside to the cities in developing countries, the proportion of people living in shantytowns and other poor areas of cities is likely to continue to rise. In Davis' (2006: 151) view, "The countryside will for a short period still contain the majority of the world's poor, but that dubious distinction will pass to urban slums no later than 2035. At least half of the coming Third World urban population explosion will be credited to the account of informal communities." Critics have seen Davis' vision as too negative[22] but nevertheless, some of them acknowledge that "without the implementation of appropriate policies, the growth of festering slums will be inevitable."[23] Other analysts of slums have expressed views similar to Davis'. A scholar of poor urban neighborhoods in Africa, for example, has said, "Increasing numbers of Africans are situated in what could be called half-built environments."[24]

Finally, the experience and resistance of shantytown women to the Pinochet dictatorship remains relevant today because throughout the world, women are primary actors in the struggle against poverty and repression. They develop survival strategies everywhere, including the joining of groups and engaging in reciprocal helping arrangements, and in many places women of all classes engage in political resistance against oppressive regimes.[25]

Methodology

This book is a work of visual sociology and oral history. Still a marginal practice within sociology, visual sociology boasts highly compelling works by authors such as Doug Harper (1982; 1987; 2001; 2009), Mitchell Duneier (1999), and Goffman (1979). It is closely related to visual anthropology, a field that includes remarkable works by Gregory Bateson and Margaret Mead (1942), Loring Danforth (1982), and James Barker (1993). Howard Becker (1986) and John Collier (1967) have produced now-classic analyses of how the visual may be used in social science.

Visual sociology has significant methodological power for communicating social stories to the outside world. I use visual images extensively in this book, primarily because they are an excellent source of data and an effective means of communicating information to readers. I wish my readers to "see" and not just to read about life and resistance in the shantytowns, and believe that the visual and verbal complement each other well in the task of communicating. To my knowledge there are no works of visual sociology on shantytown resistance to dictatorship, and I aim to contribute to filling this gap, offering images of shantytown women's resistance efforts, as well as of how they came to this resistance: their poverty, the repression, and the groups they formed.

This book draws on different kinds of visual data, each of which provides different information. First, there are photographs of shantytown life by outsiders, including researchers who studied shantytown organizations, the members of humanitarian organizations, NGO staff, exiles who had returned, members of clandestine political groups, writers of memoirs, photojournalists who courageously reported on the conditions in which the poor lived, and other members of the clandestine resistance community sympathetic to the sufferings of the poor. These photographs help us understand the women's experiences: the conditions under which they lived, their work, their associational lives, and their resistance, and such information is useful both as data to be analyzed by the researcher, and for the purposes of communicating to the reader in a vivid way. The photographs were not "neutral"; they were often tools of resistance, in that their authors used them to communicate the sufferings of the Chilean people under Pinochet to the readers of the publications in which they appeared, who tended to be exiles, locals in exiles' host countries, or members of the resistance community in Chile. Even though politically motivated, and even though they do not offer shantytown women's perspectives, I use them extensively in the book because they are almost the only photographs of shantytown life we have. I have found very few photographs by shantytown women, and I doubt that many shantytown women took photographs, especially on the subjects of repression and their poverty. Most would not have had a camera or money for film and developing the photographs.

These photographs came from numerous sources. One was the archive[26] of the Vicaría de la Solidaridad (Chile's main human rights and humanitarian organization during the dictatorship) in Santiago, where I found photographs of the workshops and community kitchens that the Vicaría had supported, and of some very early arpilleras. Another source was out-of-print, once-clandestine publications by resistance groups, and the newsletters of exile organizations that had ceased to exist. Further sources included the Vicaría's bulletin, opposition magazines, NGO publications, memoirs by shantytown inhabitants

Website Link 1.2:
During the regime, a number of courageous photographers recorded instances of repression and poverty in the country. This website describes their work and trajectory: "Chile from Within." El origen de la leyenda. http://fotografiachile.blogspot.com/2007/08/chile-from-within-el-origen-de-la.html

Website Link 1.3:
A digital archive of photographs of oppositional artwork of the late 20th century from Asia, Africa, and Latin America may be viewed on "Docs Populi," by the Organization in Solidarity with the People of Africa, Asia, and Latin America. www.docspopuli.org/CubaWebCat/gallery-01.html

and visitors, non-academic books and reports about the shantytowns and about repression, and academic books and articles. These publications were housed in libraries throughout the United States and beyond, and I was able to obtain them through the University of California at Berkeley's Interlibrary Loan Service.

The second kind of image consists of photographs of arpilleras, most of which were taken by myself, and some by other researchers on the arpilleras. The arpilleras were made by women inhabitants of Santiago's shantytowns,[27] each woman working on her own arpillera but doing so as part of a group that met between one and three afternoons a week. They express what the women wanted to tell the outside world about the conditions they and others in Chile were enduring, and about their resistance. Rather than the raw expression of women's thinking, however, they are mediated by buyers and sellers abroad and by the Vicaría de la Solidaridad, which sold most of the arpilleras for the women, exporting them to priests, Chilean exiles, and human rights activists abroad, who sold them to the public. The Vicaría asked the women to depict certain themes rather than others, and developed a system of quality control whereby it rejected some of the arpilleras. Even when the Vicaría did not make explicit orders, the women knew the kind of subject-matter it wanted, and censored themselves accordingly. Individuals selling the arpilleras abroad were another influence, since they told the Vicaría that their buyers wanted more arpilleras on certain subjects and fewer on others. Since the women made

1.11

The arpillera workshop of Villa O'Higgins, in south-eastern Santiago. Women sit around a table with the wool and scissors they use to make their arpilleras, while their children play around them. The right side of the arpillera shows raw materials and stages in the process of arpillera-making: wool, the cloth or burlap base, and the stage of placing the cut-out cloth onto the arpillera.

Website Link 1.4:
A website created by the University of St. Andrews offers access to images from a vast collection of pamphlets and posters about slavery, temperance, revivals, Mormonism and religious education, the Nonjuror movement, and the English Civil War. "Pamphlet and Polemic: Pamphlets as a Guide to the Controversies of the 17th–19th Centuries." http://specialcollections. st-and.ac.uk/projpamph.htm

Website Link 1.5:
More than 5,000 scarce and unique nineteenth- and early twentieth-century Latin American pamphlets containing political and social commentary are held at the Harvard's Widener Library. Addressed to fellow citizens, these pamphlets document the emergence of the Latin American colonies as independent states and illuminate aspects of their populations' social and cultural life. In "Latin American Pamphlet Digital Collection" by the Harvard College Library:
http://hcl.harvard.edu/ collections/digital_collections/ latin_american_pamphlets.cfm

the arpilleras primarily so as to earn a much-needed income with which to support their families, they complied with the Vicaría's orders (Adams 2005). Towards the end of the regime however, some women's compliance became begrudging, as the Vicaría began asking for subject-matter devoid of political content in order to cater to buyers who were no longer buying out of solidarity for a country in crisis, but rather seeking quality and decorativeness in what would hang in a child's bedroom, for instance. The women persisted in seeing the arpillera as quintessentially a vehicle for communicating to the outside world their social problems: "the truth about Chile," as they put it. Almost all arpillera groups ceased to exist in the 1990s, although production continued for some social entrepreneurship ventures run by middle-class professionals.[28] This book contains reproductions of arpilleras because, although mediated, they do represent shantytown women's "truth"; the arpilleras were their photographs of sorts. I began photographing arpilleras in 1994, beginning with the collections of human rights activists who had helped sell them in England, and arpilleras displayed in shops in Britain and Switzerland. When I began fieldwork in Chile in 1995, I continued to photograph arpilleras, owned by the association of relatives of the disappeared, ex-Vicaría employees, returned exiles, human rights organizations, and researchers. I later added to my dataset scanned copies of photographs of arpilleras from books and journal articles.

The third kind of visual data used for this research is in fact a combination of visual and verbal data, in the form of flyers, bulletins, public declarations, and letters produced by shantytown women and by relatives of the disappeared and of political prisoners. These documents (ephemera) give us the women's perspective, telling us about their problems, views, and concerns, what activities they organized to address these concerns, what groups existed, and where they were based. Analysis of such data yields valuable insights for the researcher about shantytown women's ideas and organizing. A large and remarkable collection of these documents is held at the Princeton University's Department of Rare Books and Special Collections, and I made digital copies of all those produced by shantytown women, as well as many produced by mixed-sex shantytown groups, relatives of the disappeared, relatives of political prisoners, and other relevant categories. With these three kinds of image, I was able to create a large, digitized, visual database that covered many different facets of shantytown women's experiences of repression and poverty, and many different anti-poverty and political resistance activities and groups. This visual database and interviews with shantytown women were the parts of my dataset that I drew on most heavily in order to produce the findings in this book.

I conducted 170 interviews, in Chile, Europe, and the United States, in 1995, 1996, 2005, and 2006. I interviewed shantytown women, the members of humanitarian and feminist organizations that helped their groups, the staff of NGOs that had worked with them, Chilean exiles who had helped sell the arpilleras they made, and European and American activists with human rights sensibilities who had also helped sell their work. I conducted these interviews in shantytown homes, in the offices of humanitarian organizations in the center of Santiago, in the homes of Chilean exiles and local human rights activists in England, Switzerland, France, and the United States, and in the homes of returned exiles in Chile. For this book, I drew mainly on my interviews with shantytown inhabitants: forty-seven one-on-one, in-depth, semi-structured interviews with shantytown women, five semi-structured group interviews with shantytown women, and two interviews with shantytown men. The remaining interviews in my dataset were not of direct relevance to this book's subject matter, but they did provide information that enabled me to build up an understanding of transnational solidarity and the work of the Vicaría.

In conducting these interviews with shantytown inhabitants, I used a snowball sample with a broad base.[29] I found my first shantytown women interviewees with the help of a Vicaría de la Solidaridad staff person who had sent their arpilleras abroad, and subsequent ones thanks to referrals by these shantytown women, by other Vicaría de la Solidaridad employees based in other areas of the city, by the staff of other humanitarian organizations, and by middle-class professionals who worked with shantytown women's organizations. The shantytown women whom I interviewed come from shantytowns in all corners of Santiago, covering the north, south, east, and west of the city. Most were of European and indigenous descent, as are nearly all Santiago's shantytown inhabitants, but did not think of themselves in racial terms. They were mostly mothers of small children at the time of the coup, and married or partnered in a heterosexual union. Some came to live without a partner in later years, through separation or widowhood.

A little over half of the shantytown women interviewed had been in arpillera groups, because many of their interviews originated in an earlier study on shantytown women's production of arpilleras. To an extent this is problematic; the interviews focused mainly on arpillera-making, and moreover, a sample of all shantytown women would have been better. However, the arpillera groups had all developed out of groups with a different purpose, in which these women had been involved, including community kitchens, knitting groups, sewing groups, unemployed people's workshops ["bolsas de cesantes"], health teams, and discussion groups. Moreover, a great many of the arpillera group members were simultaneously in other kinds of group. Finally, since between one and two thousand shantytown women were members of arpillera groups in Santiago, these groups represent a significant segment of organized shantytown women. What this book is unfortunately unable to do is present the experiences of non-organized shantytown women.

The interviews I conducted were semi-structured and lasted between one and three hours. Aiming to let the interviewees speak for themselves, I used a short list of topics to be covered. Sometimes, when the interviewee was talking about certain topics, I probed for more detailed information. The interviews were recorded and transcribed, and I coded them.

As well as conducting semi-structured interviews, I conducted a small amount of photo elicitation during fieldwork in 1995–1996 and 2005. This is a technique, described early on by John Collier in 1967, whereby the researcher asks the research subject to talk about what is in a photograph. I showed some shantytown arpillera-makers photographs of arpilleras by other groups and asked them to explain them to me. As most of the arpilleras showed women's poverty, the repression, women's organizations for coping with poverty, and their resistance, my interviewees would tell me about these subjects in the course of describing what was happening in the arpillera.

This book also draws on field notes from a year's ethnographic fieldwork. I began conducting participant observation in Chilean shantytowns in July 1995, five years after General Pinochet stepped down as President. I joined five groups of women from the shantytowns, four of which met regularly to make arpilleras. Two of these groups were based in southern Santiago, and were comprised of women from shantytowns there. Two more had formed after the coup, and contained women from a range of shantytowns and from more central working class neighborhoods, who came together once a week in a non-profit organization in central Santiago, to make arpilleras and learn how to run an arpillera-making cooperative. The fifth was a protest song group of wives, partners, mothers, sisters, daughters, and a sister-in-law of people who had disappeared; all were members of the Association of Relatives of the Detained and Disappeared. They came from a number of different shantytowns and more central working class neighborhoods throughout Santiago. A sixth group that I joined consisted of women who made embroidered pictures and lived in a working-class neighborhood in Macul, in south-eastern Santiago, that was slightly too well-off to be called a shantytown, and whose inhabitants did not think of themselves as living in a shantytown, and for these reasons I did not examine data from this group for the book.

These groups accepted me as a participant observer, in which role I watched their work and helped as much as I could without changing what they normally did. I observed them for a year, except in the case of one of the groups of women from southern Santiago, which I observed for two months. Even though I concluded the participant observation five years after Pinochet stepped down, the data gained were still pertinent to this book, as they enabled me to learn about the shantytowns and shantytown family life. While not the focus of the analysis conducted to produce this book, my field notes do inform it. For example, while walking to the bus stop with one of the women one day, I learned that shantytown families worry about burglary and so build fences, preferring metal fences to wooden ones, but not normally being able to afford them initially. Snippets of information such as this helped me better interpret the visual data. In addition to this fieldwork, and the interviews, photo elicitation, archival research, and creation of a visual database, I read memoirs by people who had lived in or visited shantytowns during the dictatorship. I did not analyze them as a body of data, but they helped me learn about shantytown life and so inform this work.

My analysis of the data began while I was in the field. I regularly wrote analytical "memos" about important themes in the interviews, later checking what I wrote by asking further questions. Once the interviews were transcribed, I analyzed them by coding them, that is, by identifying key themes and giving them a label (a "code"), and marking that code in the text. I then compared the parts of the interviews and field notes that were pertinent to a particular code, following the principles of grounded theory (Glaser and Strauss 1967). For this book, I focused on codes relevant to the experiences that shantytown women had of poverty and repression, and to their struggles against both these ills.

I approached the visual data by examining each photograph and asking who was in it, what sort of group it showed, what kind of activity it represented, and what message, if any, it contained. This analysis also produced codes, such as "Joining groups," or "Protests." The next step was to group visual images that shared the same code together, for comparison among images within the same code. To do this, I created several word documents, each containing a list of closely-related codes, and then copied and pasted photographs into them, under the appropriate codes. The result was a series of word documents headed by a code, and each containing between one and twenty photographs. The word documents were on the environment of the shantytown, the inside of shantytown homes, experiences of poverty, women taking collective action to cope with poverty, individual action to cope with poverty, repression, shantytown inhabitants' resistance to repression, and the types of group to which women belonged.

In order to analyze the visual images, I focused on one set of images under a code name at a time, examining them for what they said about shantytown women's experiences of poverty and repression, and their economic survival strategies and resistance, keeping an open mind as to the insights that they might bring, but also asking of them some specific questions. When examining the photographs under the heading "resistance activities," for example, I asked, "What are the goals of the women's resistance activity in this photograph?" (The answers might be informing about an event, or denouncing a rights violation, for example); "What means did they use to achieve their goal?" (e.g. organizing a gathering, or putting on an artistic performance); and "What do they describe as their main concerns?" (e.g. increases in the price of food, or poor healthcare). This process produced several paragraphs of writing for each code. I later merged these into the body of the text that I had written based on my analysis of the interviews. This involved adding new sections and paragraphs to chapters, and altering already-existing sections in which I discussed the same issues. I also used some of what I had written during the visual analysis as captions for the photographs.

I saw myself as having a choice about whether to structure the chapters and book around the visual images or around the themes that the analysis of textual data produced. I decided on the second option because the textual data expressed the women's understandings of their experiences and activities, whereas this was not always the case with the photographs. Also, I could make claims knowing exactly who was speaking and where she had lived when I used the textual data, but did not always have such information with the images. A change of mind illustrates this priority that I accorded the textual data. I had originally placed the photographs of men selling items in the street and working in emergency employment programs together with the images of women doing exactly the same. However, I then moved the images of the men to the part of the text that discussed men's unemployment because the interview data revealed that the women thought of men's work in emergency employment programs and as street vendors as something they did while they were unemployed, and in their minds, the men were *still* "unemployed" ["cesantes"] while engaging in this work. As the focus of the book is women's meanings and experiences of the dictatorship, I wanted to present the data in accordance with the meanings that *they* gave to their family members' situation. These meanings came through more clearly with the textual data, and so these photographs ended up illustrating the paragraphs that resulted from the analysis of the textual and visual data on unemployment.

Visual images that merely illustrate depend on the text and are subordinate to it. This is how they are nearly always used in works of sociology and anthropology, but it was not how I envisaged a work of visual sociology. I wanted to redress the balance between image and text somewhat. I examined works of visual sociology and visual anthropology to gain a sense of the extent to which the images were subordinate to text or vice versa. I paid attention to whether images were alone in a sea of text or together in groups, how the authors used captions, and how and where they analyzed the photographs. Most of the works I examined (*Balinese Character* and Doug Harper's work being notable exceptions) appeared to have photographs subordinate to text, and while this was true of Barker (1993), his approach of having several photographs together at the beginning of each chapter appeared to me to give the photographs more equal status to the text. This example made me decide to adopt this practice of making some of the images "tell a story" by themselves, in their own right, as opposed to just helping the text tell a story. I had enough photographs of some of the women's activities to enable me to do this in Chapter 4. I also adopted, on occasion, Bateson and Mead's (1942) technique of using long captions, as captions, in my view, are somewhat subordinate to the images they describe. If the writing in a caption were placed in the body of the text, this would make the photograph more of an illustration, subordinate to text. Despite these efforts, I believe I did not achieve the goal of redressing the balance overall, principally because I had analyzed and written up the textual data before the visual data, and despite my best intentions, this analysis shaped the way I viewed and incorporated the images. Furthermore, when deciding on the layout of photographs within the text, I was not always able to place photographs where I had initially intended because of the need for a page break or number of words on a page in the final book.

At the writing stage, I had to decide which images to leave out of the book. I re-examined each photograph for quality and relevance, also making the decision based on wanting to avoid repetition. Images on the same theme needed to offer new information. I chose to focus on experiences and meanings that the shantytown women shared, rather than on the differences between them. The experiences that the women had of repression, poverty, and resistance were remarkably similar, with the exception of the relatives of the disappeared, whose experiences of repression and resistance activities were different in degree and in kind, although there was considerable overlap. When it came to choosing which interview excerpts to use, the excerpt that best illustrated the point being made was the one selected for the book.

By way of background, I provide a brief description of historical facts that form the backdrop of the book. I then offer a large selection of visual images, which aims to introduce the reader to the physical environment of the shantytowns, both indoor and outdoor. The book as a whole is structured as much as possible in accordance with the sequence of steps that led shantytown women in Chile to engage in acts of political resistance. As a first step, the women experienced repression (Chapter 2) and more severe poverty than usual because of their husbands' unemployment, which resulted from the onset of neoliberal economic policies and a new national security doctrine (Chapter 3). They reacted to their impoverishment by joining groups aimed at coping with poverty, seeking jobs, engaging in entrepreneurship, adopting new consumption patterns, engaging in reciprocal exchanges, and asking their local priest for help (Chapter 4). Once members of groups, the women became involved in resistance to the dictatorship (Chapters 5 and 6). Shantytown women also resisted the dictatorship by joining groups that were not economically-oriented, and these groups, together with the ties that developed between all the different kinds of group and the women's new sense of belonging to a community, are examined in Chapter 7. Chapter 8 examines the significance of shantytown women's resistance, for the regime and for the women themselves.

The Dictatorship and What Preceded It

Unlike many socialist regimes that emerged after a violent episode during the twentieth century, Chile opted for a more peaceful route. "The Chilean way" ["La vía chilena"], as President Salvador Allende called it,[30] would bring socialism to Chile through democracy and legal means. Allende became the first democratically-elected, Marxist president in the world, taking office on November 3, 1970, and leading a coalition of leftist parties called Popular Unity [Unidad Popular, or UP]. His Popular Unity program was premised on "beginning the construction of socialism in Chile."[31] Whereas the orthodox capitalist model for economic development encouraged private capital and foreign investment, and anticipated trickle down,[32] the Popular Unity program emphasized using the power of the state to reorient resources towards the poor, through the continuation of agrarian reform, enlarging the sectors of the economy controlled by the state, and instituting social welfare programs that included giving a pint of milk a day to each child, expanding health services for the poor, creating day-care centers, and constructing low-income housing. It also aimed to bring employment for all Chileans at a decent wage level, reduce inflation, accelerate economic growth, and create a national unified education system. Importantly, it emphasized that Popular Unity would be multiparty and respect the rights of the opposition.[33] Although a change of course for Chile, this program was in some respects an extension of what had been done earlier. Chile's development strategies during the twentieth century had alternated between an export-oriented or growth-directed outward model, and a growth-directed inward model emphasizing industrialization through import substitution.[34] There had been moves towards land reform in rural areas since 1958, becoming more systematic after 1964.

The Popular Unity's plans met with severe opposition. The Christian Democrat Party slowed down change in congressional negotiations, and the delays motivated impatient rural inhabitants of the south to occupy large farms illegally,[35] often encouraged by such organizations as the Revolutionary Peasant Movement.[36] Factions within the Popular Unity coalition became apparent, with some members wanting to move towards socialism with all speed, ignoring legal constraints, and others preferring to advance through legal means.[37] There was also opposition from upper middle-class housewives, who marched banging empty pots in October 1972, as food was mysteriously absent in local supermarkets. Meanwhile, business owners concerned about nationalization shut down businesses and services, in what was known as the "October Strike," which lasted for four weeks and was settled with the incorporation of military men into the cabinet, the beginning of the armed forces' overt politicization.[38]

Allende's Chile thus faced severe economic and political challenges. Inflation rose very rapidly, and by July 1973 the inflation rate for the preceding 12 months had reached 323 percent, fueled by large government deficits.[39] As an authority on the period states, "The Chilean wage earner saw his entire 22 percent wage readjustment disappear in the first five months of 1972, and shortages of food and replacement parts led to massive dissatisfaction expressed in women's marches, shopkeepers' strikes, and continued violence in the streets."[40] Meanwhile, alarmed about the threat to United States corporate interests that Allende's expropriation policies represented, the Nixon administration carried out a program of economic destabilization, denying Chile loans and credits from both American and international lending institutions, and secretly funded opposition groups.[41]

A coup had been feared, but the ferocity of the one that surprised the world on September 11, 1973 was unexpected. It was on this day that the leaders of the armed forces stormed "La Moneda," Chile's governmental palace. Before they had seized control completely, Salvador Allende addressed the nation to inform it about the coup and his unwillingness to resign.[42] Remaining within La Moneda, he was either killed or committed suicide, a still unresolved issue. The acting Commander in Chief of the Military, Augusto Pinochet, very quickly came to head the Military Junta and continued to rule Chile until 1990.

In the weeks and months after the coup, thousands of Chileans who had supported Allende were detained by the police, military, or secret police. Of the 33,221 detained, 94 percent were tortured[43] by the DINA, Pinochet's Directorate of National Security,[44] akin to the Gestapo, and its successor, the National Center for Information [Central Nacional de Informaciones, CNI]. These institutions were responsible for much of the torture, disappearances, and arrests that occurred. Soldiers rounded up thousands of suspects, took them to Santiago's main soccer stadiums, and tortured and executed many of them; they also raided homes. The targets of this state violence were members of the government and the Popular Unity parties, the Movement of the Revolutionary Left [Movimiento de Izquierda Revolucionaria, MIR], and workers and peasants suspected of participating in extralegal takeovers of factories and estates.[45] The number killed during the regime is an estimated 1,068, not including the disappeared,[46] which currently number 1,190[47]. Many from the political left had little choice but to flee Chile, and many were kicked out, becoming refugees and exiles. As an authority on exile states, "Between 1973 and 1988, an estimated 200,000 men, women, and children—nearly 2 percent of Chile's population—were forced out of their country for political reasons."[48] In response to such repression, cells of resistance emerged throughout the nation, their organizers and members being principally women, students, shantytown inhabitants, clandestine leftist party or organization members, and trade union leaders.

The Military Junta's first political acts included the banning or recessing of political parties, the dissolution of congress, the implementation of a curfew and state of siege,[49] strict censorship and control of the press,[50] and the reversal of many of Allende's reforms. Unions soon became severely weakened[51] while leftist parties and organizations went underground and their leaders were harassed, fired, arrested, executed,[52] or escaped Chile. In December 1973 the regime issued a decree-law forbidding elections at any level, even in athletic and educational institutions.[53]

The economy was put into the hands of a group of economists known as the "Chicago Boys," whose neoliberal economic policies between 1973 and 1981 fostered the growth of nontraditional exports, consumer imports, and foreign loans.[54] They abolished all price controls, reduced tariffs, devalued the currency, slashed public spending, privatized industries that had previously been nationalized, and opened up Chilean markets to foreign investment.[55] The government responded to high social costs with a minimal safety net that targeted expectant mothers, small children, and the "extremely poor."[56] The results of such policies have been debated. Inflation and unemployment declined, although in 1980 the number of jobless was still twice that of 1970.[57] 1975–1976 and 1982 were years of economic crisis and extremely high unemployment. Protests swept the country in 1983, much as they had under Allende, and there followed an adjustment of the radical neoliberal economic policies.[58] As an authority on economic policy notes, "The change from dogmatic, orthodox neoliberalism to a more flexible, 'pragmatic' neoliberalism brought some tangible benefits. By 1985, the economy had begun to recover."[59]

Pinochet attempted to legitimize his authoritarian rule through the development of a new formal constitution, which he brought to a public referendum. The opposition was unable to mount a successful campaign against it and was hurt by the lack of an official alternative and by disagreements among parties;[60] the Chilean public voted in favor of it in 1980. The constitution reserved Pinochet the presidency until 1989, and in 1988 a referendum would be held to legitimize another eight years of power. If the public voted against him, the position of commander in chief of the army was reserved for him. When 1988 arrived, Pinochet's opposition united in preparation for the plebiscite, and the Chilean populace voted Pinochet out of power, setting the stage for democracy to take root once again in Chile.

From 1990, when the Christian Democrat, Patricio Aylwin, became president, until 2009, Chile was governed by a democratically-elected alliance of center-left civilian political parties called the Alliance of Democratic Parties [Concertación de Partidos por la Democracia, "la Concertación"], and only in 2010 was a right-wing president elected. However, Chile did not become a democratic country immediately after Pinochet stepped down; many authoritarian "enclaves" remained. General Pinochet had placed numerous reactionary judges loyal to the armed forces in the courts, shaped electoral laws to favor his followers, appointed non-elected senators that included retired military commanders, created rules preventing the president from firing military leaders, made the constitution he had drawn up in 1980 difficult to change, and instituted an amnesty for human rights crimes committed during the dictatorship.[61] He continued as head of the army, keeping present the threat of military intervention until he stepped down and became a senator for life in 1998.[62] Civilian governments were eventually successful in removing these "authoritarian holdovers,"[63] but as late as 2009 the Chilean Right enjoyed a virtual "veto power." Although in the 1990s little progress was made towards removing the shackles of the dictatorship, the changes became faster after Pinochet's detention in London.[64]

Website Link 1.6:

After the dictatorship, President Patricio Aylwin commissioned a report on human rights violations in Chile. A summary of its findings and an essay on the effect of human rights violations on families and society may be found in "Summary of the Truth and Reconciliation Commission Report" by Derechos Chile Ayer y Hoy. www.derechoschile.com/basic os/ddhhchile/rettig/english/rett igengindex1.html

The democratic transition was the product of a pact between the right-wing forces that supported Pinochet's dictatorship and the center-left sectors that took over in 1990. Its basis was the commitment to retain the neoliberal model and arguably to keep civil society demobilized so as to guarantee governability.[65] The civilian governments increased free trade policies;[66] foreign investment in Chile rose significantly between 1990 and 1999, and Chile's economy continued to depend on commodity exports.[67] At the same time there were increased public investments in infrastructure, education, and healthcare. After 1990, the economy showed structural growth and enabled almost everyone to experience improved living standards.[68]

Patricio Aylwin's administration was committed to reducing poverty and paying the "social debt" owed to those left behind. It began reforming social and labor policies within the free market framework. Many of Aylwin's programs were not maintained under the next president because of budget constraints,[69] but the president after that (the socialist, Ricardo Lagos) created new social and poverty programs.[70] President Michele Bachelet reinforced and expanded the public policies directed at the poor and disadvantaged.[71]

Poverty levels dropped after 1990 thanks to the social policies aimed at helping the most needy, and strong economic growth,[72] but in 1999, despite a decade of economic growth, almost half of Chilean households still had what many rated as poverty-level household incomes (although the official, conservative estimate was 27 percent poor or indigent). Between 1990 and 2009, Chile remained one of the world's most unequal societies in terms of wealth and income.[73] In the shantytowns, many inhabitants continued to endure hunger, low incomes, unemployment, and inadequate housing and healthcare after Aylwin became president.[74]

President Aylwin established a National Truth and Reconciliation Commission, whose final report stated that 3,197 persons had been killed or disappeared, but did not mention the thousands of tortured, detained, and exiled, or people who suffered from job blacklisting, and it failed to facilitate prosecution of these crimes. It was symptomatic of the exchange of "justice for stability" and the "pact of silence" of the 1990–1998 period.[75] In 2004, another official commission was established, and its report, called the Report of the National Commission on Political Imprisonment and Torture, concluded that torture was a systematic policy funded by the military budget and carried out in more than 1,000 detention centers in Chile, and that it had affected a much larger number of Chileans than had disappearances and executions. The army apologized for these abuses, and the navy acknowledged that a training vessel was used as a center of torture. More than 27,000 of the confirmed victims were made eligible for a largely symbolic small pension in compensation for their suffering.[76] Only in 2000 did an open debate about the regime begin to emerge in public in Chile, and there have been many acts of memory in recent years.[77]

Justice for human rights abuses was severely hampered by laws established by the Pinochet regime and by Pinochet being head of the army until 1998, thereby constituting a threatening presence that might intervene militarily or even engineer another coup. The dictatorship had left in place a 1978 Amnesty Law that protected the military and police from prosecution from human rights crimes committed between 1973 and 1978, the period during which most of the atrocities were committed,[78] but after 2000, judges in Chile began to chip away at this amnesty shield and eventually more than 300 retired officers were either in jail or facing charges. The courts are still attempting to prosecute high-ranking military officials who worked under Pinochet, but progress is slow.[79] General Pinochet himself was never brought to trial by the time of his death in 2006, although in 1998 he was put under house arrest in London on extradition request from Spain, and charged with crimes against humanity, including the killing and disappearance of more than 3,000 people. He was subsequently released,[80] but placed under house arrest again in Chile. In

Website Link 1.7:
Reports, news, photo galleries, videos, and podcasts about human rights issues around the world are available on the Human Rights Watch website, which may be browsed by region or topic:
www.hrw.org/

November 2006 he publicly acknowledged for the first time that "abuses" had taken place during his rule, but said that force had been necessary to prevent a civil-war that the Left was plotting.[81] In his last years, Pinochet lost support because it was discovered that his family had enriched themselves personally. Hence the dictatorship has been discredited, but many of its crimes are still unpunished, and many Chileans still approve of its overall goals.[82]

The nature of protest changed after Pinochet stepped down. There were almost no massive street demonstrations,[83] although in 2006 there were large movements of secondary school students,[84] and in 2007, at the initiative of Chile's largest labor union, thousands of people in different professions and cities participated in actions and demonstrations to draw attention to the widespread inequalities of neoliberal Chile, and highlight the disproportionate burdens carried by the poor and working class.[85] In 2011 there were many protests by students demanding free public education.

In the shantytowns, families were still under economic strain in the 1990s and 2000s, yet moments of massive collective expression only rarely occurred, and grass-roots mobilization dropped off dramatically after March 1990.[86] There was increased apathy among grassroots leaders and their followers,[87] and many community organizations collapsed or saw their membership dwindle dramatically in the 1990s.[88] The decline in collective action has been attributed to the fact that Concertación political parties withdrew from activity in the popular sectors as grassroots organizing was not a priority for them.[89] It has also been proposed that grassroots participation was weakened by neoliberalization, co-optation by mainstream political groups, a rise in the costs and risks of collective action at a time when democracy was seen as very vulnerable, and the fact that political parties began urging the use of institutionalized political channels for the articulation of movement demands.[90] These explanations arguably apply more to male-dominated social organizations than to women's organizations,[91] which had tended to want to distance themselves from political parties all along, however. For them, weariness with all the activity during the regime, not being able to sell their products as easily (for those in income-generating workshops), and the withdrawal of the support of humanitarian organizations, international NGOs, and people abroad were key factors in the closure of their organizations.[92]

There was some organizational life, however. In Colón, a shantytown in southern Santiago, for example, there were history workshops, senior citizens clubs, a collective kitchen, a reflection group, a Christian Base community, and annual celebrations,[93] and several shantytowns had income-generating groups (albeit severely dwindling in size), gymnastics classes, and seniors' clubs.[94] Some of the organizations that remained were asked by the government to provide services that could have been offered by the state, such as cleaning garbage from littered fields, yet their members were discredited because they lacked professional degrees.[95] There were also land seizures around Santiago, launched by the right-wing party, Independent Democratic Union.[96]

Surprisingly, shantytown women members of popular organizations were nostalgic about the dictatorship years, when in their view people had cooperated, shown solidarity with each other, and felt that their lives had a purpose.[97] Community leaders felt abandoned by political parties, disconnected from broader social movements, isolated from their neighbors, lonely, and lacking in purpose. Individuals who had not led but nevertheless participated in protests and similar activities felt that democracy brought isolation, individualism, and boredom.[98] The sense of mutual support that had characterized the protest years had disappeared by the early 1990s.[99] The shantytown women whom I interviewed were nostalgic for "the good times" of the regime, when there had been solidarity and unity. By the mid-1990s most of their groups had shut down, and those that remained had greatly dwindled in size; in 2005 the arpillera groups were no longer functioning, and some of the women were working individually and entrepreneurially, in very small operations, selling food to market stall owners and arpilleras to tourists, recycling cardboard and bottles, and even selling drugs. Others were working for an employer; one was cleaning a hospital, and another looking after a senior, for example. Two were running training centers for women, one worked for the government, and some were not working. Several participated in gym classes and seniors' groups in their neighborhoods, and some had been or were still active in parents' groups in their children's school. Their economic situation was no longer desperate, and they were no longer politically active in the way they had been previously. Most still did not approve of political parties, although one worked to help President Michele Bachelet's campaign.

New boards of representatives were popularly elected at shantytown neighborhood councils, replacing those whom the Pinochet government had appointed. However, the system whereby professionals, technocrats, and "apolitical" experts managed the economy with little input from the citizenry continued post-dictatorship, and resulted in shantytown dwellers' having little political influence.[100] The Chilean Catholic Church decreased its support for grassroots organizations after 1990 on the grounds that the government was responsible for public welfare.[101] NGOs, which had been a significant presence in the shantytowns, were co-opted into the state apparatus to different degrees, applying social programs.[102]

1.12a and b

Tall, irregular fences line shantytown streets whose surface is not yet paved, in the young shantytown of Campamento 12 Julio. In the near-absence of trees, telephone poles are prominent. Children play in the street.

The Physical Environment of the Shantytowns

Santiago's shantytowns were built by shantytown families and the government, with very limited resources. They had had minimal infrastructure and services, as the municipalities where they were concentrated had far less money per capita to spend than those of middle-class neighborhoods.[103] In many cases shantytown families had to group together and protest to have their municipal government build a school, clinic, and public telephone.

To an outsider, the shantytowns may have appeared barren. Many had rows of almost identical, single-story houses placed an equal distance apart along streets laid out in a grid pattern. There were almost no green spaces; even the rare, small plazas tended to be stretches of bare earth rather than grass, and were peppered with litter. Shantytown streets were narrow and not usually paved until several years into the shantytown's life,

1.13

The houses lining this shantytown street are identical in shape and size, suggesting that they were built by a government housing program. Normally such houses were divided in two and contained two families. They face a square with recently planted trees.

1.14

Unlike the previous photograph, this one hints at community. People have drifted towards a communal space, playing and talking to each other next to a soccer field. This space is not grass-covered or paved, and is heavily littered. There are few trees and prominent electricity poles. The houses of very similar shape and size suggest a government housing program.

1.15

There were occasionally buildings such as these in Santiago's shantytowns. This one stands in Pozo Areneros, San Miguel, in southern Santiago, not far from the center.

1.16

This house in Conchalí, in northern Santiago, has a corrugated iron roof lined on the inside with plastic or more metal, and its walls are boards of wood. It stands next to a watery ditch and the ground all around it is thick with mud. There are more single-story homes in the background. The photograph is dated August 1987.

1.17

The roof of this wooden house is of corrugated iron held down with rocks, and the only visible wall has no windows. Hardened earth surrounds the home, a ditch runs near it, and barbed wire marks the edge of the property while simultaneously serving as a washing line. The mother watches over her toddler, having recently washed his clothes.

1.18

The middle house in this photograph, with its box shape, wooden walls, and roof sloping in one direction only, is a "mediagua." The other houses in the street are also of wood, in this neighborhood in the southern part of La Granja, now the Municipality of La Pintana, in southern Santiago.

1.19

This smartly dressed woman leans against a rough-hewn wall that appears to have been made with second-hand, worn down bricks. An electricity cable emerges from the mortar. The wooden door is made from pieces of wood of different lengths, suggesting that they had previously been used for another purpose.

1.20

Like many shantytowns, this one has very few trees, prominent high tension towers and electricity poles, gritty, unpaved streets dotted with puddles, and a formidable line of high fences built to keep out burglars. At this early morning hour, almost no-one is outside.

1.21

The front of this home has been turned into a shop. Its owner has been able to accumulate enough money to have a tall, metal fence built, unlike her neighbors down the street whose fences are made of wood. The sidewalk sign that she uses to advertise her shop announces that she sells school materials, cleaning materials, cigarettes, soft drinks, zippers, sweets, and batteries. As these are small items that would take up little space to store, and require only one fridge, this business probably required limited capital.

and so, like the plazas, consisted of baked earth peppered with stones, dusty or gritty in summer, and muddy and dotted with puddles in winter. Some had a ditch with dirty water, like a drain, running along their side or middle. A few small trees lined these streets in places, but no front yards graced their edges. Instead there were fences of irregular and spiky pieces of wood originally used for other purposes, as this was all that families had managed to afford or find. Shantytown women tended to think of their fences as providing protection against burglars; but despite them, they thought it was not safe to leave the house "alone," and because of this fear, several houses had wrought iron bars covering their windows, and when families saved up some money, they often replaced their home's wooden fence with a metal one. On sunny days, the fences might be supports for washing hanging out to dry.

There were usually no cars in sight, as people could not afford them, and this made the shantytowns quiet. The low houses, unpaved streets, and lack of traffic noise gave many shantytowns the feel of a rural village. Adding to the impression were groups of children and dogs milling about on the streets, and women standing talking to their neighbor at their gate. The edge of a typical shantytown presented a bleak image of a straight line of fences of different heights in front of tiny homes. High tension towers and cables would stand out prominently over the low houses. Around the shantytown there

1.22a and b

A public toilet ["pozo negro," literally "black well"], next to an open space of baked earth and gravel in the shantytown. Such toilets were used by up to ten families.

might be an empty, flat, open, and littered space, if not a further stretch of shantytown. Often shantytowns were delimited by large streets, down which cars and buses drove, offering shantytown inhabitants a way to get to work.

Some shantytown homes were of solid construction, and had been designed according to government plans; each was the same. Others had been built by shantytown families. The family may first have had a tent (if the shantytown had originated in a land seizure) or, if the government had established the shantytown, a "mediagua," that is, a wooden hut with a sloping roof. As time went on, shantytown families saved money and replaced the tent or wooden hut with a small brick home. Some streets had a mix of brick and wooden homes, as families did not all manage to scrape together the necessary money at the same time. Many shantytown inhabitants had built part or all of their homes themselves, recycling used bricks and planks of wood. As they only had access to cheap or free materials, these were often of uneven sizes and poor quality, and the construction appeared rough. Roofs were initially made of corrugated iron, in some cases in scraps and held down by rocks. As pieces of corrugated iron provided imperfect protection from the rain, some families covered the whole structure in plastic sheeting in winter. Few houses had private bathrooms in the early years, so the shantytowns had wooden outhouses, used as communal bathrooms shared by up to ten families.[104] When the houses

1.23

A toddler sits at a rough-hewn wooden table, and a baby lies on the bed for which a curtain with holes in it will afford some privacy for those who normally sleep there. In the absence of cupboards, clothes hang from the ceiling.

were built by the government, they were small, brick structures one story high, with one family living in each half. Normally the family added rooms to increase the size of their dwelling, or built a second story later on, money permitting. In contrast to the village-like, one-story shantytowns, there were some shantytown neighborhoods with buildings three or four stories high.

The few, dispersed shops in the shantytowns sometimes consisted merely of the front room of a home. Some, called "quioscos," were simply a window that customers approached, attended by the lady of the house. They offered dry-goods such as exercise books, pens, washing liquids, zippers, batteries, cigarettes, sweets, or drinks. The occasional, very small grocery store ["almacén"] would sell a limited range of items, such as bread, milk, yoghurt, cheese, eggs, processed meat, drinks, wax, and cooked meats. The rarity of such shops meant that there was none of the color that often comes with shop windows and advertising. A small painted or chalk sign outside was often all there was to announce the place.

Many shantytowns were relatively far from the city center, and inhabitants faced long bus rides to get to work. This distance and inhabitants' economic difficulties made it too expensive for them to travel to the center of Santiago merely for leisure,[105] so those who were not working outside the shantytown tended to stay within its limits, except for occasional visits to relatives. The isolation was particularly acute for inhabitants who had

1.24

In a room whose ceiling is a plastic sheet, and at least one wall mere cloth, a family has hung up pictures of John Lennon and Jesus Christ. The older child sits on a bench in lieu of a chair.

been forcibly moved to outlying shantytowns because of the Pinochet government's policy of destroying islands of shantytown in middle-class neighborhoods, with the aim of "cleaning up" or selling the valuable land on which they stood.[106]

Shantytown homes tended to be overcrowded as they were small and housed parents, several children, and often relatives as well. Floors and surfaces were cluttered with objects due to limited room and few cupboards, and when it rained there might be large, metal washbasins and tin cans on the floor. Beds or mattresses would take up much of the floor space, and clothes sometimes hung in full view. The furniture tended to be rudimentary and of poor quality, and few pictures graced the walls, which were thin and uninsulated or poorly insulated. The inside walls were of the same planks of wood as could be seen from the outside. They might be lined with plastic sheeting in order to keep out drafts, water, and some of the cold in winter. Despite the shortage of money, most houses had a television set, and some had a modern fridge and stove, next to which stood a large, metal, bottle-shaped container of gas. There were no front or back yards; just a tiny tiled patio between some houses and the street, and sometimes a tiled space at the side or back of the house as well. These patios were cluttered, often containing a table and chair or two, as well as items for which there was no room in the house: buckets, a wooden wash basin, a large metal drum, and various plastic receptacles. However, they were often graced by a few plants eking out a living in rusty cans in lieu of pots.

Even though the shantytowns of Santiago were bleak places, the human warmth one found in some of them (see Chapter 4) may have mitigated the hostility of the environment. Some shantytown inhabitants were on friendly terms with two or three neighbors who would readily offer help when needed, some lived in lanes in which everyone helped each other, and some were members of local groups in which members were highly supportive. All was not rosy among neighbors, however. Many shantytown families were afraid of break-ins and muggings when they went out to the local street market, and so made sure the house was always guarded, and carried the smallest possible amount of money.[107] There was even a term for burglars from one's own shantytown: "domésticos."[108] In addition, shantytown parents worried about drug addiction in their neighborhoods.

1.25

Not all shantytown families were desperately poor. Some had nice-looking kitchen appliances, although their presence could hide the family's economic difficulties; they tended to be bought on credit and paid for in installments.

1.26

An older woman and young boy enjoy a quiet moment on a back patio crowded with table, bench, and metal drum. The floor is of concrete.

This mostly bleak environment of crowded homes made of poor-quality materials, muddy or dusty streets, and almost tree-less landscapes, was where the government's neoliberal economic policies and national security doctrine played themselves out in women's lives. It was also here that women of the shantytowns resisted the regime and fought poverty. We turn now to examine the repression as the women experienced it.

Two	**Living with Repression**

While some shantytown women experienced the execution, disappearance, or exile of a family member, this was not the form that repression took for most. More commonly, it manifested itself by way of a persistent military presence in the shantytowns, curfews backed by shooting, and restrictions on freedom of movement, association, and expression. The various forms of repression that shantytown inhabitants endured may be subdivided into *direct physical repression* and *non-violent repression*. Non-violent repression included constraints on people's freedoms, not immediately backed by violence. Direct physical repression involved physical violence or the immediate threat of violence by the state. It consisted of *generalized repression* and *targeted repression*. Generalized repression was repression that affected everyone in the neighborhood indiscriminately. Targeted repression was repression where a person was singled out for persecution. Both the direct physical repression and the non-violent repression derived from the regime's national security doctrine, according to which leftists were a threat to national security.[109] This chapter examines the generalized, targeted, and non-violent repression that shantytown women experienced, and then explores the *endemic* and *specific fear* that resulted from the repression, and the ways in which the repression intersected with poverty and motherhood to shape shantytown women's experiences of the dictatorship.

Direct Physical Repression

Generalized Repression

It was more common for shantytown women in Santiago to endure generalized repression than targeted repression. Generalized repression, which affected everyone in the neighborhood, included curfews backed by violence, soldiers shooting at people, military men patrolling the streets, occasional raids on homes, and the occasional presence of military vehicles, helicopters overhead, and tear gas. Shantytown inhabitants sometimes experienced multiple forms of generalized repression simultaneously.

The curfews affected the shantytown women on a daily basis for extended periods, making several normally simple activities complicated or impossible. Leaving the house became a dangerous thing to do after the appointed hour, since one risked being shot. Family emergencies also became more difficult. Nelly told me:

> At night if one of them [the children] got sick, you had to call the soldiers for them to take you to the clinic because you couldn't go out alone, because there was a curfew. Yes, there was a curfew, so when eight o'clock struck no-one could go out into the street. You couldn't go out into the street because otherwise one of them

would simply shoot you. As I say, that time I was saved, it was, well, if I hadn't gone inside they would have shot me; imagine! So those were the things that we experienced a lot.

Nelly's words suggest that activities that one had previously done freely, like going outside after 8 p.m., became life-threatening, and that if there was a family health crisis people had to make arrangements with soldiers to avoid being shot. Once Nelly almost got shot because she was just outside her house after curfew. She resented having to be inside after a certain hour and the fact that you might be shot if you did not obey, and spoke angrily about these constraints years later. The repression curtailed shantytown women's freedom of movement, in other words, and normal life was altered.

Curfew brought still other night-time discomforts. Shantytown inhabitants were supposed to have the lights off after dark. Family evening time was disturbed because sometimes husbands with jobs could not come home from work, since the lack of buses after curfew and the fact that workplaces tended to be far away meant that either they returned home fairly early or stayed overnight in their workplace. The sound of bullets sometimes disturbed the evening peace, and the risk of one smashing through one's wall caused fear. Karina told me that they could not sleep because of this, and so her family put their beds on the floor. The soldiers who prowled the streets at night sometimes broke windows with stones, as Karina witnessed in her street, and one such stone broke a window of her own home, just above where her little boy was sleeping. She told me the story:

JA: What type of repression did you have here?

Karina: Just the state of siege. [*JA*: the state of siege]. When you had to be home early. Workers had to get home early and if not, stay in the factory, because they wouldn't make it home because it was very far away, and at that time there were no buses either. We had to have the lights off at a certain time. You couldn't have the lights on until late. And they would pass by throwing stones at the houses.

JA: They would?

Karina: Yes, they would throw stones. And they said that they didn't throw any, but they did, because I saw them throw stones once. They even broke one of my windows, and the glass fell on the bed where my eldest was sleeping. So very carefully, I took out the pieces, and with a candle, because you couldn't have the light on. So what everyone started to do was make some wooden boards, and put them in the windows. To avoid the stones. [*JA*: Yes, yes, good idea]. So people started doing this in all the windows; because they only threw stones at some houses, not all. And that one time it was my turn. So that's, that's all I remember. We suffered a lot, a lot of fear.

JA: And, and you lived, this house was already built, at that time?

Karina: Yes, it was already built.

JA: Was it built in, in 1970?

Karina: Yes, it was already built. You could see that at night young people, groups, would run away, in all directions. You would hear bullets.

JA: Bullets?

Karina: Yes.

JA: Soldiers'? Whose?

Karina: Yes, soldiers who would go around shooting.

JA: At, at, at whom?

Karina: At the young people who were hanging around there, the young men.

JA: Why, for example?

Karina: Because they would go around throwing things at them, no doubt, at the policemen. Or they would burn tires, secretly. And it was safer if you put the mattresses here, on the ground, to sleep more peacefully. Because they were loud shots that you would hear. And my sister was living in Pudahuel; she still lives there, on the banks of the Mapocho [Santiago's river]. She says there were a lot of dead bodies there. Children, babies; she said it was sad to see.

JA: Were there any here too?

Karina: No, there were none here. Just that one death, of, of that lady who was having a party and a bullet hit her. And young people who were injured because they were outside doing foolish things and the police shot them. And in the National Stadium, because a lot of people came from there, injured, beaten.

Karina's words are testimony to the climate of intense insecurity that the repression created in the shantytowns. Hers was a world of gun shots, stones thrown at windows, neighbors and young men being killed, injured, or beaten, and danger if one had the lights on at night. Her words also suggest that shantytown women knew of repression going on beyond the shantytown; this knowledge would have added to the sense of insecurity. These multiple manifestations of state violence amounted to severe limitations on shantytown inhabitants' freedom, and the transformation of their neighborhoods into places in which they risked their lives. Poverty and repression intersected to produce this outcome. Outside the shantytowns, soldiers did not routinely throw stones at windows and shoot one's neighbors, for example. Men's having to stay in their workplaces overnight is a concrete instance of this intersection, in that shantytown men were more likely to work far from home and take buses to work than middle-class men, and so when the curfew caused buses to stop, they were affected differently from someone living near his workplace and able to drive a car home.

The women knew people whom soldiers had shot for being outside after curfew, and this caused them anxiety about their own children. They had neighbors who had been killed outside their homes, at the windows of their home, in their doorway, and on the second floor. Teresa told me about a young boy who lived opposite her:

JA: Did a lot of soldiers come here? What was life like in the shantytown at that time?

Teresa: Yes, they would come by here. Yes, you couldn't go out. Because of the curfew. Just there, opposite, they killed some kids because they stuck their heads out. There, at the corner, they killed another. I would just shut myself in with all my kids: "Don't go outside!" I would just shut myself in, here.

JA: At night? Starting at what time?

Teresa: At night. As early as six in the evening we had to all be shut up inside.

JA: And this lasted sort of, how many months?

Teresa: It lasted some four, five months, it must have been, yes, it lasted a long time. We were very scared, because there was no food.

Teresa knew at least three children who had been shot, and was clearly frightened for her own, forbidding them from going outside while the curfew was on. Six in the evening

2.1

Policemen keep watch during La Victoria's anniversary festivities.

2.2

Soldiers are a menacing presence along the sidewalk in La Victoria

2.3

Two soldiers with shields hide behind the corner of a house in La Victoria in the early morning. 1985. Photographer: Alejandro Hoppe, Chile. Mail: contacto@alejandrohoppe.cl Web: www.alejandrohoppe.cl

was early, meaning that the whole family was prevented from going outside for a substantial part of each day.

The curfews forced many women to take special measures not only in their daily lives, but also when carrying out new activities, such as the work involved in the groups they had joined, or going to look for family members who had disappeared. When Natalia went out very early to fetch food for her community kitchen, she had to tie a white flag to her bicycle to prevent soldiers from shooting her. The women organized the timing of their group meetings so that they would finish before curfew, and if a meeting went on too long one group slept in the church rather than risk being shot while walking home. Barbara remembered curfew as beginning quite early, and she sometimes only just managed to get home from searching for her husband in the National Stadium. She remembered walking, as there were no buses after curfew, and trying to hide as she walked.

Soldiers made their presence felt not only during curfew, but also in the daytime, during certain periods.[110] Ana said there were soldiers in her shantytown in eastern Santiago day and night, for periods of time, while Karina spoke of them patrolling every day in San Bruno, in southern Santiago. Bettina, from the shantytown of San Isidrio in northern Santiago, told me about soldiers with painted faces, who were rough with children. There were sometimes military vehicles in the streets. When the government declared a state of siege, vans of policemen arrived, there would be bullets flying, and people would run away and go home to hide, Karina said. There were also, occasionally, water cannons ["guanacos"] in her shantytown.

The states of siege, which included curfew, had yet another repercussion: shops in the shantytowns closed early and sometimes did not have enough food to sell, and this contributed to food shortages in families. There were lines for food, a problem that is widely thought of as being characteristic of the Allende years, but the words of a number of shantytown women testify to the fact that it also existed during the Pinochet era. Karina said, while describing a huge arpillera her group made:

> We put in the road as well, and the women showed where the soldiers would break windows. [*JA*: Yes.] We'd put that in too; we'd put in small white pieces, as people knew they were windows. Er, and the lines to buy things, because they wouldn't sell anything. Nothing at all! The stores would be open for a certain amount of time and then they would close, they would close. [*JA*: Why?] Because it—we were under a state of siege. What do you call it? [*JA*: Yes, a state of siege] so, people couldn't, people didn't manage to buy, they simply didn't buy anything. Instead they would give you—the bakeries would give you the uncooked bread and you would cook it here in the house. And, well, come home to hide. Because there were a lot of bullets.

Karina's words suggest that while the states of siege meant that shops stayed open only a short time, bakers, perhaps acting out of solidarity, would give people bread to eat. Her description of the state of siege reveals how repression, poverty, and gender combined to shape her experience of the regime. According to shantytown gender expectations, she, as mother, was responsible for feeding the family, and so she would go out to buy food. The repression and state of siege made this difficult as shantytown shops closed early. On her way home, the state violence caused her to have to be careful to avoid bullets; shantytowns rather than middle-class neighborhoods experienced shooting.

Many shantytown families experienced one or more raids by soldiers on their home. The soldiers would bang on the door in the middle of the night, come in with

2.4

Men and soldiers during a raid. This photograph most likely was taken in the early morning as men were being released, since raids were normally conducted in the middle of the night.

machine-guns, take men over the age of fifteen to a nearby football field or open space, and begin searching the house for weapons or documents. They would ask aggressively where the weapons were, turn the furniture upside down, turn over mattresses, and open all the cupboards, destroying things in the process and terrifying the women and children within. They would examine the books the family had, and even, Karina told me, ask about any medicines they found. Sometimes they took the children aside and asked them questions. Meanwhile, the men were kept in the open space for a few hours, their family not knowing where they were. Some were taken to the National Stadium and re-appeared after several days, or disappeared altogether. In some cases whole streets of homes were raided at the same time, and in others a single family was targeted, the latter being called an "allanamiento selectivo" ["selective raid"].

Gloria, from La Victoria, experienced three raids, Ana from eastern Santiago remembered two in the months after the coup, Natasha in Fraternidad in southern Santiago experienced "two or three" raids, while Karina in San Bruno experienced only one, and Teresa in Fraternidad experienced none although she knew that in other parts of her shantytown there were raids on every home. The shantytown of La Victoria experienced more raids than any other.[111] Gloria told me:

JA: Did it happen to you that they came in to raid?

Gloria: Yes, they raided here, yes. Well, there were a lot of raids like this, house by house, during a certain period when they had kidnapped a general, I don't remember his name. They went from house to house, going through absolutely everything, absolutely everything. My daughters had their room there, behind. They went through their books. If they saw a psychology book for example: "But what sort of psychology?" I mean, as if it were bad to have psychology books. Of course

2.5

Women and children were normally kept in the house during a raid, but they would have been able to emerge in the morning, and go to the open space where their husbands were being kept.

here in this house we have always had a lot of books, we've always been keen on studying and reading. And they would go through everything. And so when you had arpilleras we didn't know where to put them because if they caught us with the arpilleras as well, in which we would show what was happening, well, they could take us away. I mean, so we would hide them, we didn't know how, we would put them between our clothes so that they wouldn't find the arpilleras.

JA: Between the clothes in the wardrobe?

Gloria: Yes, yes.

JA: And how many times did they come in like that?

Gloria: They came in here about three times, roughly.

Gloria evokes thorough and repeated raids on her shantytown, an outcome of the military's view of shantytowns as harboring dissidents, and of La Victoria's reputation as particularly leftist, organized, and combative. Gloria's feeling that she had to hide her arpilleras in case there was a raid suggests that the phenomenon of raids destroyed her feeling of security over a long period of time, even in her home; there was no safe haven. The soldiers' questions about books point to the danger that having documents that might be mistaken for leftist entailed.

A raid was a traumatic experience, due to the suddenness, the timing in the middle of the night, the roughness of the soldiers, their destruction of one's possessions, the invasion of one's home and privacy, the mess left behind, and the taking away of husband and older sons, coupled with not knowing whether they would return. I asked Catarina, from San Bruno:

JA: And did they raid?

Catarina: They raided all the houses. Here we had a first raid, but it was during those periods when they lifted the, the curfew, to raid. It was awful. They raided, they took the men out to the street, at midnight, to the, to that place where, it was a bare field still, it had not been built on. They would even take out the young people, the children. They would leave the women in the house and the police would come in and, and men from the air force and soldiers, and go through everything. That alone made you frightened. That would convince someone who had, who had never got involved, had never got involved in anything, that things were not so natural and normal. You feel invaded in—, your privacy. [*JA*: Yes.] That was the first invasion, when you felt that the eyes of strangers, strangers' hands, touched your things, and so on. [Pause]. Well, that—, for us it was very hard, that time. And after that they were forever raiding in the shantytowns.

Catarina's words point to two reactions to raids: fear and a feeling of violation.

The trauma of the experience had repercussions on family life. In San Isidro, in northern Santiago, after Bettina's family suffered a raid, her husband did not want her or the children to leave the home. She said:

What we didn't have was a little knowledge, when we were raided, about asking for help in, in some embassy, and so that they would take us out of here. Because my husband, psychologically, was in a terrible, terrible state after we were raided. When the children were growing up, my husband wanted them just to stay there in the house, shut in, and he wanted me to not mix with anyone, with anyone at all, no-one. Because I started to participate in popular organizations secretly. When he went to work I could go out, and when he was in the house, I had to be shut in.

The raid clearly caused fear and anxiety in Bettina's husband, and the deterioration of his mental health made for an oppressive situation for her and her children. Becoming involved in groups required her to defy both his prohibition and the regime's repression, two intersecting forms of domination that constituted a formidable obstacle that she surmounted by employing secrecy.

The raids made it more difficult to participate in activities that constituted an offensive against the regime. Producing and distributing flyers or bulletins became more complicated, for example, because the raids made having anti-regime documents in the house dangerous. Making arpilleras with denunciatory messages was risky since the women sewed them at home and they could be found during a raid; the women had to hide the arpilleras they were in the process of making. Any exhibition containing dissident messages could be raided. In La Victoria, locals had built a "House of Culture" with money from France, as a place for local groups to meet, and for its opening the shantytown coordinating committee had organized an exhibition containing arpilleras, remnants of tear gas bombs, and other evidence of repression. That night soldiers came, destroyed everything, and took the arpilleras away.[112] Although being raided made anti-regime activities more difficult or risky, it could also be radicalizing. For example, local priests visited Bettina after her home was raided and invited her and her husband to form part of their local Christian base community. Wanting to understand why she had been raided, Bettina accepted, and this was an important step in a career of anti-dictatorship activism that saw her creating two arpillera groups and participating in protests and a national shantytown women's organization.[113]

Often the state's assaults were multiple and simultaneous. In San Isidrio in northern Santiago, for example, routine street violence occurred at the same time as targeted violence directed at individual families and the local church, and both took on several forms at once. Bettina painted a vivid picture for me:

JA: And what was the repression like in the neighborhood?

Bettina: It was strong repression, very strong repression. We thought there was no reason for us to have to experience such strong repression, like for example, after

2.6

Three soldiers with painted faces.

they would, whe—, when, when the dictatorship began, the streets were patrolled permanently by soldiers with painted faces. And this was really horribly rough on the children. The terror that, that they could not sort of—, sometimes they would mistreat a child who was simply in the street. And the fact that they went around with painted faces meant that you would not recognize who the person was, who was there. And they always treated people very roughly. And well, as I say, there were raids on homes here. So, we were raided and we were— and my husband was threatened as well, with, if he, well, if they found out or heard that he was still participating, he would simply disappear. So it was always quite tough. We suffered serious consequences here, like for example, the fires. The, the chapel where we started to, to participate [in groups], also, was burned to the ground.

Bettina's words point to the existence of both generalized and targeted repression. The generalized repression she mentions consists of soldiers patrolling the streets, treating people roughly, and wearing paint on their faces, which made them unrecognizable. The targeted repression includes raids on homes, her husband being threatened with disappearance, and the local church being burned down. To attack the church was to strike the community at its heart, since this was where locals came together in groups to carry out activities that enabled them to subsist, and where they discussed their problems and the regime, and it was almost the only place where they could feel relatively safe in doing so, thanks to the Church's power and moral authority. Jean Franco (1985) argues that assaults by repressive states in Latin America on priests, nuns, women, and children are transgressions on the "sanctuary spaces" of church, home, and family that offer some immunity from violation. When the boundaries of these spaces are ruptured, the meaning of these spaces shifts, reflecting the fact that they no longer offer protection from repression. This may have been true for a time in San Isidrio, but locals immediately set to work building two new chapels, the work perhaps helping to increase community cohesion and radicalization. Bettina's words also show the ways in which women experienced repression through a gendered lens. She described the soldiers' patrolling as tough on children, and her words evoke a mother's terror that her child would be mistreated by them.

Ana, whose experience in eastern Santiago was similar to Bettina's in the variety of assaults she experienced, gives us a sense of the emotions and thoughts that the repression inspired. Her words express shock and indignation with the levels of repression in her neighborhood, which she described as "terrible." It troubled her that at seven in the evening you had to make sure your children stayed indoors, since children were killed by flying bullets. She was angry that houses were raided and some families' possessions destroyed, and men taken away in the process, some never to be seen again, and she was upset that innocent people in the shantytown were killed:

JA: And what was the repression like, here in the shantytown?

Ana: Terrible.

JA: What, concretely what would they do?

Ana: Well, we had soldiers twenty-four hours a day here in the shantytown, twenty-four hours a day. And then about, the first, just after the coup, well, the first days, the first months, at seven in the evening you couldn't walk around outside in the street because they would shoot you. [Pause] So, no, it was terrible, we lived here like, like in wartime. Because with the tanks in the avenue, the raids on homes when the soldiers, in some cases, broke everything, because I don't know what they were looking for, I don't know what they were looking for.

JA: "Allanamiento" means that they would come and look for something?

Ana: Right here, they would turn the whole house upside down, break—, they would turn over the mattresses, turn over the armchairs, search, they would open the furniture, everything, drawers, everything; that was a raid.

JA: And how often did raids happen?

Ana: At the beginning, umm, about two or three times, it happened.

JA: A year?

Ana: No, just for a period of time in the year, less than a year, when it was most harsh, when the coup had just happened. Then, in that period, it was like—and some houses got it more than others. Yes. And with arrogance, they would throw the—they would take out the men; they would take them to a space, alone. For example, if there was a space, in a football field, well, that's where they would keep the men. They would leave just the women with the children in the house. And, and then begin raiding, you see, and, and anyone who rebelled or started to say things, they would take prisoner, and then sometimes there were some who never showed up again. In that period, the time of the raids.

JA: And they would come in, you were saying that they would kill people here as well.

Ana: Yes, yes, children. A neighbor from, from, from here at the back of the house. Look, here at seven in the evening you had to shut your children inside, not allowing them even to go out to the patio because the bullets were flying in all directions. And so like this, with this shoot out, there were many innocent people who died, people who didn't deserve it at all, many, many, many people here in the shantytown.

Ana's repetition of "twenty-four hours a day" and emphasis on "seven in the evening" (very early for having to shut the family indoors) suggest indignation, while her phrase "like, like in wartime" hints at outrage. When she describes the raid, her words and tone suggest anger at soldiers' arrogance and abuse: "they would turn the whole house upside down, break—." In talking of the "many innocent people who died, people who didn't deserve it at all, many, many, many people here in the shantytown," her words and tone communicate sadness and a sense of injustice, and hint at an impression of the violence as arbitrary; anyone could be killed. She experienced the environment as one of great danger, in which one risked being shot, having one's husband arrested or disappeared, having one's home raided, and having one's children killed. Motherhood shaped what the bullets meant for Ana, namely having to keep one's children inside, and it perhaps also influenced what she remembered, such as the fact that children had been killed. The situation that Ana describes amounts to an assault on the shantytown space. Soldiers in the street, tanks in the avenue, raids on homes, bullets flying, the arrest or disappearance of some men, innocent people dying, and the curfew's restrictions, constitute multiple manifestations of state violence.

How their children experienced the repression affected the women's own experiences of it. They worried about their children's fear and the ways in which the environment was intimidating for them, as when Bettina described terror caused by soldiers with painted faces in her shantytown. Gloria, similarly, was struck by her very young son's being afraid he would be taken away. She told me:

> You had to stay shut indoors because you couldn't go outside. So we experienced the repression quite intensely. And the kids, the kids were always very scared. The youngest ones, especially, got very scared, as they didn't realize what was happening. I remember one time when my son was playing with a child who lives here on this block, who was the son of a political prisoner, this little one was, this little boy. And there was a protest and the soldiers were here and they were heading in that direction, and suddenly I see both of them hiding there, there under a door. "And what are you doing there?" I ask. "We're hiding because if we don't hide, they take men away." They knew that they would come into people's homes and take men away. The kids were very frightened, and they must have been [pause] eight years old. [*JA*: Terrible]. Yes. [Pause]. The children were very much shut up in the house.

Gloria was worried about her children being constantly afraid and aware at such a young age that men were taken away. She was also, like many women, upset that they had to be inside so much. Motherhood influenced how shantytown women experienced the repression, viewing some of it through their children's eyes.

The women could not be certain about when or whom the repression would strike, and this caused a strong sense of insecurity. Karina, in San Bruno, knew that soldiers threw stones at the windows of homes and that a bullet might tear through the wooden wall of her house and kill someone, but did not know when or whether it would happen to her. Nelly and other women lived with the knowledge that soldiers shot at or arrested people when they had done nothing to deserve it. No-one knew when their home would be raided, but they knew it could happen any time. The state violence produced a feeling of not being safe anywhere, at any time.

Geographical and Temporal Variations

The women perceived that the levels of repression varied from shantytown to shantytown.[114] In La Victoria it was particularly intense, according to women from La Victoria and nearby shantytowns, several of whom mentioned its numerous raids, a statement supported by a study that noted that La Victoria was the hardest hit in this regard.[115] Gloria, who lived there, explained this in terms of La Victoria residents being organized and active in protests, and said that she experienced soldiers, tear gas, and bullets in her street. By contrast, there were some shantytowns that endured very little repression, the women said. Babette used to live in La Estrella, one of the first shantytowns in southern Santiago, at a time when retired air force men and policemen lived there, and she reported that there was no repression in the streets, all was calm, and people even had their lights on at night. A few streets away in San Bruno, it was "another world":

> *Babette*: It was people in the armed forces, there were only people in the armed forces in that shantytown [La Estrella] [. . .] the people who were in the air force, who were soldiers, who were policemen, they were from that se—, from that, let's say that socio-economic level.
>
> *JA*: Right, so what was the repression like in that shantytown?
>
> *Babette*: There was none.
>
> *JA*: When you started to make arpilleras, there was none.
>
> *Babette*: No, very little. We here, for example, when—when the protests were happening we would come over here [to San Bruno].
>
> *JA*: To protest?
>
> *Babette*: Yes [laughs]. Yes. And you know, we would run between the bullets, yes, trying to cross over. And you arrived at the other shantytown [La Estrella], and there was light, there were no fi—, there were no barricades, there was nobody in the street, it was another world.
>
> *JA*: In, in which shantytown?
>
> *Babette*: In the shantytown La Estrella, it was another world.
>
> *JA*: So there was no repression in your shantytown, La Estrella.
>
> *Babette*: No, very little. There was very little because no-one did anything, because it was just senior citizens, and on top of that people who had been in the armed forces, so it was, it was almost all people who were in favor of the dictatorship.

Babette evokes a stark contrast between San Bruno where there were bullets, protests, and people in the streets, and La Estrella's lights on at night, empty streets, and absence of barricades.

The women were also aware that the shantytowns endured more severe repression than middle-class areas of Santiago. Nora, who had lived in Simón Bolívar in south-eastern Santiago, contrasted her shantytown with a middle-class neighborhood, Ñuñoa:

> So it [Simón Bolívar] was a very bad neighborhood, with the protests. [. . .] And all this [state violence] depended on the neighborhood you lived in, because for example my parents lived in Ñuñoa, in Avenida Ossa, so it's another neighborhood, so for them this sort of thing [police throwing bombs at buildings], this—, they didn't experience things that were traumatizing.

Repression varied not only from place to place but also over time.[116] The women's words suggest that in their perception it tended to be particularly severe during periods when shantytown inhabitants were protesting in large numbers, as occurred in 1983. In the shantytown of Fraternidad during this period, but also sometimes on other days, soldiers would shoot bullets, buckshot, and pellets, sometimes every day, Natalia told me.

Website Link 2.3:
Targeted repression exists
under repressive regimes
throughout the world.
Repression in Iran is described
from the perspective of the
International Campaign for
Human Rights in Iran on this
website:
www.iranhumanrights.org/

Website Link 2.4:
Information about human
rights in China and the work
of human rights groups is
available in the form of
reports, commentary, press
releases, and videos on the
website, Human Rights in
China. The website also
contains documents by
human rights groups. See:
www.hrichina.org/

Website Link 2.5:
"Women in Iran have been at
the forefront of the human
rights movement in that
country," but have been
severely repressed by the
government. A discussion of
such repression is available
on the Amnesty International
website, "Women's Human
Rights Activism in Iran."
www.amnestyusa.org/our-
work/countries/middle-
east-and-north-africa/iran/
women-s-human-rights-
activism-in-iran

They would also drive by in trucks to frighten people, and raid shantytown homes. Nelly, who lived nearby, said they would kill young people when they protested in the street. During protests, the police sprayed protesters with tear gas and water cannons, and made arrests, and sometimes there were bullets. There was state violence just after protests as well. In the shantytown of Simón Bolívar in south-eastern Santiago, the police threw bombs at a building after a protest had taken place in the neighborhood, as Nora described:

> And then we had the horrible experience. I was, I was living with my family, and one day there was a protest, and then at night the police came, at about ten at night, and threw bombs at the building. So that was really terrible, I was almost blown out of the fourth floor, I was saying, "I'm going to jump out, I'm going to jump out."

Nora's words suggest a retaliatory action by the police, following a protest. They also communicate that she was terrified, not only because of the bombs, but also because the police had come at night, and when they were not expected; such events would have contributed to a sense of insecurity. During protest periods such as these, the shantytown women were afraid to go where the violence was. When there was shooting in the center of Santiago, for example, Natasha was reluctant to go to the Vicaría to hand in her arpillera group's work, even though not handing in work meant that her group was not paid. She was grateful for donations at such times, because they meant that her group could wait until things had calmed down.

Many shantytown women remembered the repression as having been particularly vicious on the day of the coup. Julia, from a southern shantytown, saw young people being dragged out of their houses, and remembered how one could not be out on the streets at 3 p.m. She went to visit her husband in the hospital and found it full of soldiers, some with machine-guns, and a helicopter circling overhead. The soldiers shooting in their shantytowns, the bombing of the presidential palace, and the death of President Allende remained vivid in many women's minds, and inspired fear in them many years later. Nelly felt afraid and traumatized after learning about the bombing of the presidential palace, hearing gun shots, and seeing soldiers in the street. Sixteen years after the end of the regime, she still shook:

> I was left rather traumatized because all sorts of things make me nervous, make me start to shake. Because gee, if at seven in the morning you wake up and hear that in La Moneda [Chile's White House] there is a, there is gunshot and they are killing the president or whatever they are doing, with soldiers in the street—and you are in a country that historically had not, nothing of the kind had happened, it's cause for fear.

The fact that Nelly was still shaken sixteen years after the end of the regime attests to how traumatic the violence on that day was for her. She and other women remembered numerous forms of repression and violence as occurring simultaneously on the day of the coup, both in their shantytown and in the center of the city.

Targeted Repression

In addition to generalized repression, some shantytown families experienced what I call "targeted repression," whereby a person was singled out for persecution. Targeted repression took the form of harassment, a raid just on the targeted person's home, arrest, torture, beatings, disappearance, murder, exile, internal exile, and husbands losing their jobs because they were affiliated with groups that the dictatorship wished to eliminate. It affected both families and institutions, as when the church was burned down in northern Santiago, shocking and frightening local families. While most shantytown women experienced only generalized repression, many did experience both generalized and targeted repression. Others merely knew people suffering from targeted repression, or heard of such cases, and still others were unaware that targeted repression was occurring, until they joined groups. Targeted repression could be meted out on shantytown inhabitants anywhere in the city, including workplaces, for example. In this chapter I have focused on a small number of forms of targeted repression, selected on the basis of the shantytown women's mention of them.

"They Took Him Away": Arrests

Many shantytown women endured the experience of having their husband or children detained for a few days,[117] and those who did not experience this often knew someone who had.[118] Bettina, for example, had her eldest son taken prisoner, and Ana and Barbara had their husbands detained for several days. If husbands were detained even for a short time, their wives experienced tremendous anxiety. There was also the anguish of not knowing where they were, and the strain of having to search for them on a daily

2.7

An arpillera that suggests that a woman's husband has been arrested. He is depicted in a cage-like structure, signifying a prison, on the right. Zigzag lines going from her head and the heads of most of her six children to him suggest that they are all thinking about him.

2.8–2.10

Male and female prisoners in the National Stadium.

Website Link 2.6:
Human rights violations occurring in Myanmar have been investigated and recorded on video by the organization Physicians for Human Rights, which uses the skills of medical professionals to establish the existence of human rights violations and prevent further violations and mass atrocities. A video is available at "Life Under the Junta: Evidence of Crimes Against Humanity in Burma's Chin State":
http://physiciansforhuman rights.org/library/multimedia/ life-under-the-junta.html

The organization's website also includes a library with other videos, reports, press releases, congressional testimony, statements, letters, and articles published in journals and periodicals, about human rights violations in other repressive contexts. See "Physicians for Human Rights," the left-hand margin link "PHR Library" at: http://physiciansforhuman rights.org/about/

Website Link 2.7:
One of Chile's torture centers has been turned into a museum about repression in Chile. Its website contains information about the secret police (DINA), detention centers, torture, and the victims of repression. See "Corporación Parque por la Paz Villa Grimaldi," in Spanish: www.villagrimaldi.cl/historia. html

basis. Barbara's husband was arrested immediately after the coup, for a month, and held first in the Stadium of Chile ["Estadio de Chile"], and then in the National Stadium ["Estadio Nacional"].[119] His arrest had to do with his factory's having been part of a worker take-over, and his having remained in it after curfew, together with other employees. For several days Barbara did not know where he was, until finally she received news about him from a fellow prisoner, at which point she went to the stadium every day, trying to see him. Meanwhile, she was alone with the children, not knowing what to do with them, and she suffered a raid, and felt afraid, with tanks patrolling her neighborhood. So vivid is her description that it is worth quoting at length:

Barbara: Yes, he continued working until, until 1973. Because after that they took him prisoner [*JA*: Yes?] Yes. He was a prisoner in—, he was in the Estadio Chile.

JA: You too?

Barbara: No, him. [*JA*: Just him.] Yes. One day he arrived back home—he was working at night—he arrived back here, and he said, "It seems like there are problems, that this, that and the other happened, and that I have to go because we have to look after it, because the company is ours, so we have to be there in case something happens." So he left. And after that I didn't, I didn't hear from him again. And so I was left alone here with the, with both of them. [*JA*: For how long?]

Loads of things happened. I didn't hear from him. I was alone here; there was a raid, I didn't know what to do with the two children. I couldn't go out either; I couldn't leave the house alone. And suddenly a gentleman arrived, looking sort of scared, after about four or five days. He said (the eldest child was standing there at the, at the fence), he said, "Ah, it must be here," he said. "Does a gentleman who worked in, in Fabrilán live here?" and so on. "Yes," I said, "Why?" He said, "Well," he said, "because you know," (and he was looking all around him, like this, frightened) and he said, "No, it's just that the, the gentleman is, is well, he said I should come and let you know that he is well and that he is in, in the Stadium of Chile." He said, "They let me go," he said, so, but he was all bruised and it was about three days since they had let him go, but he didn't dare go out. So he said, "I worked it out because the, the oldest child looks like him," he said, "That's how I worked it out; otherwise I would have been going around searching." So it was only then that I found out. Because I didn't, I didn't dare go out anywhere alone because the two children were small. I had one of two, and the other of four. And I didn't dare to go anywhere alone. And with the tanks going by, back and forth, doing— because they would come at night, they would conduct raids, that sort of thing, so I, I couldn't be—. And I think the worst blow for me was learning that Salvador Allende had died; it was terrible. And that everything that was happening, to see it, it was terrible. So about then—at that time a sister of, of my husband's came to live here, she stayed with the children and I started to, to go out to, to see, to look for him. Well, and then they took everyone out of the Stadium of Chile, they took them to the National Stadium. At that point I started to go to the stadium every day, early. And I was there all day search—trying to, to be able to hear the words "Yes, he's here" from someone. I could never, never find those lines of people, lines to talk to the Red Cross, so that the Red Cross could say, "Yes, they are here." [Telephone rings, recording is stopped]. So I would go there every day. Sometimes I wouldn't eat anything in the whole day, but I was there. And one day I stayed here and I had stomach problems, I had to go to the toilet all the time, I'd go to the toilet. So I said to myself, "What do I gain by staying here if—, I'm, I'm not going to gain anything because it's worse, I get sicker. On the other hand, if I am there—." And when I was there I saw all sorts of things, loads of things, things that, terrible things. So. And he has never talked and discussed—, he has never discussed what, everything he saw, everything that happened. So. Well, so many things happened there, in that—, almost a month and a bit, we were there. Well, once there was going to be an important game, with people coming to play from abroad, so, so buses started to come out by the side, like this, buses came out full of people. Some down one side, others down the other, like this. They said, "X number of people will come out by that, by that door," and so everyone would go up and down to get to the other doors. Then they would get there and they would come out by the other, they would come out by the other door. And they wouldn't let you, all the people coming out, they didn't let you approach, to talk to them, to the people coming out; you couldn't, no-one, no-one. Then, when they were two blocks away from the stadium, only then could people approach. Yes, all the people who were there like that, they would make, they would make a path for people to come out, but no-one could approach. Some came out with short hair on one side, long hair on the other, the, the, the young people, students, yes. Once one of the ones that they were taking there to the stadium escaped, he got away like this, from some detectives or something, from the people bringing him, and he tried to break free like this. And from among the very people who were waiting there, came some guys who caught him. Right there they started to beat him. Sometimes I'd arrive very early, and one of these trucks, these trucks that are closed, moving trucks, they came out from one of those, inside the stadium. And those really did, they would take out just dead bodies, and leave them there, on the ground. In the, in the pool, also, there were, on that side there were just women. You would see the women washing clothes. Once they said that they were going to, before those buses went out in all directions, they said that, that they were all on the cycle track, which was at the other end. So we all went there to wait. And you could see the people all like this, up above, making signs and things. But from there you couldn't distinguish who it was, if it was, if it was him, if it was him or not. And there, from, from, from where my husband as working, they took all of them, all of them. There was no distinction between, between the leaders; nothing, nothing.

JA: Why, were they communists, or, why?

Barbara: No, because they were in a company. [*JA*: Just because of that.] Yes, just because of that. Because they were saying that they had to give up all the, give in, abandon all the—no. They would give a time so that, at such and such a time there would be curfew and they are no—, there mustn't be any, any groups, or anything. So as there were people there, all of them there, that's why they—. They took him prisoner on the 12th, they took him. They arrived at the station and— [*JA*: The 11th of September, immediately?] Yes.

JA: And how long was he like that, disappeared?

Barbara: Well, about a, a month, or a month and a bit.

JA: And then he returned.

Barbara: Yes. One day when, when I, that time when I, I would come home up to Gran Avenida [a larger road near Barbara's home] by bus. And after that I, I wouldn't go further by bus, I had to come walking, like this, sort of half hiding, because the curfew was already on, because the curfew was very early. So sometimes, sometimes you could only just make it. And one day, since the buses started to come out on all sides, and you couldn't see anything, I was feeling very low, bitter, not knowing anything, so I said, "I've had enough of this, we're even less likely to know now. Because where are they going to go and look for the, the buses?" And I was with my two children, and suddenly I hear someone passing by, like this, banging on the, the windows like this. And I go out to, to look and it was my husband who was coming in through here, through the kitchen. And he had his pants, he was thin, with his pants tied with rope, but really thin. And that was when it ended, the, what's it called, the, the, this business of going to the stadium every day, and looking for him, and this ended with that. I could live a normal life. But afterward when he went back to work, he couldn't, because as he had been in the stadium—[JA: Him] Yes. He couldn't go on working in the same place. So they were fired for I don't know what reason.

Anxiety, fear, uncertainty, anguish, and upheaval arguably best describe Barbara's experience of her husband's arrest. What came with her husband's disappearance was almost as hard to endure as the disappearance itself; going to the stadium, for example, brought with it the traumatizing experience of witnessing someone being beaten as they tried to escape, noticing that those who caught him appeared to be regular crowd members but were in fact in alliance with the regime, and seeing trucks take out dead bodies. Walking home from the stadium was frightening in that it was after curfew so she risked being shot, and had to hide. Her husband's absence meant that she had to endure alone the terrifying experience of soldiers raiding her home and tanks in her neighborhood. Barbara's words also bring out the lack of information that shantytown women lived with regarding the repression; Barbara lacked information about her husband's whereabouts initially, what was being done to him, whether he would return at all, and why he had been detained.

Her description shows how gender, poverty, and repression interacted in shaping shantytown women's experiences of the regime. The repression involved in her husband's detention put her in the difficult situation of needing to go and look for him but also, as shantytown gender expectations dictated, having to look after the children and, since she lived in a poor neighborhood, having to guard the house from burglary. There was no respite, because staying at home she felt sick to the stomach. Her husband's reappearance did bring a welcome return to relatively normal life, but his not being able to get his job back led to exacerbated poverty.

Shantytown women who joined groups appeared to feel that the threat of arrest was always looming, perhaps in part because they heard about other people being arrested. In addition to her own husband's being held for ten days in the National Stadium, Ana knew that members of her arpillera group had been arrested or had had children and husbands arrested and held for a long time as political prisoners:

> *Ana*:   A workmate invited me, may she rest in peace; she died. A neighbor from here, who witnessed my children's birth and their growing up, and she has two children who are political prisoners. [. . .] And we took big, big risks, and thank goodness nothing ever happened to us, beyond some, some, some workmates being arrested. Well, we had the daughter of an arpillera workmate who also disapp—, well, was in prison for a long time, a "political prisoner," they were called. So the political prisoners were something we would protest about, because we were not in agreement with what was happening. And [we would protest] because of the deprivations we were experiencing. So, they were called "political prisoners." And we may have had no idea about politics, but we were protesting about what we were

experiencing. It was a way of saying something about what was happening. And one girl was in prison for a long time, as a political prisoner.

The number of arrests in Ana's immediate entourage was considerable; they existed in a neighbor's family, among workmates, and in workmates' families. In such a context, and because of their participation in groups, shantytown women felt that the risk of arrest hung over them. Ana's words also show how being in a group exposed shantytown women to information about the extent and nature of the repression. They suggest as well that group membership drew them into participating in protests (see Chapter 6); Ana's protesting about political prisoners may not have happened had she not joined the group.

The threat of death or arrest of a family member was very real for some shantytown women. We saw how Bettina's husband was warned that if he continued to be politically active, he would disappear. Cristina's husband, meanwhile, had to go into hiding in Peru and Bolivia, as he was a trade union leader and communist, and in danger. She had lived with the knowledge that someone might denounce him and he might be taken away:

> *Cristina*:   There were no economic problems but, but in my husband's case there were political problems that were serious. [*JA*: Yes.] Yes, every day here, you would hear that they had taken someone away because someone had denounced them, and that they had taken them to such and such a place.

2.11

The men in the top half of this arpillera are in prison, indicated by barbed wire. The eye with tears shows how sad they or the arpillera-maker were about this. In the bottom half, a mother and two children wave to her husband. Meanwhile, people must obtain food by begging and scavenging, alluded to by the figures in the bottom left-hand corner of the arpillera. That there was shame about this is suggested by their balaclava-like faces. Even the elderly woman on the right seems to be begging.

Website Link 2.8:

On the disappeared in Chile, see "Chile" by Desaparecidos. www.desaparecidos.org/chile/eng.html

News of people being denounced and taken away made for a very insecure existence for women like Cristina, whose husbands were involved in groups on which the regime was cracking down, such as trade unions or leftist parties. Not only their husband's life, but their own economic survival was threatened. If caught, the husband might be taken to a prison, stadium (only in the weeks after the coup), or torture center, and then killed, disappeared, sent into internal exile [as "relegados"], or eventually sent into exile abroad.

On the other hand, not all shantytown women in groups were aware, initially, of the extent of the arrests, what happened to people who were arrested, who was being arrested, or that arrests were happening at all. Moreover, many had a negative view of political prisoners. According to Catarina, a health team leader, some shantytown women saw political prisoners as something very foreign, "like an extra-terrestrial," as she put it. Her goal was to make them see that they were not different, and that one could easily become a political prisoner. When women joined groups (see Chapter 4), they became more aware of such matters through conversation with the other women who related what they had heard, and through listening to the experiences of group members whose family members were in prison. The Vicaría told them about the arrests as well, for example showing the members of the coordinating committee of arpillera groups in southern Santiago clandestine photographs of the prisoners in the stadium. A cohesive neighborhood was another source of information; in La Victoria, for example, where repression was particularly severe and there was much *esprit de corps*, a message on the wall indicated the number of arrests of locals, for all to see.

"He Has Not Reappeared to This Day": Disappearances

When people were taken away by the secret police (called DINA, and later the CNI) and their families did not hear of them again, they were known as the "disappeared" ["los desaparecidos"]. Just over a thousand people disappeared during the regime.[120] Most were men, many were young, large numbers were from the shantytowns, and they tended to be members of the Socialist or Communist party, and the Movement of the Revolutionary Left [Movimiento de Izquierda Revolucionaria, MIR], a Guevarist group. Many were taken from their homes by members of the secret police dressed in ordinary clothes, who put them into a car without number plates. Some disappeared after being rounded up during a raid, if they protested. Their disappearance resulted in years of distress and searching for the women who were their mothers, partners, sisters, daughters, or other relatives. Nadia, whose brother disappeared, told me:

> My brother disappeared on the 13th of August, 1974. Having been arrested by three members of the DINA. Including Romo. In the morning they arrested la Flaca Alejandra [a prisoner whom the secret police forced to become a spy], so that she would show them the house. My mother was alone. I had a child who was having a birthday that day. We came here. They inform us that they had arrested my brother that night. My mother tells us that three individuals had come. My brother wasn't there. She didn't understand politics because we were never into politics. As early as that morning there had been a couple kissing at the corner; this was the DINA's disguise. Hidden among their clothes they had machine-guns. They were waiting for my brother, who had gone to work. My mother offers them coffee. My brother arrives. One guy hugs him and says he is from SUMA. They had pointed a gun at him. My brother said, "Mother, DINA is taking me." The chief says, "We're going to go and talk for five minutes and we'll bring him back. Stay inside." These five

2.12 and 2.13

In the first of these arpilleras, three men in gray, signifying the secret police, arrest a man who will subsequently disappear. The onlookers are helpless. In the second arpillera, a woman sitting at home on the right wonders where a man and woman are; they have disappeared. She thinks they might be in a prison called "Four Poplars" ["Cuatro Alamos"], alluded to by four trees. On the left-hand side of the arpillera, some men are being let out of another prison called "Three Poplars" and are joining their family members. She has not been so lucky, however. This arpillera evokes the pain of not knowing; her posture indicates consternation and sadness, and the absence of others in the house suggests loneliness.

minutes are still not over. My mother sees them take him to the street corner. There was a neighbor watching, who worked for them. They put him into a red van. And that's how the nightmare that is our lives started. It was very terrible because my son was about seven years old. And he never again had a birthday. There was no time for him, because my mother would be crying, and I was busy in the Agrupación [the Association of Relatives of the Detained and Disappeared]. My mother did all the paperwork, the first year. I couldn't move, because my children were small. My mother started to have heart problems and the doctor strictly forbade her to continue with any activities. I had to leave my children alone. I had to organize things among them so that one would do the cleaning one day, be it a boy or girl; the next day if I didn't manage to cook, the other child would cook. We took turns. So that I might be able to go out all day to do the paperwork in the Comité Pro-Paz [a human rights organization], at Four Poplars ["Cuatro Alamos," a detention center]. We would go around with my sister-in-law; she had a small baby. We went to Four Poplars, to Three Poplars ["Tres Alamos," another detention center] because Four Poplars was inside. We asked in the morgue, in the clinic, everywhere. And they said "no, no, no." And I remember that once the guard in Three Poplars sticks his machine gun and moves a bullet inside it—because we didn't want to move back—to the baby's head. With the weapon. I mean that was the sort of bloodthirsty types they were, or are, because they are alive. They are enjoying the wages they receive, and everything else. We would stand in the same lines as many other people—Ana Rojas, so many others. And on such days they would make fun of us, "Bring a ticket, bring this or that," and they would eat it themselves. And they knew we didn't have any money because there was no work for us. [*JA*: You couldn't work in that period.]

I worked for 18 years—I am still contributing—for the Agrupación [Association of Relatives of the Detained and Disappeared]. I go to the Folk Song Group. I have never received a penny. And without having any way to put food in the pot. And my other brothers started to help me. But then my other brothers lost their jobs. We were dirt poor, after having had everything. My brother also experienced this, and that was why he gave himself to social struggle. That was the catalyst. He had seen how in one place they have everything, and how we were lacking food, clothing. They had brought me up in such a way that the daughter of the maid couldn't say "Tú" [the informal "you"] to me. And afterwards you realize that they are just as much human beings as everyone else. You start to value what life is. And you learn that really life is very beautiful, even though there are many unpleasant moments. That's why we clutched onto life so much, as well. There are beautiful things like gestures that people make, that in this struggle I learned to appreciate. I entered the Comité Pro Paz at the end of 1974, when my mother was already sick, and at that point they started to ask me to join them because they needed active people who would do things, who could manage paperwork, errands.

Nadia's life was turned upside down by her brother's disappearance. Her son's birthday was not celebrated again, her mother was distressed and then had heart problems, she searched in detention centers every day, where she endured abuse by soldiers and could not learn anything about her brother, and she experienced severe poverty. These changes were "a nightmare," as she put it. She resisted the state's attack on her family, however, by becoming active in the Association of Relatives of the Detained and Disappeared, where she organized denunciatory and protest activities, made arpilleras, and sang protest songs to raise awareness in others. Her words suggest that being a woman and mother got in the way of her search by making it difficult to do the paperwork

Website Link 2.9:
In Latin America there is a multi-country Latin American Federation of Associations for Relatives of the Detained and Disappeared. Its website, entitled "FEDEFAM," explains what the disappeared are, and describes the organization and its goals.
www.desaparecidos.org/fedefam/eng.html

Website Link 2.10:
There is information about the disappeared and about organizations throughout the world that focus on the issue of disappearance at the following website, which also contains links to websites on the disappeared in several Latin American countries. "Project Disappeared" by Desaparecidos.
www.desaparecidos.org/eng.html

that would enable the Comité to help her, but that at the same time she found ways around these constraints, distributing household tasks among her children and leaving them alone at home at times. With a little over a thousand disappearances, the phenomenon was not so widespread that every shantytown family suffered Nadia's fate. However, these disappearances affected more people than these families; the knowledge that one might disappear or have a child or husband disappear caused fear and insecurity in many people not directly affected.[121]

The Comité de Cooperación para la Paz en Chile and Vicaría de la Solidaridad were very important to Nadia, and to other victims of targeted repression. The Comité (as it was called) was a human rights organization set up by the leaders of various faiths in the months following the coup, to help the victims of repression and unemployment. It was forcibly closed by General Pinochet at the end of 1975, but the Cardinal of Santiago, Monseñor Raúl Silva Henríquez, re-opened it under the name "Vicaría de la Solidaridad" in January 1976, with minor changes of staff and organizational structure. The impulse behind the creation of both these humanitarian organizations was a growing awareness in the leaders of various churches that the dictatorship's repression and economic policies were having a devastating impact on certain sectors of society. In the first months of the regime, many in the Catholic Church's upper hierarchy had supported the coup, but this had changed as they became aware of the human rights violations, and many became supportive of the regime's victims.[122] The Cardinal created the Vicaría within the legal structure of the archdiocese of Santiago so as to give it a measure of immunity, and kept on most of the staff. Both organizations were very closely connected with the Catholic Church, but were entities in their own right, with mostly lay people on their staff. Many staff members were leftists who had lost their jobs after the coup and suffered persecution, and whose political ideas led them to want to help the poor and oppressed.[123]

Executions

Shantytown women were exposed to soldiers murdering people in their neighborhoods. Nelly, for example, saw young people being shot, and another time, through a fence, she saw a young man being chased down an alley, calling out for his mother, while soldiers were killing him:

> *Nelly*:   The thing is, I get scared; those sorts of things scare me. I don't get involved in that sort of thing much because I get scared. Because what happened was that when the coup happened, I was pregnant with the girl, in 1973; she was born in 1974. So I saw young people being killed, with my own eyes. And once a soldier saw me, he pointed his gun at me from the corner, said vulgar things, and told me to go inside. So from that point on I started to be afraid, I was afraid. I said to myself, "something could happen to me." And as I say, I get scared when it comes to all these sorts of things.

> *JA*:   Who would not have been scared at the time?

> *Nelly*:   At that time, yes. Because another time I was in my house doing the things I normally do—, because I wasn't living here, I was living over there in José María Caro, yes, that's where I lived. At about one, two in the morning I heard a boy, like a young man, running down the road, and soldiers were coming, so he was shouting and calling for his mother, he was calling for his mother. They were riddling him with bullets, killing him. So that too, I, yes, I saw it through a fence, I saw how they picked him up like this, like a sack of potatoes, they threw him up into a truck,

2.14

The left-hand side of this arpillera from the shantytown of Huamachuco in northern Santiago suggests that its author was concerned about executions, since a sign says "No more dead." Two other of her concerns were justice ["Justicia"] and unemployment ["No hay trabajo," there is no work]. The vehicle bears the symbol of the Chilean police, and appears to have a water cannon.

and took him away. It was all bloody where he had been. And I stayed here a long time. What I remember most clearly was when he was calling his mother, "Mom! Mom!" but they still killed him. So I saw all those things, and so I was left sort of traumatized, very shocked. I said to myself, "Gee, I hope nothing happens to me if I go to these sorts of things." When you get scared that's the way it is. When you are daring you just go. But when you get scared—I am someone who gets really scared, so, no.

Murder was close to home for Nelly. Her words suggest two kinds of fear that it caused or exacerbated: an endemic fear that was present all the time, and a more specific fear about state violence being inflicted upon her if she became involved in anti-regime activities. The regime, through violence and the fear it gave rise to, made people hesitate before engaging in resistance.

Some shantytown women experienced the murder of a family member or neighbor. Nancy, a health team leader in southern Santiago, had a daughter who was killed. Karina's neighbor was accidentally killed by a bullet when she was in the upper floor of her house, having a party. The priest André Jarlan was killed in La Victoria when a bullet hit him, crashing through the flimsy wooden walls of his room, where he was seated at his desk reading a bible. My interview with Ana was informative:

JA: And they [the colleagues in her bolsa de cesantes], did they also have husbands who were arrested, or?

Ana: Political prisoners, there were disappeared people. There are people who are still disappeared today, so, people whom soldiers killed, also, in full view and in

Website Link 2.11:
A chronology of human rights violations during the regime, a list of some of Chile's main human rights organizations, and a link to publications and more organizations dealing with human rights may be found on this website: "Derechos Chile Ayer y Hoy" www.derechoschile.com/

The link "Documentos Esenciales" contains information about the national security doctrine, Pinochet's decrees, and the Rettig Report.

the presence of, of everyone, because, for example, one arpillera workmate, Señora Ana Pacheco, her husband was killed. They, they shot him outside his house.

JA: Yes. You told me.

Ana: Yes, so, she also, let's say, was one of the members of our group. And there were many, many disappeared people who never again—Señora de Aguilera, Mr. Aguilera never reappeared.

Ana's words express the multiple forms of state violence of which some shantytown women, particularly those in groups, were aware. The woman whose husband was killed "in full view" lived in Ana's neighborhood, but executions they did not witness themselves, shantytown women sometimes heard about. Nelly, for example, knew about dead bodies that appeared, and bodies that showed up without eyes, and hacked in pieces. Gloria knew that approximately seven young people had been killed in her shantytown, and that the priest André Jarlan had met with the same fate.

Shantytown inhabitants were killed outside the shantytown as well as within, and shantytown women in groups were aware of this too. Two young adults were found dead near some blown-up electricity towers in Temuco, in southern Chile; they were the daughter and son of families living in shantytowns in southern Santiago. The young woman had been a leader in the shantytown of Lo Valledor Sur, and a member of the coordinating committee of Caro-Ochagavía. The young man was the son of a family that had already lost two sons in what had been called a clash. Natasha knew that trade union leaders in her husband's factory were shot and that her own husband was in the trade union and risked this fate. Karina's sister in the western shantytown of Pudahuel told her that bodies, including those of children and babies, appeared by the river there.

There were multiple other forms of targeted repression that shantytown women experienced in their families or knew about. Bettina, who was very active in local groups, had her home burned down, and she knew that people were tortured in secret torture centers, protesters and prisoners beaten, prisoners sent into internal exile,[124] dissidents burned alive or killed through having their throats slit, Church staff harassed, and shantytown priests expelled by the government. Gloria from La Victoria, too, was aware of many different forms of targeted repression:

Gloria: I think it was just then, in 1986, when there were lots of protests. '86, '87, '88. There were many, many protests. So at that point there was a change, and lots of things were happening here. For example, when they expelled the priests, because there were three French priests, and Pinochet expelled all three of them. So we would put all that in the arpilleras, as well, because it was what was happening here. There was a lot of repression in those years, a lot. People being killed, some teachers had their throats slit, people were burned alive. There was a period in those years when it was very tough [pause], very tough.

JA: For how long did it last?

Gloria: I think until 1988. In 1990 we had the plebiscite, the change; we started to have a change towards more democracy. I think it was about 1988, more or less. [. . .]

JA: And what other kinds of repression did you have here, in the shantytown?

Gloria: Well, they would come suddenly and take away the leaders of social organizations; they took away quite a few leaders, sending them into internal exile. They also killed a lot of young people. There are about seven, seven people who were killed in the shantytown. All young people. And that was it. They raided the church, also. There was the time, as well, when they killed a priest, André Jarlan. The repression on that day was very harsh.

Gloria's description suggests a powerful onslaught of targeted state violence. Later on in our interview, she mentioned that people were arrested, injured, and had their homes raided, and described how soldiers attacked one man in the shantytown of La Victoria:

> I remember how once something very tragic happened, which was that a soldier cut off the scalp of a young man with a knife. A *yatagán*, they call it. They cut off his scalp, sort of like the Indians; they cut it off.

Instances of indiscriminate cruelty such as this were deeply disturbing to her, and to the women in her arpillera group, who discussed it. In groups, women heard about multiple instances of targeted violence.

Many women suffered indirectly from targeted repression focused around their husband's role at work. Ana's husband, for example, was a trade union leader in the construction field; he was arrested for about ten days, after which he was never again able to find stable work that would bring him a pension. Natalia's husband was the treasurer of his trade union, and all the trade union leaders in his company were arrested, causing Natalia to live with the knowledge that this might happen to him. He somehow escaped this fate but was fired, and was only able to find short-term, occasional jobs for four years after that, until finally he found a more stable job, but one that was poorly paid. Natasha's husband was shut up in his factory for two days at the time of the coup, and the trade union leaders in the factory were shot. As he, like all the workers in the factory, was in the trade union, she was very worried about what might happen. Karina's husband was imprisoned in his ironworks for three days, while soldiers surrounded it. Bettina's husband was a textile worker and trade union leader, and as mentioned above was threatened with disappearance and was being hunted down, but thanks to a relative warning him about this, he avoided this outcome by changing jobs, but was unemployed on several occasions and their home was raided, while many of his colleagues died. Some men found their promotion opportunities blocked. Babette's husband was an electrician, and apart from being poorly paid, he had no chance of promotion or a higher wage because he was a trade union leader; she knew he risked losing his job.[125]

The organized shantytown women who knew about these forms of targeted repression were much disturbed by them. Natasha, in southern Santiago, talked of artists being unjustly killed, persecuted, oppressed, and punished, and told me that her group denounced "the repression, the murders for political reasons" in its arpilleras. Nelly was very upset that young people who protested were being killed in her shantytown. It angered her that men were taken away and taken prisoner for no good reason, and she thought there was a lot of discrimination and evil at work. The arpillera-makers in eastern Santiago empathized with political prisoners and the relatives of the disappeared, participating in protests about political prisoners, and joining the relatives of the disappeared in some of their protests. Targeted repression affected not only those who experienced it directly, but also many women who knew about it.

Non-Violent Repression

Non-violent repression took many forms. In one of its earliest decrees, the Junta prohibited the production of leftist publications. It also cracked down on expressions of dissent. This affected women who expressed ideas or distributed documents voicing opinions

2.15

This arpillera, dated 1978, alludes to letters being opened by the post office. The small words in the center read "Violated correspondence." Shantytown women were aware that packages were opened, and that they had to show post office employees what they were sending. Arpillera groups that sent arpilleras abroad had to find ways to work around this.

antagonistic to the regime's, making them afraid that they might be thought leftist, and be arrested if caught. Natasha, for example, feared she would be arrested if found with arpilleras. The shantytown women felt in danger whenever they took such documents out of their homes. Ana's group had to be very careful about where in the city center they exhibited their work, and both she and Cristina told me about how dangerous it was to take arpilleras to the center of town to hand them in, since there were sometimes identity checks on buses. Bernardita told a story that described what could happen, about a woman on her way back from the Vicaría:

> Let's see, on one occasion, one of our workmates, well, they rejected some work of hers, to be corrected. And she was carrying them [the arpilleras] in the bag here on her lap in the bus back home, because she had to alter them. And they [the police] get on and start checking everyone on the bus. But nothing, nothing serious happened. They were asking everyone for their ID cards. And they entertained themselves a lot checking a young man who had problems, apparently. And they let her be. But she was shaking like this [gestures]. She was shaking because she knew what she was carrying, she knew. A bag, here, she knew. And if they had checked that . . .

Bernardita's words illustrate the fear that people who had ideas or documents with anti-government messages had to endure, and how simple activities like taking a bus into town were dangerous for them. The mere knowledge that the police might check people, even if they did not actually do so, would have made a bus ride frightening. Her words illustrate the absence of freedom of speech and its consequences for dissident thinkers. There were still other ways in which the ban on leftist publications and parties affected the shantytown women. Post office employees would check the contents of packages, which made mailing arpilleras out of the country risky.

Another form of non-violent repression was the government's banning of leftist parties and organizations, and expression of disapproval of "politics." One consequence of this was that shantytown women believed it was dangerous to join groups, since they might be suspected of being political or leftist, and many had to be coaxed into becoming group members. Freedom of association, in other words, was restricted. Another consequence was a fear of talking about political matters. Laura, a shantytown woman who was also on the Vicaría staff, told me:

> So at the beginning there was a fear of political parties, and a fear, also, of, for example, if you talked about some problem that had to do with the general situation in the country, some women would say, "Ah, no, this is political." So they would feel very scared. So first there was a fear of political matters, because of all this campaign that there was, by the dictatorship, saying that politics is bad, that the, that the, and you had to repress—and with politicians and political militants being arrested, killed, and disappeared. So at first there was a whole fear about political matters.

Laura's words suggest that the fear about talking about political matters was widespread in groups. This fear was not in fact present in all groups, however, and many groups were sites of lively discussion about repression and government policies. The fear was arguably a function of how well the group members knew and trusted each other.

2.16

Soldiers burned posters, books, and documents that they considered leftist, such as this map of Latin America that includes a picture of Che Guevara.

Another form of non-violent repression was the government's freeze on voting, except for voting for the Pinochet government and 1980 constitution, during which the absence of freedom of expression limited the opposition's ability to influence voters, and the 1989 plebiscite. At all levels of government, leaders were chosen by the Junta and officials of their government. Even in neighborhood councils, elected representatives were replaced by military supporters. Hence after the coup, most traditional channels of political participation for shantytown inhabitants were blocked. Moreover, many political, community, and union leaders were thrown into prison, went into hiding, or fled, leaving shantytown inhabitants with no voice in the political system.[126] Politics had meant little to most shantytown women, but shantytown women in groups tended to want the regime to end and democracy to return, and they would have appreciated the chance to vote.

Fear

Endemic Fear and Specific Fears

Fear became a frequent companion. Shantytown women felt both what I term *endemic fear*, that is a pervasive fear, and *specific fears* about certain things that could happen. The curfews, people being shot, soldiers patrolling one's neighborhood, and occasional vans of soldiers and even tanks in the street made for a highly intimidating environment. This, together with the knowledge that people were being arrested, beaten, murdered, and disappeared, made people feel fear much of the time; this was endemic fear.[127] Natalia evoked it when she told me about people having to learn how to vote in the plebiscite, ". . . because people were afraid of everything, fear really gripped hold of this country." Ana alluded to it in saying that there were people who were aware of what was happening, but who would not do anything because they were so afraid, and Barbara from the shantytown of Colón suggested it when she said:

> But I didn't dare to; I didn't dare to go out anywhere alone, because both my children were small. I had one that was two years old and the other was four. And I didn't dare to go out anywhere alone. And with the tanks passing back and forth, because they had people doing—because they would arrive at night, they would raid homes, and all that sort of thing.

So afraid was she because of the soldiers and their tanks in her neighborhood that she did not go out of the house. Her words also point to the ways in which her fear was experienced in part through her motherhood; she says she did not dare to go out "because both my children were small," suggesting that if something happened to her, they would be left defenseless. Experiencing or witnessing military brutality contributed to the endemic fear. Karina and several neighbors felt afraid because soldiers threw stones at their windows. We saw earlier how Nelly's witnessing of soldiers killing young men left her "fearful" and "traumatized," in her words.

In addition to this endemic fear, shantytown women had specific fears, prevalent among which was the fear that one might be arrested or killed, or have a family member meet this fate. Dinora told me that even if they had done nothing political, people were afraid of being arrested, and that this fear wore you down. Natasha said her group members spoke about hoping nothing would happen to their family members when they went to work. She herself was afraid because her husband had been held at his factory for two days and was a union member, and union leaders in his workplace were killed; moreover, she knew about "the repression of workers," as she put it. Like her, Nelly said the women in her group were afraid that their children would be killed or arrested without having done anything wrong. I asked her:

> *JA*:   Did you talk about events that happened, like killings, things like that, in the workshop, or not? Events, say, to do with repression, events like when they slit people's throats, other events like that, or not?
>
> *Nelly*:   Ah, the *degollados* [three men whose throats were slit]. Yes, sometimes yes, because there were people who knew that in such and such a place, such and such a thing happened, and they would come to the workshop with things to say about it, and sometimes some knew and others didn't. We always talked about what was happening, saying "until when will this go on?" "Until when," we would say, were we going to be living in this situation we were in? Afraid that they might kill one of our children or that they would arrest one without good cause, because sometimes how many young people and adults were ill-treated and arrested without having done anything bad, or made any mistake! And so that was our fear, also. And in fact some relatives of some people in the workshop had been, had been arrested, they had been arrested, and some had disappeared too, I heard, as well.

Nelly's words make clear that the women were afraid that a child might be arrested or killed, and the strain was such that they wanted the regime to end quickly. They also hint at a sense of injustice about this violence, and an understanding of it as striking arbitrarily and any time. Her description illustrates, in addition, the importance of groups for the circulation of information; she mentions that group members would bring news of state violence about which others had not heard. It suggests, also, how being in groups and talking about what had happened led the women to form an analysis of the situation, and perhaps made them feel better able to handle it.

Consequences of Fear

Both types of fear prevented women from doing things they would normally not worry about doing. While normally they would walk outside if they needed to in the evening, they did not do so or let their children do so after curfew. Teresa told me that soldiers in her neighborhood had killed some children across the street, whereupon she shut herself and her children up inside the house after curfew, for the months during which it was in place. Some women were afraid to leave the home at any time, as when Barbara was afraid to go anywhere alone after her husband disappeared.

Some women feared betrayal by neighbors or group members.[128] They knew that there were secret supporters of the regime in their shantytowns and even in their groups who might report on them; these were called "sapos" [literally "toads," but meaning spies] and "infiltrados" ["infiltrators"]. Women whose husbands were leftists feared that a neighbor might denounce them, for example, as was the case with Cristina, whose husband was a trade union leader and communist, and eventually had to go into hiding. Mónica minimized the risk of betrayal within her arpillera group, but nevertheless acknowledged its existence:

> *JA*:   But you could talk freely about this in the workshop?
>
> *Mónica*:   Yes.
>
> *JA*:   There was no, no danger?

Mónica: No, no, no, no, there was no danger, no, there was no danger. Perhaps occasionally, yes, a little danger because they would bring us lots of flyers, lots of things, but—danger for those of us who were permanent, but not for the others. But they didn't pay any attention to us at all, thank goodness. So no, no, it was not a big problem.

Mónica clearly felt she could trust the women in her group, but flyers were particularly incriminating, being material evidence of dissent.

Many women were afraid to join groups that worked to produce food cheaply or earn an income. Nora from Simón Bolívar, said, "In those days you couldn't come together as a group, it was dangerous." Bettina said that people were afraid to get together because they did not trust others. The women were particularly afraid of joining groups that did something "political" or were left-wing, since the government was vilifying politics and had banned left-wing parties. Mónica told me that only half the women in her arpillera workshop joined another group that she was in, which hung up posters and banners against the regime, and built barricades; the other half were afraid. Such fears were mitigated, however, if a group was supported by a priest.

The leaders of shantytown groups were aware of women being afraid to participate in groups, and so they devised ways of persuading them. Bettina, for example, found that when she invited women to join her new arpillera group, they were nervous about it, asking her if the group would be political. Consequently, she adopted the strategy of inviting them to join personally, telling them it was a form of work, and denying that it was work that was political in nature:

> I saw that the, the most important thing for me was for people to be able to wake up and not go on dying sort of within these, within these four walls. There were a lot of people who, out of fear, would say, "No, I'm not getting into anything, anything at all, anything at all." But at critical moments they nevertheless come to someone who has a little more information, to ask them what they might be able to do. [. . .] I used techniques like, for example, inviting people to participate myself, and later working with them, offering them the chance to change our lives, to have an opportunity for work via some, some little pictures, I would say, that we were going to embroider, and so on. And as they were so distrustful, and so afraid, they would say to me, "Yes, but I'll go, but I'm very worried about it being political or something." "Nooo," I'd say, "How can you think so?" So when we had our meeting, I would explain about the arpilleras and would give each of them a blank sheet of paper and pencil, and so I'd tell them—this was inside the church, with the new group—I'd say that each of them had to draw a moment in their lives, any moment, and that afterwards we would share what we had done with the others. So people were saying that they didn't want anything to do with politics, but they were drawing their problem, and their problem was clearly related to the political moment in which we were living.

Bettina, like many women shantytown group leaders, wanted to draw women out of the house and into groups, and she knew about their fear, and worked around it with personal invitations, the promise of work, the denial that it was political, and a depiction of the work as an innocuous activity ("little pictures" and "embroidery"). She used the traditionally feminine associations and apparent innocuousness of sewing in her coaxing,[129] and a diminutive description of the arpilleras as "little pictures," which made them seem apolitical.

Puede participar cualquier
MUJER que tenga inquietud
de decir algo, o hacer algo ya sea canto, horda-
do, tejido, teatro, dibujo,
artesania.

Atrevete y muestra que puedes hacer algo diferente a:
cocinar, planchar, lavar,
cuidar niños, marido, casa etc.

Salgamos de las cuatro
paredes para: recrearnos,
compartir con otras mujeres,
aprender, conversar nues
tros problemas, ser solidarias.

Encuentro de la
Dueña de Casa.
Sabado 23 de Octubre
Zona Oriente codem

2.17

This flyer advertises a "Meeting of Housewives" ["Encuentro de la Dueña de Casa"] that was to take place in eastern Santiago one Saturday in October in the mid- or late 1980s, organized by the Committee for the Defense of Women's Rights [Comité de Defensa de los Derechos de la Mujer, CODEM]. It reads, "Any woman who is interested in saying something or doing something, be it singing, embroidery, knitting, theater, drawing, or handicrafts, can participate. Take the plunge and show that you can do something other than cooking, ironing, washing, and taking care of children, husband, house, etc. Let's get out from behind our four walls to: have a moment of recreation, talk with other women, learn, discuss our problems, be warmly supportive [solidarias]. Meeting of Housewives. Saturday 23rd October eastern Zone. Codem."

The use by the flyer's author of "Take the plunge" suggests that she is aware that shantytown women were afraid to join groups or group activities. Many shantytown women were fearful of the repression, afraid to leave their homes, and afraid to ask their husband's permission to go out to women's groups. The author attempts to persuade the women by referring to activities that are not intimidating, such as handicraft-making, singing, and other artistic activities for which women had the necessary skills. She has also chosen to give the event a name that is not intimidating, referring to it as a meeting of "housewives."

The flyer's author has a feminist consciousness, and the event itself has feminist overtones. She refers to the home as "the four walls," connoting a restrictive and limited realm from which women can escape. She says that women can show that they are capable of doing more than the housework and childcare. She is interested in promoting women's talking with other women, sharing problems, learning from each other, and being warmly supportive. The flyer ends by advocating making time for recreational activities and defending happiness as a right. Despite the influence of feminism on this event, the word "Feminism" is never mentioned, probably because the author knew that many shantytown women would not identify as feminists and did not approve of feminism. References to rights as well as women's rights suggest that the organizers of the event had a good understanding of human rights.

Like many flyers and the events they advertise, this one uses the arts, both as part of the event and on the flyer, to persuade the women to come along. The other side of the flyer, which contains information about the event, says that there will be singing, poetry, visual arts, handicrafts, and theater, and a prize for the best piece. The organizers of the event appear to want to use these art forms to promote awareness of women's rights; there are instructions saying that songs and poems must be related to "women's rights," that visual art works must denounce or express a concern related to the goals of the meeting, that handicrafts must have a caption related to women's rights, and that plays must show real situations and leave people with a question in their minds.

Shantytown women in groups were fearful about some group activities in particular, because they considered them dangerous. Ana and her arpillera group members, for example, thought that transporting arpilleras was dangerous, and that they risked arrest if they were caught with arpilleras when they were in the street. She said, talking about an arpillera exhibition in Canada House:

> In Canada House there was no problem. The problem was, if we went out into the street and they caught us, well, they could arrest us. But there we could exhibit arpilleras with any subject-matter.

Canada House was a "safe" venue, but taking the arpilleras from one's home to Canada House was dangerous. Similarly, Cristina, from a south-eastern shantytown, felt it was risky to drop off the arpilleras at the Vicaría. She said she had once been followed on her way home.

Fear set limits to what "political" activities women in groups were willing to engage in, as they considered some of these risky. When Ana was in a group that sewed for an income, for example, some group members did not dare to engage in consciousness-activities. She told me:

> We would try to raise consciousness in people about what we were experiencing, but only those of us who, who were willing to take the risk, because there was so much fear that sometimes people had an awareness, but out of fear they wouldn't do it.

Even for those who knew things were not as they should be, the fear was paralyzing. The women tended to be particularly afraid of participating in protests, because they knew that they risked arrest or being shot, and that the police would be present (see Chapter 6).

The leaders of women's groups worked to allay women's fears of participating in these more political activities. They persuaded them to participate in protests, for example, by being flexible with them. Natasha told Natalia, the leader of her arpillera group, that when it came to participating in protests, when things got violent, she would run away. Natalia replied that it was alright; the main thing was that the journalists and police had seen that people were protesting. Natalia also framed things in such a way as to make the women more likely to participate in protests, for example by telling her group that people had allowed themselves to be walked over by the military by not protesting because they were afraid of the weapons, and afraid for their families. Hence leaders coaxed and encouraged to lessen women's fears of participating in certain group activities.

There were women who were afraid to speak out in their groups about instances of repression that they witnessed or knew about, or to depict them in their arpilleras. Some women were uneasy about telling other members about certain of their protest activities. Babette, for example, did not tell her arpillera group about being involved in painting messages on walls at night. Natasha, from southern Santiago, said that her group members had a lot of information, but had to keep quiet so as not to be persecuted. She did tell her group, though, about an event that she was afraid to depict in her arpilleras:

> *Natasha*:   And one thing I never dared to do [in my arpilleras] was something that I saw, that I experienced. [. . .] I was on my way to see my daughter over there in the direction of—, because she lived over there at the intersection of Vicuña Mackenna and Romero, and a large, big truck comes down the street. It was a closed truck. [. . .] And there was a ditch or a hole, I don't know what it was, there, opposite

the market. And one man—, and both the doors at the back are opened, and my impression was this: how they were carrying dead bodies, naked, with their heads down, others with their arms tied, just like animals. It was a butcher's van.

JA: And why, and you didn't dare to put it in your arpillera?

Natasha: No, I didn't dare. [*JA*: Why?] I did confess it to my workmates, though.

JA: Why didn't you dare?

Natasha: I didn't dare because there was persecution. They knew, they knew very well that when you had some, some information to give—, they wouldn't even leave your family in peace. So because of that I said to myself, better not. [. . .] So now a lot of things are coming to light, a lot of things about which we had to be silent. For fear of being persecuted. Oh yes, how many times did they come to the house to see if we had weapons, if we had—.

Natasha felt her group was a safe space, but her arpilleras would have to get to the Vicaría and go through customs on their way abroad. Her explaining that she decided not to depict this dumping of dead bodies because she was afraid that her family would be harassed if she were caught suggests that motherhood influenced women's fear, and shaped the behaviors they adopted in response to it. Julia, from another shantytown from southern Santiago, was afraid, even five years after the regime, to depict the detention of the chief of the secret police, because she thought she might get arrested.

Some women were afraid of being in contact with certain groups. They were especially fearful of groups that were "political" or connected with the victims of repression. Natalia, for example, said that some members of her arpillera group were nervous about having much contact with the unemployed people's groups ["bolsas de cesantes"] because they were thought to be associated with the communist party. The relatives of the disappeared told me that some arpillera-makers were afraid of mixing with them. Laura, a shantytown woman who was also on the Vicaría staff, said that the women were afraid of political parties, initially. These fears of groups considered political worked against the formation of a unified resistance community.

Fear was not present to the same degree all the time, and there were actions that lessened it. Women found that once they joined a group, they became less afraid. Bettina, for example, started to "lose her fear" after joining her local Christian base community, in which members talked about what was happening. There were also periods of time when the women were less afraid, such as the late 1980s, when some began to feel less frightened about going out of their homes.

A positive outcome of the fear was that in many cases it drew people together against the regime. Evrigenis (2008) suggests that the fear of external threats shapes political groups at their founding and helps preserve them by consolidating them in times of crisis; he believes it to be an essential element of the formation and preservation of political groups, whereas its absence renders political association unsustainable. While not an essential element in the formation of shantytown women's groups, the fear did arguably contribute to groups' bonding together into a unified resistance community. The sharing of useful information, the joint actions between groups, and the expressing of solidarity were lived all the more intensely as people were afraid of being found out, and so had to act in secret. Fear was not the only glue that bound groups together; a shared wish that the dictatorship end, and shared experiences with poverty, repression, and organizing were important as well. However, the fact that it was frightening and dangerous to organize did mean that one had to work clandestinely, and so bonds with trusted individuals and groups had the added strength of mutual implication, shared understanding, and secret knowledge.

The Intersecting of Repression, Poverty, and Gender

Repression, poverty, and gender worked together to shape what the dictatorship meant for women. First, the repression impacted women's experiences of poverty. It caused shantytown families to become even poorer than they already were when, for example, it took the form of the firing or jailing of shantytown men who were leftists or trade union members; their being fired or incarcerated caused their families to become desperately short of money. We will also see how the repression shaped women's struggles against poverty, as when Natalia had to use a white handkerchief in order not to be shot when she went out to the market before the curfew was lifted to beg for food for her community kitchen. Conversely, poverty influenced the nature and extent of the repression to which women were subject. Living in a shantytown made them subject to intense generalized repression and types of repression that were not common in middle-class neighborhoods, such as raids on homes and soldiers throwing stones at one's windows. It made one likely to be shot dead if outside at night, and so shaped women's behaviors, such as keeping children indoors, or having to wave down a soldier if they needed to take a child to hospital at night.

Gender and motherhood affected how the women experienced both the poverty and the repression. When Natalia's husband lost his job because the government was cracking down on trade union leaders and this caused exacerbated poverty for the family, Natalia, who as a mother was responsible for feeding the children, felt great distress, because her children asked for food which she could not give. She joined a community kitchen, in which she used her traditionally feminine cooking skills to feed her impoverished neighborhood. She told me:

> And the, what was it called, the olla común, where we had to go out o—, on tricycles to the market to beg so as to be able to have lunch for the children of those families that did not have any way to meet their expenses, it was sort of making a plate of food for your children. Because there were families with four, five, six, seven, up to eight children. And they had to come and fetch their little saucepan, or send their children to the children's community kitchens in the church. So for us it was terrible. To wake up at four, five in the morning to go there, and with a white handkerchief so that they wouldn't shoot you. You see? So those, those were things we lived through in person.

Natalia's experiences encapsulate a larger dynamic whereby motherhood, repression, and poverty worked together to shape women's lives.

Ana, similarly, had not worked since her marriage, but when her husband disappeared for ten days, detained, and she had no money for food, she began working in her local bolsa de cesantes [a cooperative of previously unemployed people] because she needed to feed her children. She said, "After marrying I didn't work, until I found myself needing to, when my husband was arrested, and, and my children were small so I found myself needing to." Her duty as a mother influenced her reaction to the repression and its economic impact on her family. There were other ways in which motherhood impacted women's joining groups like those Ana and Natalia were in; they became members of these groups partly as a result of other mothers inviting them because they understood their situation and needs as shantytown mothers. Also, motherhood shaped what the women liked about the groups they joined; for example, they liked working in bolsas de cesantes and arpillera workshops because they could do the work at home or while being with the children.

Mothers experienced the repression as mothers in that they focused on its effect on their children, as when Bettina told me that there were soldiers with painted faces in the streets and that this was frightening for children to see, and that they treated children roughly. Similarly, Gloria was disturbed by the fact that the knowledge that men were taken away made her son and another boy he was playing with afraid. Many women saw the repression at least in part through their children's eyes.

The repression changed women's gendered daily routine of taking the children to school, picking them up, cooking, cleaning, and buying food. It pushed some women to engage in very different activities; if their husband was arrested or disappeared, for example, they went to look for him at detention sites, morgues, or government offices. We saw how Barbara spent all day, every day, outside the National Stadium when she thought her husband was there, once she had made arrangements for childcare. When Cristina's husband went into hiding in Bolivia, she and their three children moved to Chile's northernmost city to be nearer to him. The repression affected the women in smaller ways as well, as when they could not buy food during the states of siege because shops closed early.

We have seen in this chapter, then, that the shantytown women experienced direct physical repression, consisting of generalized and targeted repression, and non-violent repression. Motherhood and being an inhabitant of a shantytown shaped these experiences and how the women reacted to them. A prevalent consequence of the repression was fear, including endemic fear and specific fears, both of which effectively constrained their freedom of movement, association, and expression. In the chapters that follow we turn to the other prominent feature of the Pinochet years from the shantytown women's perspective: the unemployment and exacerbated poverty that they endured, and what they did about these ills.

Three	# Unemployment and Exacerbated Poverty

For many Chilean shantytown women, the early years of the dictatorship through to the mid-1980s was a period of exacerbated poverty due to their husbands losing their jobs, and often remaining unemployed for a long time or having recurring experiences of unemployment.[130] How they experienced this exacerbated poverty reflected the areas of life for which they were responsible as women, namely preparing meals, taking care of the children, and running the house; accordingly, their husband's unemployment meant to them not being able to buy enough food, pay the water and electricity bills, or afford their children's school fees or materials.[131] These deprivations constituted a downward cycle that was difficult to break, and together with the repression that the women also experienced, produced severe "social suffering."[132] By causing this unemployment and impoverishment, the Pinochet government's adoption of neoliberal economic policies and a national security doctrine set off a process that led women to become active in political resistance. The impoverishment pushed the women to join local groups in which they tried to earn money or procure food cheaply (Chapter 4), and becoming group members caused them to begin participating in resistance against the dictatorship (Chapters 5 and 6).

Unemployment

The husbands of the shantytown women whom I interviewed worked in a variety of blue-collar jobs. Karina's and Natasha's husbands, for example, were welders in an ironworks, Mónica's painted cars, and Catarina's made and installed industrial curtains. Bettina's worked as a textile worker in a textile factory, Babette's was an electrician, and Natalia's, Nelly's, Ana's, and Gloria's husbands were construction workers. Teresa's husband was unusual in that he was a band musician. In her arpillera group, Rosa's husband made wicker chairs and other items, Mrs. Fuentes' husband laid out basketball courts, and Lucy's had a stall in the local street market.[133]

Soon after the start of the dictatorship, many men from the shantytowns began losing their jobs. For others, this happened later, during two periods of economic crisis (1975–1976 and 1982–1983). When the man lost his job, this brought severe hardship to the family and made women feel compelled to seek paid work, and many joined income-earning groups. Women in a coordinating committee of arpillera groups based in eastern Santiago told me that all their husbands were unemployed:

> *JA*: Were you affected by your husband's unemployment?
> *Hilda*: Yes, all of us.

Hilda's words held for most of the arpillera groups that met in shantytowns, all over the city. In Teresa's arpillera group in southern Santiago, the same was true:

> *JA*:   The other women in the workshop, did they have unemployed husbands, or not?
>
> *Teresa*:   Nearly all of them. Nearly all of them. Others were separated; they had to struggle for their children, and others were single mothers as well.

Teresa's words suggest that non-married women were also having economic difficulties and sought an income by joining groups.

Shantytown men's unemployment sometimes lasted several months, or even years. Teresa answered my questions about her husband:

> *JA*:   How long did it [the unemployment] last, for those who had unemployed husbands?
>
> *Teresa*:   Well, after a time he [Teresa's husband] forgot how to work.
>
> *JA*:   But was there a period of time when he had absolutely no work?
>
> *Teresa*:   None at all, none at all. I mean, I had to go out and work.
>
> *JA*:   How long did that go on for?
>
> *Teresa*:   It lasted more than eight years, I think.
>
> *JA*:   When he had no work at all.
>
> *Teresa*:   No work at all, no work at all. I mean, he would stay with the children and I would go out and work. He was the housewife and I was the man [laughter].
>
> *JA*:   And you, with your money, paid for everything?
>
> *Teresa*:   I would pay for everything; I would give it to my kids. Luckily I found such a good home [where Teresa worked as a maid], where my boss liked me a lot. She provided clothes for my children.

The eight years that Teresa's husband was unemployed was a longer period than that which many other women describe, perhaps because he was a band musician, but reports of husbands' unemployment, underemployment, or occasional employment lasting for years were common. Teresa's words "I had to go out and work" suggest that going out to work was not something she expected to have to do, or wanted to do; she did so because she was forced to. Her joking about her husband's forgetting how to work and his being the housewife and she the man suggests that she found this role reversal somewhat absurd, and points to the influence of shantytown gender expectations that shantytown mothers should be based at home looking after the house and family, and not have to go out to earn an income unless it was essential that they do so,[134] while men were the breadwinners.

Teresa's mention of the lady she worked for giving her clothes suggests a patron–client relationship; elsewhere she mentions that this lady also gave her food. That she so valued her employer's gifts arguably suggests that the difficulty that women had feeding and clothing the family was one of the most worrying aspects of their lives when their husbands were unemployed.

Many shantytown men faced several periods of unemployment during the course of the regime. Gloria, from southern Santiago, told me about her husband:

> *Gloria*:   My husband worked in construction, yes.
>
> *JA*:   And how long was he unemployed for?

3.1

An arpillera about unemployment. Men and women wait outside a factory for work, but a sign outside the office says "Only 3 vacancies." The unemployed express despair with their straight arms drawn apart from their bodies, and open hands.

3.2

Many unemployed men have come to ask for a job at this company, where a sign says "There are no vacancies." The sign is dated March 1982, during the second major economic crisis of the dictatorship years. It says "Don't ask twice," suggesting that men were desperate and their desperation made them pushy.

Gloria: Well, one year, during that period [when she joined the arpillera workshop in about 1984]. Between 1973 and 1990 there were lots of periods of unemployment. [*JA*: Yes, yes.] And during all those times we were, we were stuck. He must have been unemployed for a year, more than a year, during that period.

A male household head's unemployment caused families great difficulty. Like Teresa, Gloria's family endured economic hardship. For most families there was little in the way of a social safety net; not everyone qualified for social security, many did not know how to apply,[135] and the amount paid was small.

Causes of Unemployment

Much of the unemployment that these women describe came about initially because in early 1975 the Pinochet government put into place a "Shock Treatment" plan of economic recovery consisting of new, neoliberal economic policies. As well as soaring unemployment, the Shock Treatment brought price increases and the decline of industrial and agricultural production, amounting to an economic crisis. At the same time there were cutbacks in the public sector, which also caused unemployment.[136] While under the previous government unemployment had reached 4.8 percent at its highest, in 1974 it was 9.2 percent, in 1975 16.8 percent, and in 1976 17.8 percent, these figures including people working in the emergency employment programs that the government set up to provide them with minimal income.[137] Unemployment remained high for most of the dictatorship years, during which the neoliberal economic policies were continued. Between 1977 and 1985, the lowest it fell to was 15.7 percent, and for three of these years, during a second economic crisis (1982–1984), it rose above 24 percent, again including the numbers in the emergency employment programs.[138] In 1983 some shantytowns had 80 percent unemployment.[139] Structural adjustment policies such as liberalization and cuts in social sector spending, at least in the short term, may have a particularly negative impact on urban poverty,[140] and analysts have suggested that unemployment hits the poor harder than it does other groups.[141] Only in the last three years of the regime did unemployment drop below 20 percent; in 1986 it stood at 13.9 percent, falling steadily to 5.3 percent in 1989. The notion of the "Chilean miracle" obscures the fact that it was only towards the end of the dictatorship and afterwards that the economy consistently performed very well.[142]

The economic policies of the regime were not the only reason for this unemployment and underemployment. The government's anti-leftist stance was also responsible. Its national security doctrine viewed Marxists as dangerous enemies that threatened the country, and the government tried to rid Chile of them by arresting, murdering, disappearing, and exiling them.[143] This persecution extended to the workplace. As early as mid-October 1973, workers who were union leaders or sympathizers of the Allende government were being summarily dismissed from their jobs.[144] Many shantytown women and Vicaría staff reported that very soon after the September 11th coup, private companies and state organizations started firing union members and other leftists. Bettina, who lived in a shantytown in northern Santiago, was informative:

JA: And your husband, was, was he unemployed for a time, or not?
Bettina: Well, yes, my husband was unemployed on several occasions, because he, as he was a trade union leader. [. . .] My husband was, er, a textile worker in the cotton factory Hirmas, as it was in those years. He worked for eleven years in the same job, so the only thing that—. So, from when he was young, from when he was very young, until eleven years after our marriage he was in the same job,

because he was a man who was sort of quite engaged, and he got politically involved up to his eyeballs, so that meant that he was sort of listed as a trade union leader. And people who had, like, this sort of background as trade union leader, no workplace could take them.

Bettina's husband's repeated periods of unemployment echo those of Gloria's husband. Her understanding of his unemployment as being due to his being a trade union leader mirrors that of other women regarding other unemployed men in leftist organizations or parties, and that of the Vicaría de la Solidaridad staff. They believed that companies were keen to rid themselves of trade union leaders, and shunned them.

It was not just being shunned or fired that led to unemployment. So, too, did the government's persecution and threatening of leftists, as this forced them into hiding. Cristina lived in eastern Santiago and her husband, a trade union leader and member of the Communist Party, had to go into hiding and was then injured by the military, and so was unable to work:

> It's a very sad, very long story. My husband was working for Madeco Copper Manufacturing Company in this country, so they were very privileged with their, their wages and things. It was a company that paid very well and everything. Everything that came from copper was—. He was working in the copper industry, and being a trade union leader, he was very badly persecuted; er, we were, he spent a lot of time in hiding. I was alone with my three small children. I have three children, the eldest is 32, the middle one is 30, and the youngest who is back there is 26. I married very young; I was 18, and at 20 I was a mother with two children. So I had no idea what a politician was, first because I never wanted to get involved much, you know. I mean, I understood very well what was happening in politics, but—. And he was a left-wing politician, he was a member of the Communist Party, so it was really, really, really terrible. So he goes, he went to Bolivia for a time, in hiding, between Peru and Bolivia. I went to live in Arica for a full year, in 1975, with my three children, to be closer to him, to be able to see him. And the people of Madeco were, as I say, a lot of people worked there; there were four thousand and something workers, workers and professionals, both workers and professionals, there were four thousand and something people. There was a great deal of persecution because they said that they were making tanks to, to confront the military with. So it was just terrible, people—, there are lots of disappeared. Luckily he is not a disappeared person, he is retired because of disability because of a serious spinal injury, a memento from the soldiers of this country, but he's alive, and that's the main thing.

While in hiding and taking refuge in Bolivia, Cristina's husband would not have been able to work, and later he was unable to work because of his spinal injury brought about by soldiers; persecution and state violence, then, were the causes of his unemployment. Cristina's description evokes the climate of mutual fear that characterized Chile; the government's fear of an enemy within, arming itself, leftists' fear of state violence directed at them, and women's fear for their husbands. Her feeling lucky about her husband's not having disappeared points to the extent to which she was living in a topsy-turvy world, in which disappearances and state violence became aspects of life that people expected.

A further way in which the repression resulted in unemployment was by men being held in detention. While in prison they lost their jobs, and although some prisoners made sculptures out of bone and avocado seeds, which the Vicaría de la Solidaridad helped sell, they were able to earn very little. Once released, these men had difficulty finding jobs, as to have been a prisoner discouraged new employers from hiring them; their old companies would not take them back. Barbara lived in the shantytown of Colón in southern Santiago, and her husband had difficulty finding work after being released from the National Stadium. She told me the story of his return home and subsequent employment difficulties after having been missing for weeks while a prisoner:

> And I was with the two kids, I was— and suddenly I hear someone going past, like this, banging on the windows, like this. And I go out and, and look, and it was my husband who was coming in through here, through the kitchen. And his pants were—, he was thin, with his pants tied together with rope. Really thin. And that was when it ended, the, what's it called, the, the, this business of going every day, going to the stadium, and looking for him. It ended with that. I could live a normal life. But after that, when he went back to his workplace he couldn't work any more because as he had been in the stadium. [*JA*: He had—] Yes. He couldn't go on working in the same place. So they were firing people because of I don't know what reason, in accordance with article such and such, I can't remember right now. For having broken law number such and such. All those things that, that happened when they—. And at that point he started to look for work in something else, and he found some work. He started to help sell for one of those men in Franklin [a flea market]; around there. [*JA*: what sort of things?] One of those men who sell things in Franklin, outside, there, like food, that sort of thing; helping him sell.

The link between the repression and unemployment is clear in Barbara's words; he lost his job while in the stadium, and then had trouble finding another. His working in a flea market, and the fact that he worked outside suggests that he was working in the informal sector. After this, he was able to find two jobs and his position became more secure. Barbara's description suggests that from her perspective the ordeal was not over when her husband was released; it had merely changed. She had been going to the stadium for weeks, hoping to catch a glimpse of him or hear about him, and now endured the anxiety of an uncertain income.

Ana's husband, in a shantytown in eastern Santiago, was less lucky. In all the years since his arrest, he had never found stable work. Ana told me:

> *Ana*: After getting married I didn't work until I found myself having to, when my husband was arrested, and, and with my small children, I found myself having to. Because he was a trade union leader in the construction industry. So, so we had—, we suffered. And from that point on, from that time on my husband has not had work, he has not had a stable job, you know, where he could belong to a, let's say, a job where he could now enjoy a pension. No, since that time he has, he has only had work on and off.
>
> *JA*:   And, and how many months was he in prison?
>
> *Ana*: About a week, a week, ten days, about that, yes.

Ana's words suggest that the national security doctrine led to her husband's unemployment, their exacerbated poverty, and her move into paid work; trade union leaders were considered undesirables. In 2006, many years after the regime, they were still enduring the consequences of the repression as he had no pension. Some shantytown women did mention other reasons for their husband's unemployment, including drug addiction, alcoholism, and illness. Mónica's husband, for example, developed cancer after having worked painting cars for several years.

Scraping Together an Income

When the men lost their jobs, many of them found one-off, very short-term work, sometimes lasting only a day. Such jobs were called "pololos," meaning literally "boyfriends." Pololos did not ensure a regular income and were poorly paid, but they did bring in some money occasionally. While I was interviewing a group of women who were recovering alcoholics and members of an arpillera group in south-eastern Santiago, one of them explained:

> Well, you know, my husband only had "pololos." "Pololos" means today you work, tomorrow you don't. For example, sometimes a week goes past without work. And this [arpillera-making] would help us put food in the pot, pay the electricity bills, often, pay the bills we had to pay here.

Rosa's words convey how uncertain and insecure work and an income were if one relied only on "pololos." From her perspective, her husband's having only "pololos" meant that there was not always enough money for food or electricity bills, which suggests that women experienced their husband's unemployment in a gendered way, influenced by their gendered responsibilities as wife and mother. Her words also show how men's unemployment led to a change in the gender regime, with women becoming the main breadwinners.

3.3

Men tried to eke out a living while unemployed, some selling items in the street, often in the center of Santiago. This man, who may be working entrepreneurially or for someone else, sells bras laid out on a piece of cloth.

Teresa's husband, also, was unemployed and only able to find "pololos":

JA: So, he wouldn't bring in any money?

Teresa: No, he didn't have work. Well, he would work but, [Teresa made a jokingly scornful sound] from time to time, when he got pololos, Saturdays and Sundays. Two days. And sometimes weeks, months would go past and he was not working.

Despite her humor, Teresa's "weeks, months" hints at an undercurrent of desperation with her husband's not being able to work full time, and having only pololos, two days a week.[145]

In addition to taking on pololos, unemployed men tried to earn some money by signing up to work in emergency employment programs. The main ones were the "PEM" [Programa de Empleo Mínimo, or Program of Minimum Employment], and "POJH" [Programa Ocupacional de Jefes de Hogar, or Work Program for Heads of Household]. The work involved garbage collection, maintaining parks and squares, and painting, plumbing, and other forms of household maintenance, mostly for their local town hall but also for other government offices. It also included secretarial or administrative work, particularly for women.[146] The programs are widely thought of by Chilean scholars as the government's way of disguising the high unemployment rates, since workers in them were counted by the national statistics agency as employed. Shantytown women tended to view

3.4

Men in an emergency employment program do unpleasant work, digging in and around the sides of a canal.

these programs in a negative light, thinking that the wage was too small for the family to live off, and that there was a risk that their husband might become an alcoholic since the men tended to go out for a drink together after work. Bettina, from a shantytown in northern Santiago, said:

> So, so, the things we talked about [in a discussion group she joined] were things directly related to our lives, things that were very critical of the regime, like the unemployment, like hunger, like the work in the PEM and POJH, where they would go out into the street to work without having anything to produce, you see? There were times when they would fill a wheelbarrow with garbage and take it and throw it away higher up the hill, so that another man could come and pick up that garbage. And as it was 1,200 pesos that they received, the men, well, during the week that—. There are always liquor stores, so the men, well, would give them their ID cards or the pay slip and order wine, every day a little wine to share. And that's why there was so much alcoholism. So when pay day came around, the men practically didn't come home because they were not bringing any money with them. Sometimes the men would say that it made them ashamed, in fact, to come home like that, with 600 pesos, 700 pesos.

Bettina's words suggest that salient features of the work from her perspective were that it was in the street, futile, poorly paid, leading to alcoholism, and resulting in some men not bringing any money home on pay day because they had spent it on drink. While many women saw the money earned as not enough to live off, some thought it was better than no money at all, and both they and their husbands signed up. As well as working in emergency employment schemes, "pololos," and selling items in the street, unemployed men went to look for short-term work in Argentina, leaving wife and children in Chile. When they sent the money home, their wives would use it to pay the water and electricity bills, as Karina and Ana told me.

Naturally, not all men in shantytowns were unemployed or underemployed. If they had skills that were in demand, and were not being persecuted, they might retain their job. Babette's husband was one of the lucky ones:

> *Babette*: Ah, well, he worked as an electrician, yes. Luckily he, he had training, he had, let's say, a piece of paper that said he was an electro—, electro—, elect—, [*JA*: —trician], electro-mechanic, let's say, electrician, right. But there were people, er, [husbands] of [arpillera] group members, of group members, who were unemployed, or who were alcoholics as I was telling you, or who were drug addicts, or who simply didn't do anything.

Babette understood her husband's qualification as having helped him remain employed. She alludes to alcoholism and drug addiction; these, together with the neoliberal economic policies, national security doctrine, and illness contributed to men's unemployment.

A "Bad Economic Situation"

This unemployment caused exacerbated poverty in already-poor shantytown families. The number of poor families in Chile increased from 28.5 percent in 1970, to 56.9 percent in 1976. It dropped after this date but rose to another high of 50.9 percent in 1986.[147] We saw above how men's solutions to losing their jobs only provided occasional, short-

Website Link 3.1:
The connection between poverty and human rights is made clear in the Amnesty International web page, "Poverty and Human Rights," which contains pertinent reports, news, and videos: www.amnesty.org/en/poverty

term, minimal, or uncertain income. Natalia from southern Santiago told me about the hardship that her husband's loss of a job caused:

JA: And what was your husband's job?

Natalia: He worked in construction.

JA: Construction, building—

Natalia: Houses.

JA: Houses.

Natalia: Yes

JA: And from when to when was he unemployed?

Natalia: When the coup happened he lost his job immediately, because he was working in a company in which they arrested all the trade union leaders and he, I don't know why, escaped this fate. He was treasurer and—, but he went to work for about two weeks, he would show up at work, but he couldn't work, they would send them back home, and later he couldn't find any work at all. He would do, as they say, occasional jobs here and there; we call them "pololos" here, small jobs, from time to time, not all the time. So sometimes the situation was hard. And so the church helped us a lot, the priests, they would make up packets of beans, lentils, things like that for us. And that's how we got by, making the food last.

JA: And until when did this situation last, with your husband's unemployment, with pololos?

Natalia: It lasted, I think about, like, four years, more or less. Of course later he would find work, but very poorly paid work. So it wasn't a job with which, how can I say, that with the money that he earned the situation got better. It was just that there was a little more, a little bit more to put into the pot. And after that, cans of food started to arrive at the churches, they started to arrive at the churches. So, [pause, dogs barking] and there you would get, you would get the basics, garbanzo beans, beans or lentils, there would be things—. So with a little bit, you could add more things and you would make a larger quantity of food. And well, those of us who were in a worse situation, with more children, they would help us a bit more. And it wasn't the case that people were making up stories about their situation, as they say, because you knew the situation that people were in.

JA: And when did your economic situation start to improve?

Natalia: It started to improve, I think after 1990, after that. You see? Because at that point the jobs became steadier, and the eldest child was finishing his studies, and the older ones were starting to do their work experience placements and they were lucky, thank goodness, they finished their work experience placements and stayed on working. They didn't earn much, but the situation was getting better for them and, well, for all of us in the family.

Natalia's words suggest that she and her family endured four years of severe economic deprivation during which they were poorer than they had previously been. Her family made efforts to survive on three fronts. The first involved both she and her husband finding other sources of income; her husband found pololos and poorly paid work, and she, as she later told me, joined an emergency employment scheme and engaged in entrepreneurship, making and selling sweets. The second was kitchen management; making food last and using cooking strategies that would make the most of a little extra food. The third was accepting donations from priests and the Vicaría.

Website Link 3.2:
Adequate food is a legally
binding human rights
obligation in many countries,
and was initially defined as a
right in the Universal
Declaration of Human Rights
of 1948. See "The Right to
Adequate Food. Fact Sheet
No. 34" by the United Nations
Office of the High
Commissioner for Human
Rights and the Food and
Agricultural Organization, both
United Nations bodies.
www.ohchr.org/Documents/
Publications/FactSheet34en.pdf

Lacking Food: "There Wasn't Enough Meat"

What did this exacerbated poverty mean to the women of the shantytowns? The meanings it took on for them were shaped by the shantytown gender expectation that they be responsible for childcare and the smooth running of the household. Primarily, the exacerbated poverty meant to them not always having enough food that they considered essential, for all the family.[148] They could not afford milk or meat for everyone, for example. For some women the exacerbated poverty meant having periods of time when they could not afford such foods for any family member. Gloria from southern Santiago answered my question about hunger:

> *JA*:   You told me you had economic problems, as was logical, your husband was unemployed. Apart from that, how would you describe your family life? Did you experience hunger?
>
> *Gloria*:   I think so, yes, yes. We went short of a lot, a lot, especially us [she and her husband], because you had to give it to the children. I mean, fruit was for the children. Milk, the same, it was always for the children. [The situation] was quite critical, I mean, everything was restricted, you couldn't buy what you needed, there were lots of things that were lacking, so [pause]. Milk, especially, was for the little ones. Apart from the fact that they would give us milk in the clinic but nevertheless, it was never enough, it was not sufficient. So, well, you didn't live well.

Gloria's words make clear her concern about not having enough food she considered important for the children. She and her husband deprived themselves to give to them, yet there still was not always enough. Statistics suggest that her problem was widespread; in 1976 the percentage of children under six years old who had been checked for malnutrition in the country as a whole was 15.92 percent, and figures remained in the double digits until 1980, after which they gradually dropped to 8.61 percent.[149]

The women experienced this lack of money for food with a good measure of pain. Gloria's saying that the situation was "critical" and the family went short a lot suggests that not being able to access what they needed caused considerable anxiety. For Natalia from southern Santiago, having to refuse a child food was heart-wrenching:

> *JA*:   And, at that time was your husband working?
>
> *Natalia*:   He was a long time without work, a long time without work, because there was no work. He was also in the government job where they paid, he was in the POJH, they paid 4000, imagine, it was $4000 a month, and $2000 that I earned. [*JA*: Ridiculous.] Imagine, how, imagine, I mean, lots of people can't imagine how we lived.
>
> *JA*:   Terrible.
>
> *Natalia*:   Meat—it was a long time since we had seen it.
>
> *JA*:   Meat.
>
> *Natalia*:   Because you couldn't buy it, there wasn't enough money, if there was enough for bread or something else, there wasn't enough for meat. And thank goodness, as I say, Holland would send us milk, and that way they could have their daily cup of milk. You couldn't give them any more because you had to be measuring it out for them to have some, for example, for them to drink their cup of milk. Because many children fainted in school sometimes because they didn't eat

3.5

This arpillera suggests that it became difficult for shantytown inhabitants to afford essentials, such as bread, sugar, paraffin, and transport costs. These goods are depicted as bags that are just out of reach, above their outstretched arms. In the lower half of the arpillera, on the left, a woman hooks up to a public electricity line illegally. Her electricity has been cut off because she cannot afford to pay the bills.

breakfast. So sometimes there wasn't enough. Often they would ask for one more piece of bread and there was none. With pain in your heart you had to tell them there wasn't any more.

JA: So they went hungry.

Natalia: Yes.

Natalia clearly felt sadness and anguish at having to refuse her children food, and perhaps also anger; she appears indignant about the wages paid by the emergency employment program (POJH) that both she and her husband were in, which were so low that they could not buy meat. Because the women could not afford enough of certain foods, donations such as the milk from Holland were very important to them, to the extent that they tended to mention them as one of the benefits of being part of an arpillera group.

Natalia and Gloria's words suggest that the women experienced the lack of money for food in a gendered way, as mothers. When they thought of not having enough food, they thought of not having enough to give their children, and it was this that caused them so much anxiety. When Nelly from southern Santiago told me about the poverty she experienced, it was her *children's* not being able to eat enough that most bothered her; she was even concerned about the fetus in her womb. She described her conversation with workmates about these problems:

So that's what we always talked about; everything that was happening. That sometimes there was no money for the electricity, sometimes the water too. Thank goodness they never cut off my water, but they cut off the water for some people, and things like that. So we would tell each other about our problems, that sometimes we didn't have anything to give the children. So sometimes right there [in the

3.6

An arpillera made by a woman from Huamachuco in northern Santiago, which suggests that she and her community suffered hunger. The sign says, "Hunger is death. We want to live." The tables and pot on the fire indicate a community kitchen, and behind stands a church. The priest supported a great many popular organizations in Huamachuco, so much so that the church was mysteriously burned to the ground.

workshop], sometimes, they would send milk from the Vicaría, and leave the milk there. So we would give the small children who came along a bit of milk at tea time, we would give the children a little bread roll, so that they came home having had their tea. So no coming home to ask for bread; none of that. Because as I say, those were critical times. I had critical periods, very critical, with my daughter. I was pregnant with her and sometimes I didn't have money for food, I didn't even have money for a bread roll. I remember that one Christmas I spent all day without a penny, nothing, without a plate of food to give her, I mean, for me to eat, because I was pregnant. So these are things that you experience directly, that you suffered. Because just as we would cry, so we would also laugh [in the workshop]. But I tell you, I had a tough time because he [her husband] wouldn't come home, he would stay outside. Imagine, me expecting my baby and without even a cup of tea, because in those years, I remember, they would sell tea bags. Not now, now they sell it by the box, but in those years they did sell them; they would sell these big blocks of compressed tea that you would buy, and they would cut them and give everyone some. So that's why, when the money from the arpilleras arrived, I would buy sugar, tea, bread, all those things to have to give her, because there really wasn't any. So, that's how it was. We would tell each other these things and cry a bit, and later we would laugh, and that way we had a good time.

Gender, and in particular motherhood, shaped Nelly's experiences of and feelings about her poverty. It was not having had food to eat when her fetus needed it and having children ask for food when she had none that was particularly difficult to bear and vivid in her mind almost a decade after the fact. It caused anxiety, which comes through in her use of the word "critical" to describe the situation, and in the earnestness with which she hoped her children would not ask for food at home. Her husband's not coming home was what she identified as the immediate cause of her hardship, since it meant that he was not

¿NUESTRO PROBLEMA?

COMO DUEÑAS DE CASA ESTAMOS ENFRENTANDO TODOS LOS DIAS EL "COMO PARAR LA OLLA", Y CADA DIA SE NOS HACE MAS CUESTA ARRIBA. ESTOS ULTIMOS MESES YA HAN SIDO REALMENTE CRITICOS PARA NOSOTROS CON LAS ALZAS DEL PAN, PAPAS, CEBOLLA, VERDURAS Y FRUTAS EN GENERAL, Y PARA COLMO, NOS SUBEN LA LOCOMOCION, ¡PARA QUE HABLAR DE LA CARNE, POLLO Y PESCADO, ¡ESOS SON PRODUCTOS PROHIBIDOS PARA NUESTROS ESCUALIDOS BOLSILLOS DE LOS QUE ESTAMOS EN EL POJH, PIMO O GANAMOS EL SUELDO MINIMO.

¿COMO AFECTA A NUESTROS HIJOS EL ALZA DE LOS ALIMENTOS?

LOS AFECTA EN LA MALA ALIMENTACION QUE TIENEN YA QUE NO PODEMOS COMPRARLE LO NECESARIO PARA QUE CREZCAN SANOS Y SE DEBILITAN PERDIENDO SUS DEFENSAS, POR ESO VIVEN CON BRONQUITIS, RESFRIOS REBELDES, DIARREAS, TIFUS, Y LA YA OLVIDADA TUBERCULOSIS. ADEMAS ESTAN CRECIENDO CON MENOS POSIBILIDADES DE UN DESARROLLO FISICO Y MENTAL TOTAL LO QUE LES DEJA EN TOTAL DESVENTAJA FRENTE A LOS HIJOS DE LOS RICOS.

¡EL PAN NUESTRO DE CADA DIA!

SACANDO CUENTAS, DAMOS UNA LISTA DE PRODUCTOS Y SUS PRECIOS LO QUE HARIAN UNA CANASTA BASICA MINIMA, PARA UNA FAMILIA COMPUESTA X CINCO PERSONAS, 2 ADULTOS Y 3 NIÑOS.

PRODUCTO	CONSUMO DIARIO O SEMANAL	VALOR UNIDAD	CONSUMO MENSUAL	COSTO MENSUAL
Leche	1 lt.	$96 lt	30 lts.	$2,880
pan	1 kg.	$106 kg.	30 kgs.	3,180
huevos	2 unidades	$13 u	60 uni.	780
azúcar	300 grs.	$110 kg.	9 kgs.	990
té	1/4 semanal	$360 kg	1 kg.	360
legumbres	1 kg. semanal	$250 kg.	4 kgs.	1.000
fideos	1,600 kgs.	$85 400 grs.	6,400 kgs.	1.408
arroz	1 kg. semanal	$115 kg.	4 kgs.	460
aceite	1 lt, semanal	$240 lt.	4 lts.	960
harina	1/2 kg. semanal	$80 kg.	2 kgs.	160
carne	1 1/4 semanal (molida y cazuela)	$490 kg.	5 kgs.	2.450
pescado	2 kgs. semanal	$180	8 kgs.	1.440
verduras	se considera una cantidad diaria	$150 aprox.	-------	4.500
frutas	1 kg.(manzana)	$80 Kg.	30 kgs.	2.400
gas	11 kgs.quincena	$1070 galón 11kgs.	2 galones	2.140
locomoción	4 (2 pasajes adultos y 2 esc.)	$50 y 15 u.	40,40	2.600
jabón baño	1 quincenal	$100 (Le Sancy)	2	200
detergente	mediano semanal	$100	4	400
pasta diente	1 mensual	$115	1	115
pasta zapato	1 mensual	$105	1	105

¡Sin Comentario!... ⟵ $28,528 !!

EN ESTA CANASTA NO VA CONTEMPLADO NI LA ROPA, GASTOS DE LUZ Y AGUA, NI DIVIDENDOS, NI UNA MISERA ENTRETENCION, NI UNA LOCOMOCION DEMAS.

¡ Y QUE PASA CON LOS QUE TRABAJAMOS EN EL POJH, PIMO o SIMPLEMENTE ESTAMOS CESANTES¡ INTERESANTE PREGUNTA PARA LAS AUTORIDADES.

3.7

A flyer produced by shantytown women in the mid- to late 1980s entitled "Campaign against price increases." The first words of text are "Our Problem: As housewives, we face the problem of 'how to put food in the pot' every day, and it gets harder every day. These last few months have been quite desperate for us, with the increases in the price of bread, potatoes, onions, vegetables, and fruit in general, and on top of all this they raise the price of transport. Never mind meat, chicken, and fish. These are forbidden products for the tiny purses of those in the POJH or PIMO [emergency employment programs] or those who earn a minimum wage." The next paragraph describes how children are affected, saying "it affects them in the poor nutrition that they receive, as we can't buy them what is needed for their growth and health, and they get weak, with their immune system weakening, and that's why they live with bronchitis, colds that don't go away, diarrhea, typhus, and tuberculosis as in times past. Moreover, they are growing up with less chance of complete physical and mental development, which puts them at a disadvantage in comparison with rich children." A chart follows, containing the cost of foods and other essentials for a family, and the words "no comment" next to the total price, which was high. The increases in the price of food were clearly a source of anxiety for the women who wrote this.

bringing her money. Nelly's words also point to the importance of donations by the Vicaría, and the importance of the arpillera workshop as a support group within which to talk about one's problems. Her mention of buying tea by the bag refers to people's inability to pay for a whole box.

In the women's view, not being able to buy food was not merely the result of their families being unable to earn enough money, it also came about because of the increase in the price of essential foods. The new economic policies had lowered inflation since Allende's day, but it was sufficiently high at times for shantytown women to experience the price rises of essential foods as threatening. That they experienced anxiety when prices rose is suggested by a flyer entitled "Campaign against price increases," produced by a group of shantytown women, about how difficult it was to buy essential foods with prices rising. In the table on the right, the authors have calculated the total monthly cost of food, saying "And what about those of us who work in POJH, PIMO [another emergency employment program], or are simply unemployed? An interesting question for the authorities!" On the left, a column entitled "Our Problem" explains that they find it difficult to buy food and other essentials because prices have risen, and asks and answers how this affects their children. This concern with the effect on their children is a further example of how shantytown gender expectations shaped how shantytown women experienced poverty, namely by making them feel distressed about not being able to feed their families properly. The opening words of this column afford yet another example: "As housewives, every day we are faced with the problem of 'how to put food in the pot' and it gets harder every day."

The flyer also suggests that their exacerbated poverty has led to their denouncing the regime. They criticize the low wages of workers earning a minimum wage or in the emergency employment programs, making reference to these wages as "squalid." The pamphlet, then, suggests that a government program that paid low wages, combined with inflation, caused shantytown women to be unable to buy essential foods, and pushed them to engage in the political act of criticizing the regime.

The women were aware of the downward spiral that the lack of food produced. The authors of the flyer say that poor nutrition leads to poor health and incomplete mental and physical development, which put children at a disadvantage. The same awareness comes across in a flyer produced by a coordinating committee called "Popular Organizations of the Eastern Area" ["Organizaciones Populares de la Zona Oriente"]. This flyer, entitled "Campaign against Hunger and Cold" ["Campaña contra el Hambre y el Frío"], says that malnutrition, poor performance in school, leaving school, illness, death, drug addiction, child prostitution, delinquency, and broken homes were all caused by hunger.

"They Cut off our Water and Electricity"

To shantytown women, the exacerbated poverty meant not only not being able to afford food, but also having their water and electricity cut off because they were unable to pay the bills. Ana, from La Gloria in eastern Santiago, discussed this with me:

JA: And when you say that you would talk about what you lacked [in your arpillera workshop], what does that mean concretely?

Ana: The things we lacked, like how they would cut off the electricity, how they would cut off our water, well, how we didn't have, let's say, the means to subsist in those days and that's why we loo—, we looked for those alternatives [joining income-generating workshops]. So, the needs we had, "Hey, I didn't pay the

3.8

When their water was cut off, or before their homes were connected to pipes, women went to public faucets with buckets. This photograph also shows how muddy streets became when it rained, how small and close together houses were, and the fact that many were built of wood with corrugated iron roofs.

electricity bill this time," "Hey, I don't have money to pay such and such," "Hey, tomorrow I don't have anything to make a meal with," and we would try to find the solution together.

JA: They would cut off the electricity because people wouldn't pay?

Ana: There was no money to pay for it.

JA: And the, the water too?

Ana: Also, yes, yes, they would cut off the water, the electricity, and there were a lot of people who would hook up to the electricity cables, they would hook up, and sometimes they would get caught and have their cables cut.

The fact that the women talked to each other about having their electricity and water cut off suggests that this caused them considerable consternation; it also points to the group's being a source of support. Hooking up to public electricity lines brought additional anxieties about risking electrocution and being caught by the utilities company. Ana's use of the phrase "we didn't have . . . the means to subsist" hints at her thinking not merely in terms her own individual problem, but rather in terms of a collective that was living below subsistence level. Indeed, the women typically became radicalized when they joined groups, realizing that many shared their problems.[150]

3.9

Fetching water at the public faucet often meant lining up. Less strong individuals, such as the boy in the foreground, carry small receptacles such as a kettle, while more muscular ones such as the two men on the right carry larger ones, and more than one. Some people in line seem to be enjoying a moment of sociability, but the cold of the winter's day, mud on the ground, and no doubt wet shoes may have made the experience of having to fetch water uncomfortable on many occasions.

3.10a and b

In these photographs, women carry not one but several receptacles of water, perhaps so as to minimize the number of trips they have to make. Two women share the burden of carrying the largest one, a saucepan on which they have put a lid to prevent spillage. The shantytown landscape is harsh and barren, almost devoid of trees, and dotted with puddles. The air is cold and slightly misty, and the sky pallid, as is typical of Santiago's winters. The women walk along an unpaved path, a phenomenon common in shantytowns, because funding for shantytown infrastructure tended to come from the local municipality, and the municipalities in which shantytowns were located were much poorer than those of Santiago's middle- and upper-class neighborhoods.

Website Link 3.3:
Much of what the women lacked comes under the category of "economic, social, and cultural rights." For an explanation of what this concept means, see "Frequently Asked Questions on Economic, Social and Cultural Rights. Fact Sheet No. 33" by the United Nations Office of the High Commissioner for Human Rights.
www.ohchr.org/Documents/Publications/FactSheet33en.pdf

Website Link 3.4:
What are economic, social, and cultural rights? What do key international organizations in the field believe is necessary to achieve them, worldwide? These topics, together with reports, news, and videos on the economic, social, and cultural rights, are discussed in "Economic, Social, and Cultural Rights" by Amnesty International.
www.amnesty.org/en/economic-social-and-cultural-rights

"Not Having Money to Pay the School"

For the women, the exacerbated poverty and husband's unemployment also meant not being able to pay their children's school fees or buy materials such as exercise books, or afford all the clothes they needed. In my conversation with Teresa, she described these deprivations, putting them in the context of her husband's irregular employment:

JA: Your husband was unemployed during that period? How many years did his unemployment go on for?

Teresa: Oh my! As he is a musician, it all fell apart. He wasn't working in anything; he stayed at home. He even worked as a maid.

JA: You mean he went to work in people's houses?

Teresa: In countryside entertainment halls, all that. In the band.

JA: Ah, he was working?

Teresa: He was working, and the work was very irregular. Sometimes there was work, and sometimes there wasn't. These holiday periods were a good time, for example, Christmas, New Year, the 18th of September [the Chilean National Day]. He worked on Fridays, Saturdays, and Sundays, in the countryside entertainment halls. Three days a week.

JA: What is a countryside entertainment hall?

Teresa: Farms where people dance, with bands. In the old days. Now they've given them another name, "Topless" or something.

JA: At that time, what were the problems you had, in your life in general, what were the difficulties?

Teresa: It was the bad financial situation; not having money to buy a pair of shoes, and the children were studying, and not having money to pay the school. The youngest, Manuel, in his case the priest got money for me somewhere called "Help and Hope." He sent a letter and told me to go there, and at that point I owed [the school] a year's fees, if I didn't pay they were not going to allow him to study at the institute. So I went there, and they went to pay the school directly. Things like that; there were always problems, with one child not having shoes, the other not having pants. And they were nearly all boys, just one girl. But we didn't lack, my family helped me a lot; in those days my parents were alive, and they were attentive to my needs. As I come from a small family, and was the youngest, they helped me a lot.

Teresa uses the common phrase "bad financial situation" to refer to her family's lack of money when her husband was working only occasionally. That she took the step of approaching the priest to ask for help with her son's school fees suggests how troubled she was by not being able to pay for his education;[151] she experienced poverty through the lens of motherhood. Many women turned to priests, because they were authority figures in the local community, and known to have contacts and some financial resources at their disposal through their connection with the Church and Catholic organizations. The organization Teresa mentions is a Catholic charity. Women also turned to priests because they trusted them (the Catholic Church had "moral authority")[152] and knew that they were generally "on their side" rather than the dictatorship's. Teresa's relying on her parents for help was possible because they lived in what in those days was a village, and probably grew their own food.

3.11

The large pink building in the arpillera bears the words, "School. Equality in Education," suggesting that in the artist's view the poor did not have access to education to the same extent as the rich. It may also refer to the military government's policy of changing the source of funding for schools, from central to municipal, which meant that schools in poorer municipalities were less well funded.

"They Had to Live with Relatives"

Many shantytown women did not have a home of their own because they could not afford to pay rent or buy, because of low wages or joblessness. In such cases, the whole nuclear family went to live in a room in a relative's house, where often more than one child shared a bed. People who did this were known as "allegados." The owners of the house sometimes built a wooden room in their small back patio to accommodate them. Shantytown women who lived as "allegadas" felt distress about this situation. There were a number of unfortunate outcomes associated with it, including overcrowding, conflict about use of water and electricity, and in some cases sexual abuse or the threat of sexual abuse of daughters by the host. Karina told me:

> *Karina*:   We talked about all the problems that the- because there were terrible problems, that made one's own problems seem like nothing.
>
> *JA*:   Like what, for example?
>
> *Karina*:   For example because of the father, well, because the father, mother [the hosts], the women, all lived together. Their mother would complain about their spending money on water, spending money on electricity, and they were fed up.

3.12

These wooden constructions stand so close together that one of them might be a room constructed in a family's patio in order to house relatives with nowhere to live. They have corrugated iron roofs and wooden walls.

So they, they would cry, because they didn't have a home to go to. And they were not saving money either to apply [to the government for a home] because there was none. And on top of this, the husband didn't turn out to be any good; he was a bit of a drunk. So they would cry about all that, there, they would talk about it to others who n—. I, at least, never had that problem because I had my house.

JA: You mean they were living with their husband in the house of—

Karina: Of their parents.

JA: Of their parents, I see. Were there a lot of people like that, a lot of women?

Karina: Yes, a lot, most of them from here lived with their parents. They didn't have a house, so that would bother them.

JA: Yes, of course.

Karina: [. . .] And one woman would also talk about how the stepfather who lived there, she was living with her step-parents; he wanted to rape her daughter. All these things came up, all these things.

That women cried suggests the extent of their desperation about not having a home of their own. While Karina mentioned the complaints and abuse they had to endure, other women talked of friction between relatives, promiscuity, overcrowding, depression, and frustration. Because of the problems, allegados tended to want a home of their own, and many joined groups of allegados. These groups engaged in protests and, once the regime was well under way, organized land seizures whereby dozens of families set up tents on unused land.

Some women, like the allegados, did not have their own home but rented a room from a stranger for the whole family, and in this situation overcrowding was also a problem. Nelly, for example, lived in a rented room with her husband and three children. These housing problems were related to the decrease in government spending; in the 1974–1989 period, per capita public social spending on housing was on average 32 percent lower than in 1970.[153]

3.13

The room is cold; the boys have crept under the blankets, one holds his hands above a flame, and both are wearing several layers of clothing. The piece of corrugated iron they have put on top of the bed suggests that the roof leaks. Items hang from the ceiling, pointing to a lack of cupboards.

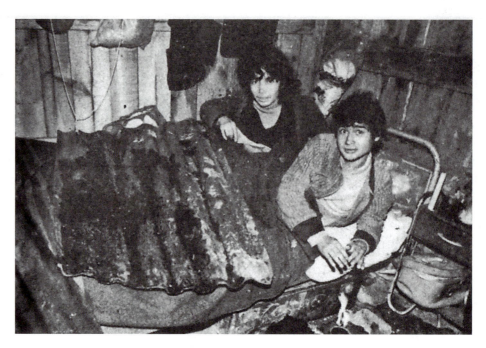

Fortunately, many women did have a home of their own, that they had bought or built over the years, sometimes after participating in a land seizure and having started off with a make-do tent. For these women, it was the quality of their housing that was distressing. Women in "campamentos," that is, new, rudimentary shantytowns that resulted from land seizures, lived in structures made out of wood and scrap metal. Once they had been in their homes for a while and saved some money, they tended to add brick walls and new rooms, so there were homes consisting of one or two brick rooms, and further rooms made out of wood and scrap materials. The luckiest families had a semi-detached brick house. Often women's homes were "mediaguas," that is, small, wooden huts built by the government. Bettina told me about her home in 1974, which she had acquired during Allende's presidency (1970–1973):

Bettina: It was a little wooden house.

JA: Of one room?

Bettina: Well, let's see, when we arrived here we had a room that was six meters long, six meters by three. When we all arrived we had what are called "mediaguas." There we had a space that measured three meters for the beds, and the other space where there was a dining room and kitchen, so we all lived that way, and that's how we raised our children.

Bettina's words suggest that there would have been overcrowding; she would not have been the only family experiencing this as she lived in a neighborhood full of similar houses at the time. Other than overcrowding, a difficulty common among women lucky enough to have their own homes was not being able to pay them off.

Problems were not limited to the confines of the home. As mentioned in Chapter 1, shantytown neighborhoods tended to lack services, paved streets, adequate sewerage systems, trees, and parks.[154] During the Allende government and later under Pinochet, one woman whom I interviewed had taken part in protests for basic services in her new shantytown, including a public telephone, school, and doctor's practice. The Pinochet government's policy of cutting back public sector spending and of forcibly moving the inhabitants of shantytowns located within the middle-class and more central areas of Santiago, and even in poorer areas such as Conchalí[155] to distant, peripheral, already-crowded shantytowns in the worst funded municipalities of the city put even more pressure on these municipalities[156] and resulted in a great many shantytown families enduring an especially severe lack of public services.

"The Only Thing I Did Was Cry and Cry": Health Problems

Mental health was a common problem among shantytown women.[157] They mentioned, as did the Vicaría staff, low self-esteem, extreme shyness, depression, and anxiety. In my conversation with Nelly, she told me that she suffered from depression and had such low self-esteem that she hardly dared to talk to anyone:

> *JA*: Participating in the workshop, basically, how did it affect you?
>
> *Nelly*: It had a good effect on me, a positive one. All good. As I say, even now it's, it was something good for me, for me to develop as a person, as a woman. Because as I say, before, I was someone who was nothing. I wouldn't talk about anything. If someone insulted me I would remain quiet. The only thing I did was cry and cry. And I didn't have the self-confidence to say, "Hey, you!" and confront the person, you understand. As I say, now I can say, "Look, you, this, that, and the other, I don't like this, I like this," and do things. Before I didn't have the self-confidence. And afterward, when I was in the workshop, I developed as a person. Now I can. If they say, "Hey, you have to go and present yourself to the President of the country and talk, and express yourself, and things," I'll go. It's something that before I, I didn't even dare to talk to a social worker, I really didn't dare, I really didn't dare, because it frightened me, it made me scared, it made me feel awkward. I didn't dare to. Why? Out of shame, more than anything, because: "What will I say?" "What will she say to me?" "Will she treat me well, will she treat me badly?" Not now. Because you have to be positive. If you go, you have to tell yourself, "It's going to go well." And the person has to listen to you. Imagine, before, when would I have been able to go to a job interview? I would not have gone for anything. But once I started participating in the workshop, no, I developed more, I, how do you say? I learned to express myself better because among workmates, you, in talking about your life, you start to learn and educate yourself, to educate yourself psychologically, intellectually. I mean, for me it was something that I'll never forget. It's a beautiful memory for, for my old age, to have been in the arpillera workshop. And if a workshop opened again, I would join one, because now it would help me a lot for therapy, because as I say, I had depression, a terrible depression, even now I am taking medicine for depression.

Nelly's lacking the confidence to talk, confront someone who insulted her, or meet with a social worker suggests low self-esteem and may have been caused in part by the relative social isolation that shantytown gender expectations imposed on women through their emphasis on women's not joining groups or going out to work. Her saying that she did not know how to talk when in a group echoes the words of many women of the shantytowns.

Some shantytown woman group leaders linked the mental health problems women experienced to the unemployment and repression. Bettina, for example, mentioned widespread fear and suspicion, which would have been caused by the repression, as well as men's getting a complex because they had problems finding work. Dinora, another shantytown organization leader, stressed the role reversal, men's humiliation, and women's mental health problems that she saw as caused by the repression and by people's not being able to meet their basic needs:

JA: And what were the shantytown women's main worries?

Dinora: The main things were the economic situation, the poverty, the unemployment, the repression. These were the main things. In other words, basic needs that were diminishing all the time, the chance to—. And on the other hand, it was a time when the topic of women's mental health came to the fore, because of this situation. It was a time of a lot of neuroses, of a lot, a lot of damage in the area of mental health, and not only women's; men's too. A great many unemployed men; this was a country supported basically by men, there was a lot of dependence of married women, on the man, on—. A working-class that was very dignified, with a very prominent space in life, came to be swept to the side, you know, and to be humiliated. The men found themselves unemployed, so you had, there was a crisis of roles, between being a man and being a woman, the man being the provider who found himself unemployed, and the woman who went out to work in whatever she could, ah, she comes to be the one supporting the family.

In Dinora's analysis, poverty, unemployment, and repression caused mental health problems for women, in particular "neuroses." Women's economic and personal survival was at risk, and hence it is not surprising that they suffered mental health problems. Like Dinora, many shantytown women experienced this role reversal as disturbing, but they appreciated its taking them out of the home and into the company of other women, and giving them the opportunity to learn.

The unemployment and not having enough money for essentials caused despair in some women, as well as in men. Bettina alluded to this when she told me about how, as arpillera group leader, she went to a group member's house to tell her that a new order for arpilleras had just come in, which meant a chance of earning some money:

So the arpilleras also taught us to feel we gained in dignity, because they also served as therapy. That was something that we really considered really important, that they served as therapy. Because it would fall to me to bring the news when they ordered arpilleras via the priests. For example, a priest would come to my house, and say, "Oh, Bettina, you know, a friend will be travelling and I want to send arpilleras. I need some thirty or fifty." So for me it was like going to heaven, hearing that. I went from house to house, the women's houses, and I would tell them. And there were times when there were tears, because the women were really downcast, as if without hope. I would say, "Look by such and such a date we need," so if there were ten of us, "to make 'x' amount of arpilleras each, five each." So the women, well, I remember that one day I came to a house, the woman was in the living room and her husband was in bed, and so I say, "You know, we have an order for arpilleras." "Oh, Lord, thank you Lord," and she starts to cry. She says, "Look, there in the bed is my husband, he doesn't want to get up, he doesn't want anything, because we have nothing to eat, we owe money in the shop," and so on. "Right, then," I say to her, "Let's start making arpilleras right away, with the little figures

3.14

The line for medical care is long at this public clinic.

[the doll-like figures that were sewn on the arpilleras].” You see, the husband specialized in making the little figures; the husband got up and started right away like, this time with some hope . . . so how was it not going to mean, well, thi—, this therapy, this, this possibility? That's why I say, well, for us it meant life and hope, life and hope because thanks to this arpillera, we would say, we give life to these pieces of cloth that could go to the garbage can. And we give life to our children, because we can buy food, we can buy an exercise book, a pair of sneakers so that they, they have shoes and can go to school. And hope in that, well, we had the hope that via an arpillera we would receive an income. And we had the hope that where that arpillera ended up, we would be communicating what was happening in, in our lives. So they meant a lot to us, the arpilleras.

Bettina's mention of women's tears, and of one woman's intense relief, thanking God when a chance to earn money opened up, is indicative of the extent of people's desperation. Her words “downcast,” and “as if without hope,” point to despair. The husband's being in bed hints at depression as well as hunger-induced weakness caused by poverty and unemployment; not only could the family not afford food, but the fact that local shops sometimes sold food on credit had plunged them into debt. True to the role reversal that

Dinora described, it was the woman in the couple who had work, and the husband was essentially her assistant, making a small part of the arpilleras. This work was vital for both of them, not only because it brought in money but also because it boosted their morale and gave them a sense of dignity, as Bettina put it.

Women from the shantytown faced still other sources of anxiety. Many were troubled by coercive, even despotic husbands who did not like them leaving the home; these they referred to as "machista." Some suffered verbal abuse and domestic violence. Alcoholism among men was another problem that shantytown women complained of, as was drug addiction, particularly among children, who took "neoprene," glue sniffing. The women also mentioned children's not wanting to attend school, not doing well at school, and becoming rebellious. These problems came on top of the unemployment and exacerbated poverty that the women were already experiencing, with the resulting hunger and inability to pay for water, electricity, school materials, clothing, or decent housing,[158] resulting in considerable anguish.

In addition to their own troubled mental health, the women had to cope with children's health problems. Catarina, the leader of a health team, saw cases of child malnutrition and scabies in southern Santiago:

> The little health room began to operate. The little health room was created to give medical care to children with problems like, [pause] to detect malnutrition, to detect all the problems a child might have [pause], problems related to food. We discovered that—the malnutrition, the big bellies, we also had problems of [pause] what's it called? That they had been abused. There were children with problems, further down the track, of scabies.

Malnutrition was not uncommon in shantytown families. A study of 339 homes in the southern low-income neighborhood of La Florida found that 36 percent of children under the age of five suffered or had in the past suffered from malnutrition.[159] Related to some of these physical ailments was the problem, noted by other women, of shantytown children's not knowing about hygiene (such as the need to wash their hands before coming to the soup kitchen), and their being dirty and wearing dirty clothes, as they could not afford soap.[160]

The women felt frustrated about not having access to good healthcare.[161] Their local healthcare center, which was free, was inadequate in their eyes. They had to line up from very early in the morning to request an appointment, and when they reached the front of the line they were likely to be told that they would not be able to see a doctor that day after all. Bettina told me:

> Because you would line up from five in the morning, you would go in at noon and they would say, "There's no doctor, the doctor's not going to come." So sometimes at, at one or two in the morning, people would make a fire and sit there so as to be there for the next day. And then the next day they [the staff] would arrive and tell them, "No, the doctor is not going to come." At mid-day. So there were a lot of cruel tricks, that we, that we experienced.

Not only did people women have to line up early and sometimes to no avail, some shantytowns just had a small hut serving as a "posta" [simple clinic], with limited opening hours, where a doctor worked in poor conditions; some had no doctor at all. The ratio of doctors to shantytown population was very low. The inadequacy of public healthcare was related to the fact that in the 1974–1989 period, the per capita public social spending on health was on average 30 percent lower than in 1970.[162] The cutting back during the dictatorship of the delivery of medicine, food, and other social services to shantytowns[163] exacerbating shantytown family hardship.

The women of the shantytowns, then, experienced the dictatorship as a time when they had difficulty putting enough food "in the pot," paying for water, electricity, schooling expenses, clothes for their children, and homes of their own, and enjoying good mental health. They understood these troubles as being caused by their husbands' loss of a job. There was a downward spiral in that these difficulties were the source of still further difficulties, coupled with anxiety. The lack of food caused malnutrition in children, for example; living with one's water or electricity cut off made life more complicated; for families who did not have a home of their own, this meant having to continue to endure living with relatives in cramped conditions, with the tensions that arose from sharing water and electricity bills; crowded homes caused conflict within families. Compounding these problems were difficulties linked to living in a shantytown, including inadequate healthcare, children on drugs, and alcoholic husbands.

Moreover, as the women's words make clear, it was not only being unable to meet their basic needs that was hard; it was also that they became fraught, anxious, and depressed. Not being able to pay their children's school fees and daily expenses made them anxious about their children's not being able to complete their education, and not being able to feed children who asked for food was a source of great distress. These emotions reflect shantytown gender expectations of women that they be the ones responsible for feeding the family and keeping the home in order; their being mothers influenced how they experienced the various deprivations.

While exacerbated poverty was widespread, there were different degrees of deprivation in the shantytowns. Some families had children who were malnourished and thin, as there was so little food, while others were slightly better off. Karina, from southern Santiago, described a family so poor that the children were without shoes:

> They were poor; the children went around barefoot. They were really, really poor, as poor as can be. Our children were never like that, thank goodness; they were decently dressed. They might lack something to eat but everything else was fine. But not them, they were, they were poor. So all these people came to the workshop, and we would help them with what we could spare, we all contributed and helped with one little thing, and another. And they were all skinny. "So many kids," we would tell her, "why did you allow yourself to have so many?" [Laughter]. It's bad to have so many if the husband is not a responsible guy.

Karina saw at least two levels of poverty in her group; families so poor that the children went around barefoot, and families whose children were well-dressed and only lacked some food. As well as illustrating the differences in levels of poverty among shantytown families, her words provide an example of the *ethos of solidarity* that was prominent in the income-generating groups. Group members believed that they should help each other, and so if a member desperately needed it, they would each contribute whatever food they could spare in order to make up a small package. Juana's description also points to the proto-feminist support that was common among the women in groups; if one spoke of her oppressive husband, for example, the others would offer a sympathetic ear, and gently proffer advice on how to resist.

Not all shantytown families became desperately poor. Babette was lucky; her husband kept his job, as did her father, and before getting married she had earned money:

JA: And your financial situation, what was it like, in those years?

Babette: Well, er, I can say that luckily mine wasn't so bad. Why? Because my husband was working. And before I got married I lived with my parents and I was working and, and I, I was paid for my work. And on top of that my father was working and, and so it was not so, so bad, the financial problem. Yes, we had a hard time, I won't deny it, but at least we were never lacking a plate of food.

JA: And when you started to make arpilleras, you, you told me that you were in a house, was it just you three in the house? Ah, so you were better off than some women.

Babette: Yes, yes. [*JA*: There were some in a very bad way.] Yes, absolutely. So, absolutely, we were much better off. Why? Because it was just the three of us living together, we had money to pay for water, we had money to pay for the electricity, to sort of eat, but we had money to eat, you see? And, and we didn't have other people in the house.

Babette's words suggest how intimately poverty was tied up with unemployment. She views her husband's, father's, and her own employment as enabling her family to suffer less than other families. The fact that Babette considered herself lucky to be able to afford water, electricity and food, and to live in less crowded conditions, suggests how bad the situation was for most.

The Pinochet dictatorship's neoliberal economic policies and national security doctrine defining leftists as dangerous, then, produced unemployment and underemployment for shantytown men, for much of the first two thirds of the dictatorship. This caused exacerbated poverty in shantytown families, which women experienced in ways that reflected what shantytown gender expectations demanded of them. Because they had primary responsibility for the running of the household and care of the children, deprivations that affected these areas, such as a lack of electricity and water, insufficient money for food, and an inability to pay school fees, were uppermost in their thoughts. The chapter that follows examines what the women did to cope with their impoverishment, and introduces us to a phenomenon that arose with the dictatorship: the mushrooming of hundreds of small groups of shantytown women aimed at procuring food or an income. Joining or forming such groups was the women's first step towards involvement in resistance activities.

Four

Surviving Poverty in the Shantytowns

How did the shantytown women respond to the exacerbated poverty they faced? They could have responded by abandonment, inactivity due to despair or, as was the case with some of the mothers in Scheper-Hughes' (1992) *Death Without Weeping*, letting a child die since, despite their best efforts, they could not feed them, while adhering to a discourse about certain children not wanting to live. Instead, they joined local groups that produced food or generated an income, and in parallel sought work with emergency employment programs or private employers, engaged in entrepreneurship, cut back spending at home, participated in reciprocal exchanges, and devised one-off solutions such as asking their local priest for help. In their groups they engaged in *direct action*, or work to solve the poverty-related problems in an immediate and direct way (the subject of this chapter), and in *applying pressure* through protests and denunciations about their poverty (Chapter 6). Because what the women did to cope with poverty was such a radical departure from their previous existence, I begin by introducing the reader to what their lives had been like previously, "within the four walls," as they put it.

Within the Four Walls

"Within the four walls" characterized the lives of a great many shantytown women before their husbands lost their jobs. They used this expression to mean that they spent most of their time at home, their lives revolving around house and children, with little outside activities and relatively little outside contact. They tended to go out only to shop for food at their local shantytown street market or grocery store, to take the children to school and back, to attend Mass, and occasionally to visit relatives or a neighbor. In my conversation with Bernardita, she communicated that it was a confined existence:

> *JA*: When did you start to work in the community kitchen?
>
> *Bernardita*: In 1976.
>
> *JA*: And what were you doing before? Were you working, or not?
>
> *Bernardita*: Before that I was like this [gestures], within the four walls. [*JA*: In the house]. In the house. In those days I was living with my husband.

Bernardita's gesture suggested the walls of a very small box, indicating her sense that she was shut up as if in a prison. This confinement, common among shantytown women, was largely due to shantytown gender expectations, which dictated that they be in charge of housekeeping and children, and not work outside or be away from home for long, even to participate in groups or leisure activities.[164] Women were responsible for all the

Website Link 4.1:
Women experience limited freedom of movement out of the home in other geographical contexts as well. See "The Status of Women in the Middle East and North Africa (SWMENA) Project. Focus on Yemen/Freedom of Movement, and Freedom from Harassment and Violence Topic Brief" and "The Status of Women in the Middle East and North Africa (SWMENA) Project. Focus on Morocco. Topic Brief: Freedom of Movement, Freedom from Harassment and Violence," both by the International Foundation for Electoral Systems and the Institute for Women's Policy Research. www.iwpr.org/initiatives/swmena

cooking, domestic tasks, and childcare. As two scholars of shantytown family life put it, the woman "organizes the daily life of the home. She takes on the domestic duties, including giving birth and raising children. She is the one who is responsible for translating the available resources into meals, clothes, a clean and pleasant environment, robust children, well-fed husbands, etc."[165] Husbands were supposed to work and provide. Compounding shantytown gender expectations, the Pinochet government promoted the type of family in which the woman was a home-maker and the husband the only provider, and messages along these lines may have influenced the women. These pressures were a barrier to becoming active in employment, politics, or the community.

Often women had worked until their marriage or first or second child, and then stopped,[166] only taking up paid work after the coup because they were forced to do so in order to earn money for essentials for the family. Ana, for example, told me:

Ana: In other words, after getting married I didn't work.

JA: After you got married.

Ana: After I got married I didn't work until I found myself having to, when my husband was arrested and, and with my children who were small, so, I found myself needing to.

Barbara, unlike Ana, had continued working after getting married, in a factory, until her second child was born and she was 28. Then she had stopped working for several years, until the mid-eighties when her husband was not bringing money home regularly.

There were some women who had never earned money in paid employment. My conversation with Karina was instructive:

JA: And you, before making arpilleras, had you worked earning money in something else?

Karina: No.

JA: Never, never?

Karina: Never, it was the first time

JA: Not even selling cardboard?

Karina: No, not even with the cardboard.

Karina had done housework for a family with whom she had lived as a girl, but her words suggest that she had not worked for a wage. The reference to cardboard alludes to the fact that five years after the coup she was collecting and selling used cardboard boxes and bottles, entrepreneurially. Despite this general trend of women not working for wages, there was one woman among my interviewees who had taken in work at home while her children were small, sewing bras and skirts for a company that gave her the cut out pieces of cloth to put together.

While shantytown gender expectations were primarily responsible for the women's not working outside the home until their husband's unemployment or imprisonment forced them to, there were a number of other related forces at work. Some husbands actively opposed their wife's working, even when they themselves were out of work. There was the additional hurdle of having to ask one's husband's permission to work, as many women felt they should. Furthermore, as they were not used to working for an income and meeting strangers; to do so was a change that required some courage. It was all the more difficult since the women tended to have low self-esteem and little confidence in their ability to work. Nelly's words, when she described her reaction to being invited to join the arpillera group, point to this lack of confidence:

> And then one day they invited me to the workshop, and I said, "Yes, OK, I'll go and see if I like it, if I get used to it." And they also told me that we would be paid for the arpilleras. "Ah, right then," I said, "That's good; if they pay, all the better then." Because in those days as I wasn't working, I didn't know how to work, I didn't know how to do anything. So that was something that was useful to me, to learn.

Nelly's idea that she did not know how to work suggests low self-esteem, related to her not having been in the labor force for some time.

Multiple other barriers presented themselves. There was the problem of what to do with the children while one worked. Some women left the children locked up at home, but were uneasy about doing so in case there were a fire and their children died trapped in the house. They also felt uncomfortable about "leaving the house alone," as they put it, meaning leaving it unguarded and at risk of burglary. Another difficulty was their belief that they would be discriminated against in the job application process because they came from a shantytown and a lower social class, especially if there was another candidate who "tenía mejor pinta" [looked more high-class], as Nanette from San Gregorio in eastern Santiago explained to me.

Not only did shantytown mothers tend not to work outside the home, they also tended not to participate in groups. Their local church, for a great many women, was the only organization to which they belonged. Most merely attended Mass, but some were active helping the priest or nuns with church activities. Gloria, for example, helped a nun by overseeing a group of children who painted on cloth, and she was also a catechism teacher. Some women were in mother's centers, groups that met once a week to learn household skills or make handicrafts, and chat together.

A significant barrier after the coup was fear. Many women were afraid of joining groups because they might be suspected of being leftists, and targeted for repression. The repression also made women afraid to go outside at times. Nanette from San Gregorio in southern Santiago contrasted the period just after the dictatorship with the dictatorship years:

> *Nanette*:   And just about at that time women started to, sort of, to rebel. They wanted to get out of the house, as there was less fear at that time, the fear had already passed as well, so women started sort of to go out of the house.
>
> *JA*:   And why were they in the house before? They wouldn't even go to the workshop, before?
>
> *Nanette*:   The thing is, there was no opportunity, and people were afraid, as well. In those days they were afraid to go out, and on top of that, as there was a curfew, and all that, people were terrified about going out. So, and also, sort of all those years, we were full of fear, very afraid.

Fear was part of what kept the women at home. When there was a curfew, there might be soldiers in the shantytown, shooting at people who went outside.

Other barriers to participating in groups before the coup and hesitating to do so afterwards were the same as those that prevented women from working for an income. Shantytown gender expectations weighed heavily. Joining groups would take the women outside the home, and carried the meaning of neglecting the children and household duties, and wasting time talking and gossiping.[167] The women lacked confidence, there was the problem of what to do with the children, and they felt uncomfortable about leaving the house alone in case of burglary. Husbands were reluctant, and this reluctance was sometimes accompanied by violence.[168] Nina told me about having to ask permission to go to her arpillera group meetings, and her husband's being suspicious and verbally and physically abusive. She sometimes adopted the strategy of taking a child with her, to lessen his suspicion:

> I, well, in my case, let's say, I was a doormat, so, the object-woman. [*JA*: A piece of furniture]. A piece of furniture. If I didn't like something, he'd punch me. So, I lived a very hard life. [. . .] I started to rebel. The truth is, I started to rebel. Because for example, to go to a meeting I had to hem and haw and beg, just like a little child, and say, "You know . . . ," and to please him as much as I could, and then say, like this, "You, er, you know, I've got a meeting at such and such a time, can I go?" Asking permission just like a little child, you see. And sometimes either they would swear at you, or they would say no. So that's where it hurt. And sometimes to be able to go out you had to take two or three children and go out with them so that, so that there would be no- because the first thing men think is that you are going to meet up with someone.
>
> *JA*:　With whom?
>
> *Nina*:　I mean, they think that you are going to meet up with someone, or a [*JA*: Ah, with a man]. Yes. So, so as not to have that type of problem you would get your youngest children and take them along. But at that point, also, the, er, woman inside started to come out, thinking "No! Why should it be this way? I'm not a little girl! I also have my rights! Because if men go out they never tell you where they are going. And they can go out at any time! Why can't I do the same?" So you start to rebel. And if he gives you a punch, you, you slap him. If he throws a cup at you, you throw the sugar bowl. Until you say, "Enough." And, and you start to rebel, you start to rebel completely. How long ago was this? Five years. [. . .] So I started to rebel because I had many years, many years of pain, in which the children saw the arguments, because in the end there was no respect even for the children. Because when a man does—is bad, he doesn't respect the children either, coming home, and the children see the arguments, the fighting, the swear words, the whole show. And they really denigrate you, without having any reason for doing so.

Nina was deeply troubled by her husband's violence, verbal abuse, denigration, suspicion, double standards, and exposing the children to his violence, and finally left him. Such behaviors on his part were powerful deterrents to her joining a group, but she did so nonetheless.

Being in prison lessened men's opposition. The political prisoner-husbands of the women who formed the Nuevo Amanecer arpillera workshop in eastern Santiago, for example, encouraged their wives,[169] who must have been finding it difficult to feed their children. Unemployment also made husbands more open to their wives joining groups in which they could earn an income, since they themselves were not earning much. Even then, though, some husbands resisted.

Despite the obstacles, some women had been in groups called "mothers' centers" before the coup. These were groups of women from low-income neighborhoods, who met one afternoon a week to make handicrafts and in some cases learn craft-making skills and skills useful for running a household. The mothers' centers were officially established by President Frei in 1968, although they may have existed in the 1950s,[170] set up by the church and charity groups with the purpose of providing a place where women from poor neighborhoods could learn a craft and earn extra money without traveling long distances or being restricted to rigid working hours that interfered with their work in the home. Successive governments used them to promote their political programs. After the coup, they came to be run by right-wing women and women connected with the military, and Pinochet's wife directed the organization of which they were part, now called CEMA-Chile.[171] Some women who were not happy about the dictatorship preferred not to belong,[172] but some such women joined because CEMA-Chile offered a package of food in exchange for work. Mónica from southern Santiago, for example, told me that she joined a mothers' center in which members sewed sheets, aprons and knitted waistcoats, because they would receive a good parcel of food for this work, but when they were able, they became independent and sold their work elsewhere.

Some women had participated in events organized in their neighborhood, before the coup. When growing up, for example, they had joined in with their shantytown's anniversary festivities, or had attended a celebration of the opening of a new, local shop. Even though this participation did not necessarily entail group membership, it brought them the experience of taking part in community life. Gloria, for example, said:

> Because these were things that you experienced from when you were a girl, in the shantytowns. I lived in a shantytown near here, and the organizing we had in those days was very good. I remember, if a bakery opened in the shantytown we were in, in La Estrella, all the leaders—[pause] including my uncle of course—went. We would all go, even the small children, to the opening of the bakery. It was an important event for all the neighbors. Or if something was organized for Christmas or New Year, we would celebrate in the street with the neighbors. People did not all stay shut up in their homes; instead they celebrated with neighbors. And in this shantytown it was the same. So those were things that—, you came [to the groups] with this training.

Gloria's mention of the shantytown anniversary and people celebrating with the baker suggest that there was strong community spirit, mutual support, and experience with working together to organize events. Her use of the word "training" suggests that these features of shantytown life provided experience that proved useful when later women working together to protect themselves and fight poverty and the dictatorship. Among the women who were group leaders under the regime there were a few who had had direct experience of participating in this community life, setting up their shantytown, or struggling to have the government put in running water, a public telephone, a clinic, a school, and other services or infrastructure. Another shantytown woman had set up neighborhood committees to campaign for infrastructure, and organized films, slide shows, and dances.[173] One women had been active in a Catholic organization, and a couple had been members of parties or organizations affiliated with political parties. Nancy from southern Santiago, for example, helped set up a health team and arpillera groups after the coup, and before it she had been in a young Catholics' group, and later in a political party.

Joining Groups

A few months after the coup, women began forming and joining groups in order to cope with their exacerbated poverty. Most prominent among the groups they formed were food-procuring and income-earning groups. The food-procuring groups included community kitchens for children ["comedores infantiles"], community kitchens for all community members ["ollas comunes"], joint purchasing groups in which members pooled their money to buy food at low cost ["comprando juntos," literally "buying together"], neighborhood gardening groups that grew vegetables[174] ["huertos familiares"], and even groups that raised rabbits. The income-earning groups included workshops ["talleres"] that knitted or made arpilleras, the more politically-oriented "unemployed people's groups" ["bolsas de cesantes," also called "bolsas de trabajo"], laundry cooperatives ["lavanderías"], and Unions of Independent Workers[175] ["sindicatos de trabajadores independientes"]. The Vicaría de la Solidaridad helped sell some of the products that the bolsas de cesantes and talleres produced.

There were also groups for solving particular problems such as not having one's own home,[176] not being able to pay one's installments on a home, or not being able to pay one's bills. One woman joked that "there was a group for everything." Within groups, women typically worked at more than one activity;[177] the talleres, for example, might knit, and make and sell bread on the side. Many groups changed into another kind of group over the course of their existence, as when a bolsa de cesantes or olla común became a sewing group, and then an arpillera group. The women called these income-earning groups, food-related groups, and groups aimed at solving particular problems "grupos populares" [working-class people's groups], "organizaciones populares" [working-class people's organizations], "grupos solidarios" [groups in which there was solidarity], or "organizaciones sociales" [social organizations]. A number of Chilean scholars call them "popular economic organizations."[178]

These groups mushroomed in the shantytowns during the regime. In 1982, analysts counted 459 "popular economic organizations," but suspected there were more than 700, amounting to approximately 80,000 members.[179] In 1984, a well-respected research institute, the Programa de Economía del Trabajo, counted 707 such organizations, keeping the membership estimate at 80,000.[180] In 1985, there were 1,125 popular economic organizations.[181] By the end of 1985, 220,000 or 16 percent of shantytown inhabitants belonged to one or more of these organizations.[182] According to a later, unpublished study by the Vicaría de la Solidaridad,[183] in 1987 there were 1,616 "solidarity organizations," as the Vicaría staff often called them, with 81,414 members. In just one diocese in the south of Santiago, there were three hundred such groups.[184] In 1990, the total number of popular economic organizations was 2,257 according to one study,[185] and according to another most of their members were women.[186] These figures belie the perception of some scholars[187] that shantytowns were a mass of unorganized individuals and a few isolated, weak, unfinished organizations. They support analyses[188] that emphasize the growing range and extension of collective actions and organizations for survival.[189]

The members and leaders of these varied groups were mostly women.[190] After the coup, joining groups in an effort to cope with poverty was one of the principal ways in which shantytown women began to organize. Many women worked in an income-generating or food-procuring group at the same time as they worked in an emergency employment scheme, for a private employer, or as a micro-entrepreneur. Some alternated over a period of time, working for an employer for some time, and later joining a "popular group." Some women worked in more than one "popular group" at a time.

In many of the groups, the women were involved in two kinds of activity: *direct action*, which involved producing what they needed for survival, and *applying pressure*, for example by making demands of the government in the hope that their economic problem would end. Some community kitchens, for example, procured and made food for the neighborhood, while also participating in street protests about hunger. One group, concerned about the increase in the price of essential foods, wrote to the Ministry of Economics about the issue, demanding that measures be taken,[191] and wrote about the problem in a bulletin. Similarly, groups aimed at solving housing problems both worked to help members acquire housing, and engaged in different sorts of protest and denunciation. One group that had carried out a land seizure produced a bulletin in order to inform people about the housing problem, for example, while another housing group created an artistic installation in La Victoria to denounce the lack of housing. In some groups, some women only participated in direct action, while in others they participated in both direct action and applying pressure.

Gendered Motivations for Joining a Group

Motherhood was a driving force in women's entry into groups. Women were responsible for feeding their children, and when their husbands lost their jobs, were in prison, were ill, or when there was no husband, they felt obliged to find ways of procuring food or money. I asked Natalia:

> *JA*:   When you joined, the priest had told you about it [the workshop], right? But what, basically, was your motivation in joining?
>
> *Natalia*:   My motivation was to be able to have a little money. Because of the poverty you were experiencing, you see, so that was the motivation of everyone in the workshops, it was to be able to take a little money home. It didn't matter what the subject-matter [of the arpilleras] was, it didn't matter what you did; the point was to take home a little money. Because everyone had children, and the children were the ones suffering from hunger, their fathers' unemployment, children who were left as orphans, because their father died, so the mother had to bear all the burden of the home. With the unemployed husbands, the money they earned was not enough, and on top of that, imagine, there were children, in my case. There were others who had more children, well, some had fewer, but the point is that everyone needed money.

Natalia's words make clear that her dominant motivation was not having enough money with which to feed her family adequately. It centered, then, on her being a woman and mother, where shantytown gender expectations demanded that women feed their children. She was not unusual; analysts have found that urban poor women spend a greater proportion of their income on household needs than men.[192]

Small children in particular made joining groups or finding some other way of earning an income urgent, in women's minds.[193] I asked Gloria:

> *JA*:   When you joined the workshop, what was it that made you want to join?
>
> *Gloria*:   Well, at that time I was participating in the Christian community. Well, really my motivation was economic. My husband was unemployed—there was a lot of unemployment in the country—and because of financial problems. I had a

small child, and I also had girls who were in school. So it was to earn a few pennies. To bring in some money because the situation was quite [pause] well, critical.

Gloria's having a small child, as well as girls in school was central to her wish to earn money and join a group. The groups were a particularly attractive form of employment for women because in many cases the work was done at home, and they only had to leave the house one, two, or three afternoons a week for their group meeting. In addition, they could normally take their children with them. The desperate need to earn money or acquire food for their families was not the only force pushing the women to join groups, however; they also had non-economic motives. They wanted to get out of the house, cease feeling lonely, distract themselves from their problems, and enjoy themselves. In addition, they were looking for the support of other women, wanted to learn something new, and wished to become less dependent on their husbands.

The leaders of groups had slightly different motivations from rank-and-file members. Primarily, they wanted to organize women, believing that only if people were organized could there be any hope of overthrowing the dictatorship. In addition, they saw groups as places in which they could raise women's awareness about poverty, repression, and gender oppression; in doing so, they were perhaps influenced by the recent phenomenon of popular education[194] whereby groups formed to analyze individual and community experiences and then took action towards change. They hoped, furthermore, that once in groups the women would participate in protests or other activities aimed at bringing down the dictatorship. In addition to these motives, they wanted to help the women feel less anguish and despair, gain self-esteem, come to see that they had rights as women, raise themselves up from their downtrodden position, and emerge from the isolation of the home. In sum, these leaders were deeply troubled by the repression, poverty, and gender oppression that they observed, and saw groups as both contributing to ending the regime and empowering women.

The leaders were women from the shantytowns. They had typically not been members of a group before joining their first group, whereupon they were ordinary group members for a time, and then were elected by the other members to be the group leader. Natalia, for example, was elected leader soon after joining a discussion group, because of her qualities; the group had first come together at the priest's initiative. Cristina had not been active in groups either, until joining a bolsa de cesantes [unemployed people's group], which became an arpillera group, where she was later elected as leader. Some leaders, however, had previously been involved in social struggles or overtly political groups. Bettina, for example, had participated in her shantytown's struggles for basic services during the Allende era. Much later on, she joined a women's discussion group that became an arpillera group. She then broke away and created her own arpillera group, and then a second one, because she wanted to give more women the opportunity to earn money by making arpilleras. She did so with the priest's support. Nancy had been active in a political party while a student; she went on to create a health team and several arpillera groups. Some leaders were roped into becoming leaders because they were in close contact with other leaders. Babette, for example, was Catarina's daughter-in-law, and Catarina asked her to help her run the health team and later set up a community kitchen that became an arpillera group.

Factors Conducive to the Groups' Existence

Certain aspects of the pre-coup social environment were conducive to the creation and survival of the groups under the regime. First, during the pre-coup period some shantytown women had gained experience with collective action, being involved in the land seizure that led to the creation of their shantytown or with struggles for services and infrastructure. In the process they had learned that it was possible to obtain what they needed by organizing and working collectively.[195] Second, when shantytowns were formed, inhabitants tended to be "solidarios" [helping each other], particularly if the shantytown had emerged from an illegal land seizure.[196] This history of solidarity had survived in the collective memory, arguably facilitating the re-emergence of solidarity within and among groups after the coup, resulting in mutual exchanges of support between groups. Third, mothers' centers had existed in the shantytowns for a decade at the time of the coup, and may have provided a model for leadership structure and for how group meetings should be conducted. The groups that shantytown women formed under the dictatorship contained many features also found in mothers' centers, including the leadership roles of president, treasurer, and secretary, the afternoon schedule, and the custom of breaking for tea in the middle of the meeting. Knowledge about the mothers' centers may have provided the women with insights useful for running their groups. Only one group member I interviewed had been active in a mothers' center, but the knowledge may nevertheless have existed among women in the community.

A number of post-coup factors also contributed to the existence of women's groups. The support of priests and nuns based in shantytowns was important. These individuals, many of whom were foreign,[197] were quick to note the devastating consequences of the regime on their parishioners, and to offer help with shantytown inhabitants' efforts to survive poverty and repression. Many priests had been radicalized by their exposure to shantytown poverty and repression, and by a socialist movement of Chilean Catholic priests.[198] Some had been influenced by Liberation Theology, a current of thought in the Latin American Catholic Church that began in the Fifties, and emphasized helping the poor and oppressed better their lives. Shantytown priests acted independently of the Church hierarchy in assisting the women with their groups. In the months following the coup the hierarchy supported the Junta, while priests were opening their doors to the victims of repression. The initial impetus for creating a group often came from the local priest, who gathered together a few women he knew from Mass, and asked them if they wished to form a group. When the Comité Pro-Paz or Vicaría de la Solidaridad provided the impetus, they first approached the local priest, and worked with him.

Priests continued to lend their support once groups had formed.[199] A shantytown priest in southern Santiago, for example, contacted the Vicaría and asked it to allow a sewing group to begin making arpilleras, selling them through the Vicaría. Many priests encouraged women to join their local community kitchen or arpillera group when their financial situation was desperate. Priests made use of their social capital, in the form of contacts with church staff abroad and in Chile, with Vicaría staff, and with potential donors, to help sell what the women produced, attract donations, and gather information. A Spanish priest in southern Santiago, for example, encouraged many local women to take their children to the local community kitchen and participate in running it, wrote letters that the women could use when begging for food in the market, and stored dry food for them. He helped an arpillera group by sending its arpilleras to friends abroad, channeling donations to it, and allowing members to sleep on church premises if their meeting went on after curfew. Nuns and lay women connected with the church were also important, creating and supporting groups, acquiring donations of food and clothing for them, and selling groups' work. In La Victoria, for example, a lay woman connected with the church set up a group that earned money by making and painting cloth bags for baguettes, which she then sent to France to be sold.

The donations were very important to the women. They consisted mainly of dried foods, milk, yogurt, cheeses, cooking oil, soap, and clothes. Priests and women religious received them from exiles, human rights activists, international NGOs, the aid agencies of foreign governments, and priests and church groups abroad, and channeled them to the women's groups that they supported. The Comité Pro-Paz and Vicaría received donations from the same sources (see below). Hence Pinochet's national security doctrine and neoliberal economic policies ironically activated transnational networks that helped undermine the regime by lending support to the resistance community.[200] Charities, middle-class individuals, and even private companies in Chile also sent donations via the Vicaría and priests. Reliance on national and international charity and the priests' and Vicaría's willingness to help them were important parts of how many shantytown families survived. Donations of milk from Holland, for example, were the means by which women in Natalia's group gave their children this food. The women valued such donations a great deal; they were one reason why they stayed in the groups.

From the women's perspective, another of the most important ways in which priests supported their groups was by lending them a room in which to meet. These rooms were a great benefit to the women because they were free, large enough for the group, on church premises where the women felt relatively safe, and close enough to their homes for them not to have to spend money on public transport. Also important to the women was the fact that they were places to which they could bring their children, and as an added bonus many churches had a patio in which the children could play, and even volunteers to keep an eye on them. Community kitchens that served food to children, groups of unemployed workers, arpillera groups, discussion groups, and groups of seniors all met in rooms lent to them by the priest.

Priests and nuns suffered negative repercussions because of their efforts. Some were expelled from Chile and others harassed. The church of San Isidrio in northern Santiago was mysteriously burned to the ground. I asked Bettina:

JA: It was in this neighborhood, that the chapel burned down? It was here, this one?

Bettina: Yes, yes.

JA: And who burned it down?

Bettina: Look, someone burned it down.

JA: Because, was the arpillera group there?

Bettina: Well, no, we were not making arpilleras yet. But we were already participating in groups. That chapel was sort of the birth place of the movement in San Isidrio. So there were already, for example, there were health groups, the workers' pastoral association ["pastoral obrera"],[201] there were children's community kitchens, which were not yet called "ollas comunes." And there were collective vegetable patches, there was rabbit breeding, there were a, a lot of activities going on there. And I guess the ones who got together most recently were the people in the workers' pastoral association. And the workers' pastoral association was really closely watched. Because the workers' pastoral association was clearly a group of [pause] Christians who reflect on the subject of, of the worker. So in those years people were starting to work on the Puebla document, which was a document

4.1

A poster advertising a fundraising event organized by the Vicaría for the comedores infantiles [community kitchens for children].

that stated clearly what forms of abuse bosses [pause] used with workers, and so on. So those years were full of conflict. And one day, at daybreak, or at midnight, well, the church caught fire, completely. Completely, completely. And so there was a big movement after this; we had to start with campaigns, to fetch bricks and everything, at that point, and as that was the, the, the main church. After that church there were one, two, three, three chapels that were built. The main church was destroyed and three more chapels were built. One for every—[pause]. So it was quite strong this, this engagement we had via the church. It was, it was one of the most combative shantytowns, as they say.

Website Link 4.2:
The Vicaría was not the only non-profit organization to support women's needlework and craft-making with the aim of enabling them to earn money for their subsistence. The organization Hand Crafting Justice works "in cooperation with women struggling for economic justice and independence in the developing world," supporting them and assisting them in their efforts to create employment for themselves in order to provide for their families and better their lives. See "Hand Crafting Justice": http://handcraftingjustice. cedris.org/index.php?lang= en&pt=c&p=aboutUs

The Church had probably been burned by agents of the government because the priest who worked there had allowed many groups to meet on its premises. Most of these groups were connected with surviving poverty, but the workers' pastoral association was a discussion group influenced by Liberation Theology which, with its stress on the need to help the poor and oppressed, would have appeared leftist and so against the interests of "national security." Ironically, the burning down of the church seems from Bettina's words to have led to yet more activism and people's coming together. Soldiers did not regularly burn down churches and this was the exception rather than the rule, but local priests did undergo other forms of harassment.[202]

The Comité Pro-Paz and Vicaría de la Solidaridad's work to help the groups was another factor contributing the groups' existence. Like priests, the Comité Pro-Paz and Vicaría de la Solidaridad helped find a market for the goods that the groups making arpilleras and sewn and knitted items produced, sending them to sellers abroad, and selling them on their premises. They also channeled donations to the groups, made available rooms in which to meet, approached a handful of reluctant priests and asking them to open their doors to groups, financed some small income-generating groups such as a laundry cooperative in eastern Santiago, and offered training in leadership, group management, technical skills, and "personal development" (self-esteem combined with consciousness-raising about poverty, repression, and rights). For example, they arranged for law professors and students to give talks about the poverty and its link to government policies to a group in northern Santiago, and showed videos of the prisoners and military brutality in the National Stadium to coordinating committee members in southern Santiago. They also provided some of the raw materials the groups needed, such as dry foods for the ollas comunes. Some of the ways in which both the local priests and Vicaría were important in the formation of local groups is clear from my conversation with Natalia:

JA: And the workshop, when you joined, you said there were five people. [*Natalia*: Yes.] So how had they started?

Natalia: The same way as me, via the church, because the news about the arpilleras reached the churches. Because the Vicaría de la Solidaridad, which Monseñor Raúl Silva Henríquez founded, started with this business of the arpilleras, and so then they started to organize people, teaching them how to make them. Sort of to help those whose need was greatest, poor people and everything. So we started to find out about everything via the church, and to integrate people. And they started to form workshops in all the shantytowns, everywhere. [. . .]

JA: And how was your workshop created?

Natalia: Because—via the Vicaría of the southern area of Santiago. They called them [the first five women members] to a meeting, because they were participating, some of them, as catechists in the church. You see? Because they would give catechism classes to children, to parents, for first communion, for marriages, and all that. So they went to a meeting and there they informed them about all this, about the Vicaría having been created. And so at that point they [the groups] started to form bit by bit. And the "coordinadora" [coordinating committee], as it is called, was created. Because Laura worked as a social worker in the southern Vicaría office, so she was the one who started to organize the women and create workshops.

The priest to whom Natalia refers played a crucial role in the creation of her group, allowing its first members to meet in his church and informing them about the Vicaría. The Vicaría then initiated the creation of still more groups in the area. Natalia's words also make clear that priests recruited group members. The priests and Vicaría were natural partners and often worked together to help shantytown women. Both were affiliated with the Church and sympathetic to the plight of the poor and persecuted. Priests were local figures of authority who were in contact with hundreds of shantytown inhabitants, making them good people for the Vicaría to approach in its efforts to organize and help the unemployed by creating groups; similarly, priests approached the Vicaría because of its contacts abroad to ask it to help sell what groups produced. The creation of branches of the Vicaría in the more peripheral areas of Santiago early on facilitated contact between local priests, Vicaría staff, and the shantytown women.

The Comité Pro-Paz and Vicaría de la Solidaridad were able to support shantytown women in these ways because they were closely affiliated with the Catholic Church, a powerful institution with some level of immunity against attack by the government. This connection protected the Comité and Vicaría from direct, violent military assault. When Pinochet wanted the Comité to close, for example, he first talked to Cardinal Raúl Silva Henríquez, rather than simply sending soldiers to destroy the organization, as he might have done with an organization not part of so prominent an institution as the Catholic Church. When the Cardinal shut down the Comité but recreated it as the Vicaría within the legal structure of the archdiocese there was little Pinochet could do because he wanted to maintain cordial relations with the Church. He limited his attacks to the intimidation and persecution of individual Vicaría staff members. Church protection made it possible for the Comité and Vicaría to help set up groups of shantytown inhabitants, while also making it more likely that women would come out of their homes and take the risky step of joining them. Cristina, a communist and atheist, expressed her feelings about the importance of this protection:

> But if the Catholic Church in this country hadn't opened its doors, we would not have been able to make it, because the dictatorship in this country was very tough [*JA*: Yes] and very hard. So you had to be sort of very brave to group together. And if the Catholic Church had not had—if Monseñor Silva Henríquez had not been willing to open the Church's doors to us, we would have been able to do very little. And the arpillera really was a denunciation in its day. Yes, it was a, it really was a, a matter of existence, yes, it was a matter of subsistence. And it was also something very, very much about denunciation, and that was something the Vicaría enabled us to do. We would not have been able to denounce our problems if we had not had the protection, the protection of the Vicaría. After that we organized ourselves really well, we created, well, workshops, I mean we created the selling team, we created a strong coordinating committee for the whole association.

Cristina's words express that the Church's protection, and specifically that of the Cardinal who created the Vicaría, gave shantytown women the courage to meet and enabled them to subsist and denounce the regime in their arpilleras. Her last words about the women organizing themselves allude to the fact they joined forces with other local groups to create a coordinating committee, within which a team made efforts to sell more arpilleras.

Being associated with the Catholic Church also conferred upon the Comité and Vicaría moral authority,[203] making it easier for them to gain shantytown women's trust, and support groups. The shantytown women trusted that priests and Comité and Vicaría staff would not betray them or let them down when they sought help. This trust derived not only from the Church's traditional moral authority, but also from its supportiveness towards those suffering under the regime. Unlike in Argentina, much of the hierarchy of

Website Link 4.3:
Non-profit organizations work to empower women around the world. One such organization in Thailand describes its work with Thai Hill tribes in nine short videos: "Thai Hill Tribes. The Work of IMPECT in Northern Thailand," on the website of the Asia Foundation.
www.asiafoundation.org/media/collection/113/1/thai-hill-tribes-the-work-of-impect-in-northern

the Chilean Catholic Church came fairly quickly to see that human rights were being violated, and made efforts to protect the victims of the regime's policies.[204] The trust the Comité and Vicaría inspired was important in a context in which many shantytown women were afraid of unknown outsiders and believed that many organizations were "infiltrados" ["infiltrated" with individuals reporting to the government]. It arguably resulted in the women's being more likely to join the groups that these institutions supported than if such groups had functioned independently, been sponsored by organizations not connected with the Church, or been run from people's homes rather than from local churches.

In addition, the Comité and Vicaría were able to attract funding, and this too contributed to their being able to support the shantytown women's groups. This funding was important because it allowed them to hire lawyers, social workers, art teachers, and other professionals who helped constitute or train many of the women's groups in subjects including leadership and organizational development. It also enabled them to open offices in the poorer areas of Santiago, and to afford premises large enough to have a room in which some groups could meet occasionally. The ability to attract funding came in part from the excellent reputation for protecting human rights that the Comité and Vicaría rapidly gained, and also from the Church connection. The Comité's initial funding came from the World Council of Churches, an ecumenical international organization based in Geneva, Switzerland, which continued to be a major funder in later years.

The Comité and Vicaría staff possessed social capital, and this too facilitated the emergence and continued existence of shantytown women's groups. They had contacts abroad, which they drew on to help sell what many of the women's income-earning groups produced. In addition, they were at ease talking with travelers and diplomats who approached them wanting to buy such products, especially the arpilleras. The relative immunity, moral authority, financial means, and social capital of the Comité and Vicaría enabled them to play an important role in the emergence and continued functioning of shantytown groups.

Also important in enabling the women's groups to exist was the support of Chilean NGOs, feminist organizations, professionals, and other humanitarian organizations. Some of these institutions provided training in how to run a group and in "personal development," and offered funding for various purposes. The feminist organization MUDECHI, for example, gave arpillera groups in eastern Santiago training in "personal development" and women's rights. The Fundación Missio, a Catholic organization, supported shantytown women's arpillera groups in northern Santiago. The ecumenical and humanitarian organization FASIC [Foundation of Christian Churches for Social Assistance] supported alcoholic women in a shantytown in south-eastern Santiago. The work of these and other institutions helped women's groups continue to function.[205]

So, too, did the international community. As mentioned above, in Europe, Canada, and other Latin American countries, priests, church groups, women's groups, human rights groups, aid agencies, and international NGOs sent donations of money and clothing, which the Vicaría and shantytown priests channeled to the women. Money from France enabled shantytown inhabitants in La Victoria to build a small building in which local groups met, for example, while money from Canada enabled arpillera groups of southern Santiago to rent a house in which to meet. Human rights activists abroad, Chilean exiles, and others in sympathy with the plight of Chile's victims helped sell the items that some of the women's groups produced. Thousands outside Chile helped by buying these products.

The exile of so many Chileans contributed to the existence of shantytown women's groups. These exiles set up organizations, some of which sent the groups donations of money and clothes. Some of this money came from their efforts to sell arpilleras, but exiles also sold Chilean pottery and made and sold meat pies ["empanadas"]. They thought of such selling as "solidarity work" whose goal was to send money to Chile to support the regime's victims and the resistance effort. Shantytown women's gender and motherhood fostered this assistance in that the exiles saw the shantytown women as indigent mothers with children, an image that fitted the trope of women and children in need of protection. In addition, Chilean exiles took it upon themselves to inform people abroad about the coup and poverty and repression in Chile, keeping the public aware and making many individuals with whom they spoke interested and motivated to help.

The regime's national security policy and use of sensational acts of violence inspired much of this international support. The blowing up of Orlando Letelier, who had been a minister under Allende and was building an exile organization in the United States, and the bombing of the La Moneda Palace (Chile's symbolic equivalent of the White House), for example, made the headlines in foreign newspapers and television news, drawing the attention of the international community to Chile. The violent nature of the overthrow of the Allende government made leftists and human rights activists abroad predisposed to help the women because they were upset by his death and the coup, having heard about his winning the presidency in 1970 as the first socialist president to come to power through democratic elections, and having become interested in how the new socialist "experiment" would turn out. Meanwhile, the national security doctrine produced a stream of exiles, many of whom supported the women in the ways described above. Support from the international community, exiles, the Comité and Vicaría, Catholic Church, and shantytown priests and nuns, then, helped the groups emerge and continue to exist.

Food-procuring Groups

Community Kitchens: "Comedores infantiles" and "Ollas comunes"

Shantytown women created and joined groups in which they procured or made food. The most common of these were community kitchens, of which there were two kinds, one preceding the other. The first, "comedores infantiles" or simply "comedores," were run by or with help from middle-class church women, and relied on donations. They aimed to feed local children.[206]

By the mid-Eighties most of these had been shut down because priests, the Vicaría, and shantytown women organizers came to believe that they were "paternalistic," fostering dependence and passivity. They were replaced by "ollas comunes," run by shantytown women alone, who acquired most of the necessary food through their own efforts, volunteering their labor.[207] The ollas served both adults and children, although sometimes the word was used when only children were served.

In the comedores, women prepared and served lunch every day in a room in the local church, and this became the main way in which many local children were fed. As well as serving food, comedor leaders sometimes taught about hygiene. Bernardita, a comedor organizer, taught that children should wash their hands before eating, comb their hair, and wash, and that children's clothes should be washed even if there was no detergent. The comedores were typically created by local nuns or priests, lay women attached to the church, or women who had been mothers' center leaders before the coup. The priest supported them by lending a room adjacent to the chapel, channeling donations to them, and deciding whether children were deserving. If shantytown parents wanted their children to eat at the comedor, they would approach the organizer, who would take note of how many children there were in the family, and inform the priest. According to Nelly, families in which the husband was unemployed were able to receive food.

The ollas built on a tradition of ollas comunes organized by striking workers, of which there were also cases during the dictatorship, with shantytown women helping these workers as a way of expressing solidarity with their cause.[208] With the shantytown ollas, anyone in the community who signed up could receive food.[209] These ollas mushroomed in Santiago in the 1980s; according to Sur Profesionales (1985), they numbered 34 in 1982 and 41 in 1984. People would come with a saucepan and empty bottle at lunchtime and line up for their helping, which usually consisted of vegetables with pasta, and sometimes milk and bread.

Local women or priests tended to be the creators of the ollas comunes, and priests helped by telling people about them and recruiting organizers. In the shantytown of San Bruno, for example, two local women created a health team with the support of their local church's council, and then started giving milk to children who did not have enough to eat. They later started making lunch, calling their efforts an "olla común," and later offered a late afternoon meal and baked bread. They made it a condition for the women running the olla that they participate in informal training in "personal development," hygiene related to preparing food, health problems, and first aid, and this training included discussion about why they needed to resort to an olla for food. The church gave food and donations from abroad, and lent them a room. Their original idea, the leaders told me, had been to organize the women. Later on, they thought that rather than give the women this food as one might gives alms, it would be better if the women did something active and participated in the effort to acquire the food they needed. Finally, still thinking that the women should be active, and wanting to continue to train the women more effectively, they created a sewing workshop, and then an arpillera workshop.[210]

There was much work involved in the daily running of an olla. First, the women had to acquire the food, and would beg for vegetables and meat at the nearest large market [the "vega"], and ask for donations from street market vendors, shops, and schools. Mónica, who lived in a shantytown in southern Santiago, succeeded in attracting donations of food by showing members of the Catholic charity Caritas the various children's community kitchen venues in her neighborhood. The priest or Vicaría usually provided pasta, oil, and other non-perishables, sometimes received from donors. The women also needed to find wood for the fire, some of which neighbors would give them.

Once the women had the food and wood, they had to transport it to the olla, do the cooking, serve, wash up, tidy up, and clean the room. Karina was part of an olla that served children in San Bruno. She had to cook twice a week and beg for vegetables and other fresh food in the market ["vega"] at six in the morning. She also had to bake bread, which she did using flour donated by the Vicaría. Her description gives a sense not only of the work involved, but also of her motivation for participating, and the prominent role of the local priest:

And as my children didn't want to go there [to the olla] (they were ashamed to be sitting at the big tables eating), the priest gave me a little piece of paper that allowed us to go and fetch the food. I had been going there all my life, but at that point I started going twice a week to cook, and out to the market to beg with a food bag, for vegetables or whatever we could get. And we'd go at six in the morning, a group of us. And afterwards, with the vegetables, we'd make the food. With what the Vicaría sent [flour] we made bread. And one day the priest said, "You know what," he said, "I'm going to close down the olla, it's better. Because the mothers are not cooperating." Because the mothers never went to do their turn. They would send the children to eat there, and it was always the same mothers who went. He closed it down and created a workshop. And he bought us knitting needles first, he bought wool.

4.2

There are so many children at this comedor infantil that several tables are necessary. The woman standing on the right looks tired; she has probably been helping with the cooking.

4.3

In this large room, several tables accommodate a great many children who are having soup. A woman in the background ladles out food.

4.4

A little girl concentrates on her lentils. She wears a cap, and the woman behind her a coat, suggesting that it is cold in the room.

4.5

Women cook food over an open fire outside, perhaps because of the smoke. Directly behind them is a shantytown chapel, a sign under its roof saying "Catholic Chapel. Christian Community of Saint Joseph the Worker."

4.6

A woman and teenage girl bring a wheelbarrow of green beans to the place where they will begin cooking. Acquiring and transporting fresh food were the first daily tasks involved in the running of an olla común (community kitchen for both adults and children).

4.7

Three women examine the beans.

4.8

The work of cutting the beans begins.

4.9

Much of the food has been chopped, but a woman in the background is still peeling.

4.10

A woman pours cut food into a saucepan. Another pan is already full, and once heated will become soup.

4.11

Standing over a large pot outdoors, each woman adds pieces of what appears to be fresh pasta.

4.12

In what is probably the area around a shantytown chapel, men and women come with their pots and pans to collect the food that the olla organizers ladle out. The pot simmers on an outdoor fire and grate.

4.13

Locals wait for their ladle of food, holding different kinds of receptacle.

4.14

As well as food, ollas comunes gave milk to children, who would come with empty bottles.

Karina's words point to the hard work involved, going to the market very early, begging, carrying the food home, and cooking. Although she does not mention it, the work of running an olla also included procuring the fuel, cleaning, peeling, and cutting the food, serving, washing up, cleaning up, and putting pans and raw materials away. Occasionally a husband helped, carrying the heavy food, fuel, or pans, for example. Karina's words also underscore the supportiveness of the Vicaría, which donated flour, and of the priest, who took measures to enable Karina's children to eat at home. His dominant role is clear in his ability to shut down the olla and initiate the activities of knitting, and later sewing and arpillera-making, to enable the women to earn an income. Karina's words also suggest that there was some stigma involved in eating at an olla. In a later interview, she mentioned that her children had been embarrassed to go because there were "street children" and "all sorts of children" there, so she would go alone, fetch their rations with a milk can, and take them home.

In a later interview Karina described the olla itself:

JA: Where was it?

Karina: Right there in the church, inside. They had a kitchen, large tins, and all the children who went to eat there— because they would give them the food right there— and the children had to bring their plates. They would line up, you would give them a large ladleful, because the spoons were big. With meat.

Karina's words evoke the work of ladling out the food to each child, and her adding that there was meat suggests that meat was something not to be had every day, and points to the lack of money for adequate nutrition in shantytown families.

Olla organizers worked in small groups, often rotating the venue from one group member's home to another, although in some cases the venue was the local church. As well as begging for vegetables and meat at the large local market ["la vega"], going there on tricycles at four or five in the morning, the women begged of local vendors, tried to earn money with which to buy food by selling items at the local street market, and baked bread.[211] The priest gave the olla organizers non-perishable food like spaghetti and beans, and the Vicaría donated some as well. Teresa described the rotating venue and her work:

Teresa: I came [to the church] asking for help for my son, and the priest spoke to me, and said "Talk to Catarina," I remember. And so I spoke to Señora Catarina. "Would you like to do the olla común?" she asked me, and it was a pot this size [gestures], a big pot.

JA: A lot of work?

Teresa: But it was four of us that did it. Let's see, María, Señora—, yes, four with Angélica. So every week one of us had to do it, all week.

JA: Every day?

Teresa: Yes, every day. And the next week it was someone else's turn. You had to wash the pot, on all sides. You'd rest for a week, then it was someone else's turn, and then it would be me again. But I had to go and fetch things from there with carts, when it was my turn to make charquicán,[212] peeling the potatoes. Señora Catarina would say: "you have to go and help Señora Teresa, to carry wood," but they were lazy, they wouldn't bring anything, or come and help either. They'd just come with the little saucepan and the jar for the milk—I had to prepare milk for them. And my husband would go and fetch the bread over in La Estrella [a nearby neighborhood], sacks of potatoes, and one roll of bread per child.

JA: Where would he fetch the bread?

Teresa: Over in La Estrella, a bakery would donate it.

JA: Donate!

Teresa: They would donate it, for all those children. Señora Catarina had it all written down, for how many. But I'd always give them more. It was one big spoon per person but I'd put more in, "Just bring a bigger saucepan, I'll give you more." So I made beans, charquicán, and spaghetti. I worked a lot, I really worked. You had to work really hard to get by.

Teresa worked hard, every day of the week, one week off, one week on, with her husband helping her. Her words hint at the solidarity orientation that some people shared during the regime, and point to how this solidarity helped make it possible for impoverished shantytown families to survive; even though her olla workmates were not helpful, a local baker donated bread, the priest opened up the possibility of her joining the olla, and she herself gave people more food than they were officially allowed.

Every day in the shantytown of San Isidrio in northern Santiago, the organizers of an olla created one committee to fetch wood, another to go to the market, and a third to cook. The Vicaría had told them that they had to fetch fresh food in the market, in shops, and elsewhere, asking people "for solidarity," and this had shocked them, because they realized that they were essentially begging. A hundred to a hundred and fifty people from the community ate at their olla.

Shantytown women participated in the running of community kitchens because they were unable to feed their children at home because their husbands were unemployed, and the children went hungry. Karina told me:

At that time all my children were small, the three of them, and my husband lost his job, and I was desperate because they were in school. The eldest would say, "I'm hungry," he would say, and a friend I had here, just behind, said, "Karina, why don't you go to the church, because there is an olla común for everyone who, for everyone whose husband doesn't have work." I went there because of her.

In Karina's words the link between men's unemployment, exacerbated poverty and hunger, and women's joining groups, is clear. In a later interview Karina said, "And so that's why I joined, there— because he lost his job and we had nothing." Shantytown gender expectations were part of the equation in that Karina's husband's unemployment led to their "having nothing" because she herself had not been working for an income, but rather had been taking care of the children at home, as these expectations dictated. The breakdown in the gender system whereby her husband was not doing what he was supposed to do (providing), enabled her to go against these expectations and join a group, becoming the family breadwinner.

The women who created the community kitchens saw them as a means by which they could help women feed themselves and their families, raise women's spirits, and enable them to gain in self-esteem, learn about rights, and come to understand the reasons for their problems. Catarina, the creator of an olla in southern Santiago, for example, viewed this initiative as a means by which she and her co-workers could improve women's situation, including the situation of women who begged for food in the street. She encouraged women in the ollas to join income-earning workshops and to feel confident about their ability to support the family, and some such women, she said, found paid work with longer-term prospects, such as cleaning homes and selling in the market. Babette, who worked with Catarina, saw the ollas as an opportunity to train women, since they brought them out of their homes and into a group. She gave the women informal training in "personal development," having them reflect on questions such as "Why am I in the olla?", "How do I feel?", and why they had such grave financial difficulties, and taught them that they had rights and obligations. From her perspective, this personal development training was an "escape hatch" for the women, who all felt oppressed and used by the system and their family members. She also talked to the women about hygiene in relation to food preparation, how to cook food with minimal fuel, and aspects of child health and nutrition. Training focused on self-esteem, financial problems, and rights, then, was part of Catarina and Babette's vision in setting up an olla.

The ollas were spaces in which organizers reflected on and discussed their poverty, and other politicized groups sometimes joined in. The organizers of a new olla in San Isidrio, for example, discussed their situation on a daily basis, and on some days male trade union organizers from a nearby olla came to talk with them about how they felt about needing to rely on an olla, and not being able to support their wives. The conversation around the table was denunciatory, Bettina said, and focused on their being tired of being trampled on, and on the unemployment, hunger, PEM and POJH schemes with their sometimes pointless work, low wages, and alcoholism that sometimes resulted from participation. In addition, the Vicaría encouraged this group to think about why they had an olla.

Shantytown women's running of community kitchens was important work because it enabled many families to survive where otherwise they would have been severely weakened by poor nutrition and lack of food. That this work was crucial was evidenced by the fact that people were generally ashamed to be seen fetching food at the olla as it showed how poor and desperate they were, yet they came in large numbers. Having food from the olla enabled people to go to school or work the next day, and to participate in acts of resistance against the regime if they were so inclined. Also importantly, the ollas calmed women's tremendous anxiety about their children's not having enough food to eat.

Despite their importance for many, not all impoverished women wanted to be involved. Many women continued to use and help run their local olla even after starting to earn money,[213] but others preferred to stop. Some felt that the other women were not doing their share of the work, and became tired of shouldering most of the burden of having to carry heavy bags of food by themselves and prepare the food at their home for many days at a time, since there were not enough women organizers among whom to rotate.[214] Others left the olla because their husband found work, or their children grew up and found jobs. Some ollas closed down when the women in them began to participate in an income-earning workshop.[215] Some women did not participate in an olla at all, despite their financial difficulties, because the nearest one was not close by, or because the people in their neighborhood did not try to solve their problems collectively. Some neighborhoods, such as Magallanes, did not have ollas because, the women explained, locals did not want to admit that they were having difficulty putting food on the table, and would shut themselves up in their homes.

The repression affected the community kitchens in a number of small ways. Natalia in southern Santiago related, for example, how, when she went to the market with her tricycle very early in the morning to beg for the necessary food, the curfew was still on, and so she had to wave a white handkerchief so that soldiers would not shoot her. The repression made many women feel that participating in the running of a community kitchen was dangerous; Catarina told me that for months after the coup it was dangerous to organize a comedor. Olla organizers saw participation in community kitchens as dangerous in part because they were a denunciation of the failures of the regime and the need for self-help. Trying to sell things at the local street market in order to earn a few pesos for their olla was a denunciation, Babette told me, because it was a way of informing market stall owners about popular groups, while hopefully gaining their support. It also showed stall owners that olla organizers were struggling to manage to produce plates of food, and not merely receiving donations, she believed. Some women carried out explicitly denunciatory activities within the ollas, and formed committees to denounce their problems.[216] The members of ollas participated in protests, for example, including hunger marches, often together with different kinds of groups,[217] and these protests were met with repression. Despite the risky denunciatory aspect and repression, the community kitchens continued, shantytown women's work in them enabling people to eat, and the women themselves to gain a sharper awareness of poverty, repression, and rights, while learning to run a group.

Other Food-Related Groups

There were many other ways in addition to the community kitchens, in which women produced or procured food cheaply on a collective basis. They created joint purchasing groups ["comprando juntos"], for example, in which each member contributed a small amount of money to a fund, with which they bought different kinds of food in bulk, cheaply. They avoided local stores and supermarkets, which tended to be relatively expensive, and shopped instead at markets. They would then distribute this food among group members, and sell some of it locally so as to build up their fund. If they had a celebration, they might use some of it to cook something special.

The women devised numerous other systems for acquiring food. In Fraternidad, in southern Santiago, there was a group whose members met once a week, each bringing what food they could from home, putting their various contributions together in a little package, and giving it to one or two group members on a rotating basis. The shantytown of La Victoria had a "leche por cuadras" [milk by the block] scheme, thanks to a donation from France. Local women organized themselves by the block, buying milk and distributing it to all the children who lived within their purview. There were community vegetable patches ["huertos familiares"] in which women and men grew vegetables collectively and therefore cheaply.[218] Some of these banded together into informal associations, one of which, based in southern Santiago, put out a bulletin called "The Seed. Vegetable Patch Group" ["La Semilla. Boletín Grupo Huertos"]. Shantytown women also raised animals they could eat; in San Isidrio in northern Santiago, there was a group that raised rabbits.

In trying to solve their food problem, shantytown women did not limit themselves to acquiring and producing food. They also analyzed the food situation and made demands of the government. One group of women, for example, organized a campaign against price increases, since they had difficulty putting a meal together because of increases in the price of bread, potatoes, onions, vegetables, and fruit, and because they could not afford meat, chicken, and fish. They produced leaflets that defined the problem, stated how it affected their children, outlined the cost of a basket of food and other essentials, and described the inadequate response of the authorities. They also suggested four measures to be taken, including forming a committee against price increases in each shantytown, conducting a study of the cost of a family basket of essentials and sending the results to the Ministry of Economics, demanding that the authorities freeze the prices of these essentials, and

4.15

A member of a comprando juntas [joint purchasing group] sells food from the window of the room where the food is stored. A local woman receives her change, her concentration suggesting that every penny matters.

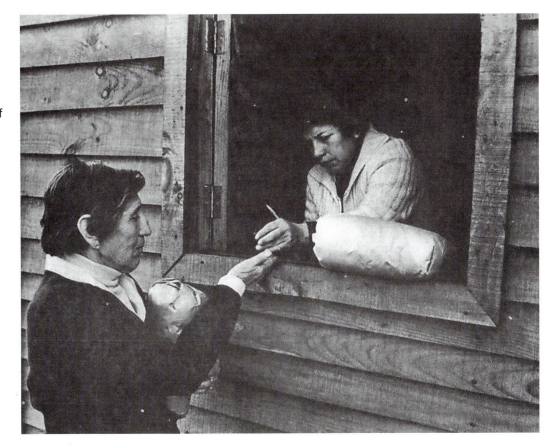

4.16

A member of the joint purchasing group kneads dough.

4.17

A member of the joint purchasing group puts freshly baked bread rolls into another member's basket.

4.18

The members of the joint purchasing group celebrating with food they have baked.

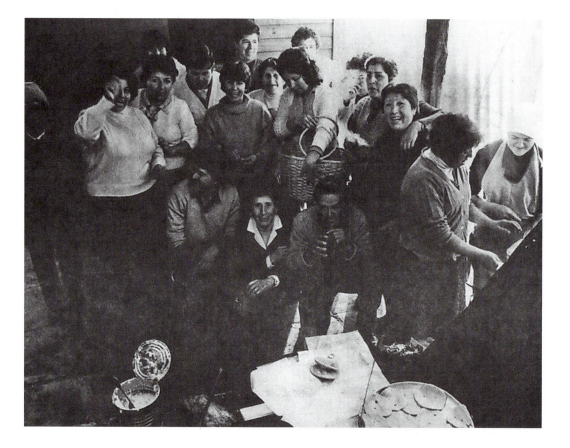

4.19

A flyer entitled "Campaign against price increases," bearing the subtitle, "Let's defend the food and health of our children." The word "Let's" and reference to "our children" suggest that the authors are appealing to their readers as parents, with the aim of getting them involved. The flyer offers examples of how gender shaped the ways in which women experienced poverty: the authors of the flyer saw the price increases as problematic for their children, their understanding that women were responsible for feeding children influenced how they appealed to their readers, and the activities that they proposed were inspired by their responsibility as mothers. The handwriting on the flyer suggests that it was made at the lowest possible cost and not by professionals but by the organizers of the campaign, probably just with paper, pen, and a photocopy machine.

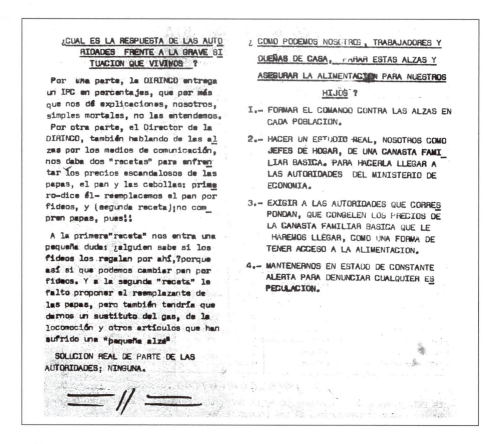

4.20

This side of the flyer depicted in Figure 4.19 analyzes the government's reactions to the price increases and proposes four measures that shantytown inhabitants could take to deal with the problem.

finally, staying alert and denouncing speculation. Other groups participated in marches about hunger.[219]

Income-Generating Groups

The difficulty that the women were having feeding, clothing, and educating their children led many of them to take the step of looking for a way to earn money.[220] There were women, of course, who had been working all along, particularly widowed, single, or separated women, and even some women with partners. But for those married women who had not been working, it was their husband's unemployment and the fact that this unemployment made it difficult to feed their children that pushed them to take the step of seeking paid work. Their search led them to local income-earning groups that operated like cooperatives, as well as to emergency employment schemes, non-government employers, and entrepreneurship, discussed later.

Arpillera Groups and other Manufacturing Workshops ["Talleres"]

Local workshops in which members manufactured something were an important source of income for many women.[221] In these "talleres," as they were called, they worked sewing, knitting, crocheting, embroidering, baking bread, making cold-worked ceramics, creating cotton sponges ["huaipe"], and producing arpilleras. They normally sold these products locally or to the Vicaría de la Solidaridad. The talleres were usually single-sex; men also had talleres, typically engaging in shoe repair and leather work. The women tended to have come to their taller "straight from the home," according to a member in southern Santiago, although this was truer for the rank-and-file members than for the leaders, and some talleres had evolved out of community kitchens.

The arpillera groups were arguably the most common kind of workshop in Santiago, with a total of one to two thousand shantytown woman members. They first appeared in 1975, and the Comité Pro-Paz helped set them up. They met two or three afternoons a week in a room in their local church, but the women did most of the arpillera work at home. In joining, the women's predominant motivation was to earn money, since their husbands were unemployed and they were having difficulty feeding their families adequately, and paying school expenses and utilities bills. There were women who joined, however, to find emotional support, become less dependent on their husband, feel less alone, learn, and contribute to local organizations. Two women from an arpillera group in Magallanes, in southern Santiago, expressed very different reasons for joining the group:

> *Sylvia*:   A friend invited me because my husband was without work. She told me that there was a workshop where I could work, earn a bit of, of—so as to be able to make ends meet. And that's how I came! Looking for, for a way to survive. That's how I came.
>
> *JA*:   And you, Señora?
>
> *Clara*:   No, not me. I came—a friend brought me along as well, because she was in the workshop. But it was more so as to get out of the house. Because all the children were in school and I was left sort of very, very alone in the house. And a little, more to be independent, because sometimes you are very, very dependent on your husband, on what he says. My husband was very like this [gestures], very *machista*. He still is, but less so. So it was like, when he came home, the table had to be laid, the food and everything had to be ready. So I joined the workshop and he gradually became less that way, and now, well, if I am there when he gets home, it's OK, if I'm not, it's OK too.

Sylvia's reason for joining the workshop was economic, whereas Clara's reasons were loneliness and wanting to become somewhat independent of her oppressive husband, who held her to task if she did not comply closely with shantytown gender expectations. Similarly, Barbara from a shantytown of Colón in southern Santiago joined an arpillera group because her sister-in-law suggested it, seeing that she was unhappy in her marriage. As these and many other women's words suggest, the initial motivation for joining arpillera groups was not political. However, many women came over time to value the chance that the arpilleras afforded to tell the outside world about the poverty and repression they were experiencing, in the hope that this would help raise awareness and support for the struggle against Pinochet.

The arpilleras typically depicted unemployment, poverty, women's popular organizations, repression, protests, and the struggles of the relatives of the disappeared. Most arpillera-makers were not relatives of the disappeared, although there were at least two arpillera groups of relatives, and several mixed groups containing relatives and non-relatives. The Vicaría and Comité Pro-Paz bought most of the arpilleras and sent them to

4.21

Women in an arpillera group in northern Santiago work with concentration. The photograph was taken in the 1980s.

4.22

Arpillera-makers brought babies and small children to the workshop meetings. The young woman in this photograph has finished basting the pieces of cloth into place, and her baby looks at her work. Next to her, an older woman, perhaps her grandmother, sews a smaller arpillera.

4.23

The outside of the same room shown in Figures 4.21 and 4.22.

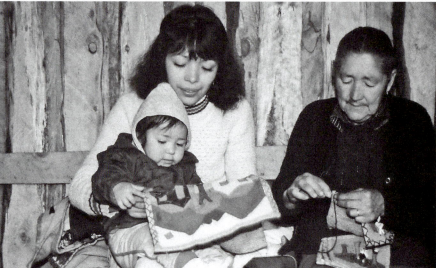

exiles, priests, and other contacts in Europe, Canada, and many other countries, who, in turn, sold them to the public.[222]

It was common for arpillera groups to have started off as a different kind of group.[223] The San Bruno workshop, for example, began as an olla, and then the women sewed, knitted, and crocheted, finally switching to arpillera-making. During our group interview, members described these changes:

JA: You had comedores as well.

Mónica: Yes.

Bernardita: They had an olla, comedores, and later they had a workshop. That's right. That was the, the way it was. [*Barbara*:   Yes]. Yes. And, as I say, in Lo Valledor Sur there was also an olla común, comedor. And that's what it all started from, that, that team which formed, and at that's when we started with the workshops.

Mónica: Right.

Bernardita: Right?

JA: Of arpilleras?

Bernardita: No, not of arpilleras right away. The arpilleras started out in about 1978. Here, in these workshops. But before that they made little squares for making blankets.

Mónica: Yes.

Bernardita: Isn't that right? They made bags for bread. Kitchen cloths.

Karina: Kitchen cloths.

Bernardita: They knitted. Waistcoats. They made long socks.

Karina: Shawls, also.

Barbara: And "Negritos José" [woolen dolls].

Bernardita: And when they got better at it [*Barbara* (sentimentally):   The Negritos José], they got better at it, they started to make little dresses for baby girls, shawls, the Negros José, the, the snowmen, the dolls [*Karina*:   Yes, the dolls] the dolls from Chiloe [*Karina*:   They were nice], the cardigans in the style of, of, what's it called? "Jacquard," "jacquard."

Mónica: We would send those cardigans abroad.

Bernardita: Yes, and that's how it was, that's how it was. And with all this, in 1978, the arpillera thing. I, I, what I remember is that they brought us an arpillera from the Vicaría.

The women in the workshop were versatile; the main goal was to earn money and they were flexible about how they did it. In performing this varied work, they used "feminine" skills, mainly sewing and knitting, that they had been taught as girls and young women. Their work was also gendered in that what they made was connected with home and children. In Puente Alto, in eastern Santiago, for example, women formed groups in which they made sheets and baked bread, before switching to arpillera-making.[224]

Often it was when a local priest approached the Vicaría, knowing that it offered more possibilities for selling the work the groups produced, that a workshop switched to arpillera-making. Alternatively, the Vicaría approached a priest, asking him to recruit women or lend a room, or to help them meet an already-existing group. The Vicaría and local priests shared a wish to help the women in their poverty. In La Victoria there was a workshop that had started out as a comedor created by a nun who worked in the church. The comedor had ended because the women who sent their children to it did not all pull their weight, and the group switched to knitting. The knitting workshop evolved into an arpillera workshop when the Vicaría de la Solidaridad sent someone to teach the women how to make arpilleras. I discussed the evolution with Gloria:

> *JA*:   And, you joined, then, for financial reasons.
>
> *Gloria*:   Yes, when I joined that group from here in the shantytown [. . .] They were doing knitting, knitting with natural wool, sheep's wool. And it was sent abroad, as well. We did designs; they were artisanal, artisanal waistcoats, jackets, eh. I joined to do that. Then came the arpilleras. They [the Vicaría staff] came, one day, to teach us and quickly, in just one day, with some explanations that they gave us, we started to make arpilleras.

Gloria's words point to the importance for the women's livelihood of an international distribution system, and to the Vicaría's pivotal role in their switch to arpillera-making. This chance to make arpilleras had opened up in the mid-1980s and was attractive to Gloria's group because it came with a new market for their work, with the Vicaría sending the arpilleras abroad. Gloria's group had switched activity, but some workshops continued with their main activity and diversified, making other items for sale at the same time, such as bread, fritters, and meat pies.

Workshops had numerous activities other than their primary work activity, on which the women placed great importance. Preparing and eating food were among them. Most arpillera groups had a break in the middle of their meetings and made tea, sometimes with bread or fritters, if they had received donations or pooled money. They sometimes served their children this food first, and then enjoyed the meal themselves, while talking animatedly. In an arpillera group in Fraternidad, for example, the women made dough and fritters when a supportive nun acquired donations of food, and in this way were able to make "delicious afternoon meals" for their children, according to Natasha, a member. The same group sometimes received donations of milk from the priest, of yoghurt from the dairy company Soprole,[225] and of milk and cheese from the Vicaría. It also saved up money during the year, and at Christmas time used it to make a large tea for the children, asking department stores and companies to donate cookies.

Another subsidiary group activity was attending very short "courses," or training sessions, which might last a whole day, or just a few hours, and took place where the group usually met, or in a room lent by the Vicaría or acquired by the organization sponsoring the training. This training was typically organized by the Vicaría, a feminist organization, or an NGO, which would send staff members or other professionals as trainers. Group leaders also provided training, as when the organizers of the San Bruno health team taught women arpillera-making so as to be able to form new arpillera groups. One of the most common courses was "desarrollo personal" [personal development], a combination of self-esteem-building mixed with awareness-raising about women's rights, repression, poverty, and human rights.[226] Other courses included "organización" ["organization," or group management], health and hygiene, nutrition, literacy, and training in the skills needed for the work the group did. Much of this training was given only to the members of coordinating committees ["coordinadoras"], which consisted of the leaders of 5 to 12 groups in the same line of work or same neighborhood. These coordinating committee members were then expected to teach what they had learned to the members of their own groups. Many women saw the training in a positive light and were proud of all the training sessions they had attended, but some had to be motivated by group leaders to participate.

Recreational activities were also an important part of group life. An arpillera group in La Victoria, for example, went to a nearby stretch of river for the day in summertime, and the San Bruno group once went to the seaside, and very occasionally went to see a play. Together, the arpillera groups of southern Santiago organized a day of plays, poetry readings, and dances, in which they all participated. Catarina, a group leader, explained these varied activities in terms of needing to disconnect from the pain and uncertainty about whether they would "disappear," while other women stressed the need for relief from tensions. A final subsidiary activity that workshops engaged in was carrying out acts of solidarity (see Chapter 5). Workshops, then, provided income, training, recreation, and conviviality.

Bolsas de cesantes

"Unemployed people's groups" ["bolsas de cesantes"][227] were another form of income-earning group, springing up just months after the coup. They were like the talleres in that they consisted of unemployed men and women tried to find a way to subsist by generating an income through manufacturing a product or offering a service. Their members mostly repaired shoes, collected recyclable materials, made sewn or knitted items, and baked bread or Chilean meat pies. Shantytown women distinguished them from the talleres, however, saying that they were "more political," and contained ex-trade union members, although in fact many bolsa members were women and not involved in leftist groups.[228] Natalia, for example, told me that they had political goals and were usually organized by the communist party. Another difference, identified in the literature, was that members helped each other find jobs, sometimes buying a newspaper together and sharing information about potential work.[229] According to Sur Profesionales (1985), there were 21 bolsas in 1982 and 33 in 1984. The Vicaría de la Solidaridad supported them by helping sell some of their products, and support also came from foreign development agencies, churches, and local institutions.[230]

In the shantytown of Simón Bolívar, women worked alongside men in a bolsa, sewing, and collecting and selling bottles and newspapers for recycling. They also produced and distributed "panfletos" [flyers containing political messages] in an effort to raise consciousness, seeing themselves as conducting a "political struggle." Cristina told me:

> *Cristina*: So a bolsa de cesantes was beginning to meet, and I go there and everything, and they tell me that they are starting to sew a few things. [. . .] We, as [the workshop of] Simón Bolívar, made our appearance in the Vicaría at that time [April or May of 1976] [. . .] but, but we were already meeting here [in her neighborhood].
>
> *JA*: What were you doing here?
>
> *Cristina*: We would go out to ask for newspapers and bottles, with carts. We would gather up the bottles, the newspapers, and sell them for our bolsa de cesantes organization in the church. There were men and women members; there were very few women, contrary to what, to what you always saw, which was that it was mostly women. We started off as very few here, but afterward there were more of us and the men disappeared; they found work in construction and couldn't go any more. We would get together in the afternoon, before curfew; we would come back just

4.24

Women weaving together using a manual loom.

4.25

Women of varying ages knitting together in a room with large, simple tables and benches, that was perhaps part of their local church.

4.26

Women sewing in what is most likely a taller or bolsa de cesantes. One woman uses a sewing machine, while two others sew by hand.

as the curfew was beginning. And we would do everything, I mean, for example, from flyers to calling on, on people's conscience, all sorts of things. We would get together as a bolsa de cesantes usually conducting a political struggle, discussing our problem, because we were unemployed.

Cristina's words show how members combined economic and resistance work in their bolsa, both earning money and producing political pamphlets. They suggest that the bolsa members saw their main problem as unemployment, and were radicalized enough to want to undertake awareness-raising, even though it was dangerous work. The repression left its mark, making members plan their meetings around the curfew.

Husbands' unemployment and having hungry children to feed were women's main reasons for joining a bolsa, as with other groups. Ana told me about how women from the shantytown of La Gloria in eastern Santiago joined local bolsas in order to feed their children when their husbands were in jail or had lost their jobs:

JA: When did you start making arpilleras?

Ana: In 1975; 1975.

JA: Ah, from the beginning.

Ana: Yes, from the start.

JA: And when you joined the workshop, what was it like?

Ana: The workshop started off as a bolsa de cesantes. [*JA*: Yes] Yes, well, we did different things. A community kitchen in the chapel of San Carlos; that's where we started to group together because our husbands started to lose their jobs, some were arrested. And we started to think how, how to make something in order to subsist.

JA: And what, what did you make at the beginning?

Ana: At the beginning we sewed, for example aprons, we repaired clothing, and then we looked for something more, which, which would give us more money, so as to be able to earn more money, and the arpillera thing started. Yes.

JA: How did it start?

Ana: Er, we star—, we started to, together, to, to think of how, how to do, well, work, and in some way, well, how to be able to make- you know, but the work that we first started to do was done using, using sacking, using sacking. And, and then we looked for, let's say, afterward we put ourselves under the protection of the Vicaría de la Solidaridad. Using contacts that other people gave us as well, because they would give us the information and we would keep going with that.

Subsistence was the initial motive behind the bolsa, according to Ana, and the difficulty with subsistence had arisen, she suggests, because of husbands' unemployment and arrest; the national security doctrine and the economic "shock treatment" made breadwinners of the women. The need for money caused them to change the focus of their bolsa's activity as economic opportunities arose, showing initiative and an enterprising disposition. Ana's words also point to the importance of the Vicaría in providing protection and an outlet for their arpilleras, and of the local church in allowing them to meet within its walls. The mention of "contacts" hints at what was a large underground network of people willing to help other victims of the regime's policies. Bolsas, then, functioned much like talleres, even doing the same work, but tended to have a more political connotation and be considered more dangerous to join.

Other Groups

Multiple other economically-oriented groups dotted the shantytown landscape. Women from San Ignacio, a shantytown in eastern Santiago, created a laundry cooperative ["taller de lavandería"] in which they washed clothes for clients for a fee. They applied to the Comité Pro-Paz for a grant of US$100, won it, and bought two wooden wash basins. Their primary motive was to earn enough money to meet their families' subsistence needs, so when they found that they were not earning enough money for all of the women in the group, they tried making sewn items, and as this did not work well either, they switched to arpillera-making. Wendy, a Comité Pro-Paz volunteer who helped them with their laundry cooperative, told me:

> When I started in 1974, at the end of the year, when, when the Vicaría[231] started with a—, it [the Comité] was just beginning to function at the area level, to deal with the problem of unemployment which had become much more serious. So people were experiencing a crisis. At that time there was about 60 percent unemployment in the shantytowns. [. . .] The Vicaría was doing some projects of 100 dollars, er, it was very little money, you see, so the Vicaría asked people to present a proposal, a very simple proposal. They were shantytown projects. So I went to work with these people and the first group was a group that created a laundry workshop. They had to create workshops that did not require much capital, because we only had 100 dollars to work with. So, a laundry workshop was formed; you know, these were people who washed for families who had to work—both the husband and wife, so they didn't couldn't wash in their own homes. So they [the workshop members] would go and fetch the clothes, wash them, and then drop them off. So I started to work with this workshop, but we had to find clients and all that, and there was not enough work for many people. It started out with five people, but there were many more in the shantytown who were looking for work. We were thinking of sewing work. We went to many factories where they gave out sewing work but it didn't work out. And suddenly the Vicaría arrived with this proposal of ar—of a craft form that they were making in Colombia, apparently. So they suggested the idea of making, well, arpilleras.

Wendy's words suggest the importance of the Comité's funding for the creation of the laundry workshop, its concern for the many people who needed work, and its willingness to suggest activities for the groups. What made what she describes possible was international and local solidarity, of which the project funding and Wendy's volunteering were examples. While the washing cooperative that Wendy describes had funding, some were more rudimentary, with two or three women getting together and using a large metal container to wash in, and wood for fuel. Natalia said, "The women would wash using a large can, making fire with wood, and they would boil the clothes and things."

There were other groups to which shantytown women belonged that were not aimed at generating an income or procuring food cheaply but were still, in one way or another, related to their economic difficulties. Housing-centered groups, for example, were created to deal with pobladores' inability to afford decent housing or difficulty paying back the money owed on their homes. These groups were called "Housing Committees" ["comités de vivienda"], "Committees of people without a home" ["Comités sin casa"], and "Debtors' Committees" ["comités de deudores"], whose members were behind with the payments for their homes, or unable to pay their electricity and water bills. Some of these

4.27

A woman washes clothes in a wooden washbasin called an "artesa." Behind her is a pot of steamy water over a fire, in lieu of a faucet. In the background, a house's number has been painted on the door, suggesting a fairly recent shantytown.

4.28

In the top half of this arpillera, the members of a laundry cooperative wash and hang up clothes. They use wooden basins and a box of soap called "OMO." In the bottom half, a woman delivers the laundry to a home in a wealthier neighborhood, indicated by the fact that a car is parked outside (shantytown inhabitants did not normally own cars). It is likely that it is also she who does the ironing for the family. OMO boxes were often used by the Vicaría de la Solidaridad as the containers in which they smuggled arpilleras out of the country.

4.29

These people sit in a tent that marks the spot they marked as theirs during a very recent land seizure. Chilean flags are just visible in the background; normally each tent had one. Living in such difficult conditions led to bonds of friendship and mutual assistance among the residents of the Campamento Raúl Silva Henríquez. The women cook together using pieces of wood on the ground.

groups organized land seizures ["tomas"], typically with the help of a clandestine political party, but there were very few land seizures during the regime for fear of violent repression; they had been more common under previous governments. Participating in a land seizure meant living in tents often made of plastic sheets in the middle of fields for extended periods, and enduring rain, mud, cold, or heat, with the knowledge that the police would probably destroy all one had, yet families with babies and small children, and pregnant women took this step.

As well as direct actions like land seizures, housing group members engaged in more strategic political activities, such as organizing street protests centered on housing, and publishing bulletins. One such bulletin explains why a group of people seized the land, and states what they wanted from the state, namely that the land be sold to them and that the state provide some building materials. It describes the ways in which the state was exerting repression, and ends by asking for support, saying that the most urgent needs of those in the land seizure were food, first aid medicines, and empty barrels and drums, and suggesting that donations be sent to a shantytown church (this indicates that a priest was lending support for the land seizure). The bulletin's authors, then, were engaging in several political activities: demand-making of the state, denunciation of the repression, and calling for solidarity.

4.30–4.32

Many individuals and families lived in the rooms and patios of their relatives' homes. Called "allegados," they did not have a home of their own, and desperately wanted one. According to the pages of this bulletin, "The Land Seizure Bulletin" [El Folleto de la Toma], produced in October 1983 by the organizers of two land seizures, 150,000 to 200,000 families in Santiago were "allegados," and 850,000 homes were lacking in the country as a whole. The bulletin describes the allegados as low-income, mostly young families, nearly all unemployed and in the PEM and POJH emergency employment programs. It evokes the right to decent housing, gives a history of the land seizure, and describes what the people who have seized land want.

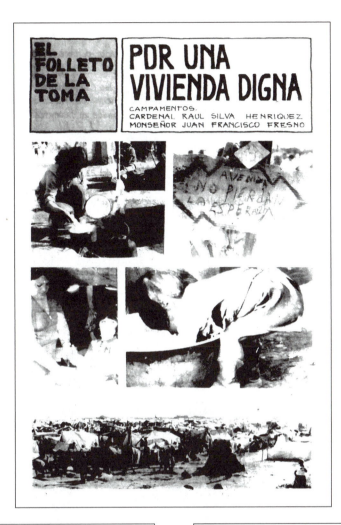

4.33

An artistic installation in the shantytown of La Victoria. A testimony to the creativity of housing groups, it spans the road, and says, "Housing is a right. Let us fight for that right." The creators are clearly radicalized, seeing their lack of housing as a right that has been violated, and wanting to motivate people to take part in the struggle.

4.34

This flyer advertises a summer camp in the shantytown of Lo Sierra. The local church helped organize it.

Women were aware that their children were suffering because of the poverty, and so organized events to make them happy, forming ad-hoc groups for this purpose. They organized annual "chocolatadas," that the giving of a bowl of chocolate to each child who came, often in the street. One that took place in 1986 in a shantytown in Concepción attracted 150 people of all ages; young people played ball in the street, two people played the guitar, and people joined in for the chorus. In some cases the shantytown women's organization CODEM organized the chocolatadas.[232] Shantytown women organized Christmas celebrations and urban summer camps in the shantytowns ["colonias urbanas"], a clever way of giving children a camp experience even though they could not afford to send them to the countryside. The camps provided the children with recreational activities and one or two meals a day, that the women made. Members of the San Bruno arpillera group helped with the camps by cooking, for example, while the members of the Magallanes arpillera group gave milk to the children in their local camp at lunchtime. In organizing such events, the women were trying to be good mothers, while ingeniously finding ways of getting around the poverty that stood in the way.

The Consequences of Group Participation

From the perspective of most women, the most important consequence of joining groups was being able to acquire food, or income with which to buy food, clothing, and schooling for their children.[233] Natalia of Fraternidad, for example, attributes being able to buy school materials for her children to her membership in an arpillera group:

4.35

Another event called "Popular Christmas" [Pascua Popular], saw women in the shantytown of Lo Valledor Sur organizing Christmas celebrations for local children, involving games, songs, dressing up, dances, chocolate, drinks, drawings, and more, as this flyer shows.

4.36

Shantytown women organize a "chocolatada," or chocolate milk treat for local children.

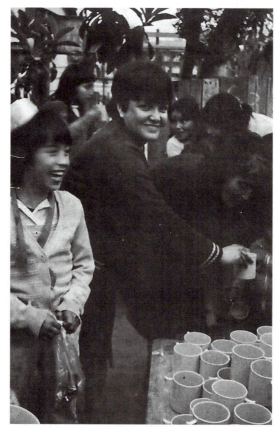

Natalia: But for me the arpillera was very important in my life, very, very important in my life.

JA: Why?

Natalia: Because as I say, I grew as a person. I gave my children an education thanks to the arpilleras, I would pay for their schooling, buy them the school materials they needed, any way I could, hunting around for where they were cheapest. So for me the arpillera was very important.

Natalia's spending the money on her children's education suggests the centrality of motherhood and children as motives for group membership. She valued highly the opportunity to develop as a person as well. The women also valued the donations of food, clothing, soap, and other essentials that group membership brought, not only for their material worth, but also for the solidarity that they embodied.

Many of the other consequences of group membership that women mentioned were not directly related to their group's overt goals. The groups enabled them to develop self-confidence; the women said that being in their group had taught them how "to have more personality," by which they meant to be less shy and have higher self-esteem. Several said they learned to "talk to others" and to stand up for themselves if others hurt them in some way. Being in groups also taught them, they thought, that they possessed worth,[234] and were able to support their family alone. Nelly commented on the improvement in her self-esteem:

> But it was very useful for me because there were teachers, as well, who would go and teach you how to be, how should I say, to be people, to have our way of, how shall I say, to show the world that we, as women, were people; we were not, well, how shall I say, it was not the case that men were worth more than women, but rather than women were worth as much as men. You understand? So that was very useful for me because the classes were sort of group classes, in groups. It made me feel better, and it made me tell myself, "I am a woman, I am a person, and I have to value myself as a person." Because as I say, men, as they are a bit "machista," they push you down. So there I started to open up, to open up, to open up a path in life.

Nelly, having not thought herself equal in worth previously, learned she was "worth as much" as a man and must value herself as a person. Her words show her understanding that women were oppressed by men, and hint at the radicalization regarding inequities of gender that went on in the groups, and the influence of feminism. What Nelly says also shows the value women gave to learning. Her mention of "teachers" is indicative of the fact that the Vicaría, NGOs, and feminist groups approached popular organizations and offered training in "self-development," which aimed to build up women's self-confidence and teach them about the notion of rights, including human rights and women's rights, while encouraging thinking about the poverty and repression.

Some women saw "getting out of the house" as an achievement that had resulted from joining groups. I asked Nicole from San Ramón in northern Santiago about this, and although she had joined an arpillera group just after Pinochet stepped down, her words evoke what many women who joined groups earlier expressed:

JA: What do you feel you have achieved with the group, or the fact of going there?

Nicole: Getting out of the house. That's a big deal. Being out of the house is good, when you go to the center [of town]. You rarely worry, thinking that the house is empty; now I don't feel so guilty leaving them [her children] alone for a while.

JA: Why is it so difficult to get out of the house; because the children are left alone?

Nicole: No, it's not so much because of leaving the children. For example, I'd leave them alone every afternoon, because I have my daughter who gets home at about three in the afternoon. The point is that you feel a heavy burden when you go out of the house and are not used to doing so, you feel like a bad mother, but after some time not so much; I just go ahead and go out.

Nicole felt that it became easier for her to be active outside the house without feeling guilty about leaving the children behind. Some women were more radical, not merely appreciating that they had come to feel able to leave the house, but also coming to think of their earlier, home-bound lives as a form of imprisonment. They talked of having escaped from "the four walls." Natalia, for example, said she "freed herself from all the four walls of the house" and discovered that she was not cut out for being at home all the time, but instead was meant to be in groups, learning and teaching others.

After having joined one group, many joined another, and sometimes yet another, or took new courses outside the group. This was partly because they had become more confident, and partly because they felt they had a right to do so.[235] Barbara, for example, had not been a member of any groups, but after joining an arpillera workshop, she became more "patuda" [literally "cheeky," but meaning daring] about joining other groups, and she joined a self-esteem workshop at her local church. Her choice of the word "cheeky" suggests slight guilt about doing something that gender expectations prohibited, but it was said with a chuckle. Natalia was even more active. She learned from her first group experience that she enjoyed group activities, being active in society, learning, and teaching others, and she wanted to do more of this. After joining a group of women in her church, she joined an arpillera group, and a little later a housing-focused group at her local church in which members tried to find solutions to the problems of not being able to make the payments on their homes or pay the utilities bills. She then became president of the parents' association in her children's school, and some time after that joined a senior citizens' club. She also began taking courses on new laws, and courses on different crafts:

JA: What was, from your perspective, the result of having participated in the arpillera workshop, in terms of your ideas, not just political ideas, but political or anything else?

Natalia: For me the result was that it really helped me grow more as a person. Because before that I was more passive, in every aspect. Yes I understood things but I didn't participate. I was in the house and everything. But once I joined the workshop it was as if I rid myself of all the four walls of the house, and I freed myself, as they say, and it was as if everything I had inside came out. So I discovered myself, and found that I was not cut out to be here in the house all the time, I was cut out to participate in groups, to learn, I was cut out to teach other people what I had learned, to be more polite with people, and so on. Yes, and from then on, I never stopped.

JA: And when did this happen?

Natalia: I started with this, as I say, this group like a mothers' center, and from then on I didn't stay in the house any more.

JA: Ah, that was before the arpilleras?

Natalia: Yes, from that time on I started to go out.

JA: Before that you had not been out to a group, nothing?

Natalia: No, I hadn't been out to a group anywhere at all. From that point on I started to participate in everything that, well, that I saw that I liked, and where I could do something with, contribute something of what I was able to do. And since then I have never stopped.

In Natalia's view, important consequences of having joined her first group were becoming active outside the home, "freeing" herself, and discovering herself. She evokes a sense of liberation from the small, narrow world of the home, and a new sense of purpose and achievement. For many women, "coming out of the home" to join the first group had been the most difficult step, whereupon they had gained in self-confidence, coming to leave behind the isolation of their earlier, house-bound lives. Ironically, then, the political repression and neoliberal economic policies had, by pushing women into groups, brought them a level of freedom they had not previously enjoyed, including a new freedom of movement, freedom to associate with others, and freedom to develop as a person.

Group leaders tended to have a leadership role first in one organization, and then another, and another. Catarina from San Bruno, for example, managed and set up a human rights committee, then a health team, then an olla común, and then an arpillera group. Bettina in the north of Santiago created first one arpillera group, then another, and meanwhile became a shantytown leader trying to improve conditions in her shantytown, helped run an olla común for people whose homes had been destroyed, worked in her local health team, became one of the directors in the parents' association in her school, and became active in the national shantytown women's organization, MOMUPO. As with rank-and-file members, becoming active led to still more activity.

Membership in some groups gave women a sense of efficacy. Women in the arpillera groups, for example, felt that they were doing important work and contributing to the ending of the dictatorship, because they saw their arpilleras as communicating to the outside world "the truth" about the regime. Most believed that the arpilleras were the only means of communicating this truth to the outside world since the media were censored; they saw themselves as important informants. One group told me they were "like journalists," and one woman used the phrase, "international pamphleteers," since pamphlets were standard means of communication in the shantytowns. Women in other kinds of groups also gained a sense of efficacy, seeing themselves as able to support their families.

Many women's marital relationships underwent some strain. The women came to think of themselves as having rights as women,[236] and as having been oppressed by their husbands. Among the rights they thought of themselves as having were the right to be treated well by their husbands, and to join groups. They became more assertive with their husbands, insisting on these rights,[237] and many began to stand up to their husbands more. Conflict resulted because husbands tended not to like their wife's leaving the house, and would become angry and suspicious of their motives. Bernardita and I discussed this:

JA: So the idea was above all to have an income.

Bernardita: Subsistence. Yes, that was the, the first idea when it came to, to working in workshops. And, well, women began to receive training there, because at the beginning it was very hard for them to leave their homes.

JA: Why?

Bernardita: Machismo. Their husbands' machismo.

JA: What would the husbands say?

Bernardita: The husbands would get angry, I mean, they could say anything. They could say that maybe she fancied the priest, and that that was why she went to the church. They said all kinds of things. But slowly they got over it, they started to learn, and the husbands started to realize that they were bringing in an income. And that it was useful. As useful as the money they were bringing in. Because there were many single mothers, widows, separated women. And those that had husbands, had husbands who didn't have work. There, there were all kinds of situations. So they [the husbands] would realize that if she participated in the workshop it was because she was going to bring in an income. And that it helped, in the most difficult periods. So the women could do it [earn an income], but the men had no possibility of doing it. So he had to stay at home with the children. But anyway, it was never many hours that the women were out, about four hours, in the afternoon.

Bernardita points to husbands' anger and suspicion being replaced by an appreciation for their wife's income, and coming to understand that her participation in a group resulted in this income. Her words suggest that it was the men's unemployment that broke down their resistance, in that it was principally because they were not working that the women's income became valuable in their eyes; their not being able to fulfill their side of the bargain intrinsic to the gender regime forced them to back down. Some husbands even came to respect and admire their wives more for what they were doing. In some cases, however, the conflict resulted in separation. Certain features of group life helped the women stand up to their husbands, especially the group's conversations about husbands' abusive behavior and ways of dealing with it, the warmth and supportiveness of other women in the group, and the training they received in personal development and women's rights.

Shantytown women's membership in groups sometimes brought a re-organization of family life; the ways housework, childcare, and income-earning were distributed among family members changed. Within these families shantytown gender expectations were changed somewhat.[238] In many families men stayed at home, looking after the children, taking them to school, and even cooking, while women went out to their groups. Ana's husband, for example, took their daughter to school, while Teresa's did the cooking. Talking of times such as Christmas, when she had to work very hard making arpilleras, Teresa said:

Especially at around this time we had to work hard, because it was all rush jobs. They were rush jobs, and you had to hand the work in quickly, and I wouldn't do anything during the day here, during the day. My husband made the food. I just concentrated on this. That's why my eyesight has failed.

Teresa's and Ana's husbands took over what were normally their wives' jobs. Women's participation in groups also meant that children's routines were changed. Bettina's children, for example, had new schedules, having to get up early because she was going out, and were introduced to new activities such as making arpilleras and participating in protests; they themselves became active in protests when they were older, telling their concerned mother that they were following her example.

With many men not bringing in any money, or much money, the women became the main breadwinners.[239] As Natalia put it, "mothers had to bear all the weight of the household" ["la mamá tenía que llevarse todo el peso de la casa"], meaning that they had to work to support the family. While many, like Natalia, were happy about the changes, there was at least one who did not consider women's having to go out of the home and work a desirable state of affairs. In response to my questions, Teresa told me about how, in her arpilleras, she depicted women working for an income washing clothes, baking bread, selling in the market, and picking fruit, and that this was what they had to do since men were not working:

> *JA*:   In the arpilleras that show people working, for example the washerwomen, what is the message there? Is it people in the PEM and POJH?
>
> *Teresa*:   Yes, because people were working as washerwomen. Just like "The Oven" [the name given to a kind of arpillera depicting bread-making], making bread, "Fruit" [arpilleras depicting the selling of fruit], working in the market selling fruit, and "fruit picking," picking fruit. It was all work.
>
> *JA*:   And those figures you did, what was the message behind that, was there an idea, was it a criticism of the government?
>
> *Teresa*:   Yes. That women had to work. Because men were unemployed. That there was no work for men, and women had to work. So that was it, you had to wash, earn money washing, in the market, making baked bread to sell. Those were the themes.

Teresa's words imply that she did not approve of the situation of women having to go out and work because of husbands being unemployed. Nevertheless, her husband's having to cook and look after the children was something she laughed about with me years later. Many men became their wife's assistant with their workshop or community kitchen work. Bettina mentions that the husband of an arpillera group member was in bed all day because he had no work and there was no food, until she dropped by with the news that an order for arpilleras had arrived, whereupon he resumed his habitual task of helping his wife make the human figures for the arpilleras. Ana's husband sewed parts of the arpilleras she made, while Teresa's husband helped her carry bread and food to the olla común. Children, too, participated in the making of arpilleras and in other work the women did.

The women devised new childcare arrangements. Those who could, took their children with them to their groups. The arpillera-makers who met in the church in San Bruno, for example, brought their children along, having them play in the church patio, sometimes supervised by young volunteers. When this was not possible, the women devised ways of having their children looked after, either by their husband or by someone else. Karina's group sometimes had to stay overnight in the church if their group meeting had gone on after curfew, whereupon the husbands looked after their children at home. It was not uncommon to have an elder daughter or relative look after the younger children while the mother was in the workshop, as well. My interview with Gloria, who had four children between the ages of seventeen and four, was instructive:

> *JA*:   And the other women, did they have children too?
>
> *Gloria*:   Yes, they also had children. We all had children.
>
> *JA*:   And how did you work things out with the children while you were in the workshop?
>
> *Gloria*:   Well, they would stay at home. Looked after by someone else. I had my mother-in-law who would look after my daughters; some were already at school. And also they were older, and they would look after the youngest. [*JA*: Yes.] Yes, generally that's what you do.

Gloria had worked out two childcare arrangements. Some women, if unable to find anyone to look after their children, would leave them alone in the house, although they did not like doing so in case there was a fire.

Group membership also enabled the women to gain a deeper understanding of what was happening to them. It helped them see that their problems were not unique to their family, and that their husband's unemployment was not his fault, but rather was caused by the regime's economic and anti-Marxist policies. They also came to appreciate the extent and nature of the repression and poverty, to understand their causes, and to learn about the concept of human rights. They learned, for example, that there were disappeared people and other categories of victim that they would not have known about had they not joined groups, as Ana told me:

> *Ana*: For me, the arpillera meant a lot, because I became fulfilled as a person, I gained knowledge about things I had been ignorant about, about what was happening outside, about daily life, let's say, about some workmates— because I had no idea what was happening.
>
> *JA*: Like what, for example?
>
> *Ana*: Well, the torture, the political prisoners, the disappeared. Because, as I say, even if my husband was arrested, this was a mere trifle compared with what other workmates were suffering. So, for example, I might have stayed shut up in my house, thinking "what happened simply happened," and I could have just shut myself up at home [. . .] Really, it was very useful for me, very, very, very much so. And useful for knowing things that, sometimes, by being shut up in the house, you don't know. You don't know, you don't know what is happening in the world, outside.
>
> *JA*: And these things, did you learn them from your workmates?
>
> *Ana*: From, from the moment I joined the, the workshop, from the moment I joined.

Ana's words point to her appreciation about having learned about the different forms of persecution that existed, and about what her workmates were enduring, and she attributes this new knowledge to having joined her group. The conversation among workmates and their attending training sessions were the main group processes fostering this learning.[240]

Being members of groups brought enjoyment, conviviality, and friendship. The women valued the conversation with other women, and the joking and laughter during group meetings, tea breaks, and group recreational activities. Workshop meetings were a pleasant and relaxing interlude during their days of strain and worry. They saw them as "therapeutic," and said that the conversation and laughter made them forget their problems or see their own problems as less severe than those of other women. They appreciated the joking, which enabled them to laugh at the situation and so feel less despair, and to mock the regime and Pinochet, which may have made these frightening oppressors seem less formidable.[241] Being in a group also offered a chance to enjoy leisure activities, as when groups saved up to go to the beach, or put on plays or dance performances. It brought a feeling of unity within the group, and in some cases a sense of being part of a family.[242] It conferred, as well, a sense of being part of a community made up of many other groups, all of one mind, wanting to end the dictatorship, and all working together towards this goal; the women enjoyed this *esprit de corps* and sense of unity. There was warmth, comfort, and fun in group membership.

Being in arpillera groups, specifically, provided a release from tensions, many women said. The chance to express their feelings in their arpilleras was something many women found therapeutic, seeing it as a "release" for their emotions. Some said that the activity of sewing took their mind off their problems. Many also found that the conversation and laughter helped them forget their troubles. Ana explained:

> But for me it was useful to learn how to make arpilleras and the, the meaning it had for me—because I could sort of develop as a person and be able to express my feelings in the cloth. I mean, so, it was like my release, it was like my way of denouncing, where I might not be able to shout, but it was my way of doing it, in the cloth. I felt very fulfilled, I felt good with my arpilleras and I really like them a lot. For my part, I feel that if it were possible to go on making them right now, I would make them. I would make them. So, it was useful to me as, like as a way of relaxing. Sometimes I was anguished or whatever, and right! I would start sewing, and would get into what I was doing. So, basically, [it was] also like a therapy.

The words "express," "release," and "denouncing" that Ana uses to describe the activity of making arpilleras all suggest that the work was a therapeutic channel for expression where others were blocked. At the same time, the sewing itself was therapeutic as it would absorb her thoughts and make her feel better.

Group leaders had a political perspective on the consequences of women's participation in groups. In their view, for the regime to be overthrown, it was necessary for people to be organized, and some created groups such as the arpillera workshops with this in mind. They thought that once in groups, they could discuss the poverty and oppression with the women and encourage discussion among women, and the women would come to understand that their problems were caused by the government's policies, and that many women shared their situation. They would also learn how widespread these problems were, and they would learn that there was gender oppression, and that they had rights, both as women and as humans. Nancy talked, for example, of women becoming aware that they were "subjects" and not "objects" to be treated any old way. Leaders also considered important the fact that groups were places of warmth and mutual support in which women had an opportunity to be listened to by sympathetic ears, and to feel the care and affection of others. They placed importance on groups having contact with other groups, seeing these bonds as "links in a chain" that strengthened resistance. Also, like the rank-and-file group members, leaders valued the fact that group membership drew women "out from behind the four walls of the home," improved their self-esteem, encouraged them to stand up to their husbands, and enabled them to escape family problems and stresses and strains for a few hours every week. In the eyes of both leaders and group members, then, group membership brought far more than income and food; it made women active participants in their communities. Vicaría staff members mention that it also gave them greater presence within their communities, in addition to recognition and legitimacy.[243]

Working for Employers

Taking jobs and engaging in micro-entrepreneurship were other ways in which women coped with their poverty when their husbands were not working. Beatriz, who lived in southern Santiago, made it clear that motherhood and husbands losing their jobs were driving forces in women's taking up paid work:

> *Beatriz*:   And I started to work in my house, because as it was, because they were such tough times, that I started to work to earn money to be able to eat.
>
> *JA*:   Your husband was unemployed?

Beatriz: Yes, my husband was not working because he was left-wing, they kicked him out of his job, so I had eight children and I had to start to work doing this [making woolen pictures] in order to be able to live, so this was the source of income that we had.

Beatriz's words make clear the link between the national security policy, unemployment, motherhood, and women's beginning to take up paid work. She involved all her children in her work, so as to be able to produce more. According to scholars Raczynski and Serrano (1992: 14), shantytown women's additional working hours through having a job did not result in a clear improvement in well-being, since they often earned little and family instability increased, but Beatriz's case and that of other women interviewed suggest otherwise: the woman's income enabled the family to survive.

The Emergency Employment Schemes

In their search for jobs, shantytown women turned to the emergency employment schemes that the government set up. The largest of these were the Program of Minimum Employment [Programa de Empleo Mínimo, PEM] and the Work Program for Heads of Household [Programa Ocupacional para Jefes de Hogar, POJH]. The work was normally in or near their neighborhood, and included cleaning schools and other public buildings, sweeping and tidying up public squares and gardens, hoeing and planting, knitting or sewing babies' clothes and sweaters, and also, Bettina told me, digging and filling up holes, and taking rubbish in a wheelbarrow from one place to another, whereupon someone else would return it to the original spot. Nelly from southern Santiago worked for the POJH program every morning, digging and planting in squares, and later on knitting babies' clothing. She told me:

JA: Were you working in the workshop and in the POJH at the same time?

Nelly: In the POJH, yes. I worked in the morning from 8.30 until 1.30 p.m., in the POJH.

JA: And what were you doing?

Nelly: There we would make baby suits.

JA: What are baby suits?

Nelly: They are little woolen waistcoats, with little trousers, with little feet, and a little hat. That's what they were.

JA: Were they knitted?

Nelly: Hand knitted. I sometimes had to make two baby suits a week, but that was later, because first I was working in town squares; yes, we would work there, in the street, yes, there we would work with, I don't know if you know what "mattocks" are, for hoeing the earth, and with spades, with sort of ploughs like this, to hoe the earth, and we worked in a town square as well.

JA: Doing the same?

Nelly: Doing the same as a man. Working just like the men, hoeing the earth, planting in the street, in squares. That's what I was doing.

JA: And that was before the arpilleras?

Nelly: Yes, it was before the arpilleras.

JA: And in the POJH, for example, how much did you earn a month, a week?

4.37

The emergency employment programs often involved hard physical labor or insalubrious work such as digging in canals and cleaning public places. In this photograph, women work alongside men, digging a ditch with picks under the hot sun.

Nelly: In the PEM, where I was, they paid 4000 pesos a month and later, when I was in the POJH, it went up to 5000 pesos; that's where I was working doing knitting. They would send us to the Neighborhood Council where there was a room, like this, big, and there they would give us things so that people could work there. And we would begin at 8.30 and leave at 1.30. We had to sign our names on the way in and on the way out too, we had to sign some books, so that they could count what we did, and it would prove that we showed up. We would sign for everything there.

The wages Nelly describes were very low, even though there were unions of PEM and POJH workers. She joined an arpillera group while she was still in the POJH scheme, found that she was able to earn more money, and so soon left the scheme. Other women mentioned that the outdoor work was physically demanding, as one had to work outdoors in the heat and rain.

The women saw the money they earned from the PEM and POJH programs as insufficient for supporting a family. Some women reported that the PEM program paid only 2000 pesos a month, and the POJH scheme 4000 pesos;[244] presumably before Nelly was earning 3000 and 5000 respectively. Wages did rise over the years, but were always low relative to the cost of feeding a family. Nelly told me:

Nelly: Because there really was a lot of, there is real deprivation, at least in homes like my home, and many of my workmates' homes were in crisis. Because there were husbands who were working in the POJH, in the PEM, so at that time it was 3000 pesos that they paid us.

JA: Per month?

Nelly: Per month, so it was very little. And then, with the POJH it went up by 2000 pesos, to make five. They would give it to you fortnightly and the rest at the end of the month. So imagine, how were we going to live with that money? You couldn't, so you had to look for another alternative, and the best alternative was to join the workshop.

Nelly found it difficult to live on the wages paid, and the arpillera workshop was an attractive alternative.

Because the PEM and POJH wages were so low, many women worked in these programs in the morning, and in the afternoon did piece-work, worked in an arpillera group, or engaged in micro-entrepreneurship. When, in about 1980, her husband left her and stopped providing for the family, Barbara joined the PEM program, sweeping and cleaning parks. At the same time, she took on piecework making bags for a woman who lived nearby, starting first thing in the morning, and having the children help her when they came home from school:

> *Barbara*:   At about that time I signed up with the, I signed up with the PEM. We started to make bags, and they paid us one peso a bag.
>
> *JA*:   What sort of bags?
>
> *Barbara*:   Shepherds' bags. With the kids we would make a hundred bags; it was enough for a kilo of bread a day. The kids went to school for half the day, and would come home to help me do this. From the moment I opened my eyes, I would start doing this. So I would quickly make some food, and start doing this. And in the whole day I made some 100, 150 bags. And I would hand them in at the corner, because a lady there would take them. And I worked in the—, and I worked a half-day in the PEM, which involved going to listen to some ladies who would talk about things that were good for you, which—, sort of giving talks, nothing else, there. [We had to] for example sweep, clean, that sort of thing. [*JA*: You had to clean]. Yes, in the sort of parks, that sort of thing. [*JA*: They were two separate jobs.] Yes, yes. But we suffered great deprivation, great deprivation.

Barbara's mention of "great deprivation" indicates how little money she was able to earn even by working in the PEM job and doing piece-work. She did not earn enough to pay for everything she and her children needed. In spending much of what she earned on bread, she was like many shantytown women, in whose eyes bread was an essential food; shantytown women had little access to education about nutrition, and it was difficult for them to afford many of the more nutritious foods. Her words hint at the centrality of motherhood to her work; motherhood was the motivation for it, determining what she spent her wages on (many men spent their minimal PEM or POJH wages on drink rather than food for the family), and influencing the work itself, in that she made bags together with her children.

Workers in the PEM and POJH schemes were occasionally forced to attend pro-Pinochet activities. Some of the women felt bad about this since they were against Pinochet, but believed that if they did not go they would lose their job. One woman told me how she and her colleagues were asked to give in their voter registration cards, whereupon they were all registered as members of a right wing party (presumably towards the end of the regime) and made to sign the relevant documents; if they did not do so, they would not receive their wages. Also under threat of losing their jobs, they had to go to events that showed Pinochet in a good light, such as celebrations for the building of new shantytown homes that his government had commissioned. Nelly told me about coercive practices like these in the POJH program:

> *Nelly*:   And when it occurred to Mr. Pinochet to go and give shantytowns [to people], everyone from the POJH had to go, we had to make sure we went, whether we wanted to or not, otherwise they would not pay us, they would not pay us for our day's work.

Website Link 4.4:
A video about Brazil, Argentina, Uruguay, Paraguay, and Chile discusses the fact that women have less secure jobs and lower wages, and generally work in the informal sector, facing a double work load. See "Southern Cone: Economic Rights for Women," a production by TV Brasil Internacional, UN Women Brazil, and Southern Cone. In Portuguese with subtitles. www.youtube.com/playlist?list =PLB00FCCBAC20405DD

JA: And what did you have to go and do?

Nelly: Accompany him when he went to give people houses, houses for the shantytowns; he would give [people] new houses. We had to accompany him when he did that. Everyone would get on buses with, to go and show that they were present, as we were workers of the POJH, when he went to give people shantytowns. And other people would slip away, they would come home, because what were we going to do there, bored? But still, you had to sign, yes, that's the other thing, because if not they would not count the day, they would put it down as abandonment of one's job, as if we didn't show up to work. So you had to do that, to work there. Yes, now there are more opportunities for women wanting to work, there are more cleaning companies, at least, more nanny positions.

Nelly's words suggest that she and her colleagues were being used to help make Pinochet's government seem legitimate; forced to go to events that suggested that he was helping the poor, they were essentially contributing to creating the impression that there was a crowd of grateful low-income citizens who liked his policies. Hence, Pinochet's problem of lacking legitimacy, such that he had to make it seem that he had widespread support, was one of many ways in which the authoritarian nature of the regime intersected with poverty, to shape women's experiences and behaviors. It was because they needed the work and income urgently that the women complied with such demands.

Working in the Private Sector

Seeking employment in the private sector was another avenue that women took. Very often they worked as a maid, which involved washing, ironing, cleaning, making meals, and looking after their employers' children. Such jobs brought not only income, but sometimes occasional donations of clothing or food, which the women found helpful for clothing and feeding their families. Teresa told me:

Teresa: I worked as a maid. I would do everything. I would stay with the little girl; she [her employer] went out to work. She had a shop selling bathroom fittings. And I would stay there with the girl, I would make them lunch, wash. Like a housewife. I did all that. I would leave my kids alone here, and be looking after someone else's children.

JA: Was that at the same time as the arpilleras, or afterwards?

Teresa: No, afterwards. We had already finished with the arpilleras.

JA: Ah, so when was it then?

Teresa: Ah, no, it was before, before we began with the arpilleras. Before, yes, because this lady had, I remember, she always gave me so much food, so much food that she had stored. She had some big pieces of furniture and everything was stored away, as she had money. And she said, "Señora Teresa, take all this food here, because otherwise it will go off." And she even brought everything here [to my house], in her car. And she gave us clothes for the children. I was working for her for seven years.

JA: Every day?

Teresa: Every day. Monday was the day when I would arrive earlier, because she would go out. I would leave everything ready and lock the door. Because I even had the key; she trusted me a lot. And she would let me, I would come home, on

Sundays I would come home earlier, to bathe the kids, and all that. And sometimes at night, and I had to come home and wash their clothes for school for the next day. That's why, I say, now I am sort of exhausted, tired. You get tired, I think. I really worked hard. That's why the kids all adore me.

Teresa worked a double shift, full-time at her job every day of the week, and then bathing her own children or washing their clothes in the evenings and on Sunday afternoons. To her this work meant struggling hard for her family, and was compensated for by her children's love, yet there is a hint or guilt or sadness in her words about leaving her children alone while she looked after someone's else's. As with Barbara above, her words point to the centrality of motherhood in her experience of work. Being a mother affected how she felt about her job, influenced the total amount of work she did every day, and determined what she saw as the benefits of her job (receiving food and clothing for the children; later on she described this employer as having "clothed my children").

As we saw with Barbara, another form of employment that women took on was piece-work, that is, work for a company, which they did in their own homes, being paid by the piece of work completed. Lydia, who lived in southern Santiago, had worked for years making clothing with a sewing machine for a company that would give her the cloth already cut out. She was still doing this work when she joined an arpillera group in the mid-1980s:

> *Lydia*: All my life I worked at home, because it was difficult for me to work outside because of the children. And I have always sewn [. . .] I have always worked in my home.
>
> *JA*: And what work did you do before?
>
> *Lydia*: Me, well, sewing. I made loads of skirts, for example, but they would give me the pieces cut out. All cut out. So I just worked with the machine. Bras, pictures.

This piece-work suited Lydia because she could do it at home while looking after the children, in line with shantytown gender expectations. Yet she clearly felt somewhat shut in since, as she later mentioned, she wanted to get out of the house.

There were still other forms of work that women performed. Some did fruit-picking outside Santiago on a seasonal basis, for agri-businesses. One woman worked for the archdiocese for many years, managing the Vicaría's storage room, as the Vicaría had come to know her through her participation in workshops. Another worked for the humanitarian organization FASIC [Foundation of Christian Churches for Social Assistance], training other shantytown women in how to make arpilleras, having been an arpillera group leader herself for a long time. Yet another took in ironing (while simultaneously working as a maid), so as to be able to afford to travel to Argentina where her husband had gone looking for work, and bring him back home. Once in Argentina, she took a job in a fruit storage company by night, and in the mornings cleaned a doctor's home.

Entrepreneurship

Entrepreneurial activities were another way in which women sought an income.[245] The women used the skills they had, which tended to be "feminine" skills that they had learned as girls and women, making drinks, bread, cakes, and other food, which they sold in public places or sent their children out to sell. They also washed clothes and ironed for customers, and sewed human figures for the arpilleras, which they would sell to arpillera group

4.38

This woman is selling items from a rough-hewn table on the sidewalk in La Victoria.

workmates. Natasha from Fraternidad, for example, took in washing while also going out to wash, iron, and clean for an ex-employer in a middle-class neighborhood. Teresa lived in southern Santiago, but her husband sometimes went to a nearby city to work, and while he was gone she made bread, fritters, fried Chilean meat pies ["empanadas"], and a popular corn-based drink ["mote mei"], which her children sold at a bus stop. She answered my questions about this:

JA: Apart from the work with arpilleras, and in the home, of course, have you worked in anything else?

Teresa: Yes. [*JA*: could you tell me?] I also worked as, as a maid. Also. And I worked a lot here in the house as well, [making] baked bread, fritters, *mote mei*. Do you know what mote mei is?

JA: No. [Teresa laughs]

Teresa: Mote mei—corn. You put it to cook with ashes from coal and some water, and then you peel the corn. And eat it. It's a little spicy. With "lejía," as the water with ashes is called.

JA: And who would you sell all these things to?

Teresa: My eldest child would go out, the eldest, and the second one. They would go out with a basket to sell.

JA: Here in the neighborhood?

Teresa: Yes. [Singing] *Mote mei pelado en mei* [laughs]. And they would go out. That's what we lived off. Because my husband would go away, sometimes he went

Website Link 4.5:
Women engage in micro-entrepreneurship throughout the industrializing world. This short article by a journalist describes a woman who sells charcoal in a low-income neighborhood of Lagos, Nigeria.
"Nigeria. Women Giving Each Other a Hand Up" by Sam Olukoya, Inter Press Service.
www.ips.org/africa/2011/05/nigeria-women-giving-each-other-a-hand-up/

to work near Valparaiso, he would find work there. And I would stay with my, with all my children.

JA: So, basically you had to—[*Teresa*:   Yes, the situation was—] put food in the pot?

Teresa: Yes. I would sell that. Then, after that—all those pains in my bones I have, are because of that. You have to wash it, to have the faucet running, and wash it because it's cold [. . .] So then when you get older, and I think that that's what must account for the pains I get here in my, in my bones. So afterwards I started to work in, baking. [*JA*: What's that?] Baking, making bread.

JA: In your house?

Teresa: In the house, here. I mean, making bread, making fritters, I would also make fried empanadas, and the children would go out and sell everything. And afterwards I, I got fed up. All that, so much kneading, with that, the back—, and that's what I think gave me the pains that—.

Teresa's words show how flexible she was in her entrepreneurial work, first making mote mei, and then bread, fritters, and empanadas. They also suggest that the work was both time-consuming and physically uncomfortable; mote mei took hours to prepare, and it involved one's hands becoming cold under a flow of cold water. The discomfort continued many years later, if she is correct in attributing the aches in her bones to this work. Teresa did this hard work so as to feed her children while her husband was away, during which time he was not able to give her money at the end of every day. With this work and her job as a maid she became the main breadwinner, since her husband's work was occasional and short-lasting. She integrated her children into the work process, an example of how shantytown children were often put to work during the Pinochet regime.[246] Teresa's entrepreneurship did not end here. She also washed people's clothes:

> *Teresa*:   I worked doing all that. I would wash other people's clothes; I also washed other people's clothes. We just had the wash basin, and we would scrub away. That's why I suffer so much in my fingers, from all that scrubbing, and washing other people's clothes, and everything. [This was] before the arpilleras. Afterwards I continued with the arpilleras and dropped everything else.
>
> *JA*:   You just made arpilleras.
>
> *Teresa*:   Just arpilleras. Yes. After that I didn't abandon my home any more, I devoted myself to my home.
>
> *JA*:   To the home, you mean, while you made arpilleras?
>
> *Teresa*:   Yes, from that point on I didn't go out to work at all. I devoted myself to my children.

Teresa's use of the phrase "I didn't abandon my home" suggests that she felt guilty about work that took her away from the care of her children and so was contrary to shantytown gender expectations, yet she had to provide for them as her husband could not.

Natalia, who lived near Teresa, also worked entrepreneurially, making cakes and sweets that she sold in the school where she worked for the PEM emergency employment scheme. She did this work so as to be able to earn enough money for food for lunch every day, but this entrepreneurship did not only represent for her a much-needed income; it also conferred dignity since it was honorable work. I asked her:

JA: What else did it [the work] mean?

Natalia: It meant, for example, the dignity of each person.

JA: What do you mean?

Natalia: Because look, because however poor you were, well, I mean now it's not that you are rich, but you had your way of living, and not because of that were you going to go about stealing or doing other things. You always had this thing of wanting to earn money in a clean way. In whatever came your way. How many women worked under the hot sun, tidying up squares, hoeing the earth! But the point was to earn money in a clean way. It wasn't much, but it helped. So I, that's why I say, if you, I, for example—, in whatever came my way. I sold sweets, I would make cakes, and so on, and sell them in the school.

JA: You sold in the school? The neighborhood school?

Natalia: Yes, in the school where I was working afterward in the PEM, I would sell them right there. And that was the money with which you brought something home for lunch every day, you see? It wasn't a lot, but it was enough to make lunch, you see.

The selling of sweets and cakes conferred dignity because it enabled her to acquire what she needed in a "clean," honest way, in Natalia's view. It also enabled her family to eat lunch every day. As with Teresa, this was not the only entrepreneurial work Natalia did. She also gave people injections and picked and sold beans:

> And at that point they started to offer, well, for example, courses in the chapel, where they would come, the Vicaría would send people, with all the support that came from organizations abroad, from other countries. So, courses like first aid, hairdressing, the idea being that people learn to do something. And I went for first aid, because I like nursing. There I learned to give injections, and so on, that sort of thing; and I still give injections, I have my clients [laughs] and so on. They [also] offered confectionery. And we started to manage, or rather to move away from the situation we were living in. You see? [. . .] I sold sweets too. As it was a school I had asked the director's permission. So I took along sweets, I would do cakes, things like that, and I sold to children, and that way I made a few more pennies. So that's how we tried to find a way to get by, as they say, whatever way we could. Then it would be the bean cutting season, where, for example, they would look for people to go and cut things in fields, and I would go to that too; and we would sell the beans we brought, to people here, by the kilo.

Natalia's words indicate an energetic engagement in a large number of different activities, both entrepreneurial and employee-based, in the effort to make ends meet: giving injections, selling sweets and cakes, picking beans, working for the emergency employment program, and finally making arpilleras. Her words also hint at international solidarity and its funding of vocational training courses, and the Vicaría's efforts to help the poor earn money.

Some forms of entrepreneurship in which the shantytown women worked were not legal, or went against the moral code. Both women and girls turned to prostitution, for example. About the neighbors whom her discussion group surveyed, Bettina said:

> Others lived, well, prostituting themselves as well, as well. So, in ways that were not right. And for us it was tough to recognize that these were our people, and that they were living under those conditions.

Bettina's learning that neighbors were surviving by doing things that were "not right" was part of a gradual process of coming to understand how severely destitute the inhabitants of her shantytown were; because many shantytown inhabitants hid their poverty, this was not immediately apparent.

Shantytown women, then, sought ways of acquiring food cheaply and earning money. For several of them, their incursions into groups, employment, and self-employment were the first time they had worked for an income since having their first or second child. In addition to such work, they found ways to acquire some of the things they needed by altering habitual ways of managing the household, in what I call "new household management strategies."

New Household Management Strategies and Reciprocal Exchanges

Women from the shantytowns changed the way they normally did things at home, so that it cost less.[247] They also engaged in reciprocal exchanges and resource pooling with neighbors and family, had their children work, and sought help from the priest.

Shantytown women changed the ways in which they acquired and consumed food. For example, they bought food on credit at their local shop, which was normally more expensive than other options and may have contributed to an increase in family indebtedness,[248] but allowed them to pay later and buy in single units, acquiring, as one woman told me, one tea bag rather than a box of tea bags.[249] They also bought food in smaller quantities and reduced their food consumption.[250] They stopped buying certain kinds of food altogether; Natalia, for example, did not buy meat for a long time, as she had enough money for bread but not for both bread and meat. If they could not afford bread, some women bought flour and lard and made the bread themselves, at home in a baked earth oven they put together, gathering sticks for fuel.[251]

4.39

A woman scavenging for food during one of the worst economic crises of the regime (1982–1983).

In some families, children and adults scavenged for food in garbage dumps and garbage cans.[252] In the relatively new shantytown of San Isidrio, in northern Santiago, the Vicaría de la Solidaridad encouraged a group of local women to carry out a survey of the economic situation of people in the neighborhood. Bettina, who participated, told me about what they discovered:

> So we had to survey our, our neighbors, the people from here, from the community. We did ten surveys each, more or less. And in the process of doing the surveys we grew tremendously, because we realized that there were many neighbors, many people who were surviving thanks to the garbage dumps. When the supermarkets sent trucks to throw away rotten food, they would come and throw it away here next to the hill. So people would collect it from there, they had their spots that they would fight over to collect that food that was already rotten. So many, many of our people lived like that.

People's fighting over spots in the garbage dump points to the extent of their inability to buy food, and their desperation. Bettina's "growing" was essentially radicalization, and coming to learn these things led her to join and later form arpillera groups in order to help people manage their poverty. As well as having their children help with the scavenging, some families had them beg.[253]

The women changed still other aspects of household management in an effort to cope with their poverty. They ceased to pay certain bills, or stopped paying installments on purchases they had made.[254] They stopped buying clothing; one woman said that it was difficult to afford shoes. They cut back on leisure activities, home maintenance, and public transportation.[255] When their electricity was cut off, many families attached a wire from their home to the public electricity lines and tapped electricity this way. This was dangerous and sometimes they were caught by the electricity company, which would cut the cables. When their water or the water in the whole neighborhood was cut off, they would go to the nearest public faucet with buckets, and stand in line.[256] Occasionally they would break open the nearest water hydrant and fill buckets with the water that poured from it.[257]

Some women developed informal, reciprocal relationships with neighbors and family members, giving each other items that they lacked. They might contact a neighbor if they did not have enough money to put together a meal, for example, and each would contribute some food or a little money to buy something, and they would cook together. Babette from southern Santiago told me:

> Then you became a housewife, a mother maybe, and it became complicated, so, "Gee, what am I going to make for lunch today? I don't have any money; well, what can I do today? And how about I go here and there and manage to do this, that, and the other?" Sometimes, among my neighbors, none of us had anything to make lunch with. Or my neighbor would call me: "Babette!" "What, Pilar?" "You know, I don't have anything to make lunch with." "You know what, I have a potato, I have some vegetables." "Ah, I have a coin, we could go and buy a bit of mincemeat." "Make me some ravioli," "Let's make ravioli." "Right!" So it was no picnic, it was not so, so easy. Even if your husband was working, they paid him very little. And on top of that if it was known that he was a leader, well, he didn't have any possibility of rising up the ranks or of earning a higher wage. On the contrary, it was more likely that they would fire you.

4.40

The maker of this arpillera shows a woman who has had to resort to prostitution, an unemployed man in despair, and a child with an empty plate (signifying not having enough to eat). In the background is a bar with a drunk man lying in front of it, alluding to the problem of unemployed men becoming alcoholics, and a factory with closed doors, signifying unemployment. Together, these elements capture the economic difficulties that many shantytown women faced.

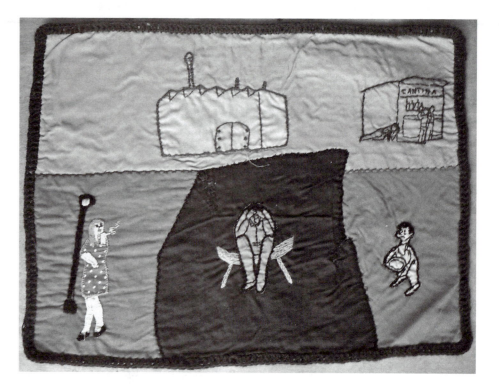

Babette's words suggest that there was considerable pooling of resources and cooperation among neighbors in the effort to secure food, even without forming a group.[258] Her husband was one of the lucky ones, not losing his job because he was a certified electrician, but Babette was at pains to stress how hard things were regardless.

Teresa, who also lived in southern Santiago, got by thanks to ongoing give-and-take arrangements with neighbors and family. I asked her:

JA: Did it happen that your husband was unemployed, at the time of Pinochet?

Teresa: Yes.

JA: And how did you manage?

Teresa: We just managed. We would all help each other. There was one [child] who was married at that stage, two who were married. And among neighbors we would help each other. When there was nothing, we would offer something.

Bonds of mutual assistance among neighbors and family helped Teresa survive.[259] Close family members, if they could afford it, would give money, food or what they could; Teresa's parents in the nearby town of Melipilla helped her family considerably. Her words "we would offer" suggest a solidarity orientation and wish to help, as well as reciprocity. In addition to reciprocal exchanges, family members who lived together pooled money. Gloria and her husband and children lived with her husband's mother, for example, whose pension kept them all going for a while.

Approaching Priests, and other One-Off Strategies

There were some things that the women did only once, or over a very short period of time, in their efforts to cope with extreme poverty. Many women approached their local priest in desperation, asking for help. When Teresa could not pay for her son's education, for example, she went to her priest, a Spaniard much appreciated for his efforts in the shantytown, and he arranged for her to receive some money from a Catholic charity and suggested she join the arpillera workshop and olla común. Mónica approached the same priest when her husband was dying of cancer and she could not afford the medicines he needed, and he lent her the necessary money every month and told her about the arpillera workshop that met in his church. She joined, and so could pay him back every time she earned money.

Another one-off strategy was selling one's furniture and other household items. Bernardita from southern Santiago was desperate because her husband was unemployed for two years, so she sold everything in the house, bit by bit, in order to survive. Finally, she sought help from her local priest:

> *Bernardita*:   And he lost his job in 1975—no, in 1973. Yes, after the coup, within two months he was unemployed. He was unemployed for two years. Two years! During which time we had to sell even the- everything. We sold everything; everything, everything.
>
> *JA*:   That's what made you venture out [of the house], isn't that right?
>
> *Bernardita*:   And that, that's when I went to the, to the church.
>
> *JA*:   Did you use to go to the church before?
>
> *Bernardita*:   To Mass, just to Mass. Nothing else. To the first—to prepare for the children's first communion. Nothing else. It was because of that, that that I joined.

Bernardita's repetition of "everything" suggests the extent of her financial need, and her desperation. It was this that pushed her to approach the priest. Mónica, whose husband was ill with cancer and needed medicine, also sold household items, behind her husband's back, and also then took the step of asking her local priest for help.

The women living in shantytowns, this chapter suggests, adopted six main approaches to the problem of exacerbated poverty. They joined groups, sought work with employers, engaged in entrepreneurship, altered aspects of household management, engaged in reciprocal exchanges with others, and employed varied one-off strategies. They typically employed more than one approach, either at the same time or sequentially. Their efforts were gendered, and shaped by their being mothers; many of them involved the gendered work that the women did as mothers and wives on a daily basis, such as making food, cleaning, washing clothes, or sewing. As mothers, the women integrated the children into the work, having them help sell food or produce piece work. Their motivations were gendered in that they centered on wanting to feed, clothe, or educate the children. Changes in the gender division of labor in the home tended to occur as a result of their activities. Having examined shantytown women's exacerbated poverty and what they did about it, we turn in the next three chapters to the resistance activities that the women became involved in as a result of joining the groups described above.

Five	**Resistance**

Resistance
Self-Protection and Community Affirmation

Shantytown women's resistance to the dictatorship was mostly quiet resistance: non-confrontational and often clandestine. Only some of it took the form of efforts that might be described as mounting an offensive against the regime. Much of it was self-protection and community affirmation: ways of holding one's ground and refusing to be beaten down that may be compared to fighting off an enemy, as opposed to moving forward with an attack. Self-protection involved taking measures to lessen the chance of being at the receiving end of state violence. Shantytown women worked to protect self and family, their shantytown, and the groups to which they belonged. Community affirmation, meanwhile, involved nurturing the values of equality, democracy, sharing, and solidarity, paying homage to individuals who had died at the hands of the dictatorship, building bridges with other groups, fostering a community of women, and celebrating shantytown and group anniversaries. An examination of community affirmation and self-protection will follow an exploration of the nature of women's resistance: incidental, and sometimes reluctant and solidarity-focused.

Incidental, Reluctant, and Solidarity Resistance

Incidental Resistance

Shantytown women's resistance was *incidental resistance*. That is, the women had not set out to participate in resistance activities, but rather became involved in such activities because the groups they joined to cope with their poverty engaged in them "on the side." Once in such groups, the women became involved in resistance activities of many different kinds, because all or most of the group participated in these activities together,[260] and leaders encouraged them to do so. The first step towards resistance for shantytown women, then, was joining a group in order to cope with an immediate problem. Even women in associations of relatives of the persecuted (see Chapter 7) had not joined their associations so as to engage in resistance, for the most part.

Group members became involved in resistance activities in a number of ways. Their leaders would learn about an upcoming act of resistance from the Vicaría or another shantytown group, or from having seen a flyer, and would inform group members, putting pressure on them to attend. Alternatively, the members of coordinating committees organized a resistance activity and encouraged group members to attend. It also happened that one group within a coordinating committee was organizing a resistance activity and would invite the other member groups to join in or lend their support. Sometimes a group member mentioned a protest activity to the rest of the group, and suggested that they all participate. Occasionally, groups participated in a resistance activity spontaneously.

Website Link 5.1:
An article in Britain's *Guardian* newspaper discusses the active role that women have taken in the uprisings in the Middle East and North Africa through their protesting, organizing, blogging and hunger-striking, and questions the extent to which there may be gains in terms of gender equality in the future. See "Women Have Emerged as Key Players in the Arab Spring," April 22 2011, by Xan Rice, Katherine Marsh, Tom Finn, Harriet Sherwood, Angelique Chrisafis, and Robert Booth. www.guardian.co.uk/world/2011/apr/22/women-arab-spring

Gloria's arpillera group, for example, spontaneously took to the streets as soon as they heard about a particularly cruel act of repression that had just occurred:

Gloria: Well, I remember that once we were in a training session in La Estrella [a southern shantytown] and they arrived with the news about the men whose throats have been slit [the "degollados"] that day, and it was that same day that they had found them, etc. And out we went; it was spontaneous. All the workshops were there. And we went out near here, in the neighborhood, and marched. We also organized some marches for the workshops, at which those of us from La Victoria would set out and join up with the other workshops. Marches about hunger too, because it was what motivated people; a march about hunger, because it was our problem. So we marched about that. And we [our various groups] would join up like that, in the avenues near here. And we even went to Gran Avenida [a nearby street] sometimes; and we'd end up in Gran Avenida where it intersects with Callejón Ovalle [another street].

JA: With the other arpillera workshops?

Gloria: Yes, all the workshops. And the ollas comunes would join in too; all the groups related to subsistence.

JA: And from the workshop, what proportion of women participated in those marches?

Gloria: I think it was not many in fact, at least from here. From other workshops yes there was more participation; maybe they were more political, the women there. But from here I think it was two or three of us who went.

JA: What was the incentive? Did someone motivate you to go or not? How did you know?

Gloria: I think there was an incentive, there was a call, I mean there were public calls, via the Vicaría and other organizations, flyers that they would drop in the streets. As we were coordinating committee members they would give us lots of flyers to distribute, because we went to meetings in San Bruno and sometimes we'd come back dropping flyers too. Lots. With a lot of paper, with lots of things to drop and do propaganda with. I mean, there was a motivation, there definitely was, on the part of the organization, to participate in these things, because it was for human rights, for justice.

JA: On the part of which organization?

Gloria: I think it came from the coordinating committee. And there was another one called the coordinating committee of Caro-Ochagavía, which was sort of at the beginning, the coordinating committee of Caro-Ochagavía which was sort of something more political where all the organizations that were, say, social organizations, came together.

Gloria's words point to three ways in which women in groups came to be involved in protests: groups marched spontaneously upon hearing about a protest, the coordinating committee to which her group belonged organized marches for all the groups represented in the committee, and groups answered public calls to protest issued via the Vicaría and other organizations, communicated via flyers dropped on the street, or distributed by group leaders within the coordinating committee. In all cases the protests were not the central activity of their group, but something they did in addition to their work. Gloria's words also show how shantytown women in groups participated in a range of protests, some about their own problems, such as hunger, and some about other people's, as with the *degollados*. Also, some focused on poverty and related problems, and others on repression. From Gloria's perspective, all these protests were about human rights and justice.

Reluctant Resistance

Rank-and-file group members tended to be reluctant to participate in some of the forms of resistance I have grouped together under the category "mounting an offensive." They participated, but often unwillingly; in such cases, their resistance was *reluctant resistance*. This was especially so with demonstrations, which put them in contact with the police and in danger of being arrested. There were a number of reasons for this reluctance, the most prominent of which were fear and concern about what would happen to their children if they were arrested, as discussed in Chapter 2. Another reason, which Gloria offers above, was "not being very political," by which she meant not being in the habit of participating in overtly political or party-related activities. Husbands' and children not "letting" them participate or not being happy about their participating lest the children be left motherless constituted still another reason for some women, although other women simply did not tell their husbands what they were going to do. Teresa's experience offers an example:

> *JA*:   And where did they have the protests, right here or in the center?
>
> *Teresa*:   In the center.
>
> *JA*:   Did you yourself go?
>
> *Teresa*:   No, I wouldn't go, they wouldn't let me go [chuckles]. No, I didn't get involved in that, not I. I—, it scared me. Once we went, with the workshop, we went to one about women. One that was similar, that they did here, I can't remember the name. Because they forced us to. It was compulsory to go.
>
> *JA*:   For the workshop.
>
> *Teresa*:   Yes, with the workshop, we had to go to—. But we went, we showed up there, we were there a little while and we, we got together, all of us, and came back. Because afterwards there are problems and—. So people went along in, to those things in the center, the, the events that the relatives of the disappeared put on and all that; we would protest about that. And that, all that was— I myself, I don't have much experience of that because I, I— that's why Señora Barbara wants you to interview Mónica.
>
> *JA*:   And you, was it your husband who didn't want you to go?
>
> Teresa: Yes, and the children didn't like it either.
>
> *JA*:   Out of fear, I imagine.
>
> *Teresa*:   Yes, out of fear. Of course they all expressed their opinion about everything, everything that was happening, but they didn't like to go like that, in—.

Teresa was prevented from attending protests because her husband and children were against it, but one senses from her words about showing up at protests briefly and coming home that she was not an eager participant. Her sense of responsibility for her children pulled her in two directions: participation in protests in order to have work and earn money for them, and avoidance of participation so as not to put her life at risk, and because of pressure from her children and husband. Some women resolved this dilemma by staying at the protest for a very short time, and attending only occasionally.

Website Link 5.2:
The United Nations body in charge of promoting gender equality, UN Women, has programs aimed at strengthening women's political participation. Its website describes its work towards "the participation and the representation of women in public spaces and in political representation systems to strengthen democracies, ensure that women can exercise and enjoy their rights and to eradicate gender discrimination." The site also contains a link to UN publications on the topic. "UN Women, the United Nations Entity for Gender Equality and the Empowerment of Women. Political Participation." www.un-instraw.org/political-participation/programme-page/

Having *young* children, in particular, made the women reluctant to participate in protests. Babette, for example, told me that she did not participate in protests much because of her children, who were small, and also because she was afraid of doing so. Similarly, Nelly avoided participation because she had no-one with whom to leave her little girl, and worried about her getting hurt if she took her along. She told me:

Nelly: I remember that once we went to the Santa Laura Stadium where there was, where we were with a group, Manuel Rodríguez, at that time.

JA: The singer?

Nelly: No, it was a group of, of, of protesters like us.

JA: Ah, of young people?

Nelly: Of young people. We would go to the center with them. But the one who participated most was Señora Natalia, she was the most rebellious. I, as I had small children, I couldn't go much. I had this one [gestures towards her adult daughter], and she was small. And the other child was a baby. So I didn't go out much, but still, I went out sometimes.

JA: And could you describe, when you went out, what was the protest like? Was it a march?

Nelly: Marches, marches; yes, it was mostly marches. Yes, because the velatorios [remembrance rituals] were something they always held at night. But [we were] in marches—, and we would march with all the young people next to us there, and us in the middle, in the center, around where La Moneda [Chile's White House] is, around there.

JA: And what was the occasion or the reason for the marches, for example?

Nelly: Well, they were about what was happening here in Chile. They were so that this ma—, the gentleman [Pinochet] would hand over control. So that there would not be so much hunger, so much deprivation. So those were the marches we did, but as he continued to have power—. With us, because people—, I thank God that that time when I went they were not throwing tear gas bombs or spraying water, otherwise I would have been all wet. That's why the fear—I didn't go because I didn't have anyone to leave her with; I didn't go very often because otherwise I might be all soaked and they could very well have knocked me over, and I would have had an accident with the girl. So I didn't go; better not go.

Nelly's having a small child and baby made her feel she could not go to marches often; her being a woman and a mother, in other words, made her reluctant to attend protests, but it did not stop her altogether. It also did not stop other women from participating in resistance activities; Babette, for example, while heavily pregnant and not able to walk well, had helped her husband block the street with sticks and stones.

When the women were reluctant, some group leaders became coercive, putting pressure on them to attend. They employed a discourse of "cooperation" and "participation," making the women feel that not to join in with protests was to be uncooperative and non-participatory, when both cooperation and participation were highly valued in the groups and resistance community. Leaders also used threats, especially the threat of not receiving work to do, which meant not being able to earn money. Ana was an arpillera group leader and member of her coordinating committee in eastern Santiago, and she and the other leaders used accusations of "not cooperating" and applied sanctions with women who did not participate in protests. We discussed this:

JA: Culturally, what rules were there in the workshop? Like this idea about sharing; what other sort of rules, ideas, did you have? How should a workshop be?

Ana: Cooperation, cooperating, cooperating, cooperation, and completing the job that we had to do. For example, when we handed in the arpilleras, if a workmate did not complete the job, she would have the work taken away from her and given to someone else who would complete the job. When we sold fritters or bread, for example, it was work we had to all share, and anyone who didn't work would not receive her share of the income. Those were the rules we had. It's the same as when we had committed ourselves to going to the protests; anyone who didn't go was punished, also. Because basically we, we, we were all involved in the same thing. So it should not be, let's say, just, so easy. Because it was hard for all of us.

JA: And what was the punishment, for example, in that situation?

Ana: We would leave her out of the—; for example, if we earned, let's see, 5000 pesos, those 5000 pesos, if there were ten of us, because we would create different groups. So if—, it was for all ten members of the group, and if one member did not participate, she would not receive her share. [. . .]

JA: And with the protests, if someone did not participate?

Ana: She would not be given work.

JA: You yourselves—?

Ana: We, we made the rules, yes.

The discourses of "participation" and "cooperation" were difficult to argue with and made women who did not join in with the protests look bad, while the prospect of not receiving work was very distasteful to the women, who needed the money urgently; hence both might be termed coercive strategies. Other leaders used persuasion rather than coercion, as we saw with Natalia earlier, who said how important it was that people protest. That coercion and persuasion had to be used at all is testimony to the fact that the fear of repression was paralyzing, and that a significant number of women participated in protests reluctantly. In some groups it was only a fraction of women who participated.

The women found ways of getting around being forced to participate in protests against their will. Some went to where the protest was going to taking place and then escaped and returned home, hid in shops, or ran into nearby parks before or soon after it began, and later did not reveal that they had not participated. Karina eloquently described her reluctance to participate in protests, the pressure put on her group by the group's leaders, and the ways in which she reacted to it:

Karina: I would always go, because they forced all of us to go. But I would come back. Since the, in the Alameda [a street in central Santiago, where protests often took place] there are so many people, I would escape and come back. Because everyone had to make their own way back. Because they would drop us off there, only, but afterwards we had to—. So that's when I; I did that bec—, because it made me SCARED; [*JA*: Yes] because my children were small, it made me scared. And I'd take a bus back home, and I'd come home; because my husband didn't know about this. My husband didn't know I did this.

JA: That you did what?

Karina: Er, go to, to the protests [*JA*: Yes], because if we didn't go, we didn't have the right to work.

JA: And why didn't you tell Señor Bernardo?

Karina: Because he would not have let me go. Because of the kids, because something could happen to me. Sometimes they had it, for example, when it was dusk; they would make us protest in a line, like this, in the streets on the way to this shantytown, with placards and everything. [*JA*: I see.] They made us walk and then when the police arrived we had to run away. Or alternatively we would not run away but look as if we were not doing anything wrong, and we were just singing. They would look at us, but they wouldn't do anything. But you still felt scared. [. . .] On Fridays they, they would take us. You had to be there at a certain time, so we would go. Here in the house I'd say that I was going, that we were going to end the workshop later than usual because there was a lot of work. But we'd go without the children, we'd leave them here.

JA: So you would leave them here. And how did you go there? Where was it? Was it protests?

Karina: In the center of town. A bus would take us, all of us, and it would leave us all in the Alameda [central Santiago's main street], and after that everyone had to see if things were rough, with everything, and you had to, each of us had to find our own way home. If anyone was arrested you had to inform them immediately because the Vicaría would get them out of jail, get the person who was arrested out. But no-one from here was arrested, no. We'd all run away.

JA: And this was during how many months, that there was a protest every Friday?

Karina: Oh, always. There was, [*JA*: Always] yes, there always was.

JA: From the beginning?

Karina: Yes, these things were always going on.

JA: If you didn't go [and protest], they wouldn't give you work.

Karina: No, they wouldn't give us work, we had to go.

JA: How would you feel about that, you personally?

Karina: Well, bad. Because if not, they wouldn't giv—, they wouldn't, I wouldn't work. But many of us would take along salt, because they would throw those things and, and salt was good, they said, to put on your lips so as not to suffocate with those bombs that they threw. I remember how once I hid with another woman in a, a pharmacy, because they were going to—we were coming back. But the police arrived, and we hid there in the pharmacy. They closed the pharmacy, they closed it immediately. So I was scared but because I had—; [*JA*: Yes, of course, yes] we were leaving. So she—, a woman would always join us and, and I remember how once we were at the hill of Sta. Lucía [in central Santiago] and we ran away up the hill. I was really frightened because [laughs] it was a lonely place, it scared us. And then we came down. [. . .] We had no idea where we had to catch the bus. So we walked a lot, until we found the street that we more or less knew, and came home. So we kept quiet, and when the moment came, they said, "And how did you come home?" "Uh, on foot, walking," we said. And we had no idea about what else had happened. They arrived all wet because of the water from the water cannon. It would knock them over, and make them all wet. And so they would congratulate us for that, just for that. That we had done our duty; we had been there.

Karina was very reluctant to participate in protests as she felt afraid, her children were small, and the police would watch her group during some of its protests. She went along to protests in the city center and her shantytown nevertheless, because of the leaders' coercion. Hers was a difficult dilemma; she wanted to do what was required to receive work and money with which to feed the family, yet at the same time going along meant that her children would be without her care should she be arrested. Hence she devised a number of strategies for avoiding most of the protest while appearing to be present in the eyes of the leaders, as did the other women, as her words, "we'd all run away" suggest. She also had strategies for managing her recalcitrant husband who was worried about the children: not telling him where she was going, pretending she was merely going to the workshop and it would finish late, and leaving the children at home. Her words also point to third-party support from the Vicaría and to her leaders' efforts at protecting the group, namely suggesting that they run away when the police arrive or look innocent and just sing while continuing to walk with placards.

While rank-and-file women tended to be reluctant to participate in protests, group leaders were eager to do so and eager for others to do so. Nancy, for example, created a health team and at least one arpillera group in southern Santiago. She had a more political background than many of the rank-and-file women and even the leaders, having grown up in a politically engaged family and been an activist in a party for many years. She told me:

> My family had always been politically engaged. When I was very young, I participated in the Catholic Youth, and after that I was a party member. Beginning in 1973, we naturally threw ourselves into what was— I wouldn't say the struggle because we didn't have— but into trying to restore democracy. Because we saw that the dictatorship was cruel, it killed people, it kidnapped people, there was no freedom of the press. What moved us was not so much love of country, but a love of humanity. And among ourselves we still care for each other a lot, those of us who are left, with whom we meet up. So what brought us to all this struggle was, rather, a commitment to humanity.

Nancy's history of political engagement suggests that she was radicalized by the time of the coup, and resisted the dictatorship eagerly. Other leaders shared her eagerness to take action. Fernanda, from southern Santiago, led shantytown adult literacy training groups, and she told me:

> I joined [an arpillera group] more to . . . to protest, as I say; well, I have it in the blood, I am a woman of struggle. I think that if there was another coup, I would be in the street, protesting.

Fernanda joined the group in order to fight the regime. Her phrase about "having it in the blood" may be a reference to Mapuche ancestry, the Mapuche being a Native People who fought valiantly against the Spanish conquistadors. Both Fernanda and Nancy were enthusiastic about resistance.

Leaders wanted shantytown women to be in groups, becoming radicalized and protesting. When women were afraid to join, they sometimes managed to draw them in by not being open about the fact that the group's activity was in fact political, as we saw earlier. They also did not tell them that the group would be engaging in resistance activities on the side. Some shantytown women joined groups and became involved in the group's primary activity quite unaware of the political nature of what they were doing. They might be described in such cases as *resisting unawares*. For example, most women joined arpillera groups for the money they would earn by selling their work, and for therapeutic reasons, and only later came to realize that making arpilleras was a political activity and form of denunciation. By then they were less afraid, having already taken the difficult step of joining a group, and were enjoying the benefits of group membership.

Solidarity Resistance

Some of the women's resistance was *solidarity resistance*, that is, resistance that aimed to help other people or express solidarity with their struggles, as opposed to resistance focused on one's own problems. The women had a word, "la solidaridad" [solidarity] and verb "ser solidarias" [being solidarity-oriented] to express this; both meant helping or supporting others, as well as expressing sympathy with their cause or plight. Groups made conscious and repeated efforts to express solidarity with the sufferings and struggles of others, and encouraged solidarity both within their group and towards other groups. Within groups, the women were "solidarias" by giving emotional support to members in distress, and material support to women in need, and by visiting members when they fell ill. Members of the coordinating committee of arpillera groups in eastern Santiago, for example, put together a bag of food for one member who was in a particularly desperate situation.

Women were "solidarias" towards other groups in the resistance community, particularly the victims of the regime's economic or national security policies, and towards those who had suffered because of natural disasters. They visited the relatives of people who had endured targeted repression both immediately after the repression had happened, and when the relatives were carrying out a protest. When an arpillera-maker's daughter from a nearby shantytown was killed, for example, Gloria's arpillera group went to visit the family in order to express solidarity. When the relatives of the disappeared held a hunger strike, the arpillera groups in eastern Santiago went to see them to express their support. When union members engaged in hunger strikes, Babette's coordinating committee went to them in order to express their support, and Bettina's arpillera group helped run their temporary community kitchen. The women's groups also expressed solidarity with political prisoners by going to visit them in jail, and encouraging others to do the same via flyers. Bettina and her fellow Christian community members in northern Santiago visited political prisoners on a regular basis. Days denominated as international human rights-related days, such as the International Day of Political Prisoners, were frequently the occasion of expressions of solidarity towards the victims of repression, and International Women's Day was the occasion of expressions of solidarity towards other women. Shantytown women also directed their solidarity at groups in the same coordinating committee, helping them with some of their activities, as when one group of arpillera-makers in eastern Santiago was making and selling fritters, and another group helped them sell.

The organizing of fundraising events was a form that solidarity often took, particularly the organizing of evenings of folk music ["peñas"]. Audience members had to pay to attend, and the money went to those in need. The Council of Christian Communities of Valledor Norte organized a peña for the benefit of a young woman who had been burned by soldiers and almost died. There were peñas for "relegados" [people sent to jail in distant and often hostile corners of Chile], for someone who could not afford to visit their relatives, for someone who had to have paperwork done, for someone who was ill, for the unemployed, and for alcoholics. Normally the beneficiary was in the same

5.1

This flyer, produced by shantytown women of southern Santiago in the mid- to late 1980s, reads, "Freedom for Women Political Prisoners. Saturday 8th March. Visit them in the Prison of San Miguel. 9.30 a.m. Women of the southern zone." Its authors are encouraging readers to show their solidarity towards the prisoners. Producing the flyer was in itself an act of solidarity, in that it was done to help the women in prison. With this gesture, the authors of the flyers were simultaneously affirming and strengthening their ties with the prisoners. The date, International Women's Day, was a time when it was common to link up with other groups of women and build community (see Chapter 6).

coordinating committee as the organizers of the peña. Some peñas included poetry and theater, as well as song, and the selling of fritters. I discussed this with Babette:

> *JA*:   And, and as a workshop what other activities did you organize or what else did you express solidarity about?
>
> *Babette*:   Well, for example, there was a peña [evening of folk music] for a comrade who was in a bad way, or who was sick, or who, or who had been sent somewhere and he didn't have support, or the family didn't have the support needed to be able to travel, and we'd do a solidarity peña. Or [*JA*: For a comrade of—] for a comrade in, in, it might be in, in a social organization or—, but one that was part of our organization [the coordinating committee], one that was part of our organization.

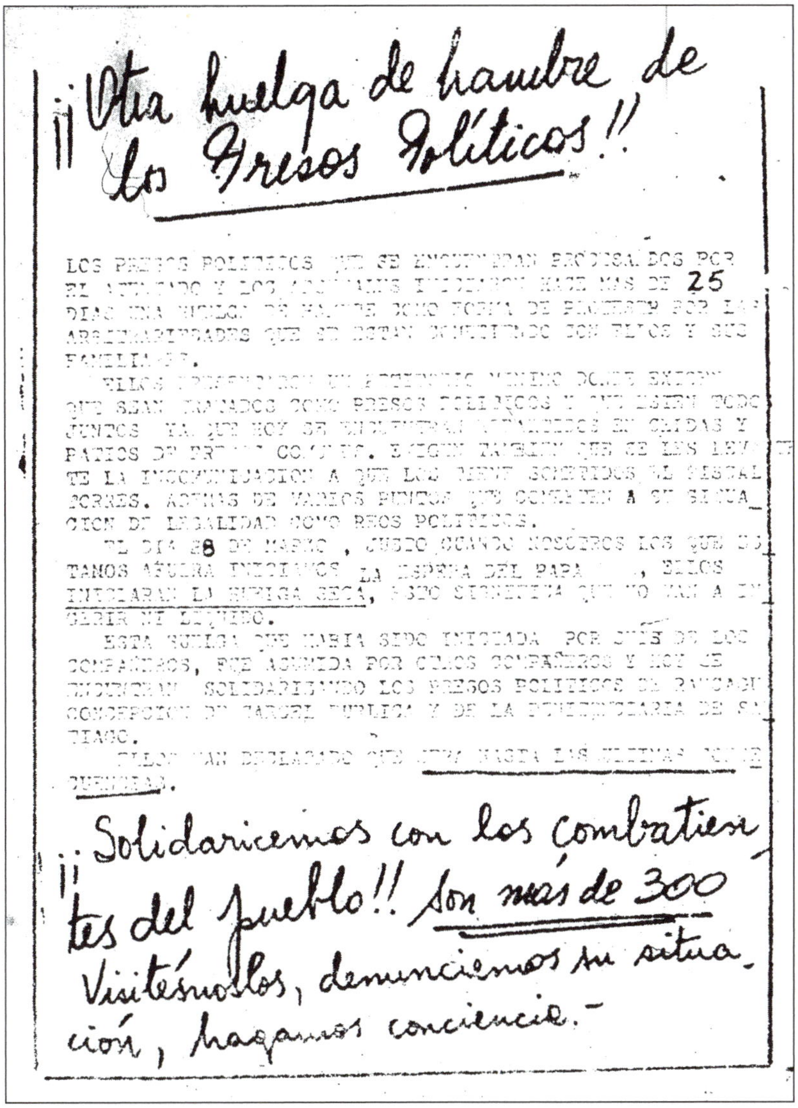

¡¡Otra huelga de hambre de los Presos Políticos!!

LOS PRESOS POLITICOS QUE SE ENCUENTRAN PROCESADOS POR EL [illegible] Y LOS [illegible] HACE MAS DE 25 DIAS UNA HUELGA DE HAMBRE COMO FORMA DE [illegible] POR LAS ARBITRARIEDADES QUE SE ESTAN COMETIENDO CON ELLOS Y SUS FAMILIARES.

ELLOS [illegible] UN [illegible] MINIMO DONDE EXIGEN QUE SEAN TRATADOS COMO PRESOS POLITICOS Y QUE ESTEN TODOS JUNTOS YA QUE HOY SE ENCUENTRAN [illegible] EN CELDAS Y PATIOS DE [illegible] COMUNES. EXIGEN TAMBIEN QUE SE LES LEVANTE LA INCOMUNICACION A QUE LOS TIENE SOMETIDOS EL FISCAL TORRES. ADEMAS DE VARIOS PUNTOS QUE COMPETEN A SU SITUACION DE ILEGALIDAD COMO REOS POLITICOS.

EL DIA 28 DE MARZO, JUSTO CUANDO NOSOTROS LOS QUE ESTAMOS AFUERA INICIAMOS LA ESPERA DEL PAPA, ELLOS INICIARAN LA HUELGA SECA, ESTO SIGNIFICA QUE NO VAN A INGERIR NI LIQUIDO.

ESTA HUELGA QUE HABIA SIDO INICIADA POR [illegible] DE LOS COMPAÑEROS, FUE ASUMIDA POR OTROS COMPAÑEROS Y HOY SE ENCUENTRAN SOLIDARIZANDO LOS PRESOS POLITICOS DE RANCAGUA, CONCEPCION, DE CARCEL PUBLICA Y DE LA PENITENCIARIA DE SANTIAGO.

ELLOS HAN DECLARADO QUE [illegible] HASTA LAS ULTIMAS CONSECUENCIAS.

¡¡Solidaricemos con los combatientes del pueblo!! Son más de 300

Visitémoslos, denunciemos su situación, hagamos conciencia.–

5.2

Shantytown women organized and participated in solidarity events aimed at helping people less fortunate than themselves. For example, a coordinating committee of women's groups in the south of Santiago called "Caro-Ochagavía Women's Front" encouraged readers to give support to political prisoners who were on a hunger strike. They suggested visiting them, denouncing their situation, and raising public awareness about them. This is a page from the bulletin the Women's Front produced (Boletín de la Mujer, Frente de Mujeres Caro-Ochagavía 1987 issue 8). The same organization produced a document that explained that political prisoners were people who were fighting for the rights of Chileans, enduring torture, and often losing their lives in the process. It enjoined readers to visit them in jail, with the words, "Have we ever thought about how we who are organized can support them?" and "Do we devote enough time to our jailed comrades? Let us not forget that . . . it is our duty to struggle for their freedom." A photograph accompanying the text showed protesters holding a banner demanding freedom for political prisoners, and there were drawings of someone behind bars with a dove in the foreground, accompanied by barbed wire and a clenched fist.

JA: And what else?

Babette: Er, for example, at that time we would do—, there was, well, the organization of the unemployed, which was also part of the coordinating committee of the shantytown. Yes it was, as I say, from everywhere, young people, adults, the unemployed, alcoh—, alcoholics anonymous, or what we were in charge of, the health field, regarding the, the consumption of alcohol, drugs, all that sort of thing. We would, as I say, we would put on a peña for these groups, for someone who needed it, or who had to travel to see their relatives and didn't have money, or they had to send money to have some documents drawn up, or someone had to do paperwork, for example, and they didn't have enough money with what they had saved. And so, we did . . . some fritters, and you would pay a certain sum and serve yourself, and that money was gathered together. Later we would keep accounts and take the money to the people who needed it. Those who knew how to play the guitar and sing would do it, and so on.

JA: And these things, would you do them as a workshop?

Babette: Also, we also participated as a workshop.

As Babette's words make clear, there were numerous peñas, helping people with a variety of problems. She organized them as member of the coordinating committee of Caro-Ochagavía, a mixed-sex coordinating committee of popular organizations in southern Santiago. Members of her arpillera workshop, which was part of the coordinating committee, joined in with the organizing.

Another solidarity activity was the organizing of campaigns to help certain groups. These involved numerous activities and some lasted several days. For example, several shantytown women's organizations in eastern Santiago organized a campaign for people whose economic situation was more desperate than their own. The campaign included both direct action, such as giving donations, and more political activities such as discussion sessions on the social and economic reality of the shantytowns, presenting the Ministry of Economics with a proposal based on a survey about poverty, and a form of "mass action" (not described). In the flyers that the organizers produced, the problem was framed in terms of rights, namely the right to eat. Organizing such events together resulted in the strengthening of ties between organizing parties, and between the organizers and those being helped.

The women's emphasis on solidarity extended not only to groups who were victims of repression and poverty, but also to individuals whose homes were damaged by bad weather. Bettina, for example, helped local people whose roofs blew off in strong winds, causing the inside of their homes to become drenched with rain. She helped run a soup kitchen for them, with food that the priest obtained from the Vicaría or archdiocese, while those afflicted took refuge in the church. Mónica also helped people whose roofs were leaking during the rainy season, setting aside some arpillera group earnings to buy coal to help keep the afflicted warm, and fetching dry mattresses. She told me:

> . . . A certain amount [of our funds] for the workshop, a certain amount to buy food with which to help people, all those sorts of things. For coal, because when it rained here, lots of people had water coming into their homes, people with children, and so on. Right, so, the priest would take charge, doing things here and there. I would ask for mattresses here and there, we would, there were a lot of young adults. . . . So we had to buy coal, and we would buy it by the sack. And the young people, because I had young people, there were about fifteen young people in the church,

CAMPAÑA
en contra del
Hambre y del Frío

9 al 22 de Julio

ORGANIZACIONES
POPULARES
ZONA ORIENTE
COPO

Pan y Techo para los más Pobres

5.3

A coordinating committee of shantytown groups in eastern Santiago, called "Popular organizations of the eastern zone" ["Organizaciones Populares Zona Oriente"], organized a campaign to bring food and shelter to the poorest people in their area, in what was an extended case of solidarity resistance. It was entitled "Campaign against hunger and cold," ["Campaña en contra del hambre y del frío"] and took place in mid-winter, between July 9th and 22nd one year in the mid- to late 1980s. Like many such events, it aimed to denounce and raise awareness, as well as help. The organizers programmed seven concurrent activities: first, collecting food, clothing, shoes, roofing, medicine, money, wood, wire, nails and other materials, all of which would be distributed among subsistence organizations in the eastern area. Second, discussion sessions on group leadership, health, nutrition, legal problems, and the social and economic reality of shantytown inhabitants. Third, the repair, by teams, of houses, roofs, walls, and sewage drains. Fourth, local groups serving beans, chocolate milk, and other types of food, while dialogue took place among participants. Fifth, a discussion session among shantytown women, organized by a feminist NGO. Sixth, fundraising evenings of folk music and dance [peñas], cultural events, and arts competitions; and finally, a "Massive Public Action" in which the whole area would be involved. The organizers planned to give the Ministry of Economics a proposal about needs in terms of food, and the results of a survey about the nutrition of shantytown inhabitants. A local church assisted with the event, acting as a center for the collection and distribution of food and other goods. Like many groups, the leaders of the campaign placed great importance on strengthening local groups and encouraging more people to join groups, as well as on creating links with other organizations or sectors, such as professionals, students, trade unions, and the church. They also considered it important to inform the public about the problem of hunger and inadequate shelter, framing their struggle in terms of rights, including the "right to eat."

Website Link 5.3:
World news, current discussions, and publications about women's participation in politics are available on the website "iKnow Politics" by the International Knowledge Network of Women in Politics. www.iknowpolitics.org/

young people who helped a lot. Someone's house would be flooded; they would go to the house with, with picks, spades, and so on, to the homes of people who were really badly flooded. Another would run to fetch coal, in a can, because it would not burn. And another would deal with a wet mattress or with situations where there was no mattress. And so on. We worked very well, like this.

Mónica's words point to solidarity from the young people's group she ran in her local church, and from her local priest, as well as her own solidarity. She and the group seem from her words to have been highly motivated to help others. Mónica undertook a number of other charitable actions. She cooked food for seven seniors in a room in the church. She took note of which families in her neighborhood were in dire need of financial help and suggested to the priest that part of a fund be given to them. She helped young people addicted to drugs, talking to them, advising them, and trying to get them involved in activities. She worked with groups of small children ["patotas"] on Sunday afternoons, having them play, write, and make little figures. She helped with the week-long children's summer camps in the shantytowns ["colonias urbanas"], cooking meals for the children. Lastly, she helped people without homes who organized land seizures, even though she already had a house. Her words illustrate how some women, already poor themselves, went out of their way to help others who were even poorer, and how the priest was often a partner in their efforts.

More than merely working in accordance with the value of solidarity, many of the women's groups had an *ethos* of solidarity, meaning an understanding that members would and should support each other, and other members of the resistance community; that it was their duty.[261] They felt this support should be extended to other groups in their coordinating committee, and to workers, political prisoners, relatives of the disappeared, people poorer than they, and people without adequate housing. This applied particularly to times when people were trying to overcome grief after state violence, coping with natural disasters, and protesting. Gloria said:

And also, sometimes we had to be solidarity-oriented ["solidarias"] with other people from other groups, from another organization, or we had to be solidarity-oriented with what was happening in other workshops. If you had, for example, if something happened in another shantytown, we would go over there to express solidarity with the people there. When something happened here, also, we had to be present. It was a way of saying "we are united." There was a lot of unity as well. That was another value that we lived by a lot: unity. Despite the differences that there might be, not so much within the workshop but at the shantytown level, ideological differences let's say, we still experienced unity, which doesn't happen as much now. Because we all sort of had something in common: the dictatorship. We were all against that. So then there was more unity.

JA: And those values, solidarity, sharing, how did they come to be so strong in the workshop? How did they arise in the workshop?

Gloria: I think they arise spontaneously, they arise spontaneously. I don't know. [pause] . . . They arise spontaneously. Well, here in the shantytown, which originated as a land seizure, we have been living by these values for a long time. Everyone who participates in a land seizure has to experience solidarity, has to be united, has to know how to share. Because there was no water in our homes. You had to fetch water, and so on. So I think all these things sort of arose naturally. And I also think that sometimes it's something sort of typical of poor people [pause], that if you don't have these values, we are not capable of surviving. Which is something that sometimes, these days, we miss, because there is more individualism, everyone is shut up at home. Or now it's as if the ego is stronger, so people are doing things more to boost their ego than to be solidarity-oriented. So things are experienced in a different way, organizing is experienced in a different way.

JA: And did anyone come and give talks about the importance of being solidarity-oriented, or not?

Gloria: No, I think not [pause]. It just happened. And you realized when it was no longer present, and we had to do something to remedy it. And sometimes some problem arose, or was identified by someone, so then we had to see what had to be done at that moment. "What shall we do?" we asked.

JA: You talked about expressing solidarity with others. Can you give me an example of what sort of problems there were?

Gloria: Well, when, for example, when they killed someone. I remember that they killed a *compañera* who was very young, in the shantytown of Lo Valledor. She was the daughter of a workmate from the workshops, and she would participate [in organizations], and they killed her. Well, we all went there, all the workshops set out to go there, to express solidarity, to be with the family. That was a way of expressing solidarity. Also, sometimes, if there was someone who was very much in need of money, we would put together a packet of food, with what each of us could afford we would make up a packet and take it to that person.

JA: [Pause] What other ways of showing solidarity were there?

Gloria: Well, I think being solidarity-oriented in an economic sense. Or if there was someone who was ill, as well, to go and see him, to go and see that person who was sick [pause]. In that sense. That's what you saw most of, in fact.

That there was an ethos of solidarity in Gloria's group is suggested by the phrase "we *had to be* solidarity-oriented with people from other groups," which indicates that the group felt it was an imperative, and the phrase "we had to do something to remedy it" [when solidarity temporarily disappeared], which suggests that groups saw this as a temporary problem that had to be solved. Gloria mentions two ways in which groups practiced solidarity: by visiting people who were victims of repression or illness, and by putting together packets of food. That expressing solidarity was a political act and not merely a private act of kindness is suggested from Gloria's saying that being solidarity-oriented with other groups was a way of saying "we are united." In her eyes it affirmed togetherness in a shared cause, that of ridding the country of the dictatorship. That she actually felt unity with other members of the resistance community is suggested by her referring to the woman who had been killed as "compañera." Solidarity and unity went hand in hand, in her view.

Despite the ethos of solidarity, the reality sometimes fell short. Three women described limitations to their group's solidarity orientation. Barbara said that solidarity was much talked about in her arpillera group, but there was less of it in practice. Teresa helped run a community kitchen for adults in which some of the women who were supposed to participate in the work often did not do so, and Karina experienced the same in another community kitchen:

And one day the priest said, "You know what," he said, "I'm going to close down the community kitchen, it's better. Because the mothers are not cooperating." Because the mothers never went to do their turn. They would send the children to eat there, but it was always the same mothers who went.

Karina's words point to the lack of solidarity among the mothers, some of whom were freeloading and not contributing. However, Karina does, like Barbara and Teresa, mention solidarity-oriented behavior within her arpillera group. Solidarity was not always given, but it very often was, and the intention was always there.

Expressing and encouraging solidarity strengthened the resistance community in a number of ways. It promoted contact with other groups and helped maintain and strengthen bonds in that community; acts of solidarity knitted people together. It fostered *esprit de corps*, unity, and cooperation in the struggle against Pinochet, and a sense of collective identity (see Chapter 7). Joining others during their protests and being visited by other groups, for example, fostered a sense that there were people beyond one's circle of acquaintances who shared the same views. This arguably raised confidence that overthrowing the dictatorship was possible, and helped give people the courage to continue in their struggle. Babette told me:

> *Babette*:　We also did work regarding political prisoners. Yes, we also had a whole, the workshops, the health teams, the women's groups, the arpillera-makers, they all had, well, we had a, a sense of social engagement.
>
> *JA*:　And what did that mean, exactly?
>
> *Babette*:　"Social engagement" meant if you could lend support— for example, my husband was a trade union leader. It didn't matter, it didn't matter— and my workmates went and, and we lent our support for a few days. They lent their support, at the, the place where they were having the hunger strike.
>
> *JA*:　Yes, who was doing it?
>
> *Babette*:　Well, my husband, [*JA*:　Yes] you see? And workmates from, from the coordinating committee went and gave support to the hunger strike for a couple of days. I mean, we were present in all— in one way or another, we were present. And that's why I say, I mean, sometimes we ourselves organized. Er, for this struggle in March, we'd say, "You take care of the, of the entertainment, you take care of the content, you take care of the dance part." Right, on another day, the day of political prisoners, the international day of political prisoners, we paid homage to political prisoners, or we made contact with other groups, other organizations and went down with them together, and, and we did different activities, but all related to social issues.
>
> *JA*:　Yes, interesting.
>
> *Babette*:　We did everything like that, that's why I was saying, everything together, everything was a chain, [*JA*:　yes, yes, yes] one link with another link, and we were joining forces.
>
> *JA*:　What other activities did you do apart from these? It's very interesting. As a workshop, I mean.
>
> *Babette*:　Well, for example, vis—, vis—, visiting political prisoners.
>
> *JA*:　You would go and visit.
>
> *Babette*:　Yes, we'd visit. There were workmates, too, as you were asking, I don't remember any in my neighborhood, but from the other workmates I remember that they had workmates whose, whose husbands, their husbands were, were disappeared or they were prisoners. [. . .]
>
> *JA*:　And these things, would you do them as a workshop?
>
> *Babette*:　Also, we also participated as a workshop.

Babette's words about links in a chain and "joining forces" suggest that helping groups in this way produced bonds, a sense of community, and a feeling of strength. Her mention of "being present" points to the importance of being there to support others, and she emphasizes that all the popular organizations had a sense of social engagement, suggesting that they all gave solidarity. The shared ethos of solidarity, then, enabled shantytown women in groups to know that they could rely on the solidarity of others in the resistance community, and to feel supported.

Ana from eastern Santiago spoke to me in detail about her group's solidarity resistance, and because her words suggest the consequences of this resistance and give a concrete sense of what it involved, I quote her in full. The resistance she describes is participation in demonstrations about the problems of other groups who had suffered targeted repression, in particular exiles, the disappeared, political prisoners, and those who had been killed in the National Stadium. Only one of her group members was directly affected by these problems, having a family member in jail for political reasons.

Ana: We would go to the protests; to the protests. We'd arrange things with the San Ignacio workshop, and other workshops. And we would participate in International Women's Day. We would help the comrades of the detained and disappeared, er, the political prisoners.

JA: Doing what?

Ana: With protests.

JA: In the street?

Ana: In the street. We would participate in the *velatones* [remembrance ceremonies that involved lighting candles], all the activities that there were at that time; I can hardly remember some, but we participated actively.

JA: And did the Vicaría make you participate? Or, or did the Vicaría put pressure on you, or not?

Ana: No, no, the Vicaría never put pressure on us. The Vicaría only protected us, supported us, but the Vicaría never forced us to do anything; no, no, it was totally independent.

JA: And how did you know, for example, that there was going to be a protest? Who would tell you about it?

Ana: Because of the dates.

JA: But how did you know, for example, that there would be a . . . protest on such and such a date?

Ana: Because it's something you don't forget, it's something you don't forget. The 11th September, for example, is something that no-one forgets.

JA: Yes.

Ana: You understand? I mean, no—, no-one would tell us about anything. We would organize ourselves, as women, in relation to what we were experiencing, but no-one would say, "Do this, do that."

JA: Right. But how did you know where to go?

Ana: Because we would make arrangements in the workshops.

JA: Ah, you would organize your own—

Ana: Yes, yes, we would organize ourselves; for example, we would say, "Right, let's go to Avenida Grecia at 8 in the evening." Right, and, and, "And we'll do such and such, and such and such." Where they would make the fires, where they—, the banging of saucepans, at first, so—; but that was something we would organize ourselves, in the group.

JA: And who would organize you? The leaders of the group, or?

Ana: It was us; just ourselves.

JA: All the women in the group.

Ana: All of us, all of us; well, each one of us, well, would suggest something. Among ourselves, among ourselves we, we would organize ourselves to say what we were going to do. And, for example, International Women's Day; everyone knows International Women's Day, and we knew that at such and such a time, or—. Well, we didn't have the information ourselves, about anything, but we would arrange things with other workshops, for the time when we would meet, what we'd do, and we'd arrange things with the other workshops. Yes.

JA: And what, what form did your protests take? Concretely, what was it like?

Ana: Let's see; so, we would go out to march, we'd take along, well, banners, er, about the cause that we were involved with at the time. So, for example, the banner of the—, of political prisoners, of the exiled, of the disappeared . . . So, at the beginning we participated more in the sense that, well, what was happening, we would, we would plan it and help. For example, the comrades of the detained and disappeared, the exiles. So we, well, it was a minority of us, perhaps, but we all joined with the bigger groups to, to, to help. So, for example, all the prisoners in the National Stadium, on the day of, I can't remember at the moment, but we had a day, "Hey, on such and such a day, we'll meet at the National Stadium and have a *velatón* [lighting of candles] in the street." Or, "On Avenida Grecia at such and such a time, we'll get together and have a velatón," or "Let's go walking from here, to join with the other workshops or with the other groups, to go to, to such and such a place," where there was a march.

JA: What is a velatón?

Ana: A velatón is when you light candles.

JA: And, and did you carry the candles in your hand or put them—?

Ana: We would start marching with the candles in our hand and we'd light them and put them in a line on the edge of Avenida Grecia or at the edge of the National Stadium. It was for all the fallen, that's what the meaning of the velatones was.

JA: And what other sorts of protest did you participate in?

Ana: That was the—; yes, that was giving support to other groups.

JA: And in a protest what proportion of women from, from the workshop went, participated?

Ana: All of them.

JA: All of them went.

Ana: All of them, all of them, it was very strange if someone couldn't go for some special reason, but all of them went, all of them, yes.

JA: And how did you feel, doing protests? Didn't it make you frightened?

Ana: Attacked by police, the water cannons; well, you had to seek refuge wherever you could. It happened to us many times that we had to go to the center and we would seek refuge in, in some shop. Well, no, it was—the water cannons would knock us down onto the ground, all that, we put ourselves in great danger, great danger.

That solidarity resistance was habitual for Ana's group is suggested by the fact that they had placards ready for use, for each cause. Her use of the word "comrade" suggests that her group felt fraternity with these victims and survivors, or saw them as fellow leftists or fighters for the same cause. Meanwhile, her clarity about which days were typical protest days and when and where to go suggests shared knowledge and a sense of community. While in the early years her group joined in with the protests of these groups, in later years they also organized protests themselves, coordinating things with other workshops so that they went to the venue or marched together. Both approaches would have nurtured bonds between groups and helped build up a sense of community among anti-Pinochet organizations; solidarity resistance, then, was important in its long-term consequences, as we shall see in Chapter 8. We now turn to the first of three types of resistance activity in which the women engaged: self-protection.

Self-Protection

Partly in response to fear, shantytown women put considerable effort into protecting themselves against the repression. They worked to protect their groups, their shantytown, their families, and themselves. This self-protection was an important part of shantytown women's resistance, in that it enabled their groups to avoid danger and thereby continue with their activities.

Protecting the Group

Using Information from the Resistance Community

Knowing that organizing was dangerous, the women adopted a number of strategies to protect their groups. One such strategy was to engage in a particularly dangerous activity only if they had information that enabled them to proceed with confidence. They would not meet with strangers, for example, unless trusted individuals assured them that the strangers were safe to meet. The women in arpillera groups felt at risk of being betrayed by people posing as buyers, particularly when these people came to their homes, and so were careful to allow only "recommended" people to come. Cristina, one of the first arpillera-makers, who lived in Simón Bolívar in eastern Santiago, said:

> My role was to check them [the arpilleras] over, to do the quality control. Well, to sell arpilleras to people, in other words; to open up possibilities for someone to come. All this was clandestine, so it had to be people who were recommended, if they were buying arpilleras. Not just anyone could go and buy arpilleras. Now it's open, now they sell them anywhere, and they sell anything, but in those days it wasn't. We were very, very careful.

Groups worked to minimize risk if they had to come into contact with individuals whom they did not know. Those who did the recommending, in Cristina's group's case, were normally members of the Comité Pro-Paz and Vicaría, who had many contacts within the anti-regime community. This points to the importance of networks and of the anti-regime community for groups' protection; shantytown women's groups tapped into this community for information that would help ensure their safety. It was often the case that organizations in the resistance community helped each other, acting in secret and keeping things safe for each other. There was a conspiracy of silence vis-à-vis outsiders and an ethos of solidarity within the community.

5.4   **Shantytown Women's Resistance**

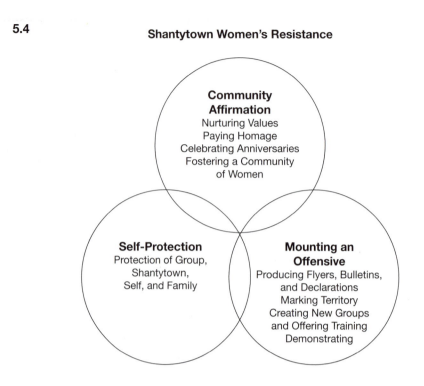

When they went out to sell their arpilleras by knocking on doors, Cristina's arpillera group first sought information about whom to approach, and were given the names of people likely to buy. These individuals would have been sympathetic to the cause, and so unlikely to denounce them. She said:

> So they, they [the Comité Pro-Paz] took the first steps for us, doing *peñas* [fundraising folk music performances] and things to raise money to be able to buy materials, things to be able to— because we couldn't sell our product. So we would go from door to door, but imagine, who was going to buy an arpillera that was a denunciation? So you would go from door to door, but doors, doors that they had given you information about. I mean, "Go to such and such a place, because this, this friend, because he might buy it."

Cristina's words show how, as above, her group took the preventative measure of heeding information that would help them lessen their exposure to risk. They also suggest that the resistance community was made up of a web of people whose membership in the community was not known to all, but communicated as need be, and secretly. This information could be important for the safety and success of cells within the community. Finally, her words suggest that this community constituted a "circle of trust." Cristina knew she would not be betrayed when she followed up the contacts given, and that people known to be against the dictatorship could be trusted. Groups within the resistance community shared secret information and acted in solidarity, and this helped ensure safety.

Employing Secrecy and Disguise

The employing of secrecy and disguise was another way in which the shantytown women protected their groups. There were groups that did everything secretly, and so could be called clandestine groups, and there were groups that were secretive about the more dangerous parts of their work but not about other aspects, and so could be termed semi-clandestine.[262] The women in arpillera groups, for example, kept the fact that they made arpilleras secret from neighbors, yet when they sold bread or fritters as they sometimes did with their group to augment their funds, they did so openly. Shantytown women were especially likely to employ secrecy when they were outside their homes, vulnerable, and carrying denunciatory documents.

The women would hide dangerous documents that they transported, owned, or stored. The arpillera-makers, for example, considered it dangerous to take their work to places in or near the center of Santiago, since this involved walking down streets where there might be soldiers, and so some hid the arpilleras under their clothes. A woman from the eastern zone described concealing them under her skirts when she went to hand them in, comparing 1995 to the years of the regime:

> At least now we have freedom. In Pinochet's day we had to do things secretly, we worked secretly. We would even prick our stomachs because we had to hide the arpilleras next to our panties, actually. There are a few positive things [today]; now we can get together for a meeting here without it involving any risk to us. In those days you couldn't.

This brief description affords an example of how groups employed a strategy of hiding dangerous material, sometimes at considerable discomfort to themselves. While not being explicit about the method employed, Ana told me something similar, namely that her group would hand in their arpilleras "secretly" and "quietly" in the Vicaría area office in Plaza Ñuñoa, which was between her shantytown and the center of the city. The women also hid dangerous materials that they kept in their homes. In La Victoria, for example, arpillera group members hid their arpilleras while they were in the process of making them, in case their home was raided; they believed that the consequences would be severe if the soldiers found them. Gloria would hide her half-completed arpilleras between the clothes hanging in her wardrobe. Another woman hid one in the oven.

In order to protect themselves, groups also disguised the nature of the work they did, representing it as something else. Natalia, for example, would use the post office to send strongly denunciatory arpilleras to a buyer in Europe, and she developed a number of techniques for eluding the notice of the post office staff, to whom one had to show the contents of one's packages. These included disguising the fact that she was sending anti-regime messages:

JA: Was there very violent subject matter too?

Natalia: Yes.

JA: Like what, for example?

Natalia: Well, for example, when they would beat people in the center, you know. There were arpilleras with tires on fire also, the smoke going up, or showing when the guanaco sprayed water at people, all those things. So, well, they were violent. When they sent them, well, they knew how to send things, eh. They would send them by mail, by air mail or by boat very often, things [themes] that wouldn't attract attention, for example, the themes of—.

JA: What do you mean?

Natalia: No, because you see as they checked everything, in those days, they had to be well camouflaged, as they say.

JA: The subject-matter?

Natalia: Yes.

JA: Ah, how would you do that?

Natalia: You would wrap them up and send them, for example, as "embroidered handkerchiefs." This is what you would write on the papers you sent. Because sometimes we had contact with people abroad, we as individuals, as members of the coordinating committee, or as a workshop. And we would send them by mail.

JA: Directly?

Natalia: Directly. So we would go to the post office and you had to do all the paperwork. And you would show some of them. Because in the post office they asked you to show them what it was.

JA: Yes.

Natalia: So we always made up the packages right there in the post office, you see. But those other ones that we took along, we would keep separate. We would show everything that was kindergartens, vegetable patches, and other things that didn't show the violence in Chile. So then when the packages were ready to go, we would put them [the denunciatory arpilleras] in the middle.

JA: Ah, in the middle of the innocuous ones.

Natalia: Yes. And that's how we would send them.

JA: And to whom, to whom would you send those that—

Natalia: We sent a lot to Sweden, because Sweden was a country that helped organizations in Chile a lot.

Natalia's words show how groups disguised aspects of their work that were suspect as something innocuous and acceptable. What she did in the post office involved four different strategies: describing the arpilleras as something innocuous on the form that was stuck onto the parcel, showing the post office staff only those arpilleras that had innocuous themes, moving to the side to wrap the arpilleras up in their packaging, and slipping the more political ones in among the innocuous ones. Her words suggest that she had done this more than once; this was a routine that she had worked out for protecting the group.

Groups also used disguise to make some of their group activities appear other than what they really were to any outsiders who might see them. Groups of women who did not feel safe during their meetings, for example, tried to make the meeting seem like an innocent gathering. The members of one arpillera group brought hair dryers to their meetings so that if soldiers suddenly came in, they could pretend that they were attending a hairdressing class.[263]

Women used "secret" or "underground" venues for some of their group activities. These were places that they and others in the resistance community thought of as safe spaces, as well as spaces where anti-regime voices might be heard. If the arpillera-makers wanted to exhibit their work, for example, they used Canada House [the "Casa Canadá"], an exhibition venue connected with the Canadian consulate, or a theater, the Teatro El Angel, which Ana described as being "like an underground."

Often groups used several strategies together. As well as choosing "safe" venues, for example, groups adopted other self-protection practices within them. When Ana's arpillera group exhibited its work in the Teatro El Angel, for example, it chose to exhibit the sharply denunciatory arpilleras ("strong arpilleras" as she called them) less prominently than the less denunciatory arpilleras. The less denunciatory arpilleras portrayed soup kitchens, people learning to read and write, laundry cooperatives, kindergartens, the "rondas" [children dancing in a circle], and fruit picking, while the "strong" arpilleras portrayed raids on homes, and other forms of state violence or repression. Ana's group would put the less denunciatory ones on top of the pile and the "stronger ones" below. Towards or just after the end of the regime, when the group exhibited and sold arpilleras in the Mapocho train station, which had been converted to an exhibition space, and Quinta Normal Park, they avoided displaying "strong" themes. She told me:

> *Ana*: And before, as I say, in the difficult years, they would invite us. There was Canada House [Casa Canadá], Angel Theater [the Teatro El Angel], the Mapocho Station [a train station-turned-exhibition space], where we went about two times. [We exhibited] in Quinta Normal [a park] on about two occasions, also; we went to exhibitions there.
>
> *JA*: The Casa Canadá, who organized that?
>
> *Ana*: It was an association of women in the Casa Canadá, yes.
>
> *JA*: But how could you exhibit at the time of the dictatorship?
>
> *Ana*: Secretly.
>
> *JA*: Ah, they were secret exhibitions.
>
> *Ana*: Secret.
>
> *JA*: Not open to the public?
>
> *Ana*: Well, for example, in the Stat—, in the one in the Teatro El Angel, er, there we had all sorts of things, all sorts of subject matter, strong, not strong, er. But there it was in a, like in an underground place. So there we had the pretty ones on top, and below the, the stronger ones. And in the other exhibitions it was the same. In the Casa Canadá there was no problem. The problem was if we went out to the street and they caught us, they could take us prisoner. But there we could exhibit any sort of subject-matter, anything. And in the, in the Mapocho, in the Mapocho Station, also—there we didn't have strong subject matter either, or in the Quinta Normal exhibition. But in the Teatro El Angel we did, there we had exhibitions with, let's say, with strong subject-matter.
>
> *JA*: And what do you mean by not strong subject-matter?
>
> *Ana*: The pretty things, the children's community kitchens, the literacy classes, the washerwomen, the kindergartens, the children dancing in a circle. Those were the not strong themes—the vegetable gardens, all those things, let's say, that are not strong. The strong ones are the rest, what I was saying before, the raids on homes, all that.
>
> *JA*: And these, these exhibitions, were they in the 1970s, or in the 1980s?
>
> *Ana*: I think until 1980—something.

Ana's words show that groups simultaneously employed the strategy of hiding, in this case hiding more denunciatory arpilleras under innocuous ones, and using venues considered safe. They also suggest that there was shared knowledge in the resistance community about which venues were safe and which were less safe. This knowledge gave groups more freedom of expression as safe venues meant that the women could exhibit more sharply denunciatory arpilleras.

Hence, many shantytown women's groups operated with caution in several aspects of their work, since they felt in danger. They were operating in a clandestine or semi-clandestine way when they employed secrecy and disguise, relied on information from the resistance community, hid dangerous documents, and used safe venues. There were certain situations that groups considered especially dangerous, and they employed extra care while engaging in them. For many groups, contact with strangers and taking denunciatory documents to public places where there was surveillance were two such situations, that were cause for putting into practice one or more self-protection strategies. The danger and need for special care contained a positive side; the fact that contact with people outside the resistance community was dangerous, and that there were "safe" venues, created a sense of an "inside" and an "outside" to the resistance community. It arguably helped bring about a feeling of unity and a sense of shared understanding and experience within the community.

Secrecy characterized a host of other activities that women employed or participated in, both in all-women groups and in mixed groups. For example, Babette was involved in a group that wrote messages on walls at night in order to inform people about up-coming protests. They would paint the messages secretly, and she would keep quiet about it, even in her arpillera group. A Vicaría employee showed the coordinating committee of arpillera groups in the southern part of Santiago a video of people being arrested and taken to the National Stadium. This video had been made secretly, and was circulating in the resistance community secretly. Gloria was involved in an organization that was secretly intended to replace the Neighborhood Council in La Victoria (whose leaders were chosen by the regime). The name chosen for it was "Comando Poblacional" ["Shantytown Commando"], which was meant to camouflage its being a replacement, as creating a parallel organization would have been subversive.

Protecting the Shantytown

Raising the Alert

Shantytown women worked to protect their neighborhoods by raising the alert about soldiers approaching, helping neighbors in need, and even talking to soldiers. Gloria, for example, would go to the street corner periodically to look out for soldiers and warn her neighborhood if she saw some coming. In addition, she and her local priest approached soldiers to talk to them. She told me:

> There was a lot of fear, also; a lot of fear of the repression. The most you did, if you were not more involved in the church, which is where we created the organization of the "Shantytown commando," was go and stand watch. Some people had less contact with that sort of thing, with that sort of organization; the most they would do was keep alert while in the house, and if something happened, then help someone involved. For example, in my case, living here, the priest told me to be alert, to see what was happening, and if anything happened, to work out how I might inform others, because we didn't have phones in those days; how to inform others if soldiers were coming this way and there was repression. It meant sometimes going to look from the street corner, to see what was going on; that sort of thing. In other words, the least one could do was help. Or if you were, [pause] well, as I participated in the Christian community, sometimes also, I was a little more, I'd go out with the priest to try to talk to the soldiers; we'd go out. But it wasn't people in the workshop doing this because they were in the workshop, but rather each of us did it more individually.

Gloria's keeping watch and informing people about soldiers approaching were activities aimed at protecting her neighborhood.[264] Her words suggest that there was an ethos of helping others and a strong sense of community. They also hint at the women's need to be creative in devising ways to raise the alert if danger was on the way, given the constraints caused by their poverty, such as not having telephones. Lastly, they indicate that shantytown women had third-party support in their self-protection efforts in the form of their local priest, who helped organize such efforts; and they show how Christian community members participated in political activities.

Building Barriers

Women participated in shantytown efforts to block key streets into the shantytown to make it difficult for soldiers and police vehicles to enter. One way they did so was by building barricades. Together with men, women would roll tires out into the road, adding pieces of wood and rubbish.[265] Nora, who lived in Simón Bolívar, told me:

JA: Did you come together spontaneously or arrange to meet in a house? How did you do it?

Nora: No, no, just spontaneously. You know, in those days you couldn't meet, it was dangerous. So as you would see, everyone knew, so if you saw some movement, when, for example, they had banged on a large thing that all the avenues have, there in Américo Vespucio [a large street]— So they would bang it in a certain way, and it was so as to get together.

JA: How interesting. And people knew where to go?

Nora: Yes, they knew all the places.

JA: What would you do when you heard that?

Nora: Everyone would come down, as there are only buildings round there, everyone would come down, each person bringing what they had; for example they would bring tires, things to burn.

JA: To make the barricades. And was it when the police came, or at any time?

Nora: Normally on the 11th of September [the anniversary of the coup].

Nora later added that sometimes there were barricades on the 10th and 12th September as well. Her words suggest there was considerable community spirit, and a sense of community territory, with "everyone" coming to the street with material for the barricades. They also point to the existence of secret messages that the community understood, with a banging noise meaning that it was time to build a barricade, and to the existence of shared secret knowledge, such as the knowledge of where to go. Sometimes shantytown women helped make barricades while the police were shooting. The members of the coordinating committee of arpillera-makers from eastern Santiago told me:

Hilda: I often ran in the street with tires so that, so that others could do their—.

Miriam: Do you know, she [Hilda] couldn't hear, she couldn't hear, she was deaf. Now she can hear because she has a hearing aid, but in those days she would pick up a tire and the bullets were whizzing past her, and she wasn't hurrying because she couldn't hear. A bullet could have killed her, and she couldn't hear.

Hilda: There is a workmate of mine here still, the others have left, who would say, "Hey, Hilda, you have to go there." "OK," I would say, but I didn't know where.

5.5

This flyer from the mid-1980s sports a drawing of a barricade, showing the tires, old metal barrels, and pieces of wood that were used to build them. It also points to three types of activity that went on during protests: the banging of pots, the shouting of phrases, and the throwing of projectiles. A coordinating committee of shantytown groups, the Command of Popular and Social Organizations, produced the flyer, which is a call to participate in a protest.

"Pick up those tires and go there, to the avenue." I would cross over there, with the tires. And worse than that, they would laugh at me. So that was what it was like. Now everything I hear hurts me.

Miriam: If you think about what we've been through, all the good things and bad things, and everything that has happened . . .

Hilda: It was terrible here, what we went through.

Hilda rolled tires onto the street at great risk to her life, with bullets flying. Even if she could not hear the bullets, her involvement, given the police presence, suggests the extent of her determination to protect her neighborhood. Sometimes the barricade-building was a smaller and less dangerous affair, conducted with just one or two other people. Babette, for example, describes putting rocks, sticks, and stones into the street with her husband, to make it difficult for military vehicles to penetrate her neighborhood. Another form of barrier that women helped create was the dropping of twisted nails ["miguelitos"] onto the street at night. These would fall with the sharp part pointing upwards in such a way that the tires of buses would puncture, and traffic would stop.

5.6

The remnants of a barricade in La Victoria, with a tire still burning.

5.7

Locals have used blocks of cement to form a barrier across the street. Young men throw projectiles at a military vehicle.

Marking Territory

Another way in which men and women protected their shantytowns was by marking their territory, making it clear in this way that the shantytown was their space, and that soldiers were intruding, and arguably strengthening a sense of belonging to that neighborhood, for local inhabitants. Among the most common forms of marking territory was the painting of murals, which happened in many shantytowns.[266] Shantytown inhabitants painted murals in teams, some of which were called "brigades" ["brigadas"]. Some such teams contained only men, others women as well as men, and still others only women. Their themes, which were very varied, included imprisonment, torture, death, exile, a wounded peace under threat from state violence, unity, struggle, and being attacked but not defeated. Many contained messages about the importance of not capitulating, the importance of not forgetting the dead, the need for Pinochet to go, the desirability of voting against him in the plebiscite, and the need to end the repression. Often they made reference with pride to the founding and survival of the shantytown, referred to the shantytown's anniversary, mentioned the sufferings of locals under the dictatorship, and inspired and encouraged people to keep fighting the regime. Most murals communicated a strong sense of community, suggesting an "us" (the people of the shantytown) versus a "them" (soldiers and the government).

In addition to murals, shantytown inhabitants produced written messages without visual images on the walls of their neighborhoods. These included messages about the amount of poverty and repression endured by the local community, about inhabitants who had been killed by state violence, and about the community's struggles, and contained injunctions to keep up the struggle and not lose hope. Shantytown inhabitants also wrote messages in chalk on the surfaces of their streets, indicating that the shantytown was a particular kind of space. In La Victoria, for example, huge purple letters on the surface of a road said "Area of Freedom," telling the reader that he or she was on someone's territory, where certain principles applied. They suggested an "us" and "them," and reminded the inhabitants that their community valued freedom, thereby building community and affirming the community's values in the process of marking territory and distinguishing this space from that outside.

5.8

Locals have used chalk to write "Area of Freedom" on the surface of this street in La Victoria.

5.9

A mural by an all-women team of muralists called "Brigada Laura Allende." It reads, "Just go, nutcase . . . now," referring to Pinochet.

5.10

These messages on walls in La Victoria inform passers-by about the amount of repression and poverty endured in the shantytown. The upper message says, "La Victoria 1957–1987 = 70% unemployment. 27% child malnutrition (1–7 years of age). 3000 families without homes. Lack of medical care." The second message says, "Disappeared. Political prisoners. Exiled. 7 people murdered. Expelled priests. Raids on homes. This is why we are fighting until we achieve victory." As the authors remind readers why there is a struggle, it is reasonable to surmise that their goals were to raise awareness, radicalize, and make people want to join in. The messages are also an example of community affirmation, in that they remind the reader of the successful founding of La Victoria in 1957 from a land seizure, despite repression, and appeal to the readers' pride and sense of community.

Protecting Self and Family

Women's wish to protect themselves and their families gave rise to a range of practices. When soldiers came, they hid behind houses or ran home. After curfew they stayed indoors. If their group meeting went on too long and curfew began without them noticing, Karina's arpillera group stayed in the church overnight, putting mattresses on the floor, rather than go home and risk being shot. The priest would come and reassure them. In La Victoria, women worked at their arpilleras secretly after dark, putting black curtains up at their windows, and using candles rather than the electric lights so as not to attract soldiers' attention. Natalia told me:

> Because we were all born in a free country, and suddenly there was such a harsh coup, so tough, such that you had to— to work you had to, well, close everything, have it be dark inside at night, so that they would not come by and see why you had the light on so late. There were people who, for example, would even work by candlelight at night, making arpilleras; in La Victoria for example, which was a shantytown where they [soldiers] treated people really terribly. So they always say that what they did, since they lived surrounded by soldiers watching over them all the time, was put black curtains in the windows, blocking out everything so that no light would be seen, so as to be able to work till late.

Natalia's words offer an example of shantytown women's use of disguise as a form of self-protection, not of themselves, but of their houses (making their house appear to be one in which the lights were out, when they were not). They also point to the women's creativity in finding a way to lessen the danger to themselves and their families. While this and staying in the church were measures women took to protect themselves from harm that came from being part of a group, many women tried to protect themselves and their families by simply not becoming involved in any groups, particularly ones that might be construed as political.

The women also took measures to protect themselves when participating in protests. Some took salt and lemons to lessen the effects of tear gas. Others hid from soldiers or the police; Karina, for example, once took refuge in a pharmacy, and on another occasion hid on Sta. Lucía Hill, in downtown Santiago. She told me:

> But many of us would take along salt, because they would throw those things and, and salt was good, they said, to put on your lips so as not to suffocate with those bombs that they threw. I remember how once I hid with another woman in a, a pharmacy, because they were going to—. We were coming back but the police arrived, and we hid there in the pharmacy. They closed the pharmacy, they closed it immediately. [. . .] So I was scared but because I had— [JA: Yes, of course, yes]. We were leaving. So she—, a woman would always join us and, and I remember how once we were at the hill of Sta. Lucía, and we ran away up the hill. I was really frightened because [laughs] it was a lonely place, it scared us. And then we came down.

Karina's description points to three strategies for lessening the danger while at the protest venue: hiding in shops, coming prepared with a homemade remedy against the tear gas, and running away into a park.

Some women were aware of the need to protect themselves psychologically from the strain of poverty and the repression. In some cases, joining groups was a strategy they consciously adopted with this aim in mind, or that they encouraged other women to adopt.

Natalia, for example, joined a group that met in her church so as to "distract herself" from what was happening. Some group leaders, like Catarina, were aware that groups could help in this way, and tried to foster these beneficial effects. While talking about creating groups in southern Santiago, she mentioned wanting women to forget their difficulties, and described the groups as helping women disconnect from the pain. Both the leaders and members of groups had similar goals in mind when they organized group recreational activities. These activities, which included outings to the river in summer, regular tea breaks in the middle of group meetings, end-of-year workshop anniversary parties, and International Women's Day dance and poetry performances, were the occasion of laughter and joking. The humor was in itself a form of resistance,[267] enabling the women to laugh at Pinochet, and see their own difficult situations in a more light-hearted way. During International Women's Day, women's arpillera groups in southern Santiago organized a recreational event involving Hawaiian dancing and a play, and this and similar activities took their minds off the lack of money and other troubles at home, and relieved their anxiety, since there was enjoyable conversation and laughter.

As well as working to protect themselves, shantytown women took action to protect their families. Babette threw cans of water and wet sacks over tear gas near her door, to prevent it from coming into the house. Women boarded up their windows and put their family's mattresses on the floor as a safety measure, since there was sometimes shooting at night, and soldiers threw stones at the windows to break them, as we saw earlier. They made their children stay indoors after curfew because of the bullets, not even allowing them into the patio. In these small and varied ways, the women protected themselves and their families.

Community Affirmation

Community affirmation, in the sense of celebrating, preserving, and strengthening community, was a second form of resistance in which shantytown women in groups engaged, by way of many different activities. In the face of threats to their community from repression and new values promoted by the regime, activities of community affirmation were important in maintaining the will to resist, keeping morale high, and preserving community cohesion.

Nurturing Values

Many groups of shantytown women tried hard to nurture certain values. These values were solidarity ["solidaridad"], in the sense of expressing sympathy with and lending support to others as discussed at the beginning of the chapter, conviviality ["compartir"], meaning spending time talking with others and sharing resources, unity (within and between resistance groups), equality of treatment (within groups), and democracy. What underlies all these values is care and concern for others as opposed to focusing only on one's own needs or problems; they are social in orientation, fostering collectivity. Some of these values had been prevalent in the Allende era; the value of solidarity, for example, had existed in many shantytowns created from land seizures then and earlier, with neighbors helping each other survive.

Nurturing these values was a form of resistance in that the women viewed them as contrary to values that the regime and neoliberal economic system were fostering, namely individualism, egotism, and competition. These new values were a threat to their own, in their eyes, in that people could become individualistic, selfish, and competitive. Hence they saw themselves as needing to nurture their own values, and they tried to have their groups be spaces of anti-individualism, anti-egotism, and anti-competition. The Vicaría, other humanitarian organizations that helped shantytown women, and some priests encouraged these values in the women's groups, and also in other groups, as when Rodrigo, a priest who visited political prisoners, insisted that they work together and be solidarity oriented when producing items to be sold by him.

These values guided much inter-personal behavior within shantytown women's groups. Gloria's arpillera group, for example, put into practice the values of sharing, equality of treatment, and solidarity. Members shared out donations of food equally among themselves. If one member knew a sewing technique that the others did not, she would teach it to them. Members also helped newcomers make their first arpillera. If a member arrived with something to spread on bread, she would share it with the others. If another was unable to buy food, the others would each contribute what they could spare. If someone was ill, the group would visit them. If a member wanted to talk about her family or economic difficulties, the others would listen sympathetically and offer suggestions. Gloria answered my questions about this:

JA: The values you had, what might they have been?

Gloria: I think solidarity was a very important value. "Compartir" [sharing and conviviality] too, and trying to be fair as much as possible. If food arrived— because in those days food came from the Vicaría, just as it did from Caritas, we'd receive flour, milk, and so on [pause]— so all that would be shared out in an equal way.

JA: When you say shared, can you please explain that?

Gloria: Well, sharing, in that if I have something, I don't know [pause] for example, if a workmate arrived with something to put on bread, she shared it with the others. Or also sharing what we knew; a member who knew more helping another who knew less. Or she would help her make her arpillera, giving her ideas; trying to teach each other. That was mainly what it was, trying to teach each other. Because sometimes a new person would arrive and you had to teach them how to do the work. I remember when I joined [pause], I didn't know much about knitting, and they taught me, the workmates taught me, they taught me how to knit. They had the patience to teach me. So that's what we shared.

JA: And could you describe solidarity a little more for me?

Gloria: Well, it's like being—. It's related to "compartir" [conviviality and sharing] also, isn't it? To be solidarity-oriented ["solidario"] is to be generous, to help others. [. . .] And we would talk about that sort of thing. [They were] conversations of women, from the shantytowns, about how we saw things, the situation, how we managed. There were some whose husbands were alcoholics, it was a really big problem, and we also talked with one of them a lot, to give her support. And there was a lot of supportiveness in our group. I mean, it was a time when people were very solidarity-oriented.

Gloria's words suggest that group members made a conscious effort to help each other, to teach and share what they had with each other, and to keep to a principle of equality of treatment; solidarity, "compartir," and equality of treatment were important to them. This made for a warm and supportive environment, an oasis as compared with the outside world of hunger and repression. Nurturing these values was also a way of creating a space of refusal or dissidence vis-à-vis the regime. Moreover, the values of democracy and equality enabled microcosms of democracy and socialism to be preserved within the authoritarian context. There was a sense among Vicaría staff that people's tendency would otherwise be to forget how democracy, in particular, operated; in the groups it was kept alive.

Velatorios and Other Ways of Paying Homage

Shantytown women paid homage to people killed by the armed forces. There were several ways of paying homage, one of the most common of which was the placing of candles along the street where the fallen had lived or been incarcerated, or in other designated places, by night. The action was often preceded by walking in a group to the designated place, sometimes with a lit candle in hand, sometimes without. Often repeated annually on the anniversary of the person's decease, these rituals were called "velatorios" or "velatones." They bore some similarity to the placing of candles in front of portraits of the Virgin Mary or Jesus Christ, or in front of "animitas," small shrines sometimes found in quiet spots in Santiago. The velatorios were carried out with equal solemnity, and in near-silence. In another velatorio, women in arpillera groups based in eastern Santiago paid homage to the prisoners who died in the National Stadium by putting candles on the sidewalk in a line, just outside its outer walls, along Avenida Grecia.

The velatorios were collective expressions of mourning, in which people expressed regret for the loss of the deceased individual, and so they were a form of remembrance ceremony. At the same time, they were statements that there was a community in support of the victims, which condemned the regime's actions. As such they were a form of community affirmation. The velatorios were also reminders of the state violence to which the resistance community was subjected, and a form of condemnation of this violence. When a woman on the second floor of her house in San Bruno was killed by a soldier's bullet, neighbors placed candles on the street on the anniversary of her decease, which kept her present in people's memories, while reminding them of the violence of soldiers in the neighborhood.

The velatorios were inclusive events that brought in people from other neighborhoods and groups. Gloria's description of people's paying homage to the French priest André Jarlan evokes this inclusiveness. He had been very active in helping the poor in La Victoria, and had been killed by a bullet shot at the wooden walls of his home by a member of the state security forces:

> When they killed a priest, André Jarlan, the repression was very harsh here, on that day. So [pause] when we went to see what had happened and everything, we had to go in the dark. And it was priests—because the lights had been cut off. That's the origin of the famous velatón that we have every year. People remember because you had to put candles out so that people could come into the shantytown. People from other places who heard about it would come, and it was all dark, so they put candles in all the streets and people could come in, they could see. That's the origin of the "velatorio" as we call it, in which every year we try to remember; although it's fewer people every time, who do this.

The velatorio Gloria describes was a moment of contact between La Victoria and other shantytowns, when these other neighborhoods expressed their solidarity. Karina, in a nearby shantytown, knew of André Jarlan's death and the tradition of lighting candles, and on a yearly basis after his death she would light a candle in the street outside her own home, even though it was not in his shantytown.

5.11

Locals paid homage to the priest André Jarlan, killed by a policeman's bullet in La Victoria, by sticking crosses and pictures on the walls of his house.

5.12

A "velatorio" in memory of the disappeared. The photographs show their faces, and bear the words "Where are they?" a phrase often used by the Association of Relatives of the Detained and Disappeared in their protests.

Velatorios were not the only way of paying homage; participating in "liturgias" was another. These were church masses with political content, after which attendees might walk with banners. Shantytown inhabitants paid homage by painting murals on shantytown walls, depicting the words or face of the person who had been killed. They also created flyers, wrote articles in bulletins, and participated in marches in homage of the dead. Like the velatorios, these other forms of paying homage combined remembrance, protest, and community affirmation.

Building Bridges and Fostering a Community of Women

As will be discussed further in Chapter 7, shantytown women worked to build bridges among shantytown organizations. One way they did so was by forming coordinating committees, and once these were established, working to strengthen them by, for example, advocating unity among the groups within them. Five women's groups from southern Santiago came together in October 1988 to fortify the "Coordinating Committee of Caro-Ochagavía Women's Front" ["Frente de Mujeres de la Coordinadora Caro-Ochagavía"], since they felt that some of the directors were "inactive." They created a new directorate, and developed short-term and long-term work plans. The same group also worked to promote unity within the broader organization of which it was a part, the Coordinating Committee of Caro-Ochagavía, by writing a letter saying that it was necessary to strengthen the Coordinating Committee. The women had first analyzed the symptoms of weakness and then thought of solutions, which they listed in their letter. They thought that there were too few organizations in the coordinating committee, not enough effort being put into increasing the number of organizations, and thus into mobilizing, and a tendency to think in terms of political parties, which divided the organizations. They asserted that it was the job of the directors of the coordinating committee to strengthen ties between organizations and save the coordinating committee, and they suggested that the coordinating committee invite all the organizations in the area to a large meeting. These suggestions reflect their efforts to fortify the links between the organizations within the coordinating committee.

Sending greetings to other organizations and attending "liturgias" (political masses) and other events that brought many groups together were other ways in which the women built bridges. An arpillera group in Puente Alto, for example, sent a letter of greeting to trade union members on May 1st [Labor Day in Chile], and when these trade union members had a gathering with speeches in a square in the neighborhood, the women went along and read the letter to them. Chapter 7 provides more detail.

Shantytown women organized many events that aimed specifically to bring women together to discuss their rights and problems as women. The leaders of many women's organizations from the shantytowns and middle-class areas organized a very large gathering of women in one Santiago's Caupolicán Theater, for example, so as to assert a joint desire for democracy, and make a statement about women being united against the regime, and constituting a significant force. On a smaller scale, the Caro-Ochagavía Women's Front organized a "Meeting of Women," and the feminist group Committee for Women's Rights [Comité de Derechos de la Mujer, CODEM] organized a "Meeting of Housewives" at which shantytown women discussed women's rights, women's history, human rights, and other political matters. CODEM also organized large "National Meetings of Women from the Shantytowns" ["Encuentros nacionales de mujeres pobladoras"], which brought many women together to discuss the current political situation, the role of women's organizations in popular movements in Latin America and Chile, the importance of women's struggles in Chilean history and in the present, and the development of local

5.13

The "Southern Zone Women's Front" ["Frente Zonal Sur de Mujeres"] organized an event for International Women's Day, on the evening of March 7 1986, in a park in the center of Santiago.

5.14

In this flyer from the mid- to late 1980s, the Caro-Ochagavía Women's Front advertises a "Women's Gathering," ostensibly aimed at bringing women together, but probably intended as an awareness-raising event. The support of a local church is manifest in the word "Parr," standing for "parroquia," or church.

5.15

There were a number of protests that were the outcome of a coordinated effort of many women's groups. On December 29 1984, for example, shantytown and other women's groups such as the feminist group MUDECHI protested about the regime at the Caupolicán Theater. The banner of the coordinating committee of Caro-Ochagavía in southern Santiago is visible on the left.

coordinating committees. At one such meeting, women decided to participate in the national strike, demand the dissolution of the National Center for Information [CNI], reject the Councils of War, and support indigenous women.[268] In having women discuss these topics, CODEM was raising awareness and radicalizing, but also encouraging the existence of women's organizations, and fostering resistance and support between organizations and between women.

Shantytown women organized cultural events and demonstrations on International Women's Day, and these too were an assertion of the existence of a community of women. Their groups became active sometimes weeks before the day, organizing an event, sometimes in conjunction with other groups, and encouraging other women to attend by producing flyers. The arpillera-makers' coordinating committee of southern Santiago, for example, put on a play, dance performance, and poetry readings, interacting with the other arpillera groups in the process. It was also common on International Women's Day to go to a park in central Santiago, where the Folk Music Group of the relatives of the disappeared performed dances and songs alluding indirectly to the disappearances. There was also more open denunciation of human rights violations, and for this reason the police

Website Link 5.4:
Other repressive contexts also give rise to organizations that promote women's rights. One such organization, Kurdish Women's Rights Watch (KWRW) aims to support and promote women's rights in the Kurdish community, whether in Kurdistan or in the diaspora. Its website describes its work, and the "Articles and Reports" link contains information about honor killings. See "Kurdish Women Rights Watch" at: www.kwrw.org/about.html

sometimes came with tear gas and water cannons. Before they showed up, however, women in different groups had the opportunity to meet and talk, building bridges and strengthening alliances.

Celebrating Anniversaries

Lastly, shantytown women helped organize and participated in anniversaries of their group and shantytown. These were rituals that affirmed the unity and power of their community or group. Anniversaries of the founding of their shantytown involved numerous festival-like activities that brought together all the local social organizations, and nearly all the shantytown's inhabitants. In the shantytown of José María Caro, local organizations, many of which were women's organizations, planned activities for children, a marathon, a procession of all the social, cultural, and sports-focused organizations of the shantytown, and a closing ceremony, and invited artists of the shantytown to join in. For one of La Victoria's anniversaries, Gloria's arpillera group exhibited their arpilleras alongside an exhibition of weapons of repression and newspaper cuttings about the repression, in a "House of Culture" that had just been built with French money. They worked with other resistance groups in order to do so. Such activities affirmed and produced community.

Shantytown women's resistance, this chapter has suggested, was mostly incidental resistance, growing out of their joining groups in order to cope with their poverty (Chapter 7 briefly examines groups they joined to cope with the repression). Some of it was reluctant resistance, and in some cases the women even resisted unawares, at least initially, and some of it was solidarity resistance, engaged in to help others rather than themselves. The resistance activities in which the women participated may be grouped together in three categories: self-protection, community affirmation, and mounting an offensive, the first two of which were the least confrontational. Shantytown women protected their shantytowns, their groups, their families, and themselves, with activities that included raising the alert if soldiers approached, building barricades, marking territory, using information from the resistance community, and employing secrecy and disguise. They affirmed community by nurturing values, paying homage to the fallen, building bridges, fostering a community of women, and celebrating anniversaries. In sum, resistance is not limited to "offensives"; it includes actions to shield and strengthen one's community or group.

Six   Mounting an Offensive

6.1

This flyer, produced in the mid- to late 1980s by shantytown women of southern Santiago, reads, "Woman: Talk to your neighbor in the armed forces and demand that they stop being instruments of death and repression of their people. Your child requires it of you. Women of the southern zone." The authors, identifying themselves as women, appeal to readers as mothers with children in need of protection. They simultaneously condemn state violence and aim to incite action that will lessen it.

Shantytown women mounted an offensive against the regime. They produced and distributed flyers about upcoming resistance activities, put together bulletins with articles about the poverty and repression, wrote "open letters" and letters to ministries, produced public declarations containing criticism of the government, created groups so as to radicalize other women, and participated in demonstrations. In many of these activities, the arts played an important role. While some of this offensive was directed at the regime, most of it targeted third parties, as when the women produced flyers prompting other shantytown inhabitants to participate in the national strikes, or participated in street protests so as to make their grievances known to foreign journalists.

Fighting with Documents

Shantytown women churned out a great deal of written material that amounted to a considerable resistance effort. They produced flyers, bulletins, open letters, declarations, one-page leaflets ["separatas"], and letters to various ministries, which contained denunciations, information, condemnations of the government's actions, demands, and

Website Link 6.1:
Posters and pamphlets are widely used by political groups. A digital archive of such documents produced in Latin America and the Commonwealth countries may be viewed on a website by the School of Advanced Study at the University of London, by clicking on "Gallery." Commonwealth and Latin American Archives Project. Political Archives. http://polarch.sas.ac.uk/pages/intro.htm

incitement to protest. Most referred to poverty, the repression, human rights, and resistance. The coordinating committees of shantytown groups were normally the authors of these documents, except in the case of bulletins, in which rank-and-file group members were also involved.

Producing Flyers

Shantytown women produced and distributed flyers, seeing this as an act of resistance against the regime. The word they used for this was "panfletear," and they called the flyers "panfletos." A dropping of flyers was also referred to as a "volanteo"; "volantes" were small flyers. "Dropping" is a more accurate word than "distributing" when it came to flyers, because the women normally dropped them on the street and quickly walked away, because it would have been dangerous to have been caught handing them out. Locals knew to pick them up.[269] Gloria, for example, as a member of the coordinating committee of arpillera workshops in southern Santiago, would receive flyers to distribute during coordinating committee meetings, and on her way home to La Victoria she would drop them on the ground. Sometimes, however, the women stuck them on trees and gave them to group members. The arpillera groups in eastern Santiago communicated the danger and secrecy they employed when they told me about putting up a fight:

JA: And what other things did you do to "put up a fight," as you say?

Miriam: All sorts of things. Taking to the streets, flyers. You had to go around secretly with the flyers, because if they caught you with a flyer, you'd get locked up [put in prison].

JA: What are the flyers?

Lydia: Papers, propaganda.

JA: From a party?

Lydia: No, against Pinochet.

Juana: Everything we did was against Pinochet, because we wanted to get rid of the dictatorship, because it was too much. [. . .] But all of us would go out, we'd go to the embassies, we'd do those—in fact, there were also flyers that we'd stick on the trees.

These words suggest the fear the women felt about distributing flyers. The women's adopting precautionary, self-protective measures illustrates how mounting an offensive and self-protection often went hand in hand. What the women say also shows how they saw distributing flyers as an anti-Pinochet activity, and one in which they engaged with the express purpose of ousting the dictator.

The flyers were small pieces of paper the size of one's hand, but sometimes half a page or a full page in size, and usually hand-written and photocopied. To make them, the women would write out the contents on a piece of paper, and if the flyer was intended to be small they would repeat the contents several times on a page, make multiple photocopies, cut the pages into the small flyers, and give them to coordinating committees and groups to distribute. It was also common for women to distribute flyers given to them by other groups.

Most commonly, the flyers incited resistance, by informing readers about a resistance activity and encouraged them to attend, while at the same time stating what the authors of the flyer wanted, such as "Food for our children," or disapproved of, as in

6.2

This flyer, produced in the mid- to late 1980s by a group called Feminine Front [Frente Femenino], reads "No more dictatorship. For the right to life: food for our children, decent healthcare for everyone." The "No" followed by a plus sign may simultaneously mean "vote 'no' in the plebiscite." Like many flyers, this one was written by hand, by someone who most likely had not had the opportunity for much education.

6.3

This flyer, produced by the Coordinating committee of Caro-Ochagavía Women's Front in the mid- to late 1980s, calls on women to participate in a march to the center of Santiago as part of the prolongation of the national strike. It depicts shantytown women as powerful, with its image of a determined woman with one arm raised, and it its assertive language, "Shantytown women denounce and announce." The phrase "against repression" is typical of the brief statements so often found on flyers, describing what women wanted or were against.

6.4

Some flyers, like this one produced in the mid- to late 1980s, invite women to participate in an event on International Women's Day and include statements about what the authors and their presumed audience want. These authors, the Women's Department of the Confederation of Construction Workers, say, "We fight together for peace, democracy, and life." They add, "We want to decide about our lives and our maternity!" and "We want to end all forms of repression, torture, and death!"

6.5

This flyer simultaneously encourages women to participate in political action and makes demands. Produced by the "Rosario Ortíz Popular Union of Women" [Unión Popular de Mujeres Rosario Ortíz] between 1987 and 1989, it calls on women to demand justice for the disappeared and freedom for political prisoners, and to say "no" to impunity. Both the word "disappeared" and "political prisoners" are in the feminine, suggesting that this group is particularly concerned with the welfare of women. At the same time, it announces that the national strike will take place and it informs about a meeting in the Theater of Sta. Laura to be held on the evening of International Women's Day. The drawing shows a combative woman, with a star in her hair, like that of Che Guevara or Mao, suggesting that she is a leftist.

POR LA PAZ DEMOCRACIA Y LA VIDA
LUCHAMOS UNIDAS

MARTES 10 DE MARZO, 18:30 HORAS, AL CENTRO

A CELEBRAR EL "DIA INTERNACIONAL DE LA MUJER"

¡QUEREMOS DECIDIR SOBRE NUESTRAS VIDAS Y
NUESTRA MATERNIDAD!

¡QUEREMOS PONER FIN A TODAS LAS FORMAS DE
REPRESION, TORTURAS Y MUERTES!

DEPARTAMENTO FEMENINO
CONFED. DE LA CONSTRUCCION

MI DIA. LAURA
8 MARZO 19°°HRS! MUJER EXIGE:
- JUSTICIA PARA LAS DETENIDAS DESAPAR.
- LIBERTAD PARA LAS PRESAS POLITICAS
- NO A LA IMPUNIDAD
-¡EL PARO NACIONAL VA!
Unión Popular DE MUJERES "Rosario Ortíz"

POBLADOR DE LA VILLA
- POR EL DERECHO A LA SALUD
- POR UN SALARIO JUSTO
- POR UNA EDUCACION DIGNA, PA-
  RA NUESTROS HIJOS.
APOYA LA HUELGA GENERAL
    DEL 18 DE ABRIL
¡NO A LAS ALZAS!
¡NO AL COMERCIO DE LA EDUCACION!
¡BASTA DE LAS AMENAZAS DEL
TIRANO!

6.6

(foot of facing page)
This flyer, produced in the mid- to late 1980s, calls on inhabitants of a neighborhood to participate in the general strike, in the name of the right to health, fair wages, and decent education for our children. It reads, "Poblador of the Villa [some shantytowns were called "Villa" followed by a name]. For the right to health, for a fair salary, for a decent education for our children, support the general strike of 18th April. No to price hikes! No to the commercialization of education! For an end to threats by the tyrant!"

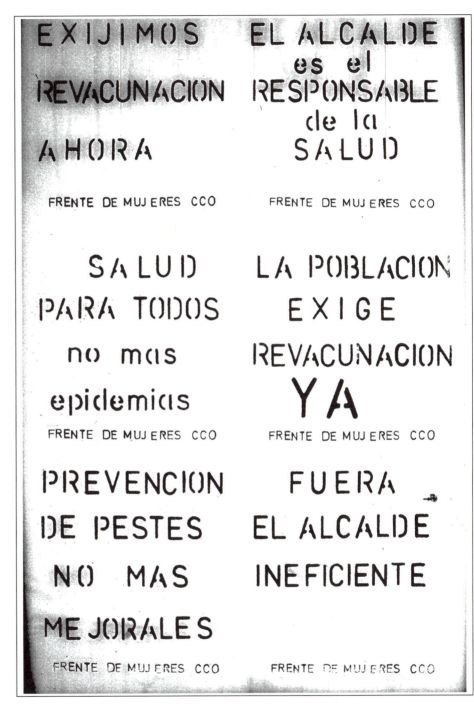

6.7

The Coordinating Committee of the Caro-Ochagavía Women's Front produced this flyer, which makes demands of the state, saying, "We demand vaccinations now," "The mayor is responsible for our health," "Health for everyone, no more epidemics," "The people demand vaccinations right now," "Prevention of epidemics, no more Band-Aid solutions," and "Out with the inefficient mayor." Mid- to late 1980s.

Website Link 6.2:
This website offers digitized posters produced by movements for several causes. It also contains links to archives of political posters, pamphlets, and ephemera. Center for Political Graphics. Click on "Exhibitions." www.politicalgraphics.org/home.html

Website Link 6.3:
Posters from the former Soviet Union, Cuba and China may be viewed at "The Chairman Smiles" by the International Institute of Social History. www.iisg.nl/exhibitions/chairman/cubintro.php

"Against repression" or "Enough repression!" The resistance activities included demonstrations, national shut-downs, International Women's Day events, meetings of women, and expressions of solidarity towards certain groups. The Women's Department of the Confederation of Construction Workers ["Departamento Femenino Confederación de la Construcción"], for example, produced flyers announcing an International Women's Day event that they organized, and also stating, "We want to decide about our lives and our maternity," "We want to put an end to repression, torture, and death," and "Let's struggle together for peace, democracy and life." The women who wrote flyers also incited resistance by telling people what to vote for during the plebiscite, and by encouraging them to make demands of the state for justice, freedom, and the end of impunity. There were, in addition, flyers that drew attention to a problem, and called for support in dealing with it. Flyers, then, were normally directed at other shantytown inhabitants, and many were essentially a call for support for the resistance in the face of a formidable enemy whom the women could not hope to defeat alone. However, the women also produced flyers making demands, intended for the municipal government. Sometimes these were demands for immediate services from the government. One flyer, for example, demanded a vaccination campaign, preventive healthcare, and the expulsion of an "inefficient mayor."

Many flyers made explicit reference to rights. They mentioned that women had the right to "happiness," referred to the right to decent housing, water, electricity, education, and health, and quoted part of the Universal Declaration of Human Rights. One flyer, for example, called on inhabitants of a neighborhood to participate in the general strike in the name of the right to health, fair wages, and a decent education. Another called on shantytown women to fight for their rights, while inviting them to a protest in the Caupolicán Theater. The rights it referred to are the right to food, decent housing, water, electricity, and an education and healthcare for their children; these were the problems that shantytown women were most concerned about. The protest referred to was most likely the well-known Caupolicán Theater protest in which dozens of groups of women participated, drawn from both working and middle-class.

Another "genre" of flyer was the flyer targeted at soldiers. These aimed to make soldiers question what they were doing, and come to recognize that it was wrong. The authors clearly hoped that soldiers would start thinking about their use of violence against fellow Chileans, and refuse to shoot, or defect. They normally had a photograph of a soldier or soldiers in a non-aggressive pose, and a question or request about not shooting their own people. Murals were another medium for the same messages; a mural in La Victoria, for example, showed a soldier with the words, "Soldier, whom are you defending by shooting at your people?" The soldier was portrayed not as a vicious or aggressive person, but as a young man who was somewhat confused or lost.

Producing Bulletins

Bulletins were another weapon of resistance that shantytown women used. They were usually produced by a team within a coordinating committee. Members of the groups represented by the coordinating committee contributed articles, tips, news, poems, or jokes. The work involved included writing an editorial, conducting interviews, collecting articles, acquiring paper, printing, and distributing to coordinating committee or association members. The contents of bulletins suggest that the producers and authors aimed to inform, radicalize, incite participation in particular resistance activities, provide a moment of relaxation and pleasure, and make readers feel better. The bulletin of the arpillera coordinating committee of southern Santiago, for example, contained short articles about the repression, interviews with popular organizations, injunctions to participate in the

6.8

This flyer, produced in the mid- to late 1980s by a "Women's Committee," calls explicitly on shantytown women to defend their rights. It reads, "Shantytown Woman: We call on you to defend your rights: to decent housing, to water and electricity, to the education and health of your children. We await you on 29th December in the Caupolicán. Women's Committee S/C." The handwriting on the flyer suggests that it was written by a shantytown woman who has not had the opportunity of an extensive education. Her mention of "rights" suggests that she and the women in her group are radicalized, seeing their problems not as personal issues but as related to the government, and seeing the existence of these problems as a violation of their rights. A large protest such as the one that took place in the Caupolicán was dangerous and many shantytown women would have been afraid to participate. The writer of the flyer has attempted to persuade women to come to the protest by naming what shantytown women most cared about: not having a home of their own, having their electricity and water cut off since they could not pay the bills, not being able to send their children to school because they could not afford school materials or fees, and not having access to good healthcare since the local clinic often turned people away if they had not begun to line up at the crack of dawn, and the doctors treated patients rudely. The author appeals to the women as mothers, mentioning the education and health of their children.

6.9

This flyer, produced in the mid- to late 1980s and signed "Chilean women," is aimed at persuading soldiers to rebel and not shoot against their own people. It says, "Soldier. Enough vacillating. Join your companions at arms. Fight together with your people."

6.10

A page from the bulletin produced by the Caro-Ochagavía Women's Front, containing a cartoon and caricature. Its title, "Humor: We mustn't lose it" ["El humor: no hay que perderlo"], suggests that it was important to the authors that readers see the funny side of things, and perhaps also that they have a few minutes of relaxation while reading the bulletin. The cartoon shows a nurse wearing handcuffs and a soldier pointing a machine gun at her, and the caricature shows Pinochet reading out the new list of exiles who were allowed to return to Chile, but the names he reads are names of Chilean heroes of centuries past, foreign celebrities, Santa Claus, and other absurdities. The humor makes Pinochet seem less threatening. These cartoons are an example of shantytown women's groups' use of the arts in their resistance work. Another page in the same issue of the bulletin used song. Entitled "Let's all sing together now! About the Pope's visit," it contained the words of a song by the famous folk musician Violeta Parra, which "depicts the reality of our country very well," according to the author of the page. Both the cartoons and song seem to be used to raise people's spirits or provide a moment of relief from tension, as well as to celebrate the positive in their lives (in the case of the Pope's visit). Mid- to late 1980s.

6.11

The front page of the bulletin produced by the Women's Front of Caro Ochagavía, in southern Santiago. The assertive pose of the woman in the drawing and sentence "Women Mobilize for their Rights" suggest both a level of consciousness about rights being violated, and a wish to encourage readers to become active in demanding that their rights be met. Mid- to late 1980s.

general strikes, recipes, tips for making the most of meager resources, jokes about the regime, and occasionally poems. Any arpillera group member could contribute.

Awareness-raising about repression and failing economic policies was one of the goals of the producers of bulletins. The coordinating committee of groups in Clara Estrella/Sta. Olga, two shantytowns in southern Santiago, for example, produced a bulletin called "Shantytown Information Sheets" ["Informativo Poblacional"]. The very name indicates that they aimed to provide information. The first page of the October 1987 issue featured an article about the regime's restrictions on freedom of speech, its constraining of people's ability to act, its view of strikes as illegal, its repression of strike organizers, and the daily increase in repression that resulted in a loss of security for all. A second article on the same page discussed the increase in the price of essential foods and transport while wages stayed the same and many people were unemployed, stating that it was miraculous that people managed to eat every day. It continued by mentioning the excess of wheat produced in Chile, which the government was selling at very low cost to other countries, and ended with the statement that only by organizing could shantytown inhabitants face the price increases and human rights abuses, and it enjoined the reader to distribute the bulletin. This bulletin, then, aimed to raise awareness about the evils of the regime, and to encourage readers to take action.

Another bulletin, the "Women's Bulletin" [Boletín de Mujeres] produced by the Caro-Ochagavía Women's Front ["Frente de Mujeres Caro-Ochagavía"] provided information about the regime's failings, and about human rights. Its March 1987 issue,[270] for example, contained news about particular acts of repression including the beating of a priest by armed men, information about women's history and rights, descriptions of the poverty and repression that existed in Chile together with mention of their consequences, criticism of the government's budget and statistics, and information about the deterioration of the health of shantytown families.

Some bulletins encouraged readers to express their discontent publicly. The same March 1987 issue of the "Women's Bulletin," for example, contained a call to protest and an exhortation to motivate others to protest. This call to protest was couched within an editorial on the Pope's upcoming visit that explained the importance of using this visit, describing it as an opportunity for the Chilean people to publicize their problems, express themselves *en masse* without censorship, and protest. The editorial contained denunciatory language, including "the pain of a people subject to the tyranny of a fascist dictatorship," "an anguished, humiliated, tortured people," and "with the pope's visit, people gain the right to express themselves on a massive scale without censorship." It also talked of "accelerating the end of the dictatorship." With these words and phrases, it expressed in a direct fashion its disapproval of the regime and encouraged others to express similar views publicly.

Many articles were opinion pieces combined with encouragement to organize. For example, a page in the same bulletin discussed the deterioration in the health of shantytown families, and asked when shantytown children would be properly nourished, when healthcare would really be a right, and when recreation, preventative healthcare, and an improvement in the environment would become a reality. It called for women's being organized and unified in popular organizations, so as to struggle for the rights that were their due. There were also pieces that combined news with a call for action. The last page of the bulletin, for example, announced a hunger strike by political prisoners and called on readers to lend their support by visiting them, denouncing their situation, and raising awareness. In producing bulletins, women were informing readers about the negative consequences of the regime's policies, and calling for action to oppose the dictatorship and support its victims.

Making Public Declarations

Shantytown women made "public declarations" in which they denounced aspects of their circumstances that they considered unacceptable, expressed disagreement with a step taken by the state, and openly criticized and accused the regime.[271] The Caro-Ochagavía Women's Front, for example, wrote a letter dated 27th October 1988, in which it expressed disagreement with the high court's decision to chastise a judge who had denounced torture, and called on organizations and political parties to suspend this measure.[272] Another public declaration by the same group denounced the existence of a measles epidemic and demanded that the Ministry of Health take a series of measures.

Another form of declaration was the "separata," a one-page leaflet. An organization called "Women of COAPO" produced a one-page leaflet addressed to women, called "The Shantytown Family," in October 1986. It criticized the regime's discourse about the family as the pillar of society, and stated that shantytown families were lacking in essentials for their basic needs, and deprived of their rights, including the right to food, work, decent housing, education, happiness, and health. It deplored the fact that shantytown families now had to pay for education and health, rhetorically asking how they possibly could as they were impoverished, with most shantytown inhabitants working in the emergency employment schemes. It expressed sorrow that many shantytown homes had their water and electricity cut off, and tea and bread were the only daily food, not even available every day. It accused people in government of enriching themselves, destroying what the working-class had built up, and instigating "State Terrorism." It expressed the need to train and struggle until Pinochet was no longer in power, and then to work until they had built a fair and egalitarian society where their basic needs would be met, and all would have equal opportunities. They would create laws to maintain the happiness of the majority, the exploited. These declarations openly criticized the dictatorship, stated what the women wanted, and pointed out what they lacked, in what was a bold assertion of rights and disapproval. The women would have distributed them as anonymously as they could, and hidden them before doing so.

Scrawlings on Walls, Murals, and Arpilleras

Shantytown women scrawled information on public, outdoor walls at night, creating what were called "rayados." This form of expression was not new; it had been employed under the oppressive rule of an earlier president, Gabriel González Videla (1946–1952).[273] Under Pinochet, the rayados tended to be incitements to resistance, particularly encouragement to participate in a demonstration, giving the time and date. The women who made them would hide this even from the members of other groups they were in. Babette told me:

> *Babette*:   Well, we'd go and do rayados on the wall. Yes, you'd do this kind of thing. But it wasn't, it was, it was more secret, you see? I mean, if you wanted to go, you'd tell people there [in your arpillera group], if you didn't want to, you'd keep quiet about it because it wasn't so good if the others knew what you were doing at night.
>
> *JA*:   Ah, you would do that at night.
>
> *Babette*:   Yes.
>
> *JA*:   What would you write, for example?

```
Á LA  OPINION PUBLICA EN GENERAL :

                                    La  ORGANIZACIÓN TALLERES SOLIDARIOS POPULARES,
del SECTOR CARO, denunciamos y repudiamos  el CONSEJO DE GUERRA, ya que como  o
mujeres, madres, esposas e hijas,  no podemos dejar de  manifestar el dolor y
angustia que nos  aqueja  como pueblo.

                                    POR ESO EXIGIMOS :  que no se aplique el CONSEJO
DE GUERRA, porque consideramos que no estamos en guerra.

                                    TODA PERSONA TIENE EL DERECHO A SER  JUZGADA
POR TRIBUNALES DE  JUSTICIA ORDINARIA.

                                    Nuestra Organización que lucha por los derechos,
no puede quedarse  sin denunciar estos  atropellos que sufrimos como pueblo,
en que no se respetan  los  DERECHOS  HUMANOS : el DERECHO A LA VIDA, el
DERECHO  A LA LIBERTAD y el  DERECHO A LA JUSTICIA.

                             Fraternalmente


Stgo, 27-Abril-1984                        TALLERES SOLIDARIOS POPULARES
                                                  SECTOR  CARO
```

6.12

A public declaration produced by the Women's Front of the coordinating committee Caro Ochagavía and the coordinating committee of Solidarity and Popular Workshops of the Caro Area [Talleres Solidarios Populares Sector Caro], made up of women in southern Santiago. It reads:

> TO PUBLIC OPINION IN GENERAL:
> The organization POPULAR SOLIDARITY WORKSHOPS of the CARO NEIGHBORHOOD denounces and repudiates the COUNCIL OF WAR, since as women, mothers, wives, and daughters we cannot fail to express the pain and anxiety which afflicts us as a people. FOR THIS REASON WE DEMAND: that the COUNCIL OF WAR not be used, because we consider that we are not at war. EVERY PERSON HAS THE RIGHT TO BE JUDGED BY ORDINARY COURTS. Our organization, which fights for rights, cannot fail to denounce these violations which we as a people suffer, in which HUMAN RIGHTS are not respected: the RIGHT TO LIFE, the RIGHT TO FREEDOM, and the RIGHT TO JUSTICE. Fraternally, Popular Solidarity Workshops of the Caro Neighborhood. Santiago, 27th April 1984.

The Council of War judged harshly any suspected dissidents, sometimes condemning them to death without fair trial. The document is remarkable in its assertiveness, with the words "demand," "denounce," and "condemn," at a time when the population had been witnessing harsh repression of protesters during mass protests. It suggests that the authors have had considerable discussion on the matter and reached a consensus, and indicates clearly their understanding of rights and of part of the state's repressive apparatus. With the words "mothers, wives, daughters" they emphasize their family roles, perhaps as a protective shield.

DECLARACION PUBLICA

El frente de mujeres de la coordinadora Caro-Ochagavia
y las organizaciones sociales de la Zona Sur ; frente a la
sanción aplicada al juez Garcia-Villegas por denunciar la
tortura en Chile. Cree un deber hacer llegar su más irrestricto
apoyo y considera increible que el más alto tribunal sancione
al juez Garcia -Villegas por decir la verdad. Llama a las
organizaciones y partidos politicos a exigir la suspension
de la medida.

Atentamente

FRENTE DE MUJERES

COORDINADORA CARO OCHAGAVIA

Elizabeth Henriquez   Luisa Delgado   Loreto Guajardo

Coordinadora   Organizacion   Difusion

Santiago 27 Octubre 1988.-

6.13

A public declaration by the Women's Front of the Coordinating Committee of Caro-Ochagavía, in which the women express their disapproval of the fact that sanctions have been applied to a judge who stated that torture was occurring. It reads:

> PUBLIC DECLARATION:
> The Women's Front of the Coordinating Committee Caro-Ochagavía and the social organizations of the Southern Zone, in response to the sanction applied to the judge García Villegas for denouncing torture in Chile. Believes it a duty to communicate its wholehearted support and considers incredible that the highest tribunal punishes the judge García-Villegas for telling the truth. Calls upon organizations and political parties to demand a suspension of the measure. Sincerely, Women's Front, Coordinating Committee Caro-Ochagavía. Santiago, 27th October 1988.

6.14

This writing is an example of a "rayado," a message scrawled on a wall, written by the national association of trade unions, the majority of whose members were men. It calls upon people to protest, saying, ". . . to the park at 5 p.m. C.N.T. [Comando Nacional de Trabajadores, National Workers' Union] A.C. 4th. Flyers also calling people to the park have been posted just above. The photograph was taken in La Victoria.

6.15

A mural by an all-women team of muralists called "Brigada Laura Allende." It shows women voting "no," that is, against the continuation of the dictatorship in the 1988 plebiscite, and incites readers to do the same, appealing to them as women.

Babette: Well, [*JA*: You personally, for example] I mean, we'd call people to protests. Yes, so we'd write, "Protest, 11th August, at such and such a time." And we'd rotate, one person here, the other there, and so you'd give a signal, and, and we'd start to produce the rayados. I'd do rayados; I remember that I'd do rayados.

Babette's words suggest that because it was dangerous to make statements against the regime or help organize protests, the groups making the "rayados" organized themselves to minimize risk, having someone stand guard and give the signal, while others stood in strategic places. These were self-protective measures taken during activities the women judged to be especially dangerous, akin to women's hiding their arpilleras under their skirts while taking them to the center of Santiago.

Highly politically engaged women produced and distributed numerous different forms of document, of different shapes and sizes, on an on-going basis. Mónica and a group of 15 to 20 women, for example, put up posters against Pinochet, hung up banners, and distributed flyers. She told me:

Mónica: We'd go out here and there, and you know why. It was like—

JA: What were you doing?

Mónica: Sticking up posters, ah, against the president. The truth is that we were against the president.

JA: Of course. But what were you doing?

Mónica: We would stick up posters, go out to make barricades [chuckles], go out to do lots of things, to put up big banners. All that sort of thing. It was a group of us, not all of us. Not all of us. Just a group. It was a little group of about 15 or 20. We had meetings about this too, to plan things, how we were going to do it, and who was going to do it, because we didn't go out just any old how. All that sort of thing. The conversations ran like this, "You are going to do such and such. And who wants to do this other thing?" And we'd agree and, and go out. That was our work. Not our work; our ideals. Because those are ideals, not work. Those we—, were the ideals. And would you believe, I am still working against the governments that exist? Because it is my ideal and no-one is going to take it away from me.

JA: Was it the same people as were in the workshop that worked with, doing this, too?

Mónica: Many of them. Many from the workshop and many from outside. Many from outside. The ones from the workshop, I'd say it was half the workshop. Because half, the other half were afraid, saying, "I don't go out."

The messages that Mónica's group produced were statements about the wrongs of the regime. The fact that they were communicated in a number of different media speaks to the women's resourcefulness and determination to express their views. Mónica's words also point to how carefully planned such protest activities had to be, and how paralyzing fear could be, dissuading some women in the arpillera workshop from participating.

Arpillera-making, in which between one and two thousand women engaged in the shantytowns, was initially something the women did as a form of earning money. However, the women who joined arpillera groups very quickly came to see themselves as denouncing the poverty and repression that they and others were experiencing, calling

6.16

This arpillera, which Chilean exiles have made into a postcard, denounces hunger. Children wait for their food at a table lain with forks, while a woman oversees a steaming pot. The red church indicates that this community kitchen operates in a room within the local church. The women who cooked and served at the comedores sometimes included both local mothers and middle-class church volunteers, which may explain why the woman overseeing the pot has blond hair (blond often signified "middle-class" in the arpillera lexicon). The arpillera-makers made their inability to afford food and their struggles to produce or procure it cheaply central themes in their arpilleras. Many arpilleras depict sharp increases in food prices, children begging, people looking for food in garbage dumps, and small, local grocery stores with signs saying that they would not sell food on credit, a reaction to so many people's asking to pay later.

their work "una denuncia" [a denunciation]. Knowing that their arpilleras were sent abroad, some arpillera-makers referred to themselves as international "pamphleteers" ["panfleteras"] and "journalists." They believed that their arpilleras enabled the outside world to learn "the truth" about what was happening in Chile, when other avenues were blocked by the regime. This denunciation was initially motivated by the Comité Pro-Paz and Vicaría's asking the women for arpilleras that showed what was happening and illustrated the Universal Declaration of Human Rights, for which these organizations provided the women with copies of the document. However, most women soon came to want to denounce themselves, feeling that they were doing something important that also allowed them to express themselves. Some remained focused on the money and did not much mind what they were asked to depict. The arpilleras are further discussed in Adams (2000, 2001, 2002a, 2002b, 2005, forthcoming).

Website Link 6.4:
On uprisings in repressive contexts in North Africa and the Middle East, see the following articles by the Middle East Research and Information Project:
"No Exit. Yemen's Existential Crisis" (May 3 2011) by Sheila Carapico, "The Reawakening of Nahda in Tunisia" by Graham Usher, "Libya in the Balance" by Nicolas Pelham, "Algeria's Rebellion by Installments" by Azzedine Layachi, "A Revolution Paused in Bahrain" by Cortni Kerr and Toby Jones, and "Revolution and Counter-Revolution in the Egyptian Media" by Ursula Lindsey.
www.merip.org/mero

Demonstrating

Demonstrations are the facet of resistance to dictatorship most often portrayed in the media, yet they occupied Santiago's shantytown women far less than other forms of resistance. Only occasionally did the women take to the streets to participate in marches ["marchas"], funeral processions, and protests in squares.[274] These tended to be organized by groups at the more politicized end of the spectrum, such as associations of relatives of the persecuted, trade union organizations, feminist groups, or large coordinating committees. Many took place in the center of Santiago, others in the shantytowns themselves.[275] They ranged from the local to the national; the largest were mass protests initiated by a trade union in 1983, in which hundreds of groups and thousands of individuals participated. The smallest were based in a shantytown. There were days in the year that were understood as days for protesting, and there were standard places, such as the center of Santiago, or Avenida Grecia for groups based in eastern Santiago. When the coordinating committees came into being in the latter years of the regime, it was frequently they who informed the groups about protests, encouraged them to join in, and told them where and when to meet.

These demonstrations focused on a variety of issues, mostly falling within the categories of poverty and repression. There were demonstrations about the lack of housing, the problem of hunger, changes in education policy, and the murder of certain individuals. The women participated in protests on more than one issue; Gloria, for example, told me about a march about hunger that took place in the streets in and near the shantytown women's neighborhoods, in which she and all the arpillera workshops and social organizations participated. She also participated in marches expressing discontent with the "municipalization" of schools [schools coming to depend on local, municipal funds], and in marches protesting the fact that three male leftists had had their throats cut by agents of the dictatorship (they were known as the "degollados"). When the news arrived about their murder, a protest occurred spontaneously, she said; her workshop and other arpillera workshops that happened to be in a training session joined the protest, together with some community kitchens. Similarly, the arpillera workshop of La Gloria, together with other arpillera groups, attended International Women's Day demonstrations year after year, participated in "cacerolazos" [saucepan-banging], and lit fires in the street ["fogatas"]. On days of national significance such as the anniversary of the coup, they marched with banners stating the cause about which they were protesting, be it the disappeared, exiles, or political prisoners. They sometimes joined the relatives of the disappeared or the relatives of political prisoners in their protests in order to show their support, as well. Organized shantytown women, then participated in a variety of demonstrations and street protests for different causes.

As protests were usually met by police violence, the women were afraid of participating. They risked arrest or being shot, and often there were water cannons and tear gas. Nina, who had been in a knitting group in her local church in La Torre, said, talking about herself and her family, "Well, I practically wouldn't go out. We wouldn't go out because the protests were so ugly in those days; I mean it was very dangerous." The sense of danger and fear was such that the leaders of some income-earning groups felt they had to put pressure on group members to join in. Some members succumbed, while others still did not participate. Teresa and Karina were afraid of going to protests in the center of Santiago, and Teresa resisted pressure to do so from group leaders, because of fear:

> Of course they forced you to, yes; don't you remember how right there, don't you remember that Karina was saying the other day that she would hide and not go? And I wouldn't go; I was very scared about that sort of thing.

Fear caused Teresa to avoid going, and Karina to hide once she got to the center of Santiago where the protest was taking place. The leaders of the coordinating committee and some group leaders threatened the women with less work and therefore less income if they did not join in. They tended to believe that it was important that as many people as possible participate in protests. There were some groups in which fear reduced participants to only two or three in number, and others in which all members joined in with the protesting, planning how they would go about it beforehand, at their workshop meeting. One way around the repression was to take advantage of an event that was less likely to inspire state violence, to turn it into a protest march. Funerals of individuals killed by the armed forces sometimes became protest marches, as when André Jarlan, the French priest from La Victoria, was killed and a funeral was held for him in the center of Santiago. Thousands marched there from La Victoria and other shantytowns, carrying placards and shouting.

While they were actually in a protest, the women felt intensely frightened. A woman in Gloria's group was so terrified when she saw the policemen appear at an International Women's Day celebration that she ran away as fast as she could. Natalia shook all over when she saw the crowd of policemen during a protest, but she would tell herself that it was necessary to go out into the street so that foreign journalists would know that all was not well in Chile, an example of how the women sometimes thought of third parties as their main audience. She said:

JA: And until what year did you personally continue to participate in protests?

Natalia: No, I participated always, until they ended.

JA: And when was that, in 1990?

Natalia: About 1990. And of course at the beginning you would shake all over, because you would find this scrum of policemen, oh, it was terrible, it really was. But I would say, "if you don't go out into the street, you won't gain anything by talking in your house, because no-one will hear you." Because if you were in the house and were speaking against Pinochet, who was going to hear you? [*JA*: Yes.] No-one. While if you were shouting in the street, then yes, even if they didn't want to, they were going to hear you all the same. And as there were a lot of foreign journalists, that was the idea; that they realize what was happening in Chile. Yes, because ambassadors and so on, representatives of the government to the United Nations would say that in Chile there were no killings, no disappearances, that the country was wonderful, when it was not like that. [. . .]

JA: Who would encourage you to go?

Natalia: Just we ourselves. Because we would say, "If we don't do something, who will?" Men went out into the street very little; men were always staying at home. They didn't dare [to protest] because they knew that men would get it much worse than women. For example Laura herself was in prison for five days.

Natalia's words show that the fear was such that she had to work to control it, reminding herself of why she was protesting. One goal was to get the truth out about the regime, and thus counter the version of events that government representatives were disseminating. Natalia also mentions that men did not protest in the street as much as women because they were more likely to be targeted for violent repression, another example of the overturning of shantytown gender expectations that prescribed that women's "place" was in the home and away from politically activism (Chapter 4).

6.17

Marchers beginning their walk from La Victoria to the center of Santiago for André Jarlan's funeral. André Jarlan was a priest in La Victoria, killed by a soldier's bullet in 1984. Women and men from his and other shantytowns joined the march from their homes, forming a large procession moving towards the city center. In the process, they shouted their demands.

6.18

Marchers and their banners as they walk from La Victoria to the center of Santiago for André Jarlan's funeral.

Natalia and Natasha, both from southern Santiago, gave graphic accounts of what it was like to participate in a street protest. Their arpillera group would learn about the protests from flyers ["volantes"] dropped on the ground for people to pick up, and from a Spanish nun who lent her support to the group, encouraging it to participate. The women would show up at the appointed place, which might be downtown or near their neighborhood, and protest, burning tires so that vehicles could not pass, shouting anti-Pinochet slogans, throwing stones, and banging saucepans. They carried placards that said they wanted freedom, jobs, and an end to the repression. They also participated in protests organized by workers and politicians about certain laws, about the repression, and about murders by the state. For a time these protests occurred fortnightly, but there were larger protests once a month. Although the women normally set out to the protest together, they came back individually as they became separated in the fight with the police. I questioned Natalia about such experiences, and her vivid description is worth quoting at length:

JA: And the political participation that you mentioned, what did you do, for example?

Natalia: Well, as far as politics was concerned, it was when there were protests. And we all participated in beating saucepans, pots.

JA: What would you do with the saucepans?

Natalia: Go and shout against Pinochet for example; that kind of thing.

JA: The protests, what form did they take? I have never seen one here.

Natalia: No, because now—

JA: Now there aren't any [laughter].

Natalia: It involved going to the center usually, or it took place in the shantytowns themselves, but most of them were in the center, and it involved coming together in a certain place and then, at a certain time, we would start, we would start to shout, to throw stones and all that. So then you'd have a big battle, as they say, because the police would come with tear gas, there was fighting with the police, all that sort of thing. We'd burn tires so that the traffic wouldn't be able to pass, all that. So we'd all participate because it was what we wanted, that Pinochet go, as soon as possible.

JA: Yes, and how many times a month or a year did you participate, for example?

Natalia: There was a period of time when we did so very frequently, almost every week, every fortnight. The biggest ones were once a month. And cars without number plates would show up and start shooting, and things like that, you see; they were very unpleasant moments, because how many people died without having anything to do with this sort of thing? A bullet would hit them, and there they'd drop.

JA: And these protests in which you participated, when you did you start to participate, what year?

Natalia: I started as soon as they started. Yes we were already in the workshops, because all this was started by this member of parliament, Rodolfo Seguel, you see. He was a miner, he worked in the mines, so he was fired from the mines because he was a leader and was struggling for the workers, so at that point he was the one who started with the toughest protests against Pinochet.

JA: In 1983?

Natalia: Yes, more or less around then.

JA: And until when did you personally continue participating in protests?

Natalia: I participated always, until they ended.

JA: And when was that, in 1990?

Natalia: About 1990. And yes, at the beginning you would shake all over because you would see all this scrum of policemen. [. . .]

JA: And who would inform you that there was going to be a protest?

Natalia: The shantytown leaders, people who participated in more advanced groups than ours; so they would drop flyers.

JA: Where?

Natalia: In the streets, anywhere; and from the flyers we would know that on such and such a day, at such and such a time there would be a protest. And people would go there.

JA: And what proportion of your workshop would go?

Natalia: Many.

JA: Like how many, roughly?

Natalia: I think, for example, [*JA*: Half, or more?] more or less; many women.

JA: Who would encourage you to go?

Natalia: We'd encourage each other. [. . .] Nadine was another real fighter in the workshops, but they never took her away, because she would fight with the police and everything, and she was [Natalia makes a sound of admiration] so brave, she had Mapuche blood [the Mapuche were a Native people who fought the Spaniards very bravely], I would tell her. She was really brave. She would end up with swollen eyes where they would beat her, but they never managed to take her away.

JA: And how, did you go together with the women of the workshop, to the protests?

Natalia: We would all set out together, but afterward—.

JA: By bus, or how?

Natalia: No, with any means of transport. Then, to come home, each one of us came any way she could, because we would all end up lost, with everything that had happened, so each of us would come back wet, sometimes, from the guanacos [water cannons] and everything, with tear gas bombs that they would throw.

JA: And would the Vicaría encourage you to go, or not?

Natalia: No, not for that; it wouldn't get involved. The only thing they would say was that if anything happened, if anything happened to us, we should tell them. If they took someone prisoner, if they beat people, things like that; in that sense they would help, but encouraging people to go, no.

The women engaged in varied activities during protests, including building barriers in the street, shouting anti-Pinochet slogans, and banging saucepans, as Natalia's words show. They felt tremendously frightened since the state reacted with multiple forms of violence, including beating people with batons, spraying tear gas, water, or water with acid, and shooting at people from vehicles without number plates. Consequences for the women could range from swollen eyes, to arrest and being held for several days. The banging of saucepans to which Natalia referred was a form of protest that upper-class women had used during the Allende era to protest his rule, during the "march of the empty pots." During the mass protests of 1983, such saucepan-banging was referred to as a "cacerolazo." Women banged away from inside their homes, standing by a window so the noise could be heard, and outdoors, the din signifying their discontent with the regime. Another activity, which Natalia does not mention, was "serving as nurses," as one woman put it, meaning helping the injured after protests.

As well as marches, there were gatherings of different groups in one place. Speeches were given, and often there was an artistic performance with a political message. We saw above how International Women's Day was the occasion for such demonstrations, beginning in the 1980s in a park in the center of Santiago, and attracting women's groups of all kinds. In another kind of gathering, groups might stand with placards in front of a government building in their neighborhood, for example, shouting phrases related to their grievances. These typically focused on local concerns, such as the lack of employment in the neighborhood, and the inadequacies of the healthcare system. When Bettina and others from her neighborhood protested about these issues holding placards in front of their municipal government building, their protest was met with repression, and people were arrested. She said:

> Then, when I was forming a group, people would participate; they would participate. Well, especially when there were things going on here, because in our popular groups our, our mission was always sort of to discuss what was happening here in our municipality. Like, for example, the fact that there had been so much unemployment and that companies had come to set themselves up in the municipality and didn't give men from here the opportunity of employment. One way of denouncing was, we would go to the square in front of the town hall, and would stand there with signs. Sometimes it was whole mornings that they made us wait, and afterwards they would not let us come in. They would bring their shock units; there were arrests. And so we experienced a lot of repression here in the municipality. Also [protests] about the clinic, because you would line up from five in the morning.

Bettina's words suggest that even when people demonstrated mildly, the state responded with violence. They also suggest how participating in groups was radicalizing; the discussing of their problems would have aided this radicalization.

Many of the resistance activities in which shantytown women participated, including both leaders and the rank-and-file, could be placed under more than one of the three types of resistance (self-protection, community affirmation, and mounting an offensive). In producing bulletins, for example, shantytown women were informing (mounting an offensive), encouraging people to express solidarity with other groups (community affirmation), boosting morale, and making people laugh at the situation (both self-protection). Not all the activities in which they engaged were what one traditionally thinks of as resistance, but where they served to strengthen resolve, inform, or protect, they were chipping away at the regime's power, and so deserve this name.

Creating New Groups and Offering Training

There was one resistance activity in which group leaders, in particular, were involved: creating groups and offering the women in them training so that they became radicalized. When group leaders created and ran new groups, it was so as to help fellow shantytown mothers survive and escape "the four walls," but they also had more political reasons.

Website Link 6.5:
Women struggling for democracy, freedom, and women's rights in Afganistan have created the Revolutionary Association of the Women of Afganistan (RAWA). The organization's website contains news about women in Afganistan, rights-related art work, and a description of the organization's activities. "Revolutionary Association of the Women of Afganistan" www.rawa.org/index.php

Website Link 6.6:
The page "What Are Human Rights?" on the website of the United Nations Office of the High Commissioner for Human Rights explains what human rights are and includes links to the Universal Declaration of Human Rights, to a list of human rights issues, and to information about people's struggles for human rights. www.ohchr.org/EN/Issues/Pages/WhatareHumanRights.aspx

They believed that to oust the dictatorship it was necessary that as many people as possible be organized. In addition, they wanted women to understand that their problems were caused by the regime, and to become active participants in society, for which they used the term "participar," meaning to come out of the home and join groups. They also had feminist and therapeutic motivations, although few would have called themselves feminists; they wanted to raise women's self-esteem and teach them about their rights as women so that they would be less oppressed by their husbands and family duties; they wanted women to gain the support of group members and be able to share their problems; and they wanted to provide the women with a form of therapeutic relief from their difficulties, if only by giving them the opportunity to vent their feelings and relax for a few hours a week. Among the new groups that leaders created with these goals in mind were the arpillera groups. Catarina and Babette, who were the leaders of a health team and then community kitchen in San Bruno, created several of these, seeing them as better serving their goal of having women understand that the regime was the source of their problems, and that many women shared the same problems. Babette told me:

> Later on, the mothers had to go to the workshop and, and I learned that by doing so people came to understand that we shared the same enemy. So it was necessary to get together, and what better weapon for women than education and organization [being in a group]. So at that point we started to do, we started to integrate people, and do—, to work on the arpilleras.

Babette's words illustrate the political motivations that many group leaders had for creating groups, namely that women become radicalized. Later on, Babette told me that she saw the arpillera groups as a better way of raising women's awareness of their problems and their link to the regime than the community kitchens, because one could give the women training in personal development and have more discussion at arpillera workshops, while sitting around a table making arpilleras, than while cooking and serving food. Meanwhile Nancy, who created arpillera groups alongside Babette, understood the arpillera groups as a form of protest against the repression.[276]

A tool that group leaders often used to raise awareness was the "personal development workshop" ["taller de desarrollo personal"]. This innocuous title was an umbrella term for various activities aimed at radicalizing women, both in terms of understanding themselves as victims of the regime's policies, and as victims of a system that oppressed women. It included teaching women about women's rights and value as a person, raising their self-esteem (so as to empower them), teaching about the extent of the poverty and repression and how they were caused by the regime, and teaching the women about human rights. When Nancy and Catarina offered self-development training to women's groups in southern Santiago, they told them that they were subjects and not objects that could be treated any old how, and they tried to raise their self-esteem.

As well as talking to the women, the personal development workshops involved leaders encouraging women to discuss their economic and repression-related problems, and subjugation as women. In the community kitchen that Babette helped set up, she drew women into thinking about how they felt about their lives, and about why they were in the community kitchen. When the group turned into an arpillera group, Babette continued this training, having women think about who they were, what they were worth, why they did not send their children to school, and why they were in the arpillera group. She also communicated to them the idea that women had rights and obligations. The personal development training was not always called "a workshop"; sometimes leaders used the term "personal development" to refer to their encouraging of conversations in which

Website Link 6.7:
News, videos, and reports on the different ways that women's rights are violated today are offered in "Women's Rights" by Human Rights Watch:
www.hrw.org/en/category/topic/women

Website Link 6.8:
Like the shantytown women of Santiago, women in Tibet work toward raising public awareness of the abuses faced by Tibetan women in their region. One of their organizations, the Tibetan Women's Association, contains videos about Tibetan women's struggles, an overview of the organization and its projects, and publications.
Entitled "Tibetan Women's Association," its website is:
www.tibetanwomen.org/about/

6.19

For shantytown women who were group leaders, the arpilleras were a vehicle for organizing women into groups, where they could become radicalized. For the women who joined the groups, they were initially a way of earning money, but soon came to be a vehicle for telling the outside world about the suffering the dictatorship brought. This arpillera shows four men, symbolizing the military junta, beating up a woman who symbolizes liberty, and who is carrying a basket of bread for her children, alluding perhaps to mothers' having difficulty feeding their offspring.

women thought about these issues. In addition, group leaders organized "Summer Schools" in which attendees could take courses with different names but mostly involving discussion about rights and the regime.

Group leaders were not the only ones giving personal development training and raising consciousness; Vicaría staff or Vicaría contract staff also did so, as did a feminist organization of middle-class women, MUDECHI, coming to arpillera groups and talking about rights. Shantytown human rights groups called Human Rights Committees ["Comités de derechos humanos"] did the same, in addition to having the women discuss instances of repression. Group leaders normally collaborated with these organizations in this effort. Leaders, then, created groups and worked to improve women's self-esteem, and raise awareness about the evils of the regime and concept of human rights. One consequence was that the women came to see how their problems were linked to the regime's policies, and that their rights were being violated; they became radicalized.

Website Link 6.9:
Articles, news, and videos on gender equality and women's rights of particular interest to young people are available on "Young Feminist Wire," by the Association for Women's Rights in Development (AWID). http://yfa.awid.org/

Website Link 6.10:
Women's organizations in other repressive contexts also use the arts for their cause. This websites contains examples of artwork made by the Revolutionary Association of the Women of Afghanistan (RAWA). Songs, posters, stickers, bulletins with visual images, greetings cards, and T-shirts may be seen on: www.rawa.org/payam.html The following web page contains poems: www.rawa.org/poems.htm The following website contains RAWA songs: www.rawa.us/rawasongs/index.html

Website Link 6.11:
An Egypt-based association of Arab women aiming to promote Arab women's active participation in social, economic, cultural, and political life uses poetry towards its cause. See "Poems" on its website, "Arab Women's Solidarity Association United": www.awsa.net/literature/poems.html

6.20

A handwritten note from a pocket on the back of the arpillera above, which reads, "This woman is freedom and she is being beaten down by these four men who want to take away her basket of bread that she has for her children, the people of Chile."

The Arts in Resistance

Art featured prominently in community affirmation and women's efforts to mount an offensive, often being used to raise both funding and awareness, and having the effect of bringing people together around an issue related to persecution or poverty. Women from the shantytowns, usually together with men, organized "artistic-solidarity performances" whose goal was to encourage people to give material and moral support to those in need. The artistic component served both to attract people and provide a performance they felt it worth giving money for. For example, the Caro-Ochagavía Coordinating Committee, composed of both women and men from southern Santiago, organized an event advertised on flyers with the words "Artistic-Solidarity Event. Enough Internal Exile" ["Acto artístico-solidario. Basta de relegados"]. The price for attendance was 15 pesos, and the money would have been used to help the prisoners or their families. While raising money, it also raised awareness and support for political prisoners who were sent to prisons in remote and inhospitable regions of Chile. The peñas were one such "artistic-solidarity" event, using song and sometimes dance to put on a show in order to raise money (see Chapter 5), but "artistic-solidarity" events could center on other art forms as well.

Shantytown women occasionally used film to inform people about the repression that was occurring. The Association of Relatives of Political Prisoners, for example, organized an evening showing of a film by a young woman who had been shot, teaming up with the Association of Artists of La Victoria in order to do so. The venue was the House of Culture of La Victoria, a meeting place for local organizations, and admission

6.21

Many women's organizations organized activities in which women were encouraged to reflect on their position as women. The Caro-Ochagavía Women's Front organized a "Summer School of Women Inhabitants of Shantytowns," to take place in 1988 over the course of six evenings, each evening session lasting an hour and a half, the venue being a shantytown school. The front section of the flyers says, "Shantytown Women's Summer School. Women have a voice to speak out with and rights to conquer."

The flyer goes on to explain that participants in the summer school could choose one of six courses, among which was one about the position of women according to the law, and another about the role of women in society. While these courses appear to have a feminist orientation, others seemed to reinforce women's traditional role, one being about the importance of keeping the home clean and providing nutritious food for the children's health, and another about common illnesses in the family and how to treat them. The program also included two sessions not directly related to women, but that might be called "radicalizing" in another way. One was about the characteristics of people in shantytowns, how to obtain decent housing, and the laws regarding the neighborhood associations that were run by people in favor of Pinochet. A second course focused on what popular organizations exist, and why they emerge. Three of the courses were to be taught by members of the NGO, Committee for the Defense of Rights of the People [Comité de Defensa de los Derechos del Pueblo, CODEPU]. For an hour and fifteen minutes after each session had ended there was to be theater, song, and film, some of which were chosen perhaps in part to stimulate thinking about the situation in Chile, as seems the case from the choice of the film "The Great Dictator" by Charlie Chaplin.

The authors of the flyer introduced the summer school in such a way as to avoid alienating women who were afraid of anything political or did not like the word "feminism," saying, "The Shantytown Women's Summer School [is] a way of acquiring training so as to improve our quality of life together with our family and to take on an active role in the society in which we live." Men were also invited. As an incentive for women to participate, the organizers had arranged for activities to keep children happy while the women were in class.

Website Link 6.12:
Activists use music as a medium of expression for their discontent with repressive practices in other contexts as well. This article describes a rap musician's work in Ramallah: "Music Runs into Walls" by Ray Smith of the Inter Press Service: www.thescavenger.net/arts/music-runs-into-walls-715.html

was free; this was above all an awareness-raising effort. Other art forms were also vehicles for raising awareness. We saw earlier how an art competition organized by CODEM was the medium for awareness-raising about human rights and bringing women together; one of the rules was that the art works had to be about human rights. Shantytown men and women also, as described above, made murals to raise awareness; there were some in La Victoria that informed about political prisoners and torture.

Shantytown organizations occasionally put on artistic events that were several days long and involved several different art forms. The nature of these events suggests that they would have raised awareness, built bridges, and affirmed community. A group calling itself "Organizations of Clara Estrella and Santa Olga" [two shantytowns], for example, organized an eight-day cultural and political event between 1987 and 1989, involving an exhibition about human rights, an exhibition of "handicrafts, visual arts, and photography," a homage to the Nobel Prize-winning poet Pablo Neruda, a meeting with workers in connection with the national trade union, a play, mural-painting with chalk for children, and a traveling music and dance troupe that would visit all the shantytowns in the area. The nature of these events suggests that attendees would learn about human rights and workers' problems, and celebrate a communist and leftist icon (Neruda).

There were numerous arts-based meetings whose main goal appears to have been to bring people together. The Caro-Ochagavía Women's Front, for example, organized a "Shantytown Poetry Get-Together," which cemented links between cells of resistance; women's organizations in the area attended, as did the relatives of the disappeared and the relatives of political prisoners, while a human rights organization, a community of nuns, and the Vicaría's southern area office collaborated in the effort. The Theater Company La Carreta ["Compañía de Teatro La Carreta"], a mixed-gender group, organized an evening event entitled "Poets in their first Shantytown Get-Together" in the southern neighborhood of Sta. Rosa, which brought poets and other locals together. Shantytown women also used music to gather people together, as when a women's organization organized a "Song Festival for Women." Bringing people together in this way allowed for the exchange of information about repression and social problems, the building of bridges between cells of resistance, and the affirmation of shantytown community and creativity.

There were several other ways in which shantytown women and men used the arts as a form of resistance. The bulletin of a shantytown women's organization included cartoons depicting Pinochet and soldiers saying ridiculous things, thereby communicating the ineptitude of the dictatorship. These same cartoons enabled readers to laugh for a moment, hence providing a moment of relief from tension and restoring perspective for readers. Photographs often accompanied articles in shantytown women's bulletins, providing visual evidence for what was said. The relatives of the disappeared used photographs on their pickets in part to show that the disappeared person had really existed; the photographs were evidence of sorts. Groups sometimes added an attractive drawing to their flyers about events, with the aim of attracting more people to the event. They also used drawings to lend potency to a shocking message; a Guernica-like drawing illustrated a flyer about political prisoners, for example. The inhabitants of La Victoria copied the words of the poet Pablo Neruda about humble people triumphing onto a wall next to a street, where they served to raise morale and encourage people to go on struggling. A poem in a bulletin told women to go out and struggle, serving the same purpose. This plethora of artistic forms and venues in nearly all cases fortified the resistance community, even if only in small ways and sometimes indirectly.

The arts could be used successfully as a resource for a number of reasons. Art-making or listening to music were not overtly political acts, and so could attract frightened

6.22

Flyer advertising an arts-focused event called "Second Solidarity Marathon," a seven-hour afternoon and evening performance of music, dance, poetry, and theater for solidarity. It was organized by the Shantytown and Cultural Coordinating Committee of San Gregorio, a shantytown in the south of Santiago, and took place in the local church, with the priest's support. The flyer asks for food, medicine, clothing, or 20 pesos as an entrance fee, all which would be used to benefit locals in need. It dates from the mid- to late 1980s.

6.23

The Caro-Ochagavía Women's Front organized a song festival ["festival de la canción"] aimed at women. The local priest cooperated, allowing local participants to sign up for it on church premises. Many flyers, like this one, included art works such as drawings or poems. The art helped attract attention, made the flyers appealing, aroused emotions, and sometimes carried messages through symbolism. It dates from the mid- to late 1980s.

Poesia Poblacional

Con el titulo de "TODAS IBAMOS A SER REINAS", el Frente de Mujeres de la Coordinadora realizó su Primer encuentro de Poesía Poblacional, en donde participaron las organizaciones de mujeres de todo el sector, en conjunto con madres de Detenidos Desaparecidos y las compañeras Presas Políticas.

Este encuentro de poesía se pudo realizar gracias a la colaboración de SEDEJ, CODEPU, Comunidad Hermanas Espiritú Santo, SEPADE y Equipo de Solidaridad Vicaría Sur.

MUJER

Mujer que vives
entre tablas y barro
sin agua, sin luz,
sin sol, sin esperanza,
sin un futuro mejor.
Mujer mira a tu alredor
ves tus hijos que
juegan y juegan
sin darse cuenta
que vida les espera.
Mujer que puedes ofrecer
a tu hijo el día de mañana
en esta sociedad tan mezquina
que te mantiene
marginada de los demás.

Mujer, sale, mira
hacia el horizonte
y sale a luchar;
a luchar sin decaer
lucha por una vivienda
digna
en donde tus hijos crezcan
donde vean entrar
la luz del sol
donde florezcan tus rosales en completa liber
(tad.

Poesía participante en el encuentro.

Comité de Mujeres
Clara Estrella - Santa Olga.

Autora: M.E.N.

6.24

A page from the Women's Bulletin of the Caro-Ochagavía Women's Front from the mid- to late 1980s, describing a "Shantytown Poetry Get-Together" that had recently taken place. Local shantytown women attended such events and produced poems, some of which, like the one here, indirectly denounced the regime or proclaimed that it was necessary to struggle. The Get-Together had been organized by the Women's Committee of two southern shantytowns, together with the Association of Relatives of the Detained and Disappeared, and the Association of Relatives of Political Prisoners, an example of the links between groups discussed in Chapter 7. Several local shantytown women's groups participated.

Peña Artística
Sábado 23 - 20 hrs
Parroquia Lo Espejo
Invita: Coordinadora

6.25

Many types of shantytown group organized peñas [fundraising folk music performances], sometimes for themselves, but often to help others. By attending, people were expressing solidarity and contributing money. This peña was organized by the Coordinating Committee of Caro-Ochagavía, made up of women's and men's groups in southern Santiago, in the mid- to late 1980s.

women and men afraid of participating in something political. The appeal of the arts cuts across age groups and political sympathies, and as most shantytowns hosted few artistic events, and their relative rarity made them attractive to people and drew them in. Artistic performances were something one could charge for, and so they were effective when it came to raising funds. Many artistic events could not be subject to repression as easily as overtly political activities, since political messages could be hidden and the event itself could be portrayed as merely an artistic event. This made the arts an effective medium for conveying such messages, and it made producing them relatively safe. Lastly, the arts could arouse emotions, and this helped stir people up, adding an emotional charge to any wish to struggle against the regime that they might already have.

This chapter and the previous one have explored the resistance of shantytown women: self-protection, community affirmation, and mounting an offensive. The most aggressive of these was the last; it involved producing documents that incited protest, informed about the country's problems, accused the regime, and made demands, as well as demonstrating and, in the case of group leaders, creating groups in which they attempted to radicalize the women. Most of this resistance, except for the demonstrations, was quiet resistance, as opposed to overt confrontation with the state. It was varied, extensive, energetic, creative, and ambitious, including as it did the goal of overthrowing the regime. In it, the women used many different methods and media: the arts (drawings, photography, cartoons, music, poetry, theater, dance, murals, and arpilleras), the written word (flyers, bulletins, public declarations, and letters to ministries), symbolic political actions (such as lighting candles), celebrations, gatherings, street protests, creating groups, visiting other victims of the regime, campaigns, and training sessions. The fact of living in a shantytown and being impoverished shaped this resistance by influencing the kinds of repression to which the women were subject. It also produced constraints on the resistance, around which the women had to work. Meanwhile, motherhood affected how the women felt about resisting and what they did while engaging in resistance activities. We turn in the next chapter to the ties that women developed with other groups, and to the women's coming to feel part of a community of resistance.

Seven

Ties Between Groups

Shantytown women came to develop a feeling of membership in a community of resistance within which there was strong unity and all thought alike. This occurred because they developed ties with other groups, including both informal ties and ties formalized as coordinating committees. These ties were with other economically-oriented groups like the ones discussed in Chapter 4, and with repression-oriented groups and groups focused on women's rights. This chapter introduces the repression-oriented groups very briefly, and then discusses the development of ties and women's coming to feel part of a community of resistance.

Repression-Oriented Groups

The repression prompted many shantytown women to join groups. The most prominent of such groups were the "Associations of Relatives" of the disappeared, of political prisoners, of the executed for political reasons, and of exiles. These groups contained both shantytown and middle-class women and a small number of men, who worked to find out about their loved ones, save their lives, improve conditions for them, or raise awareness about the problem. There were also repression-oriented groups that grew out of people's being injured during protests in shantytowns (health teams), and having to endure raids and soldiers in the streets (discussion groups).

Associations of Relatives of the Persecuted

Women who had endured targeted repression directed at a family member formed and joined associations of "relatives," which were among the first anti-regime groups to protest in the streets.[277] These included the Association of Relatives of the Detained and Disappeared, created in 1974, the Association of Relatives of Persons Executed for Political Reasons, created in 1975,[278] the Association of Relatives of Political Prisoners, the Association of Relatives of Internal Exiles, and the Association of Relatives of Political Exiles.[279] All were composed of both shantytown and middle-class individuals, and mostly women. Together, these associations of relatives made up a large part of what is sometimes referred to as the human rights movement, one of the most dynamic collections of people resisting the regime.

The Association of Relatives of the Detained and Disappeared, the most vocal of these groups, started because the relatives began meeting each other as they waited in lines outside prisons, morgues, or government offices to inquire about their disappeared. They came to realize that they had all experienced a disappearance in the family,[280] and grouped together so as to share information and support each other. It was not long before

7.1

Members of the Association of Relatives of the Detained and Disappeared walk past policemen in central Santiago, showing photographs of their disappeared. While their expressions are defiant, the tense fingers of the two women furthest to the left suggest fear.

they were taking action to inform Chileans and the outside world about the disappearances, and demanding that the government tell them where their "disappeared" were. Most Association members were women from the shantytowns, although there were middle-class women and a handful of men as well. Their headquarters were in a room in the Vicaría's building in the Plaza de Armas in the center of Santiago, and they had local chapters in several shantytowns.

The Association organized a wide range of activities aimed at informing the Chilean public and foreign countries that people were disappearing, finding out where their disappeared were, and later seeking justice. These included hunger strikes, chainings to fences around Congress and other prominent buildings, political music and dance performances, candlelight vigils, and demonstrations in public places at which they would stand with placards or banners. They also made arpilleras, which they sent out of Chile via the Vicaría and other routes, regularly gave news about the disappeared to embassies, and participated in political masses called "liturgias," after which they might carry banners and shout slogans demanding to know the whereabouts of the disappeared. The Association produced a bulletin, flyers demanding information and denouncing, posters, and booklets about the problem of disappearance, and wrote letters with information about the disappearances to prominent military personnel and members of the public chosen at random from the phone book.[281] The flyers and placards with which the Association demonstrated almost always showed the face of a disappeared person and the words "Where are they?" sometimes accompanied by his or her age, family status, and job.

7.2

Partly because of the government's denial, much of the work of the relatives of the disappeared centered on affirming that disappearances had happened. One aspect of this work was producing flyers. This flyer from the mid- to late 1980s states that 119 of the early disappeared did in fact disappear in Chile, contrary to what the government had had published in newspapers. The flyer also demands information and pays homage. The large words in the center read, "We demand a reply from Pinochet. Association of Relatives of the Detained and Disappeared." The words on the left say, "Homage to 119 Detained and Disappeared. Seven years ago with the publication of the magazine "Lea" in Argentina and the newspaper "O Dia" in Brazil, Pinochet attempted to describe as dead 119 Chileans who were detained and disappeared in Chile. This was a farce set up by Pinochet." In July 1975, Chilean newspapers had stated, citing these Argentine and Brazilian publications, that the Chileans in question had died as a result of armed clashes with the police in Argentina and murders by their own comrades, in several Latin American countries and France. It was subsequently discovered that these foreign publications had never existed. This was an attempt by DINA (the Chilean secret police) to cover up the fact that disappearances were occurring, undertaken within the framework of a cooperation agreement between the secret police of Southern Cone countries, called "Operation Condor." In this flyer, the relatives of the disappeared were forthright in their condemnation of Pinochet and demand for information. Other of their flyers give information about had disappeared, when, and where.

7.3

Relatives of the disappeared have chained themselves to a fence and policemen are cutting the chains. This photograph was published in 1987 in the magazine of the Chile Solidarity Campaign, *Chile Fights*, based in London.

7.4

Many protests took place in parks. This flyer from the mid-to late 1980s begins with the words, "Everyone to the park. 19th November at 5 p.m. For bread, for democracy, for Chile." The bottom half of the page announces five new disappearances, and contains a photograph of a relative of the disappeared holding up a placard displaying a photograph of her disappeared. The reference to democracy, Chile, and bread perhaps may perhaps have been intended so as to appeal to a wide audience. These concerns were on the relatives' minds, of course, and the suggestion of bread refers to the impoverishment that many of them endured, since it was often the breadwinner who disappeared. Needing to search for them, they had little time to earn an income.

7.5

Relatives of the disappeared protest holding up a banner and placards showing photographs of their disappeared and bearing the words "Where are they?" Late 1980s.

7.6

The Association of Relatives of Political Prisoners ["Agrupación de Familiares de Presos Políticos," AFPP] produced this flyer with the faces and names of prisoners, stating that the dictatorship wanted to murder them, and saying "Let's save their lives." Mid- to late 1980s.

7.7

On March 27 1987, members of the Association of Relatives of Political Prisoners chained themselves to the fence of the Congress building in support of a hunger strike by political prisoners.

7.8

The cover of a bulletin produced by the Association of Relatives of People Executed for Political Reasons. Its drawing suggests sadness.

The Association of Relatives of Political Prisoners is less-known but was also very active, often organizing events in partnership with the Association of Relatives of the Detained and Disappeared, as well as with the Chilean Human Rights Committee, other human rights organizations, and an organization of political prisoners. Its overarching goals were to save the lives of political prisoners and their relatives, and improve conditions for the prisoners. Within the Association, a Committee for Life had as its goal to organize activities aimed at acquiring information and demanding punishment of those responsible for murder or acts of brutality against prisoners.

An important part of the Association's work was raising public awareness about political prisoners. The Association produced flyers informing people about the political prisoners, put on video showings in shantytowns, and organized an itinerant exhibition about the situation of political prisoners at the Chilean Human Rights Committee; it could be borrowed on request. It contained testimonies, photographs, poetry, and handicrafts made by political prisoners. The Association also produced public declarations. In a public declaration dated 25 October 1985, for example, together with the Association of Relatives of the Detained and Disappeared, it announced the decision to terminate the occupation of the church of San Francisco, and described the solidarity they had received. The declaration went on to denounce the repression and the persecution of the brother of a political prisoner, said that the Association would continue with actions aimed at saving the lives of political prisoners and their relatives, and asked for people to be aware of the situation of political prisoners and their relatives. It also organized "acts of solidarity" for political prisoners and acts of denunciation of the murder of particular prisoners, and made flyers asking people to participate.

The Association also demonstrated in varied ways. Members occupied the Belgian consulate in Santiago for a day and the Church of San Francisco for several days so as to draw attention to the repression to which prisoners and their relatives were subject. They also engaged in hunger strikes, chained themselves to fences, and organized demonstrations throughout the year on the subject of human rights. Furthermore, they organized and participated in acts of homage. One took the form of a day-long cultural event for a painter, an ex-political prisoner killed five years earlier; it included an exhibition of his work, a forum on art and politics, art and exile, and art and prison, and an exhibition for justice and freedom of creation. In addition, every Friday relatives of prisoners who had been killed asked the chief of police that the guilty be handed over; in the process, some were arrested. Some of the events the Association organized involved informing, demonstrating, and paying homage, all rolled into one. A "Day for Human Rights," which it organized with the relatives of the disappeared and other human rights organizations, for example, included a "march for life," vigils and velatorios, the reading of the Universal Declaration of Human Rights in different parts of Santiago, and the making of murals in shantytowns on the subject of International Human Rights Day.

Lastly, beginning in 1985, the Association published a bulletin called *Hoja Quince*, which contained articles announcing beatings, raids of prison cells, and punishment of prisoners through solitary confinement, mentioning the response of prison authorities when relatives spoke to them about such punishments, discussing the policy that prison managers had of punishing prisoners and sending them into solitary confinement, and denouncing the repression to which relatives of political prisoners were subject. The bulletin also gave information about political prisoners who had been moved from one prison to another and about the release of a political prisoner, informed about an attempt by the CNI to kidnap someone as they left prison, announced prisoners' and the Association's hunger strikes to protest the repression carried out in prisons, informed about the Association's activities and other activities in which it had participated, and called on people to become involved

Te invitamos a una Jornada el dia 15 de Noviembre. Para recordar a todos Los compañeros asesinados en Falsos enfrentamientos.
Bajo el Lema

"Constructores de La Vida Combatientes de la libertad."

Parroquia; Sn Cayetano: La Legua.
    11 Hrs, Misa
    17 Hrs. acto artistico Cultural.
    Ana maría miranda. Rebeca Godoy. Raul Acevedo.
Comité: D. Humanos La Legua.
Agrupación: Familiares de ejecutados Politicos.

7.9

Flyer from the mid- to late 1980s advertising a remembrance day for executed individuals, organized by the Association of Relatives of People Executed for Political Reasons together with the Human Rights Committee of the shantytown of La Legua. The events of the day included a Mass and an "artistic-cultural performance," pointing to the importance of art in resistance activities. This would have been a day not only of homage, but also of community building. The writing on the top left reads, "We invite you to a day-long event on the 15th November. To remember all our comrades murdered in false confrontations, under the slogan: "Constructors of Life, Constructors of Freedom." The authors refer to "falsos enfrentamientos" [fake clashes] because the government occasionally claimed that individuals the armed forces had killed had died in clashes either with the armed forces or with other leftists.

in activism "for life" and for the freedom of political prisoners, and to give them solidarity and support. It also stated that during the "month of political prisoners" there were many acts of solidarity towards the political prisoners, and described these acts as people's response to the "terrorist" policies of the government, "which uses repression to stay in power, and prolong the state of hunger, misery, unemployment, and lack of housing."[282]

Another association, the Association of Relatives of Persons Executed for Political Reasons, produced flyers demanding justice and punishment of those guilty of the executions, and put together a bulletin entitled "Life will prevail over pain and death" ["La Vida Prevalecerá por sobre el dolor y la muerte"], of which there were 16 issues by 1987. It also participated in events jointly organized with the associations described above, as when it partnered with the Chilean Writers' Association on one occasion, and with the Human Rights Committee of La Legua [one of Santiago's shantytowns] on another to organize a day of events in memory of resistance fighters killed by the state, including a Mass in the morning and an artistic performance in the evening.

Forming into groups brought the members of associations of relatives many benefits. Together, they could confront the state with more impact than if each member worked alone. They could pool their skills, as when the artistic talent of one member of the association of relatives of the disappeared combined with the writing skills of other members enabled them to produce a booklet explaining the phenomenon of disappearance. They could draw on each other's experience with organizing protests, generate numerous creative ideas about how to protest, and pool knowledge about how the DINA [Chile's Gestapo] was operating. It was by coming together, for example, that the relatives of the disappeared discovered that the DINA had first targeted the socialists and members of the left-wing group MIR [Revolutionary Left Movement], and later the communists. Being in a group also made the women feel less afraid, and gave them the courage to protest. Meanwhile, they could share information about support available to them.

Being organized into groups turned the relatives into visible entities that other groups could approach in solidarity, which made members feel supported and less alone in the struggle. It also made them targets for material forms of solidarity, and for professional expertise such as legal help. Their being in groups was also good for the resistance community as a whole, in that they provided an example for other groups, some of which copied their effective techniques, and it gave other groups heart, showing them that they too could struggle against the state.

Their protest activities were successful in drawing attention to the forms of persecution that they endured. When the Association of Relatives of Political Prisoners engaged in a hunger strike at in the Australian Embassy, for example, the ambassador promised to inform his government and outside world. When, in 1985, the associations of relatives of political prisoners and the disappeared occupied the church of San Francisco in Santiago, they succeeded in persuading the head of the Vicaría de la Solidaridad to promise to visit prisoners: meanwhile, the International Red Cross expressed concern about the prisoners and relatives, and there were a great many manifestations of solidarity and support vis-à-vis their demands, including the simultaneous occupation of the Chilean consulate and Red Cross in Brussels. With such activities and the attention they attracted, the associations of relatives were a constant thorn in the government's side.

Two other human rights organizations in which women participated alongside men were the Human Rights Committees ["Comités de derechos humanos"] and branches of the Committee for the Defense of People's Rights [Comité de Defensa de los Derechos del Pueblo, CODEPU]. Both had units in the shantytowns, in which women were active. Their main activities were the recording and denouncing of incidents of repression and other human rights violations, the raising of awareness about targeted repression and human rights, and the support of popular organizations in their struggles for rights.

Health Teams ["Equipos de Salud"]

Health teams mushroomed in Santiago during the regime, being run by shantytown women and based in shantytown churches. Born of the repression, they came about in part because one could not take someone hit by a soldier's bullet to a government-run neighborhood clinic because they risked arrest. They treated people injured during protests; health team members, together with a doctor, often found themselves taking an embedded shot from a shotgun out of victims' skin. Gloria from La Victoria said:

> And what we organized here, well, was the "milk by the block," the "collective food-buying groups," and there were health groups too, that were organized for the protests. Because they would treat the injured. Because you couldn't take someone wounded by a bullet to the clinic because they would arrest him, so you had to be careful with that too. So health groups were organized in the shantytowns.

Gloria's words suggest that the health teams were a response to the repression, manifested not only in the form of bullets, but also in the arresting of protesters who went to clinics. In some cases, as with Gloria's, it was shantytown women who created the health teams, in others, nuns, recruiting shantytown women with medical experience. The Vicaría helped coordinate them.

The health teams also responded to medical needs that went unmet because of government cutbacks in social services, acting in this respect like an alternative medical service, involving shantytown people taking the initiative to create what the government did not provide, as was the case with the community kitchens. Shantytown women complained that one had to line up from 4 or 5 in the morning for "a number," in order to be seen by a doctor, only to be told, often, that the doctor was not coming that day or would not be able to see them. Health teams aimed to offer basic healthcare for adults and children. Bettina, who worked in one in San Isidrio, would see people who were ill as they came in, collect information about them for when they went to see a doctor, and at the same time recommend groups they could join. She would also give injections, treat people, and help them understand how they were meant to take their medicine.

Nancy and Catarina, both from shantytowns in the south of Santiago, created and ran a health team with the idea that it would help compensate for the inadequate health services provided by state-run neighborhood clinics. Catarina explained:

> . . . the lines for the healthcare center, when you had to arrive to [pause], to be in line at dawn to get a number at the healthcare center. So that's why health groups were created, in the churches as well, afterwards.

Catarina's words make clear that there were not enough doctors for the local population at her shantytown clinic, and one senses her frustration. They also point to the support of local priests, and their importance in the continued existence of shantytown health teams. Catarina and Nancy's health team started out as a side-line to the local comedor [community kitchen for children], checking the children who came for malnutrition, abuse, scabies, and lice, before turning its attention to adults.

Catarina and Nancy's health team did not limit itself to checking for and treating health problems; it also provided some teaching and sought to raise awareness about the ills of the regime. Catarina and Nancy made the women whose children ate at the comedor attend training courses about first aid, about how to treat children for common ailments, and about hygiene while cooking. Awareness-raising was part of these classes; Babette, who worked in the health team, encouraged the women to think about the situation they were in, and how they felt about it. She told me:

> *Babette*:   And after that I got married, you see, and I joined a health group [*JA*: Yes] where, where we, we treated people with a doctor [*JA*: Yes], at the time of the protests. So, we would participate. We gave medical treatment, so we would take out the shot, all that sort of thing. And I was living in the home of someone who, who, who was in the coordinating committee, the coordinating committee of this neighborhood; someone who was the leader of the, of the, of the health team, and so she said, "How about if you take charge of the women?" "Yes, OK," I replied, "I'll take charge of the women side of things. So, what shall I do? Well, let's, let's organize the women."
>
> *JA*:   Who said that to you?
>
> *Babette*:   Catarina.
>
> *JA*:   Catarina; and where, who was Catarina, was she in the health group?
>
> *Babette*:   She was in the health team, yes.
>
> *JA*:   The Vicaría's?
>
> *Babette*:   The Vicaría's, yes, yes. And it was the neighborhood's too, because they were involved. In every neighborhood you had health groups, and they were coordinated by the Vicaría as well.
>
> *JA*:   OK, so Catarina said, "Let's organize the women."
>
> *Babette*:   Yes. "Help me organize the women." Because she was an experienced leader. I was just starting out. I was about eighteen, eighteen or just twenty-one years old, so I was a little unwilling. "OK," I said, "I'll help you, I'll help you." "Right," she said, "Let's start." And, and "Let's start with personal hygiene." We started with lice. And at that time there was a lot of scabies, because children were weak, perhaps, so—. And after that we saw that the women, well, were capable of doing other things, and we saw that they were very keen to do new things, so I started to learn about the arpilleras, and I started teaching arpillera-making.

Babette's account suggests how widespread health teams were. Health teams had indeed mushroomed in the shantytowns; according to the research institute Sur Profesionales (1985), there were 22 health groups in 1982 and 72 in 1984. Babette's account also points to the existence of coordinating committees of health teams and to the Vicaría's assistance with creating the links between health teams. Babette's words shed light on shantytown women's organizing more broadly as well. Her mention of Catarina's suggesting that she organize the women by teaching them about health problems shows how interested group leaders were in helping women solve their problems and in bringing them together, or "organizing them," as Babette puts it. They also offer examples of how one shantytown women's group could grow out of another, and of how much shantytown women valued learning, not having had the opportunity for much education while growing up. Babette's team realized that women had mental health problems, primarily anxiety and despair, and with this in mind they created arpillera workshops, thinking that these would help the women relax and earn some money. They gave the women in the arpillera workshops training on health and "personal development," and encouraged discussion about state violence and the women's anguish.

Discussion Groups

Women formed and joined discussion groups in which they tried to understand the repression. One such group was created in San Isidrio, a shantytown in northern Santiago, and in it, women both discussed their situation and listened to talks by professionals about the economy and other matters relevant to their poverty. Bettina had accepted an invitation to join this group because she wanted to understand why her home had been raided by soldiers, and why there was repression. Referring to it as a "grupo popular" [popular group], she told me:

Bettina: And after that they invited me, someone invited me, because they were getting together in the chapel, with the support of the Vicaría. They came to invite me to participate in a group of women.

JA: And who came to invite you?

Bettina: A, a woman who, who had already, who had started; and she had been invited by the Vicaría. A woman came to invite me; a neighbor, rather, a neighbor from, from here, from the community. So she said that she had come to invite me to participate, if I wanted, in a group of women, a popular group, and so on. I had had experience of groups before, in a mothers' center, you see; a mothers' center, which is different from popular groups because in mothers' centers you just learn to make things with your hands, you see? And you have tea and save up money to, to go on, on an outing, that's a mothers' center. But the point of popular groups was to go and discuss what was happening in each of our lives. It was to take up a topic related to development. Like, for example, that first time, when I arrived in that group, the topic was economic, about economics, and there was an economics teacher teaching that topic. And I remember it so well; he drew a circle, and that circle was divided up, and we realized that health had a little bit of money, of resources, this other part had a little, and so on, but what had most was the part that the government administered. And we started to, I mean I at any rate, started to become very interested, because my house had already been raided. In those days I was not participating in, in social matters, or political things, or anything, I was a mother and housewife. So I was interested in a lot of things, and with the raid this desire to know why awoke in me. Why this? Why that? And so on . . . So on that occasion I found that the topics that were being discussed were topics that really interested me a lot. And from that point on I started to give my opinion, I started to, to participate in a way—absolutely fully. And within one month of having joined they choose me as president of the group. So, well, I started to, to take on the fact that I was president of the group and to participate a lot more, and later, more or less in 1980—, let's see?

JA: Sorry, the group, was it an arpillera group?

Bettina: No, it was not an arpillera group yet, it was a group of women. They were called popular groups. It was just to go and reflect, to discuss topics and so on. And so more or less in, I'm talking about '74, '75, they invite us to receive training in arpillera-making. Because already by that stage there was a lot of unemployment. We were already doing the olla común, you see. And we were also, well, looking for ways to subsist because people—; you see, the Vicaría did an exercise with us, before the arpilleras, it did an exercise with us so that we might grow and so that there might be a lot, a lot of empowerment, among us. And it gave us a number of surveys to do, surveys to see how our people were surviving, our families. So we had to conduct the surveys with, with our neighbors, with the people from here, from the community. More or less ten surveys each. And in the process of conducting the surveys there was a huge amount of personal growth, because we realized that there were lots of neighbors, lots of people who were surviving thanks to garbage dumps. . . . Others lived prostituting themselves as well, so, trying to work in ways that were not right. And for us it was tough to recognize that these were our people, and that they lived in these conditions. And at that point the Vicaría gives us the chance to learn this skill, to make arpilleras.

As Bettina's description shows, her group discussed development, the national budget, what was happening in members' lives, and how people in their neighborhood were making ends meet. They were being radicalized in the process, as is suggested by what Bettina says about coming to see that people were surviving thanks to garbage dumps, prostituting themselves, and trying to work in ways that "were not right." The Vicaría supported this radicalization process both by sending professionals to the group to explain about economic policy and other matters, and by encouraging the women to conduct a survey of their neighborhood; it then initiated the arpillera group. The local priest was supportive as well, allowing the group to meet in his chapel. What Bettina says she valued from the group was coming to understand the repression, and learning.

There were many other discussion groups in the shantytowns, most of these having a religious focus, being called, typically, "comunidades cristianas" ["Christian communities," or in scholarly analyses, "Christian Base Communities"]. These were small groups that met at their local church to discuss the Bible, often making links between what they read and their own lives and misfortunes.[283] They put on additional activities as well. So as to raise money for a young woman from the shantytowns who had been burned by soldiers and had almost died, for example, the Council of Christian Communities of Valledor Norte organized a fundraising evening of folk music and dance that people would pay to attend. There were still other religious discussion groups of which shantytown women were a part, such as the Workers' Pastoral Association, in which members discussed the economic, political and social situation in Chile with an emphasis on the situation of the worker, and leftist, Catholic groups, such as the Catholic Action Workers' Movement ["Movimiento Obrero de Acción Católica"].

Besides the discussion groups, health teams, and associations of relatives, there were still other groups whose goal was to cope with the repression. Human Rights Committees [Comités de Derechos Humanos] were present in many shantytowns, keeping track of the repression locally, and raising awareness about all forms of human rights violation. They produced flyers containing testimonies about human rights violations that had occurred in the area and demands for justice. They also organized remembrance days ["jornadas"] for fellow anti-regime activists killed by the state. One such day, organized by the Human Rights Committee of the shantytown of La Legua together with the Association of Relatives of Persons Executed for Political Reasons, had as its purpose to remember "comrades murdered in fake clashes." The local priest lent his support; the event took place in La Legua's church, and included a Mass at 11 a.m. There was also an artistic performance in the evening.

A group called the Rosario Ortíz Popular Union of Women [Unión Popular de Mujeres Rosario Ortíz] encouraged women to participate in various forms of protest in connection with the victims of repression. It produced flyers enjoining women to demand justice and freedom for the disappeared and political prisoners, and say "No" to impunity. The same flyers also announced that the national strike was on and that there would be a meeting of women in the Theater of Sta. Laura on International Women's Day.

Other Groups

Women-Focused Groups

Shantytown women formed and joined groups focused on women's rights or women's issues.[284] The "Committee for the Defense of Women's rights" ["Comité de Defensa de los Derechos de la Mujer," CODEM] was an organization with branches and members in shantytowns in just over a dozen of Chile's cities, and there was even a branch in the exile community of Grenoble, France.[285] Created in 1981, CODEM's main goal was for women to become active subjects in society and autonomous, as opposed to shut up at home in their traditional roles, subjugated by "machismo," as Briant (1987) put it. CODEM also aimed for a society in which women's rights would be recognized and ensured, struggled against machismo and a traditional conception of men and women's roles, and aimed to fight side by side with men against the dictatorship and human rights violations. Its leaders thought it necessary for some of these goals to be achieved that women emerge from their homes, join groups, receive training, and work for an income. In Santiago's shantytowns, members organized events aimed at raising women's awareness of their rights as women, as well as their understanding of human rights more broadly. The art competition discussed earlier, advertised as a get-together for housewives but encouraging the production of art on the subject of human rights, was one such event. CODEM members also visited female political prisoners, organized "chocolatadas" [yearly events in which local mothers organized to acquire and give chocolate to children] in the shantytowns, and produced a bulletin containing articles about women's situation and rights, including their "sexual rights." CODEM was raided at least once, in Concepción, Chile's main southern city, in 1986.[286]

There were also "Women's Committees" in several shantytowns, and women's units within trade union federations, such as the Women's Department in the Confederation of Construction Workers ["Departamento Femenino Confederación de la Construcción"]. In the latter years of the regime, Casas de la Mujer [literally "women's homes," that is, women's centers] started appearing in the shantytowns. They offered local women training in "personal development," aspects of women's lives such as female sexuality and menopause, handicraft-making, and other skills. Some also offered day care. Women created these centers with the aim of training women and raising their self-esteem. They were normally set up and run by shantytown women who were aware of women's rights and barriers to equality between men and women. One staff member, for example, told me that the staff of her Casa de la Mujer saw Chilean society as "machista" and husbands as authoritarian and violent; she wanted to help women value themselves as people and gain a sense of their rights. The Casas de la Mujer normally had NGO support and funding, and sometimes NGO staff conducted the training.

Political Parties

It was common for the shantytown women with whom I spoke to disapprove of political parties. Parties of the Left continued to operate despite Pinochet's ban, albeit in a clandestine fashion, as did political groups such as the Revolutionary Left Movement [Movimiento de Izquierda Revolucionaria, MIR] and the armed unit of the communist party, the Manuel Rodríguez Patriotic Front [Frente Patriótico Manuel Rodríguez].[287] Most of these women had not been members of parties or of other overtly political organizations, and even women whose husbands were members of left-wing parties or trade unions were not themselves involved in such organizations. Teresa, like many other women, stressed her non-involvement, using the word "politics," by which women typically meant political parties and their activities:

> *Teresa*:   Here well, I am passive, I don't get involved in anything. But some [women] are political and they like to get involved in politics. Not many, not many. There is no-one who is really, really political [in her arpillera group]. [. . .]
>
> *JA*:   Were you in some political party?
>
> *Teresa*:   No.
>
> *JA*:   Why don't you like politics?
>
> *Teresa*:   Well, because politics, well, we have never sort of, no-one in the family has liked politics.

Teresa's saying that she does not like to be involved in politics and is not political was typical of the shantytown women I spoke to, even if they were engaging in other kinds of political behavior such as producing and distributing denunciatory documents or arpilleras. Fabiola, a younger, single woman from southern Santiago, also described herself as "not involved in politics":

> We are not involved in politics, on any side. We have not been involved, in my family. We don't know any more about politics than what you see on television and from what I have heard from the women in the workshop. The workshop is where I have learned more about politics, really; more so than from the television. [. . .] And about politics I can't give an opinion, because we have never been political.

The conversation in shantytown women's groups enabled women to come to understand more about politics, and they valued this. Fabiola's manner of speaking suggests that she was not ashamed about not being "political."

Many organized shantytown women were reluctant to be members of political parties because they saw them as insincere and mercenary, and were suspicious of them.[288] Barbara, for example, thought that political party leaders took advantage of people, as they had of her mother who had come to Santiago from the saltpeter mining towns in Northern Chile:

> *Barbara*:   My mother always went around selling *El Siglo* [the communist newspaper], and, and doing raffles and that kind of thing, so he [Barbara's husband] says that I, I'm the same as my mother. And I'm not because I don't, I tell him I'm not involved in any party, or anything. My mother was, she had always liked that sort of thing; the whole family was always in favor of the communist party, always.
>
> *JA*:   And you, never.
>
> *Barbara*:   I didn't like it, I didn't like it.
>
> *JA*:   Why?
>
> Barbara: Because I have always had bad experiences with people. There are good people, like —. For example, my mother didn't know how to read or write. That's why they would send her to, to drop flyers and that kind of thing. And people with, with more education, and all that, all the more so, and they always liked to order others about, to order them to do things, then they ordered— . . . Because of that experience I have never liked it. I mean, if I have to vote, when it is time to vote I will have to vote. But I have never liked the ideas they have. Because I saw what the democracy was and I know that you always have to—; to have something, you

Website Link 7.2:
Another context in which women's levels of civic engagement is low is Morocco. There, women exhibit low participation rates in civic or political organizations, and few women take part in activities to express their views on social and political issues. See "The Status of Women in the Middle East and North Africa (SWMENA) Project. Focus on Morocco. Civic and Political Participation Topic Brief" by the International Foundation for Electoral Systems and Institute for Women's Policy Research.
www.iwpr.org/initiatives/swmena

always have to work, you have to, you have to earn something, working. Working. Working honestly. And they, no, it seems that they want things to be, to be given to them, to be given to them. So I don't like that. Because I know that when something requires an effort, you value it. But if it doesn't require an effort, you don't value it. So I think it's—and I have always seen things that are sort of, that, that there are people who put on airs as if they have had to work hard, and that it's people from the shantytowns who go out and, and fight, and go out to, to complain and protest, and then others say, "We did this, that, and the other." I don't like it, I have never liked that; I have never liked those things. That's why I have never liked it. Yes in, in, for example if they had an election here for, for a mayor, and there was someone from the communist party and from the UDI, and from Renovación Nacional [both right-wing parties], and there was only one from the communist party and no-one else, I would vote for the communist. Before voting for the UDI or for right wing parties. I would vote.

JA: But do you feel more left-wing than right-wing?

Barbara: Right-wing, never, with what I have lived through; with what I have lived through, no.

Barbara, like several shantytown women, was critical of political party leaders, seeing them as ordering people about, wanting things to be given to them, putting on airs, and taking credit for things shantytown inhabitants did. Similarly to Barbara, Nina of La Torre, who had been the president of a knitting group at her local church, as well as of another knitting group and an electricity services group, said "I just have an opinion [political opinion]. But no, I do not get involved in parties."

Barbara's words about having to work are an expression of the common view among shantytown women that no matter which party is governing, one has to work hard to survive. The shantytown women I spoke to mostly believed that parties did not really change anything in people's lives. I discussed this with Francesca, from Fraternidad:

JA: Did you participate in a party, or not?

Francesca: No, it doesn't interest us. We're fed up with politics. Ultimately, whichever party wins, you have to work really hard.

That life was the same regardless of which party won was a common sentiment at the time of my 1995 interviews, along with the idea that politics was dirty and politicians deceitful, and that women in shantytowns had been tricked by political parties in some way.

There were barriers to political party membership for shantytown women, quite apart from their own suspicion and negative experiences. Shantytown gender expectations dictated that men, not women, be members of parties. There is a hint of this in Barbara's husband's accusing her of being involved in political matters. Another barrier was the fear of being involved in anything political,[289] or in any kind of organization. In some workshops there was a taboo about pushing party politics onto other group members. There was also pride associated with being independent of a party, even if there was acknowledgment that one or two group members were party members. Several groups emphasized that they participated in protests as members of their group, "without a color" [party affiliation], or said that they went to protests of their own accord. Taboos, fear, gender expectations, and pride at one's independence made for formidable obstacles to party participation. Nevertheless, there were, of course, shantytown women who were "involved in politics"; Fernanda from southern Santiago, for example, had been part of an overtly political left-wing group, but kept her membership secret to almost all her arpillera group colleagues even five years after Pinochet stepped down, and did not reveal it to me.

In addition to the repression-oriented groups, women-focused groups, and economically-oriented groups discussed in Chapter 4, there were other groups that counted shantytown women among their members, but whose members were mostly men. These included groups of young people in the shantytown,[290] underground trade unions,[291] and groups effectively replacing the Pinochet-dominated Neighborhood Associations [Juntas de Vecinos]. Gloria, for example, was in the "Comando Poblacional" [Shantytown Commando] of La Victoria. This group, created as an alternative to the Neighborhood Association, would hold meetings to organize marches and other events, and discuss matters pertinent to the shantytown, such as what had happened during recent protests or raids. The Commando also organized milk distribution, joint purchasing groups, and health groups that would tend to the injured after a protest. Women like Gloria became less afraid of political groups or simply had more exposure to political groups as a result of joining her first group, a knitting group that became an arpillera group, and this may have made it easier for her to take the step of joining the more combative Commando.

Ties Between Groups: A Resistance Community

Coordinating Committees: "Coordinadoras"

Many shantytown women's food-procuring, income-generating, and other groups joined together, forming umbrella organizations, or coordinating committees, called "coordinaciones," or more commonly "coordinadoras."[292] These consisted of one or two representatives from each group, out of a total of five to 12 groups. There would be a coordinating committee meeting once a month, normally. The groups represented in the coordinating committee were typically from the same area of the city and engaged in the same activity; for example, 12 arpillera groups in the "southern zone" of Santiago formed a coordinating committee of arpillera groups. There were also, however, coordinating committees made up of different types of group in the same area; these might bring together bolsas de cesantes, a health team, an Alcoholics Anonymous group, groups of young people, and arpillera groups, for example. Lastly, there were coordinating committees at the metropolitan and national levels. MOMUPO ["Movimiento de Mujeres Pobladoras," Shantytown Women's Movement] was one such organization, bringing together shantytown women's organizations from all over Santiago. Among its goals were to help subsistence groups financially and offer training in organizational skills, women's rights, and health.[293] There was also a National Committee of associations of relatives of political prisoners. Some of larger coordinating committees were female dominated, others male-dominated, and still others mixed sex.[294]

Coordinating committees arose and increased in number mostly in the 1980s. According to Sur Profesionales (1985), there were five coordinating committees in 1982 and 12 in 1984.[295] One of the main reasons that they formed was that the leaders of the groups represented within them and the Vicaría staff, who supported many groups, thought that unity was a source of strength, and that when groups were connected this would increase the chances of being able eventually to overthrow the dictatorship. In addition, they wanted to raise women's awareness about the causes of their poverty and the existence of human rights violations, and thought that bringing groups together helped this happen. Coordinating committee members organized workshops and "jornadas," that is, discussion and awareness-raising days, for the members of the groups they represented. They also organized fundraising activities, such as the selling of fritters

7.10

A flyer produced by the Coordinating committee of the Caro-Ochagavía Women's Front, demanding better healthcare for women giving birth. The flyer uses a motherist discourse and Pinochet's own discourse of defending the family. It reads, "Let's defend the family! We demand that Chinchón [a nickname for Pinochet] guarantee our safety when we give birth. We want to give life without losing our own. No deaths while giving birth as happened with mothers in the Hospital of San José." Humor as a form of resistance is evidenced in the choice of nickname for Pinochet, and in the drawing. Mid- to late 1980s.

["sopaipillas"] and evenings of folk music, in these ways collecting money for individuals who had to travel to see relatives in prison camps, or needed to pay bureaucrats to produce documents, for example. At their meetings they often discussed problems in the groups they represented, recent repressive acts by the state, and whether or not to participate in resistance activities to which they had been invited.[296]

The coordinating committees of arpillera groups carried out quality control on the arpilleras made, took them to their main buyer, the Vicaría, went to fetch payment from the Vicaría and hand in work for which the Vicaría had requested changes, and made efforts to find additional buyers. They also organized training, leisure, and protest activities for the groups they represented. The leisure activities included a poetry contest, a "Latin American encounter," outings in the summer, and cultural events on International Women's Day. Coordinating committee members attended meetings ["encuentros"] of shantytown inhabitants, as occurred, for example, on December 14 1985, when the Vicaría organized an "Encuentro" called "Shantytown Inhabitants for a Life of Dignity" ["Pobladores por una vida digna"].[297] In addition to these activities, when approached by organizations offering training, it was the coordinating committee members' job to motivate the women in their groups to participate. It was also their responsibility to inform their own group members about what had been said at the meetings; for example, telling group members what training courses the Vicaría was offering, and telling them about the Vicaría's decisions regarding how much it would pay for the arpilleras.

Some coordinating committees were subdivided into teams. In the arpillera coordinating committee of southern Santiago, for example, one team was responsible for organizing training, and another for conducting quality control, taking the arpilleras to the Vicaría, bringing back the money, distributing the money to all the coordinating committee members, receiving new orders for work from the Vicaría, and communicating these orders to the coordinating committee members. A further team produced a bulletin about what was happening in each shantytown.

Coordinating committee members often participated in events of a political nature organized by other groups, and they typically encouraged the members of their groups to do so too. They sometimes visited other groups to express solidarity with their cause, as when Babette and fellow members of her coordinating committee in southern Santiago went to support trade union hunger strikers. The same group paid homage to political prisoners on the internationally denominated day of political prisoners. Coordinating committee members also shared information about events of a political nature, for example giving each group representative "volantes" [flyers] about protests that were going to take place, for her group members. They also dropped flyers in the street so that anyone could learn about what was happening.

Coordinating committee members attended meetings with Vicaría staff to receive training. Some of this training was politically-oriented; coordinating committee members learned and talked about events in Chile, including the repression, policies regarding schools, laws regarding work, political changes, human rights, the dictatorship, poor healthcare, the Constitution, and the plebiscite. The Vicaría showed one coordinating committee clandestine videos about political prisoners in the National Stadium, and people being arrested in their homes. After learning about these topics from Vicaría staff, coordinating committee members would pass on the information to the women in their groups. Coordinating committee members also received training from the Vicaría on building up self-esteem and managing groups. A health team in southern Santiago and a feminist organization called MEMCH also trained them.

The "Coordinating committee of Caro-Ochagavía Women's Front" was made up of women's groups in an area of southern Santiago. These groups included the Committee of Shantytown women of San Bruno ["Comité de Mujeres de San Bruno"], the Committee of Women of Lo Sierra ["Comité de Mujeres de Lo Sierra"], the Committee of Women of Avenida La Feria ["Comité de Mujeres de Avenida La Feria"], the Arpillera Workshop of San Bruno ["Taller de Arpillera de San Bruno"], Non-Organized Women ["Mujeres no Organizadas"], and the Catholic Action Workers' Movement ["Movimiento Obrero de Acción Católica"]. The minutes of a meeting of October 27 1988 announced that it planned to give training to its member groups, help develop these groups, and "mobilize for the re-conquest of women's rights." It planned in the longer term to set up a school and kindergartens.[298]

Its activities were far broader than this, however. It produced flyers demanding the re-vaccination of shantytown inhabitants, other forms of preventative healthcare, the expulsion of an "inefficient" mayor,[299] and better medical care for women giving birth, as well as flyers encouraging women to participate in a march to the center of Santiago and in the extension of the national strike. It produced a document explaining who political prisoners were, stating that they suffered torture, harassment, and murder, and encouraging people to visit them. It made "public declarations" such as one (October 27, 1988) expressing disapproval of the high court's decision to punish a judge who had denounced torture in Chile, and calling on organizations and political parties to demand the suspension of this action. Another of its public declarations denounced the measles epidemic and demanded a series of measures from the Ministry of Health. It produced a bulletin, called

"Women's Bulletin" [Boletín de las Mujeres], organized a "Summer school of women inhabitants of shantytowns" in which women would discuss their economic and political situation and women's rights, and it organized "Meetings of Women" [Encuentros de Mujeres] in churches. It organized a "Shantytown Poetry Get-Together" together with the relatives of the disappeared and the relatives of political prisoners, and a "Song Festival for Women" [Festival de canción para la mujer]. Finally, it wrote a letter to the leaders of the largest coordinating committee in the area stating that this coordinating committee needed strengthening, and suggesting how this should be done.

For some of its activities, the Women's Front partnered with human rights organizations, priests, religious groups, and the Vicaría de la Solidaridad. For example, it had members of the Committee for the Defense of People's Rights ["Comité de Defensa de los Derechos del Pueblo," CODEPU] teach three courses in its summer school. It joined with this same organization in organizing a shantytown poetry get-together, together with a community of nuns and the Vicaría office of southern Santiago. It often worked with local priests, as when priests allowed people to sign up for an event by coming to the church, or lent a room on church premises for some events.

Ties Not Formalized

Apart from forming coordinating committees, shantytown women in groups struggling against poverty or repression developed ties that they did not formalize, with a wide variety of groups engaged in the same or a different activity, and having anti-regime sympathies. These included other shantytown women's groups, mixed-gender shantytown groups, shantytown men's groups, associations of relatives of the persecuted, groups of artists, middle-class women's groups, NGOs, and Vicaría staff. Such ties, together with the coordinating committees, produced a network of groups all over the city and beyond, amounting to a large and connected resistance community, which extended to foreign countries.

Groups of shantytown women were able to form these ties with other groups partly because many resistance activities drew groups together. Groups met each other, for example, during protests or at shantytown anniversaries. Ties also formed because local priests or the Vicaría fostered the coming together of groups, as when the priest in San Bruno organized a party to celebrate Chile's national day, inviting groups of seniors, young people, and arpillera-makers that regularly met under his roof. Some ties developed because groups actively sought contact with other groups, as when the relatives of the disappeared asked the Vicaría staff to help them meet with the arpillera-makers in order to inform them about the disappearances, or when underground politicians approached arpillera groups before the plebiscite to talk about the situation in Chile, or when actors and musicians came to the shantytowns to perform and talk about their experiences. Ties developed, in addition, because some group members also belonged to other groups, as when some arpillera-makers were also in the association of relatives of the disappeared, or because their husbands belonged to other groups, as when Babette's coordinating committee helped her husband's trade union. Lastly, ties between groups formed because some groups gave training to other groups, as when some relatives of the disappeared went to the shantytowns to teach women's groups how to make arpilleras, or when shantytown women from southern Santiago visited political prisoners and relatives of the disappeared to learn how to make arpilleras. The ties with middle-class women's groups formed mainly when middle-class feminists approached and offered training in "personal development," women's rights, or human rights, or when other middle-class women's groups were present at the same protests, or invited shantytown women to participate in protests.

Towards the end of the regime, for example, middle-class feminist groups and the arpillera groups in eastern Santiago worked together to produce a list of points about what women wanted from the post-dictatorship government. Concepts like women's rights helped link women's groups together across class.

Already-existing ties were strengthened through solidarity resistance and community affirmation (see Chapter 5), as when one group supported another's fundraising activities, lent support when another group was protesting, visited a group directly affected by state violence, or sent greetings to another group on Labor Day or other days of significance. Bonds also grew stronger when groups joined together in coordinating committees; some women called the members of other groups in their coordinating committee "compañeras," and said a friendship would develop. When the committees organized events or training, or simply carried out regular activities such as quality control of the products their groups made, these were times of conversation, sharing problems, and joking, during which ties were strengthened.

Not all groups wanted links with each other, however. Natalia told me that her arpillera group did not want ties with certain local groups that were "more for politics," and she said that while some arpillera group members who were in political parties identified with such groups, this was not true of all members. Her group did not meet with the bolsas de cesantes, for example, because they "had a political goal" and "were usually organized by the communist party, and people were afraid to be with communists," as she told me. Conversely, the relatives of the disappeared found that some shantytown arpillera groups were afraid to spend time with them, attributing this to the fact that they were being persecuted by the regime. In addition, there was some rivalry between groups, as when the coordinating committee of arpillera groups in eastern Santiago was angry with an arpillera group based in Melipilla for claiming that they were the first to come up with the idea of the arpillera; they did not socialize together at meetings. Some groups found it difficult to work with others; some shantytown woman leaders found it hard to work with trade unionists, for example. Links between groups were not always harmonious or desired, but there were far more accounts of constructive relationships and warm ties of solidarity than otherwise.

A Sense of Community

The formalized and non-formalized ties between groups made the women feel part of a community made up of many other groups and individuals, all sharing the same enemy, and all having shared experiences of repression and poverty. They viewed this community as being all of one mind in hoping for the regime's end, all working towards ending the dictatorship, and they felt a sense of tremendous unity within it. The San Bruno arpillera group evoked this while telling me about events in which they participated:

Karina [in a nostalgic tone]:   Gatherings, gatherings.

Bernardita [also nostalgic]:   The peñas. With peñas; the peñas.

Mónica: Also.

Karina: Before it was very lovely. Now—

Barbara: People were more united, more together, we were all thinking about the same thing, it was more fun.

JA: You mean this group, or—

All together [energetically]:   No, everyone, everyone, everyone, everyone!

> *Barbara*:   The whole country, the whole country had the same idea, about the same person, and everyone was struggling for the same thing and, and we did important things for the same thing.
>
> *Teresa*:   And it stopped there.
>
> *Barbara*:   Now everyone has gone their own way, and—it's all disintegrated. And all the—we had big organizations, and so many people got together—.

These words evoke an intense sense of group belonging, and of joint activity with a shared goal. They also suggest pride at having been able to bring together large numbers of people, and form large organizations. They hint at *esprit de corps*, a warm feeling of community, and excitement about all these groups struggling together. Analysts have suggested that unity within a community, exhibited by shared understanding, mutual support, and reciprocity in relationships, determines social cohesion, which is an aspect of social wellbeing.[300] That the women experienced wellbeing from the unity they describe is suggested by the fact that in 1995 they said with regret that they had felt "alone" since the end of the regime when their groups began disintegrating, and that groups hardly went out or did anything any more.

The sense of membership in a community was strong in part because the cells within it shared knowledge, and this knowledge was secret. The secrecy was due to the government's hostility to opposition, and to its strategy of violent repression, which made for a dangerous environment for dissenting groups. There was a substantial body of knowledge that was known to the community but kept within it, including knowledge about who was anti-regime, knowledge about plans for protests, and knowledge about secret meeting places and secret underground venues for expressions of dissent. Such a situation, where the safety of one depended on the secrecy of another, and the danger posed a risk to both oneself and one's network, fostered and lent intensity to many of the activities in which the women engaged, and to the feeling of belonging. The San Bruno group told me:

> *Mónica*:   No, but those were good times.
>
> *Barbara*:   But I thought that they were very intense.
>
> *Bernardita*:   Pressured.
>
> *Barbara*:   Yes. Because we all had to go around sort of secretly. These things were done sort of secretly.

Barbara's phrase "we all had to" suggests that she had a sense of all members as engaging in the same behavior, and sharing an experience. She makes a causal link between having to go around and do things secretly, and the intensity of experience. The repression, in causing the need for secrecy, contributed to this intensity and the feeling of belonging in the community within which there were shared experiences. The sense within and among groups that all were fighting a common enemy further fostered a sense of community. It brought about cohesion within and between groups, as well as cooperation, and solidarity. Babette told me, for example, that if there were arguments in her group the women soon made up, remembering that there was a common enemy to be fought.

The shantytown women believed that within this community there was a worldview that was contrary to that of the regime, and thought of it as a shared, alternative truth. In their view, this truth was the correct understanding of the situation in Chile. They talked of knowing "the reality" of the regime with its repression and poverty, while others did not, and spoke of the arpilleras as communicating this truth to outsiders. There was also a sense that this truth was dangerous to reveal or to be known to hold, and so it was a semi-secret truth. I asked a Vicaría employee, Imelda, about this:

> *JA*:   This web—the people from here, the people abroad who sympathized, what was the glue, what was the thing they had in common? Apart from the obvious, being against the dictator? Was there anything else?
>
> *Imelda*:   As I was saying—solidarity. Like any word that suggests a society that is more educated, more moderate. Many also—like the affection that existed between us, the people who confronted this together, collectively. I think there was a lot of affection as well. I think that was the glue. The truth—the hidden truth. I mean, we knew- the people of the arpillera, we knew things that it was not necessary to speak about, you understand? I mean, I think that the most similar thing to this at that time was the symbol of the fish.

Imelda's words suggest that all people connected with the arpilleras had a sense of shared truth, that was a secret truth, and that this bound them together (along with affection and solidarity). The fish that she refers to was the secret symbol of Christians in ancient Rome; they too had had shared values and a sense of collectivity in the face of an oppressive social environment.

Within the community, there was a shared, secret symbol that indicated membership in the community and sympathy with its wish for the end of the dictatorship. This symbol, known and understood as such by members of the community but to few people outside it, was the arpillera. Imelda said:

> I associate it [the arpillera] with what the fish might have been at the time of the catacombs. This was the symbolism, if you like. Of identification, of complicity. I mean, you sometimes didn't know who you were meeting with. For whatever reason, you formed new relationships with people. I, for example, moved house in 1974. So you start to have new neighbors. And you have no idea who these neighbors are. I, personally, was in a very difficult situation because I wasn't living with my husband; my husband was in hiding, and so on. And the fact that a neighbor—I saw an arpillera in a neighbor's house in a totally new neighborhood—, it was as if, "It's alright!" [tone of relief]. I could feel safe, you see? I could say what I liked. I mean, it was that, that strange. I mean, it was a lot of things together. As if you needed very few words to know what was happening there.

The arpillera in her new neighbor's home indicated to Imelda that she was on safe ground and could express her views. As a symbol of membership in the resistance community, it signaled complicity and identification with that community and its views; those who knew about it shared a worldview in a hostile environment in which they were persecuted, as had the Christians in ancient Rome. Partly due to this, the women who made arpilleras had something of a special status in the community.

The strong feeling of community and the *esprit de corps* that came from sharing a common enemy and having to work in secret made some shantytown women look back on their years in groups under the dictatorship as "the good times." "People were more united, more together" and everyone thought in the same way, as the San Bruno group had told me. The women had enjoyed feeling part of this corpus, and derived a feeling of strength from it. They sorely regretted its loss when it disappeared and when there was relatively little contact with other groups due to many having disintegrated, five years after Pinochet stepped down.

These had also been "good times" because there had been more solidarity than after the regime when, in the women's eyes, people were individualistic, selfish, and materialistic. The San Bruno group explained:

> *Fernanda*:   Because despite the sorrow, the hunger, the suffering, it was lovelier, it was nicer.
>
> [. . .]
>
> *Barbara*:   There is a lot of selfishness.
>
> *Fernanda*:   There is selfishness, there is ambition, I mean, people who have something want it just for themselves; that's it. Before, everything was shared, people would give things, would help each other, help each other, they would open their doors; there was more solidarity. Now, no. And you notice that you have to, the country has to suffer for those things to return. That's the way it is. I wouldn't say everyone, I wouldn't say everyone, but the majority: there is that selfishness, that rivalry, that envy, and I think that par—, part of society, more the people who are higher up. The selfishness of this, of capitalism, and all that. And you know that poor people are there too, but they have nicer values. Solidarity, going to help; and they are values that you just can't buy.

In Fernanda's view, the post-regime period was characterized by selfishness, ambition, rivalry, and envy, and the past by helping each other, giving things to each other, and solidarity. However, while there was much that women in groups missed after the regime, there was also much that they were thankful to have behind them. Many women remembered the fear, repression, intense poverty, and danger.

In sum, when the women talked of the dictatorship as "the good times," they referred to the fact that there had been a sense of unity among groups within the anti-regime community. They regretted the groups' dwindling in number and size, the cessation of solidarity, conviviality, sharing, and training, and the rise of individualism and egotism. They missed the high levels of activity of the earlier period, and many actions undertaken to help others. They also missed not being listened to any more, and having been forgotten by the international community and by the politicians whom they had helped.[301]

A Collective Identity

As a consequence of the ties between groups, and even simply of having joined a group, the women came to think of themselves in collective terms: as all poor and all enduring repression. Cristina described the members of her arpillera group in this way:

> We were very poor, very poor, all of us. Unemployed husbands, disappeared husbands; so people who had never had anything to do with politics, were finding out for the first time that their husbands were arrested for political reasons, but they had no idea why. So this thing [the dictatorship] brought, caused a great upheaval.

Her words "we were" and "all of us" point to the extent that she thought of herself as part of a collective in which members endured the same deprivations and state violence. However, the women also emphasized that some members of the groups had suffered targeted repression when they had not, or worse targeted repression than they had, or were poorer than they were. This did not stop them from thinking they were all in the same boat; it was a matter of degree.

Another aspect of the collective identity was the idea that what they endured was a violation of their rights. Bettina referred to "our lives" as made up of rights violations, violence, and injustice:

> *Bettina*:   I think that the main thing was that we took advantage of this means of expression [the arpilleras] to communicate to other countries about what our lives were like. All the injustice, all the human rights violations, all the forms of violence that we had to confront, and all the participation, also, that we women might be involved in.
>
> *JA*:   And what were your motivations for wanting to communicate?
>
> *Bettina*:   We wanted to communicate because knowing, I mean, thanks to the training workshops, we knew that, well, what was happening here, in our country, was a human rights violation. Like for example in those years we wouldn't even talk about quality of life, you see; just about being alive, never mind how you lived. Like for example domestic violence, which in those years was not talked about; the problem was that we didn't have, well, the right to health, that we didn't have doctors, that there was no education, that there was none of this, that, and the other. So the purpose was to denounce, in a way, you see? That was the way of communicating, that was it, the interest in communicating, denouncing a situation that was happening and that in some way we were contributing towards [by saying] what could not be spoken.

Bettina understood herself and the other women in her group as all enduring a denial of their basic rights, of which she mentions two, health and education, and alludes to two more, justice and personal security. Moreover, in their arpilleras they represented themselves within the context of the shantytown, the suggestion being that the whole community suffered from the deprivation that was the arpillera's focus. The collective identity was not passive, however; it included a notion of themselves as resisting. Like the arpilleras, the flyers and bulletins described in Chapter 6 referred to rights as denied to everyone in the community, suggesting that their authors had a sense of collective identity.

The collective identity as victims of repression, human rights violations, and the regime's economic policies had not always existed; it developed as an outcome of the women's being in the groups. Ana, for example, told me that she had also known little about the existence of political prisoners, torture, and disappearances; she attributed this to being shut up in the home. Not all were like her; Cristina, for example, was aware of the political persecution early on, in part because her husband, a communist, had had to go into hiding in 1975, and also because she had helped people find their disappeared relatives, while assisting the Comité Pro-Paz in 1973–1974. But many shantytown women described themselves to me in ways similar to Ana. Once they joined groups, they heard about the various forms of targeted repression from group mates or from the relatives of political prisoners or of the disappeared with whom their group came into contact. They also learned about them at their training sessions, typically organized by the Vicaría or other rights-oriented organizations. Ana said:

> *Ana*: Because there we had many women who were ignorant in many ways; ignorant because we spent all our time in the house with the children, but we didn't

see what was going on outside. It might be that one's own problem was simple compared with the problems of others, of other women who were going through worse things, like their husbands being disappeared to this day, even, or like sons who had disappeared. So the, the fact of being in your world of the house, with the children, well, well, you might have had a fright because your husband was arrested, but luckily he returned, and life goes back to normal, and you think that nothing is happening outside, that everything outside is fine, but it's not. So those day-long training sessions were useful because we would talk about all these matters, all these matters, like that some workmates were worse off than others, and we'd try to find a solution. That's what they were for, those meetings of women, those training sessions that they did . . . For me the arpillera was very important because I developed as a person; I gained knowledge that I didn't have, about what was happening outside, about daily life, let's say, about some workmates who had things going on that I had no idea about.

JA: Like what, for example?

Ana: Well, the torture, the political prisoners, the disappeared. Because, as I say, although yes my husband was arrested, it was nothing in comparison with the sufferings of other workmates. And I, perhaps, would have stayed shut up in my house, and what happened to me happened, and I would have just shut myself up at home.

Ana's perception that being at home all the time was the reason for the women's prior ignorance, while joining groups brought new knowledge about state violence, was shared by many women. The training sessions were not the only cause of this change; conversations with workmates[302] were important as well; Ana heard directly from workmates about the torture, political prisoners, disappearances, and other problems that shantytown families endured. Contact with the repression-oriented groups furthered this awareness. When the relatives of the disappeared came to visit them or teach them how to make arpilleras, for example, the women learned about the extent to which the repression affected other communities.[303] Similarly, when the women visited political prisoners, they learned what they were enduring. The women did, as Ana's comparing herself to others indicates, distinguish between the repression they suffered and the repression others suffered, but they came to feel that they all endured some form of repression.

A final component of the women's collective identity was being leftists. The women called themselves "de izquierda" ["of the Left"]. This, like the awareness of rights and repression, was not an identity that they had held previously. Ana told me that she used to have minimal understanding of Left or Right before joining her local bolsa de cesantes. When she had voted for Allende, it had only been because when she was a child he had come to her region giving out sweets and she had liked him, and moreover, her father was pro-Allende:

JA: What was your political position before joining?

Ana: The truth is I had no idea about anything; I had none. And I'd have arguments with my husband because he'd arrive home late because of his meetings, because he'd go out because they'd call him and come and pick him up here. So that bothered me, because he was with us very little. But I never participated in anything, except for a few gatherings they had at the party level, or—. They were active, and once I think he took me along so that I'd shut up, because he was not doing other things, he was in these gatherings. But, but I had no idea, I had none. Let's see, I didn't know how to define left and right wing, I had no idea, none at all, none at all, none at all, none at all, none at all, none at all.

JA: None at all. And which party was he in? The communist party?

Ana: Communist.

JA: But you would have voted, I suppose. Did you vote for Allende, for example?

Ana: Yes, yes.

JA: I mean, even so, did you feel more sympathy for the Left, or not?

Ana: The thing was that I had no idea, my dear; I had no idea if I was right or left-wing. I mean, it was because I liked him and because I was a girl when, when Salvador Allende traveled in a train to the south, giving out sweets, giving out balloons and goodies, and as small children we would go to the station because we knew that he was going to come by and that he would give people things, sweets for example. I knew—, and because my father was a railway worker, my father was, he worked with the railways. So they were, let's say, in favor of Allende in those years, but I was small. So when I voted, I voted for Allende, but without knowing anything about anything. Now I have worked it out and am clear about what I want and the direction I'm heading in. But not in those years. So after having joined these solidarity workshops; let's say that there, things became clear for me and I began to realize what, what was happening. And right now, of course, I'm not so clear about what's going on, but I think I know more than before.

Ana used not to have a political position or understand the difference between left and right-wing, even though her husband was a communist and her uncle had been a leftist, as she later told me. This changed, however, and she came to see herself as understanding these differences, and as she later told me, became left-wing.

Not all shantytown women saw themselves as leftists, however; some supported the regime. Babette's old neighborhood, La Estrella, contained retired members of the armed forces who were in favor of the dictatorship. In Cristina's neighborhood of Simón Bolívar, most people put out flags on the anniversary of the coup. About the shantytown of Colón, Barbara told me:

but there are always very poor people here. I don't know; how come they defend the—And they put a blindfold over their eyes and didn't see—. No, there are people like that.

Some people, even in Colón, which had a reputation for being leftist and combative, defended the regime and so would not have called themselves "of the Left."

Shantytown women, this chapter has suggested, developed a collective identity and strong sense of being part of a community, all of whose members were anti-dictatorship, and within which there was unity and solidarity. These developments came from their joining groups and forming ties with other groups, including the many groups aimed at coping with the repression and focusing on women's rights. The plethora of repression-oriented groups is testimony to the fact that a national security doctrine coupled with state violence targeted at shantytown families encourages women in shantytowns to form groups and so add building blocks to a community of resistance. In the next chapter I analyze the ways in which shantytown women's groups in Santiago constituted a significant force undermining the regime (in part because of the construction of an anti-regime community) and brought about changes in the women's lives.

Eight   Surviving Dictatorship

Dictatorships shape almost every facet of the lives of the poor. They affect what they are concerned about, how they feel, and how they behave. To women who live in shantytowns, a dictatorship means repression and increased poverty, if the new economic policies that a dictatorship brings in cause unemployment. Santiago's shantytown women became distressed about not having enough money with which to feed or educate their children, and about having their water and electricity cut off. This pushed them to leave behind their home-bound lives and begin to work for an income or join food-producing groups, even if shantytown gender expectations required them to spend their time at home looking after house and children. Dictatorships also mean repression, to shantytown women, and this repression causes them to worry that their family members might be arrested or killed, and to live with fear and insecurity as their almost constant companions. The repression affects their routines and their movements. Dictatorships are such powerful shapers of the poor's experience, that one might add "degree of authoritarianism" as an additional dimension to the theory, developed by Patricia Hill Collins, that race, class, and gender intersect to shape people's lives.

Poverty and repression interacted during the Pinochet era, to produce particular experiences. One's level of poverty, for example, affected how one experienced repression. Repression in the shantytowns tended to be more continuous, intense, intrusive, and extensive than in middle-class neighborhoods, even though there were variations between shantytowns,[304] because the Pinochet government thought that the shantytowns harbored people with political sympathies different from its own, and ideas that were dangerous. The intensity of the repression and contrast with middle-class neighborhoods helps explain why there are such marked differences between accounts by the poor and by many middle-class individuals of what the dictatorship was like, with some of the latter stressing that it brought order to Chile, while shantytown accounts suggest disorder, a turning of normal life on its head.

Gender and motherhood shaped shantytown women's experiences of repression and poverty, and their efforts to fight both these ills. For example, these women experienced the threat of state violence as a threat to their children, as well as to themselves. They worried about their children being arrested or killed, and about their feeling afraid. They objected strongly to facets of the violence that were damaging to their children, and were concerned about how these affected them. Hence Bettina was concerned and indignant about the presence of soldiers in the streets of her shantytown in large part because these military men treated children roughly, and because their painted faces made children frightened. Many women made efforts to keep their children in the house after curfew lest they be shot, and felt saddened that they had to be indoors so much. Before engaging in protest activities, they thought about the consequences for their children. They were reluctant to participate in street protests, for example, in large part because they thought there would be no-one to care for their children should they be arrested. Being a mother shaped how they experienced the repression, and how they felt about aspects of their own resistance.

Gender also affected the ways in which women experienced the repression in that men, more than women, the targets of state violence. When shantytown gender expectations push men to go out and work and women to stay at home, and dictate that men be politically active but not women, then men are more likely than women to be the leaders of political parties and trade unions. Because of this, under a dictatorship that considers the Left an enemy, they are targeted to a greater extent than women, suffering arrest, disappearance, murder, exile, internal exile, and harassment. Shantytown women more commonly experience these assaults as "wife of," "partner of," "mother of," "sister of," and "daughter of," although they are targeted as well. Under Pinochet, some of these forms of repression brought the women periods of intense anxiety about not knowing where their husbands were, and days or even years of searching while having to make arrangements for childcare and ways to earn an income while they searched. Women, then, experienced targeted repression in gendered ways.

Just as gender shapes experiences of repression, so too does it shape experiences of poverty. Motherhood impacts how shantytown women react to their exacerbated poverty when their husbands lose their jobs. They experience their economic difficulties as mothers responsible for their children's well-being, feeling "pain in their soul," as Natalia put it, at having to turn down a hungry child's request for more food, for example. In Chile, such sorrows and anxieties were part of what pushed them out of the home and into groups or employment. Once in groups, new motivations for being in the group developed, such as enjoying the company of other women, and appreciating the support they received when they shared their problems, and these too were gendered. Moreover, joining groups led to a new gender role for women, that of family breadwinner, and a reversal of the old system of women at home looking after the children and men out in the workplace. Gender, then, profoundly affected women's experiences of exacerbated poverty, and what they did to alleviate this poverty affected their roles in the family.

Poverty, repression, and gender were also intertwined when it came to resistance. In many cases, resistance of a political nature and struggles against poverty became blurred during the Pinochet era. Some aspects of the struggle to survive poverty, such as the community kitchens, were simultaneously a statement of the regime's failures and an act of defiance in the face of its ban on organizing. Merely to organize was to resist, in a context where repression, fear, and an awareness of the government's view of "politics" as undesirable acted as powerful disincentives. Meanwhile, the fact that the women were being good mothers, trying to feed their children, softened the subversiveness of what they were doing, and drew some reluctant women into these groups.

Shantytown women's organizations aimed at surviving poverty also constituted political resistance in that they engaged in protests and other political activities on the side. In addition, they provided a forum for the exchange of information about the evils of the regime and for the development of ideas about human rights, and were places in which members gave each other courage and support in their struggles against repression as well as poverty. If struggles against poverty were simultaneously forms of political resistance, the inverse was also true in some cases. Marching about hunger, for example, was a political act that asserted that the government was unable to solve important problems, and it was also an attempt to combat one's poverty. Poverty and political resistance were inextricably bound together.

Resistance

Women of the shantytowns engaged in resistance against the Pinochet regime as the result of a process that was set in motion by the government's neoliberal economic policies and national security doctrine. These brought about widespread unemployment in the shantytowns, and repression, both targeted and generalized. Shantytown women whose husbands were unemployed or in prison found that they were unable to feed their families, send their children to school, or pay for water and electricity. One of their responses to this crisis was to join groups in which they could obtain food or earn an income, or find support with managing the consequences of repression.[305] Once in these groups, the women were drawn into resistance activities because the groups tended to participate in such activities "on the side." Their resistance, in other words, was *incidental resistance*, as opposed to resistance that they had set out to engage in. For some women, it was *reluctant resistance*, particularly when they were likely to be confronted with the police, as was the case with protests. On such occasions group leaders sometimes persuaded or coerced them into participation. However, shantytown women's resistance was mostly quiet, non-confrontational, unobtrusive, and small-scale, and much of it was performed in solidarity and sympathy with the causes and protests of others, as *solidarity resistance*.

The many different resistance activities in which shantytown women engaged may be grouped into three broad categories: self-protection, community affirmation, and mounting an offensive. Self-protection involved taking measures to lessen the chance of being at the receiving end of state violence or other forms of repression. Shantytown women worked to protect their neighborhoods by keeping watch for soldiers approaching, building barriers in the streets, and marking territory. They protected themselves and their families by staying inside after curfew, boarding up their windows, and hiding and slipping away during protests. They protected their groups by using secrecy and disguise, gathering information before meeting with strangers, hiding dangerous documents, and using safe venues for their activities. Efforts to protect one's neighborhood, group, self, and family are part of what constitutes resistance to dictatorship; they are among the ways in which people resist a dictatorship's onslaughts.

Community affirmation, also a form of resistance, entailed a series of activities emphasizing and fostering unity. Women nurtured the values of solidarity (in the sense of giving support), democracy, equality, unity, and "compartir" [sociability and sharing] within their groups. They did much work to express and encourage solidarity with the struggles and causes of others, having as they did an *ethos of solidarity*. They paid homage to the fallen by lighting candles in certain public places at night, and by producing flyers, participating in funeral marches, and creating murals. They also built bridges with other groups, participated in group and shantytown anniversaries, and fostered the creation of a community of women.

Shantytown women's resistance took the form, lastly, of "mounting an offensive," that is, activities aimed at contributing to the effort to overthrow the regime. The women put out statements expressing their views, directing these at the government, other resistance groups, and their communities. These statements took the form of declarations, letters to ministries, open letters, flyers, bulletins, and the arpilleras, all of which informed, accused the government, made demands, or incited protest. The women also took part in demonstrations, and created new groups in the belief that it was necessary for people to be organized for the dictatorship to be overthrown. In these groups, the leaders or others they made arrangements with offered training about repression, poverty, human rights, and women's rights, and worked to strengthen women's self-esteem and sense of efficacy, in the hope that this would lead them to participate in protest activities.

In all three forms of resistance—self-protection, community affirmation, and mounting an offensive—shantytown women used a wide variety of methods and media: symbolic political actions (such as lighting candles or chaining oneself to a fence), the arts (drawings, photography, cartoons, music, poetry, theater, dance, murals, and arpilleras), the written word (flyers, bulletins, statements, denunciations, demands, open letters, letters to ministries, and declarations), gatherings, protests, talking to groups, visits, campaigns, celebrations, and training sessions. Shantytown inhabitants, including women, used the spaces of shantytown walls and even the surfaces of streets in their struggle, to mark territory, inform, and encourage people to continue the fight.

Fear was a significant impediment to resistance. Shantytown women were often afraid to join groups, produce overt criticisms of the regime, or participate in protests. However, group leaders found ways of overcoming the barrier of women's fear. Some used persuasion, stressing how important it was that journalists and others understand the reality in Chile, while others used coercion, forcing group members to attend protests by threatening less work and therefore less income for women who "did not cooperate." The women responded to the coercion by devising strategies for seeming to participate fully while minimizing the amount of time they were at the protest, showing up and quickly slipping away or hiding, for example. Leaders circumvented women's fear of joining groups and participating in activities outside the home by making their groups or activities sound innocuous, as when a feminist group organized what was really an attempt to raise awareness about human rights under the guise of an art competition for shantytown women, and advertised this event as a "Housewives' Get-Together." Similarly, a leader who created two arpillera groups persuaded local women to join by answering in the negative their questions about whether the groups involved "something political," and by making arpillera-making seem harmless, describing it as the making of "small embroidered pictures" using sewing, a traditionally feminine, and therefore non-threatening, skill.

It is ironic that it was during the repressive Pinochet era, when the government discouraged any form of dissidence or independent organizing, that many shantytown women first became members of groups in their community, and politically active in ways other than via voting. This happened for a number of reasons. Often it was the repression itself that fostered this political engagement, as when it led to the disappearance of a relative, or their husband's losing his job. This produced a breakdown in the gender regime in many families. With men not able to be the breadwinners that shantytown gender expectations demanded they be, the women turned to groups as one way of supporting their families or coping with persecution and began participating in resistance activities on the side. Once they were in their first group, their fear lessened and they tended to join one or more additional groups. In the groups there was discussion about one's experiences and about women's position in society and women's rights, and this caused the women to feel that they had a right to be in groups, rather than engaged in nothing but childcare and housework. The fact that the creators of groups were shantytown women themselves, who understood other women's fears and knew how to get around them, also facilitated women's joining groups and becoming involved in resistance against the dictatorship.

Another important factor that contributed to the phenomenon of shantytown women's becoming members of groups and active in resistance during the dictatorship was the backing of a powerful institution able to stand up to the Junta to an extent: the Catholic Church. Catholic priests in the shantytowns were supportive, lending rooms, recruiting women into the groups, channeling donations to the women, storing food, and helping sell what the groups produced. The women's food-procuring, income-earning, and some repression-oriented groups tended to meet on shantytown church premises, where the women felt safe from repression since they saw churches as sanctuaries, and priests as respected local figures with the Catholic Church's protection. This made it easier for them to come out of the home and into groups when they were afraid or unaccustomed to doing so. Closer to the Church hierarchy, the Vicaría de la Solidaridad, a humanitarian organization created within the Catholic Church to help the victims of repression and poverty, and its ecumenical predecessor, the Comité de Cooperación para la Paz en Chile, also offered support. Vicaría and Comité staff, many of whom were lay leftists, asked shantytown priests to help the women's groups, offered grants to help groups become established, channeled donations to the groups, offered them technical and leadership training, sold some of the groups' products for them, and worked to raise the women's awareness of the extent and causes of poverty and repression.

Support from Chilean exiles, sympathetic priests and citizens abroad, journalists reporting on Chile, international and Chilean humanitarian organizations, and other resistance groups in Chile was also important. The women benefited much from the solidarity of others, and fortunately were operating within a resistance community in which solidarity was readily given, both locally and transnationally. This community, like the women themselves, had an ethos of solidarity, which arguably was the glue that bound it together, in addition to a shared wish that the dictatorship might end. The women felt and appreciated both the solidarity and unity of this community during their attempts to survive poverty and resist the regime.

The Consequences of Group Formation

Chipping Away at the Regime's Power

Shantytown women's resistance did not result in an overthrow of the dictatorship and had no immediate or obvious political effect on the Pinochet regime. As happened with dissidents in China,[306] rarely if ever did shantytown women succeed in visibly weakening the regime or directly changing government policy. The dictatorship came to an end largely because Pinochet had written into the 1980 constitution that in 1988 there would be a plebiscite on the continuation of the dictatorship. In this plebiscite, a majority of the Chilean population voted against the dictatorship thanks to the combined efforts of resistance groups (shantytown women's and others), political party leaders, and intellectuals.[307] Shantytown women who were group leaders had contributed to this outcome over the previous years by quietly creating groups, fostering discussion about rights and the causes of poverty and repression, building bridges with other groups, and encouraging shantytown women to participate in various kinds of resistance activity. This caused thousands of shantytown women to understand the regime as having policies responsible for their poverty and the repression they endured, and to see themselves as having rights, which the regime was violating. The small, quiet, behind-the-scenes activities in which these leaders and shantytown women group members participated helped build up a resistance community and led to the exchange of ideas within it that contributed to a majority vote against a continuation of the Pinochet regime in the 1988 plebiscite.

Even small groups like community kitchens, which do not appear to chip away at the power of a regime and seem merely to be helping people survive, erode the power of a dictatorship by raising awareness about the link between group members' poverty and

8.1

An arpillera that suggests that its author had some knowledge of human rights. Its dominant themes are the closure of trade unions and male unemployment. Along the top it quotes from the Universal Declaration of Human Rights, saying, "Art.23(4) Everyone has the right to form and to join trade unions for the protection of his interests." The top right of the arpillera shows a factory with the sign "No vacancies," referring to unemployment. The top left alludes to exploitation at work; an employer offers work, but without benefits. The trade union building has an "x" over the door, meaning that it was closed. The bottom half shows a woman washing clothes in a basin, and says "my wife works," and again, there is a closed trade union. The author suggests that while the men are unemployed, the women are working.

8.2

Detail showing that the arpillerista had learned the words of the article from the Universal Declaration of Human Rights, and thought about them sufficiently to make an arpillera about them. Such arpilleras were often ordered by the Vicaría, who encouraged the women to learn the articles of the Declaration.

the repression and the government's policies, about how widespread poverty and repression are, and about human rights. In women's groups this happened through group conversation, contact with other anti-regime groups, and the "personal development" training and talks about rights that the women received from group leaders, Vicaría staff, the members of feminist organizations, and at the end of the regime from anti-dictatorship political leaders who came to talk to them about why a continuation of the dictatorship was undesirable, and to teach them how to vote, which some women claimed they had forgotten how to do after so many years. If the women had been isolated in their homes, they would have been much harder to train, because they would have been difficult to reach.[308] The Peruvian writer Mario Vargas Llosa (2001: 233) wrote, about Peru under authoritarian president Fujimori:

> What is needed is a multi-party and popular mobilization, capable of resisting the infinite forms of intimidation and blackmail of the authoritarian infrastructure which, as happened in Chile against the Pinochet regime, could win over national and international public opinion to the cause of democracy, removing from the blindfolds that prevent them from seeing the true face of the Peruvian regime.

Women's joining groups was a component of the "popular mobilization" to which Vargas Llosa referred, successfully winning thousands of people over to the cause of democracy. Bringing with it as it did conversations with other women and other groups, in which women heard each other's experiences and neighborhood news,[309] it enabled thousands of women to see what people not in groups did not always know, namely that the regime was violent and had policies damaging to the poor. Hence the hundreds of groups that shantytown women created were arguably responsible for the anti-dictatorship votes of thousands of women. The women's groups also made others aware of the evils of the regime, as when the women sent abroad arpilleras about poverty and repression, or raised awareness among those in their neighborhoods through the making of flyers and public declarations.

The arpillera in Figures 8.1 and 8.2 offers an example of how grouping together resulted in the radicalization of group members. Its subject matter (the right to form trade unions, male unemployment, exploitation, and the closure of trade unions) and the article from the Universal Declaration of Human Rights make it clear that its author was aware of human rights, repression, and widespread unemployment. The Vicaría asked the women to produce arpilleras on these themes, and in doing so the women would discuss the issues depicted, gaining a heightened understanding of them in the process. Radicalization in arpillera groups also happened, as in other groups, because the women talked about their problems and realized that others shared them, and because the Vicaría, a feminist organization, and at least two NGOs led discussions and offered talks on poverty, repression, and rights, even making some arpillera groups learn the articles of the Universal Declaration of Human Rights. Lastly, it happened because being in groups exposed the women to visits by relatives of the persecuted, who related their experiences, and it exposed them to groups of women from other shantytowns, with whom they could discuss their problems. In these ways, groups produced a growth in women's awareness about the nature of rights, the extent of repression and poverty, and the link between their problems and the policies of the regime.

The fact that shantytown women created and joined groups was important in several other ways as well. The women tended to develop and nurture bridges between groups, and it was these bridges or ties that produced a resistance community as opposed to a mass of isolated groups.[310] These ties helped create unity and cohesion within the community. Since they allowed for an exchange of information and ideas, they also contributed to the development of a consensus about the need to bring the dictatorship to an end. The communication that ties facilitated also fostered shared values, goals, and symbols within the community, and this strengthened it and increased the potential for joint action.

The ties also fortified individual groups. The relatives of the disappeared, for example, felt heartened by the moral support they received from the arpillera groups, and political prisoners would no doubt have felt encouraged by Bettina's group's visits. In addition, the ties boosted morale by making shantytown women's and other groups in the resistance community see that they were not alone in their experiences or struggle. Being in contact with each other made it more likely that when one group protested, others would lend support, either by joining it or by expressing or encouraging solidarity. In a context of state violence such support helps make resistance possible, as the sense of not being alone may increase courage and lessen fear.

The resistance community was strengthened when women joined groups in yet another way: the women changed in ways beneficial to this community. As we saw in Chapter 4, being in groups boosted women's self-confidence and self-esteem, mainly because of the "personal development" training and the support of other women that they received. Greater self-confidence made it more likely that they would join or create still other groups, and when they did so, this increased the number of cells of resistance. Joining groups also made the women gain a sense of efficacy, coming to believe that they could, together, change things; a population with a sense of efficacy is more likely to struggle and win than one without. At the same time, joining groups caused women to develop a collective identity as "left-wing," "anti-dictatorship," members of "the poor," and victims of repression and human rights violations.[311] This helped put them in a frame of mind that made it more likely that they would participate in protests and other political acts that in different ways weakened or criticized the regime.[312]

Being in groups also caused shantytown women to develop skills that helped strengthen both their organizations and the resistance community. The women talked of gaining leadership skills, group management skills, the ability to carry on a conversation (a skill many thought they did not have), and the confidence to talk to foreigners and middle-class people without feeling intimidated. They also learned to organize and to advertise activities, and some learned to write articles, public declarations, and letters making demands of ministries, and to produce bulletins. In these ways, being in groups gave people skills that helped build up civil society.[313]

Being in groups made the women less afraid, as mentioned above, and so more likely to participate in resistance against the regime. Many shantytown women had been fearful of joining groups, particularly groups that might be construed as political. Having been inactive in community life for so many years, in a context in which gender expectations demanded that they stay at home, many were also timid about stepping into community activities. Once coaxed out of their homes and into groups, however, they became less afraid, and seeing others do the same, they became emboldened. A fearless population is more likely to resist than one paralyzed by terror, and so group leaders' drawing people out of their homes and into contact with each other was an effective strategy in terms of encouraging resistance.

Consequences for the Women and their Families

There were personal consequences of great significance to the women, of joining groups, as explored in Chapter 4. What the shantytown women appreciated most about having joined groups was the access to money or food that it brought, and especially the fact that it enabled them to feed, clothe and educate their children. Grouping together also enabled them to access donations of food and clothing, which they appreciated greatly, as they did the conviviality, friendship, conversation, and relaxation it brought. In some cases it was therapeutic, they found, in that the conversation and laughter during group meetings lessened their sense of being oppressed by their problems, and the work itself was absorbing and relaxing. They enjoyed the sense it gave them that they were part of a community in which everyone wanted to end the dictatorship and was working together towards this goal, in unison.

Being in groups made women gain a sense of self-worth, and the arpillera-makers in particular gained a sense of political efficacy, seeing themselves as communicating the truth about Chile to people abroad, where other channels of communication were closed, and viewing this as important for the undermining of the regime. These women appreciated the fact that they had gained an opportunity to denounce what was happening to the outside world, as it brought not only a sense of contributing to the effort to end the dictatorship, but also emotional release.

Many women saw their having emerged from the home and joined a group as an achievement, and some felt, more radically, that their earlier, home-bound life had been a form of imprisonment within the restrictive "four walls." They left behind them their old isolation and restricted freedom of movement, and came to think that they had a right to participate in activities outside the home and to join groups. Often they joined more than one, and in becoming more involved in community life, gaining presence and status within their neighborhoods. The women did not all think of their having joined groups or entering paid employment as liberating, however; there was at least one woman who thought of it as an undesirable situation caused by the problem of their husbands' unemployment.

Joining groups changed women's roles in the family, forcing new divisions of labor. The gender regime within their families was temporarily altered;[314] unemployed husbands "allowed" women to work and join groups, even if they did so reluctantly. The women became more assertive with and independent of their husbands, learning how to do so from other group members' experiences and suggestions, and becoming confident about doing so in part as the result of the personal development workshops, in which they were told about women's rights. The other group members supported them in their new assertiveness.

The groups were places of mutual moral and material support among members, where women shared their problems, consoled, advised, learned from each other, and even gave food to members in a desperate situation. In them, women experienced conviviality, warmth, enjoyment, and a release from tensions. The groups also attracted the support of NGOs, humanitarian organizations, and the church, and put the women at the receiving end of international solidarity. This support was not only materially useful; it also boosted their morale, giving them the courage to continue struggling to survive and resist the onslaughts of the repression, and made them feel less hopeless or desperate about their situation. Partly because of this support, the women came to feel part of a broader community of resistance in which there was solidarity and unity, all members against the regime and working towards ending it.

When the bombs fell on the presidential palace on the day of the coup, this was the beginning of far-reaching changes for the women of Santiago's shantytowns. The dictatorship's neoliberal economic policies and national security doctrine caused exacerbated poverty and violent repression, and changed these women's daily routines, concerns, and fears. These policies pushed them into groups, which helped them survive the impoverishment and state violence, and transformed their sense of self, position in the family, and involvement with public life. Crucibles of learning and new experiences, the groups drew the women into political activities in which they had not imagined participating. Within them, the women contributed to the ending of the dictatorship.

Constraints and Flaws in the Dataset

Some constraints encountered at the data collection stage limit the analytical power of this work. Unfortunately, hardly any of the photographs presented are by shantytown women, despite my concerted efforts. I believe that few women from the shantytowns took photographs or possessed cameras; cameras would have been one of the items they would have tried to sell when desperate for money. Most of the photographs used for the book were taken by middle-class male and female researchers; human rights-oriented, middle-class, male, professional photographers; or anonymous photographers who were probably members of leftist clandestine groups, since they gave their photographs to exile organizations and to clandestine leftist groups to publish in their newsletters. Photographs by shantytown women would have presented a shantytown woman's (the photographer's) perspective on her experiences and resistance, in line with the book's goal. Fortunately, however, the visual database contains a very large number of flyers, bulletins, posters, and arpilleras produced by shantytown women's groups, and these do reflect their perspective.

Another constraint I faced was that the photographs I was able to acquire were often of poor quality. Many come from the bulletins or newsletters of shantytown groups, clandestine groups, and exile groups, in which images were not reproduced to a high standard because such organizations tended to have minimal funds and no or limited access to high-quality printing facilities. Some printing would have been done in secret, using unsophisticated equipment, in back rooms in people's homes. Moreover, nearly all these groups dissolved after the return to democracy, making it difficult to find the people who might have the negatives.

A further constraint was that there are few images in existence of certain aspects of shantytown life under Pinochet, meaning that there were few images to analyze for these topics, and to choose from for inclusion in the book. Images of state violence and other forms of repression occurring in the shantytowns, especially, are in very short supply. Not only is it likely that few shantytown inhabitants owned cameras, but also it would have been very dangerous for individuals to take photographs of soldiers in their neighborhoods, raids on homes, arrests, and the like. There are also few photographs indicating that healthcare was poor in the shantytowns, one of the women's main complaints. It took a great deal of searching and following up references to find as many photos as I did on such topics, yet I found only a small number.

A further problem was that in the books, newsletters, and archives from which the images are drawn, there was often limited or no information about which shantytown the photograph shows and when it was taken. Also, the photographer's identity is often not mentioned; this may have been partly because of the repressive nature of the regime and the fact that photographs showing poverty and repression would have been subversive, making it dangerous to include such information. Many of the flyers and bulletins that the women produced, however, did mention their group's name, especially when the activity advertised was not obviously subversive.

These flaws in the visual dataset are considerable, yet it is unlikely that it would have been possible to construct a visual dataset on the topic of shantytown women's resistance to dictatorship and their experiences of repression and poverty, made entirely out of images produced by shantytown women, always labeled with the photographers' names and the location and time of the photograph, and on all wished-for topics. The repressive context, for one, worked against this. The thorough searching I did, in a wide variety of places including shantytown documents in archives, women's organization newsletters, Catholic Church publications, clandestine political group newsletters, humanitarian organization newsletters, publications of exile organizations, books on the shantytowns, and collections of arpilleras, at least yielded many images pertinent to a great many facets of the lives of women from the shantytowns.

In addition to these shortcomings in the visual data, there are shortcomings connected with the interview and textual data. All the women interviewed had been in groups, and the data suggests that women in groups have different experiences and viewpoints from women not involved in groups, and may be more radicalized. Their experiences of poverty and repression would have been the same or similar for both categories, but the nature of their struggles and resistance would have been different. It is possible that non-organized women engaged in more resistance "of the mind" while appearing inactive or indifferent, as Skidmore (2004) has eloquently shown for Myanmar. My findings, therefore, apply to organized shantytown women, and not to unorganized shantytown women. However, compensating somewhat for the bias towards organized women is the fact that at the beginning of the dictatorship most of the women interviewed were not in groups and never had been, and during our interviews they told me about this period of their lives. In addition, the visual data include many photographs of women who were not in groups, or at least not photographed in a group.

A little over half the shantytown women interviewed were members of arpillera groups, as this had been a criterion by which I had originally selected them. This produces a bias towards women in arpillera groups. Compensating somewhat for this, however, is the fact that nearly all the arpillera groups had evolved out of another sort of group, and women in arpillera groups were or had been in one or more other groups, especially community kitchens. Also compensating to an extent is the fact that I interviewed relatives of the disappeared who lived in shantytowns but had not made arpilleras, and shantytown women who were working in NGOs, the government, and a local women's organization, and had not made arpilleras. Moreover, the visual data were not limited to arpillera groups, but rather included images of women in a very large range of groups.

The interview data are also problematic in that being about the past they are affected by selective recall, memory loss, and confusion about dates. As Narayan, Pritchett, and Kapoor (2009: 8) state, "Subjective data, especially subjective data about the past, are subject to a variety of distorting factors. These include biases in recall,[315] the ways in which individuals frame narratives about themselves,[316] sensitivity of responses to the research method and questions,[317] social context and power structures,[318] and just plain errors. An additional concern in poverty studies is the incentive facing poor people and poor communities to give answers that "please" in the hope of gaining funds and programs. Added to these problems is that of distrust, especially so soon after the end of a dictatorship, when people might still suspect outsiders of being able to endanger them.

I tried to limit the impact of these problems in several ways. In most cases, I began interviewing the shantytown women once I had already been observing their groups for quite some time, and this meant that they knew and trusted me and were more open than they would otherwise have been. I did, however, conduct a group interview with the relatives of the disappeared very early on in the fieldwork, and the women were fairly guarded, and there were shantytown women whom I interviewed without having observed their groups. In these cases I took several measures to lessen the likelihood of the above problems occurring. I mentioned who had referred me, and if it was a trusted organization or person, the referral acted as a guarantor of my trustworthiness. I waited until the interview was well under way before asking sensitive questions or questions about which distorted information might be given, so that the interviewee had had time to relax. It sometimes happened that the interviewee could not remember the date of a particular occurrence, and so I would ask them how old their children were at the time, which they usually did remember, and later I would ask them the birth dates of their children. It did happen on one occasion that a woman whom I interviewed once in 1995 and again in 2005 described the same thing slightly differently, and I used her 1995 account as it was closer to the time she was describing. If I noticed that an interviewee had given me information that contradicted what another had said, I checked with third parties and asked questions during participant observation.

All the problems described above were lessened in their impact by the use of more than one method. The visual and archival data, for example, served to check the validity of the interview data and provided new, complementary information. The texts that appeared alongside photographs in the shantytown bulletins and exile and leftist organization newsletters were helpful for the same reasons. For example, there were references to unemployment, poverty, and to strategies for surviving poverty in all three kinds of data, and they pointed to the same experiences. Meanwhile, my year's participant observation of varied groups enabled me to experience shantytown women's groups at first hand, and helped me understand many aspects of shantytown life that were alluded to during the interviews and in photographs. The combination of visual data, interview data, photo-elicitation, archival data, and participant observation field notes, I believe, helped correct the weaknesses that using only one of these datasets would have yielded, and made for a well-rounded and rich database.

Notes

1 All names and place names are pseudonyms, except for La Victoria, for historical accuracy, and a couple of others for which the real name does not compromise any individual.

2 The municipalities of which they are part were spending less than 4,000 pesos per inhabitant per year in 1984; by contrast, the municipality of Providencia, a middle-class neighborhood, spent 10,949 pesos per inhabitant per year (Morales and Rojas 1987).

3 Income levels and quality of housing and infrastructure vary within these impoverished areas (Hardy 1986).

4 I use "solidarity" as the women use it, to mean concretely helping others, expressing ideological support, and showing sympathy if another person or group is afflicted. Bell (2002: 32) notes, "North Americans usually understand solidarity as political support for people engaged in justice movements. Haitians, like other Latin Americans, expand the definition to include neighbors' sharing burdens and supporting each other's personal struggles." Her expanded definition is close to aspects of the women's.

5 In addition, there is "resistance of the mind," eloquently described by Skidmore (2004) in relation to the Burmese context.

6 "Leftists" and "the Left" are taken to mean those in favor of social justice, having a preference for state intervention to promote social and economic equality, and to an extent supportive of class struggle.

7 Corporación José Domingo Cañas 1367 (2005); interview with Nora; conversations with middle-class Chileans.

8 Single, widowed, lesbian, or separated women may join groups, by contrast, because they have lost their job due to their government's change in policies, or because the main breadwinner in their family is in jail or disappeared.

9 Teresa Valdés, Clarisa Hardy, Claudia Serrano, and Dagmar Raczinski, however, are among those scholars who have produced excellent work analyzing women's coping with poverty.

10 See, for example, the edited collection by Jaquette (1989), Dandavati (2005), and Franceschet (2005) on Chile, and Bell's (2002) study of women's resistance in Haiti under military dictatorship (1991–1994), which focuses on village women.

11 See M.E. Valenzuela (1991); Serrano (1988); Palestro (1991); Kaplan (1990).

12 See, for example, Campero (1987); Leiva (1996); Oxhorn (1991, 1995); Schneider (1991, 1995, 2000); Salman (1997); Donoso (1991); and Finn (2006).

13 Tironi (1987).

14 See Dubet (1989); Salman (1997); and Campero (1987).

15 Valenzuela (1984).

16 Skidmore (2004) explores this topic in a chapter of her book on Myanmar.

17 See, for example, Agosín (2008), and the testimonies in Sepúlveda (1996).

18 See Bayat (1997); Early (1998); Eteng (1997); Hoodfar (1998); Bantebya Kyomuhendo (1999); the edited collection by Makinwa (1987); Matshalaga (1997); Blondet (1995); Solinger (2002); Zheng (2003); Stokes (1994); Van der Winden (1996); Machado (1994); Meikle (2002); Turner (1994); Weston (2004); Hao (2005); and Potts (1999). On Chile, see Valdés et al. (1993); Sabatini (1995); Hardy (1986, 1987); Raczynski (1984, 1985); Chuchryk (1989, 1991); Dandavati (2005); Schild (1994); Fisher (1993); Díaz (1985); and Schkolnik (1988).

19 Policzer (2009). He states, "Authoritarian regimes have been by the far the most successful and common sorts of regimes in history, and they don't show any sign of becoming extinct. Democracy has made advances in recent decades, but by 2007 only 90 of the world's 192 countries were classified as "free countries" that enjoy the civil liberties and political rights associated with democratic regimes (Freedom House 2008). Also, authoritarianism is not restricted to states. Many if not most armed non-state groups, including guerrillas, rebel groups, criminal gangs, terrorists, and national liberation movements, are more authoritarian than democratic (Policzer 2006). Such groups exercise de facto, if not de jure, control over large numbers of people and territory" (Policzer 2009).

20 Davis (2006) bases his assertions on the first global audit of urban poverty, the UN-HABITAT's *The Challenge of Slums* (2003). In this study, UN-HABITAT defines a "slum" as characterized by overcrowding, poor or informal housing, inadequate access to safe water and sanitation, and insecurity of tenure, and estimates that there were at least 921 million slum-dwellers in 2001, and more than one billion in 2005.

21 The five great metropoli of South Asia (Karachi, Mumbai, Delhi, Kolkata, and Dhaka) alone contain about 15,000 distinct slum communities whose total population exceeds 20 million, notes Davis (2006: 26).

22 See, for example, Angotti (2006).

23 Gilbert (2009: 35).

24 Simone (2004: 425).

25 See, for example, Bell (2002); Abusharaf (2009); Shami (1997); Blondet (2002); Lind (1997); Feijoó (1996); and Arditti (1999).

26 This archive contains documents about human rights violations and poverty under the dictatorship.

27 A small minority of arpillera-makers were members of the Association of Relatives of the Detained and Disappeared. Mostly working-class, there were a few middle-class women among them. These relatives of the disappeared made a great many arpilleras, but were outnumbered by women from the shantytowns who were not relatives of the disappeared. There were also political prisoners, a handful of exiles, and a group of men who made arpilleras.

28 Adams (2005, 2001, 2000).

29 A snowball sample is one in which interviewees recommend other interviewees.

30 Allende (1971); Sigmund (1977: 130–131).

31 Oppenheim (2007: 36).

32 Oppenheim (2007: 22).

33 Oppenheim (2007: 37–38).

34 Oppenheim (2007: 20–23).

35 Sigmund (1977: 139).

36 The rural branch of the Revolutionary Left Movement ["MIR"].

37 Wright and Oñate (1998: 3).

38 Wright and Oñate (1998: 4).

39 Sigmund (1977: 234).

40 Sigmund (1977: 176).

41 Qureshi (2009); Oppenheim (2007: 72).

42 Oppenheim (2007: 79).

43 A government report on torture under the dictatorship was produced in 2005. See: Chile. Comisión Nacional sobre la Prisión Política y Tortura. 2005. *Informe de la Comisión Nacional Sobre la Prisión Política y Tortura*. Santiago de Chile: La Comisión.

44 Schneider (1995: 75–81).

45 Wright and Oñate (1998: 4–5).

46 Comisión Nacional de Verdad y Reconciliación, Chile. 1993. *Report of the Chilean National Commission on Truth and Reconciliation*. Vol. 2. Phillip E. Berryman (trans.) London: University of Notre Dame Press.

47 Victoria Díaz, Agrupación de Familiares de Detenidos-Desaparecidos, personal communication, February 19, 2009.

48 Wright and Oñate (1998: ix).

49 Wright and Oñate (1998: 5).

50 Sigmund (1977: 262).

51 Angell (1991: 188).

52 Valenzuela (1991: 25).

53 Sigmund (1977: 262).

54 Drake and Jaksić (1991: 5).

55 Wright and Oñate (1998: 6).

56 Montecinos (1997).

57 Silva (1991: 103).

58 Silva (1991: 111).

59 Silva (1991: 113).

60 Valenzuela (1991: 53).

61 Alexander (2009: 27); Paley (2001).

62 Silva and Cleuren (2009); Paley (2001).

63 Alexander (2009: vii, 30).

64 Sorensen (2009: 6).

65 Silva and Cleuren (2009: 20).

66 Alexander (2009: 2).

67 Alexander (2009: 14, 16).

68 Foweraker (2009: 35).

69 Alexander (2009: 11).

70 Alexander (2009: 19).

71 De la Maza (2009: 261); Alexander (2009: 32).

72 Silva and Cleuren (2009: 11).

73 Paley (2001: 89); Alexander (2009: 12, 19–20).

74 Paley (2001: 89).

75 Alexander (2009: 8, 28).

76 Sorensen (2009: 5); Alexander (2009: 30).

77 Alexander (2009: 27, 28).

78 Alexander (2009: 29).

79 Sorensen (2009: 3).

80 Alexander (2009: 28).

81 Alexander (2009: 32).

82 Policzer (2009: xv).

83 Paley (2001).

84 Silva and Cleuren (2009: 22); Alexander (2009: 20); Navia (2009: 321).

85 Alexander (2009: 20).

86 Paley (2001); Foweraker (2009: 34).

87 Posner (2009: 59).

88 Paley (2001); Adams (2002a, 2002b, 2003).

89 Paley (2001).

90 Hipsher (1998); Olavarría (2009).

91 Hardy (1987).

92 Adams (2002a, 2002b, 2003) and field notes.

93 Paley (2001).

94 Adams (2002a, 2002b, 2003) and field notes.

95 Paley (2001).

96 Klein (2009); Olavarría (2009); Paley (2001).

97 Adams (2003).

98 Paley (2001).

99 Paley (2001); Adams (2002a, 2002b, 2003).

100 Paley (2001: 20).

101 Foweraker (2009: 36).

102 Silva and Cleuren (2009 :15).

103 Morales and Rojas (1987: 99).

104 Budnik (1986).

105 Alvarez (1988).

106 Morales and Rojas (1987).

107 Participant observation field notes.

108 Alvarez (1988).

109 See Constable et al. (1991).

110 The same occurs in other authoritarian contexts. In Myanmar, soldiers appear on the streets in cities during periods of political tension, and in many towns and rural areas in the ethnic states they are a constant presence (Fink 2009: 143). In Guatemala, while the army claimed victory, the guerillas refused to admit defeat, and the battlefield was quiescent but political repression continued, taking the form of selective repression, militarization of daily life, and relentless economic insecurity. The town of Xe'caj was under constant surveillance by military commissioners, civil patrollers, and spies (Green 2004).

111 Corporación José Domingo Cañas 1367 (2005).

112 Several years after the dictatorship, some of the arpilleras were anonymously returned.

113 How joining groups brought about radicalization is discussed in Adams (2000).

114 Schneider (1991, 1995), who notes that levels of combativeness varied between shantytowns, found that the most combative were those in which a political party's work in popular culture before the coup created a skilled generation of grassroots militants capable of maintaining community support.

115 Corporación José Domingo Cañas 1367 (2005).

116 Policzer (2009).

117 The arrest of dissidents is widespread under authoritarian regimes. In China, organized political dissent results in the arrest of labor activists (Lee 2003), for example.

118 The principal victims of imprisonment, as well as of concentration camps, torture, disappearances, and executions, were male manual workers (Fisher 1993).

119 Both were soccer stadiums.

120 The phenomenon of disappearance occurred under repressive regimes throughout Latin America. In Guatemala alone, for example, there were an estimated 42,000 disappeared (Green 2004).

121 Interviews with Bettina, Margarita, Natalia, and Teresa.

122 Smith (1982); Sigmund (1986).

123 Lowden (1996); Vicaría de la Solidaridad (1991).

124 See Barbera (2008) on internal exile, Bolzman (1996) on exile, and Weinstein and Lira (1987) on torture.

125 Work-related resistance incites repression under other authoritarian regimes as well. In China for example, in Solinger's (2004) analysis, now unemployed and impoverished workers experience intimidation. The state alternately promises favors and funds to compensate the jobless, and battles and jails protesters. The workers retreat into a crushed quiescence.

126 Fisher (1993).

127 On fear, see Politzer (2001), Green (1999), Scheper-Hughes (1992), Scheper-Hughes and Bourgois (2004), Corradi et al. (1992), and Taussig (1987). The experience of living in fear was not unique to Chile; "violence and fear suffused people's everyday lives," as Green (1999) found in her study of Mayan widows in the Guatemalan countryside three years after the civil war.

128 Fear is pervasive in other authoritarian contexts as well. In Myanmar people live with fear, and community life is damaged by concerns about monitoring and surveillance. A climate of suspicion makes political organizing difficult; activists find it hard to expand their networks beyond a small group of close friends because they do not know who can or cannot be trusted. Even non-activists have cause for concern, since informers and agents can make trouble for people against whom they have personal grudges (Fink 2009: 139). In Peru under Fujimori, some of the most pernicious and enduring effects of the violence were the loss of security, the internalized fear of unrest and instability, and the lack of trust between people (Blondet 2002: 292).

129 In other authoritarian contexts also, women have attempted to make their activities sound innocuous. In Aceh, one of the most active women's NGOs struggling against Indonesian domination decided to use the name "Flower," a feminine, unthreatening name, to disguise its real political objectives (Siapno 2000: 281).

130 Meanwhile, widows, separated, and single women had had to struggle to survive all along, and the economic crises made matters difficult economically for them as well.

131 While these are women's concerns, they are also basic needs.

132 Das (1997).

133 Interviews with Ana, Karina, Nelly, and Teresa.

134 The same has been found in other studies of the urban poor in Chile (e.g. Ruiz-Tagle and Urmeneta 1984: 104).

135 Raczynski (1985).

136 40,000 public employees lost their jobs in the first six months of 1975 (Smith 1982).

137 Teitelboim (1990).

138 Teitelboim (1990).

139 Fisher (1993).

140 Moser (1996).

141 Lozano and Feletti (1996).

142 Autocratic leaders in other countries have adopted similar economic policies upon taking power, with similar consequences. In Peru, for example, Alberto Fujimori put in place a structural adjustment program two weeks after taking power. As in Chile, this resulted in recession and hunger (Barrig 1990).

143 Constable (1991).

144 Smith (1982). See also Bouvier (1983) on the dismissal of leftist workers for political reasons.

145 The employment situation of the poor is similar in other contexts. In China, the poor experience employment insecurity and casual work (Hao 2005). Unemployed workers eke out a living in the service sector in the streets, or in the informal sector; all are severely strapped financially (Solinger 2004). In Iran, few of the migrant poor squatters studied by Kazemi (1980: 54) were fully employed in regular wage-earning occupations; the overwhelming majority held a wide variety of temporary menial jobs, or were unemployed. However, in low-income areas of Harare, Zimbabwe, four years after a structural adjustment program was introduced, nearly all people surveyed had a formal sector job or lived in a household headed by someone with a formal job (Potts 1999).

146 Ruiz-Tagle and Urmeneta (1984).

147 Montecinos (1997).

148 Mid-1980s surveys show that about a third of families living in "extreme poverty" did not satisfy their basic nutritional requirements (Vergara 1990: 59).

149 Teitelboim (1990). As in Chile, in Harare, Zimbabwe, the urban poor did not eat what they would like at meals, and endured food and clothing shortages (Matshalaga 1997). The urban poor in Benin City, Nigeria also suffered nutritional inadequacy (Atuanya 1987).

150 Adams (2000).

151 As in Chile, the poor in China experienced restricted access to education because they were unable to afford school expenses (Hao 2005). Similarly, in Harare, structural adjustment-related costs meant that either the poor or their children had to leave school, or could not stay at the school of first choice, or had not been able to take their exams (Potts 1999).

152 Lowden (1996).

153 Raczynski and Romaguera (1995).

154 The same has been true in other authoritarian contexts. In a low-income neighborhood in Harare, Zimbabwe, infrastructural services were poor, there were insufficient transport facilities, clean water and other sanitary services, and clinics had long queues and delays for those seeking medical attention (Matshalaga 1997). In Iran, there was an absence of paved streets, inadequate public transportation, and other social services (Kazemi 1980).

155 Ramirez (1988: 18).

156 Morales et al. (1990); Morales and Rojas (1987).

157 Interviews with Catarina, Nelly, Ada, Barbara, Bernardita, and Vicaría staff members.

158 Raczynski et al. (1984).

159 Cereceda and Cifuentes (1987).

160 Interview with Bernardita.

161 In Iran also, medical and health facilities were lacking (Kazemi 1980). As in Chile, in a low-income neighborhood in Harare, Zimbabwe, people seeking medical attention faced long queues and delays at clinics (Matshalaga 1997).

162 Raczynski and Romaguera (1995).

163 Smith (1982).

164 On shantytown gender expectations, see Hardy (1987); Valdés (1991); and Sabatini (1995).

165 Raczynski and Serrano (1985).

166 Interviews with shantytown women. Other studies have also found that women of the shantytowns did not work outside the home for an income after getting married (Raczynski and Serrano 1985).

167 Interviews with Magallanes group, and the Vicaría staff member Rita.

168 Men's opposing women's joining groups is a phenomenon present in other authoritarian contexts as well. In Uganda, men resisted women's involvement in any form of mixed public life or associational activity, and even women-only organizations proved to be too threatening to some men (Tripp 2000). In Haiti,

husbands and male partners often opposed women's political or social participation. Many men objected to "their" women working with other men, told their wives they should not neglect "women's work," and did not like them leaving the house, although there were some husbands who encouraged their activist wives (Bell 2002: 95).

169 Interview with Cristina.

170 Fisher (1993).

171 Valdés and Weinstein (1993).

172 Interviews with Mónica and Isidora.

173 Quoted in Fisher (1993).

174 Jansana (1989).

175 Ramirez (1988).

176 For analyses of such groups, see Campero (1987); Donoso (1991); Hardy (1987); and Razeto et al. (1990).

177 In Uganda, also, women formed organizations that engaged in several activities. There were organizations, for example, that combined income generation, savings, social welfare, farming, cultural, and other activities (Tripp 2000).

178 Razeto et al. (1990).

179 Razeto et al. (1983).

180 Chateau et al. (1987).

181 According to Leiva (1986), whose study was based on Vicaría figures (Vicaría de la Solidaridad, 1986).

182 Sur Profesionales (1985).

183 Quoted in Donoso (1991).

184 Interview with Catarina. A diocese ["decanato"] was the name Santiago's Catholic Church gave to a collection of neighborhoods in Santiago.

185 Razeto et al. (1990).

186 Hardy (1987).

187 Arraigada (1988); Valenzuela (1984).

188 Valdés (1987); Leiva (1986); and Schneider (1991).

189 In other authoritarian contexts women also cope with poverty by forming groups. In Uruguay, women organized community kitchens and neighborhood associations (Valdés 2000). In Peru, working-class women participated in community kitchens, mothers' clubs, and "glass of milk" committees between 1989 and 1992 (Blondet 2002). In Haiti, low-income rural women pooled money, resources, and labor, and shared food. They created thousands of groups, and their forms of mutual support ranged from encouragement to counseling for rape survivors, rotating child care, and revolving fund loans (Bell 2002).

190 See Donoso (1991); Hardy (1987); and Bustamante (1985).

191 Such demand-making occurs in other authoritarian contexts as well. Some migrant poor neighborhoods of Tehran, Iran, for example, occasionally presented petitions to high officials, after the eradication of a settlement and housing compound, or when they perceived such threats to their homes (Kazemi 1980: 81).

192 Beall (2004).

193 Interviews with Cristina, Nelly, and the Magallanes group.

194 Freire (2000).

195 A study of the urban poor in Guayaquil, Ecuador found something similar: that often it is to obtain basic infrastructural services in squatter settlements that community organizations are first formed, and although "women do not necessarily see themselves as natural leaders they play an important role in the formation of such organizations" (Moser 1992: 24).

196 Interview with Gloria.

197 Smith (1982).

198 Smith (1982).

199 The contributions of local priests to shantytown organizing receive mention in Smith (1982) and Oxhorn (1995).

200 Adams (forthcoming).

201 These were groups that discussed the Bible in relation to the lives of workers.

202 See the memoirs of Herreros (1991), a priest in southern Santiago.

203 Lowden (1996).

204 Smith (1982).

205 Similarly, in Peru, institutions supported shantytown women's groups in important ways. Mothers' Clubs supported the community kitchens that were organizing at the end of the 1970s, receiving donations from Caritas, the Catholic Church charity (Valdés 2000). Priests and NGO professionals lent their assistance as well (Barrig 1990).

206 There were 121 children's community kitchens in 1982 and 93 in 1984 (Sur Profesionales 1985).

207 The phenomenon of the urban poor pooling voluntary labor in order to survive has been noted in other contexts as well, as found in a cross-country study (Beall 2002).

208 Interview with Bettina.

209 For a detailed study of ollas comunes, see Hardy (1986). Gallardo (1987) has also studied these organizations.

210 Interview with Babette.

211 Interview with Babette.

212 Teresa defined *charquicán* in this way for me: "pototoes, potatoes with pumpkin, mince meat, and now that there is corn, you put in corn, and beans, the green kind."

213 Interview with Bettina.

214 Interview with Teresa.

215 Interview with Bernardita.

216 Interview with Nancy.

217 The coordinating committees of the various popular groups in an area tended to organize the protests.

218 Similarly, a study of a low-income area of Harare found that the poor practiced urban agriculture as a survival strategy, and some took up rural agriculture (Matshalaga 1997).

219 In other authoritarian contexts, as in Chile, shantytown inhabitants have taken to the streets to protest about the lack of essentials. In Peru, for example, many of the

129 shantytown protests in Lima between 1980 and 1986 demanded drinkable water (Barrig 1990: 186).

220 Raczynski and Serrano (1985); Montecinos (1994).

221 Even though some of these activities were the same as those in bolsas, described below, these groups were not called bolsas, but rather "talleres" [workshops], "talleres laborales" [work groups] or "talleres solidarios" [workshops in which there was solidarity]. According to Sur Profesionales (1985), there were 215 such workshops in 1984. However, as there were at least 40 arpillera workshops alone at that time, the figure is likely to be an underestimation.

222 See Adams (1998, 2000, 2001, 2002a, 2002b, 2003, 2005, forthcoming).

223 Similarly, in Uganda, women organized themselves into groups that adopted different functions as the demands or needs of the group changed over time (Tripp 2000).

224 Interview with Imelda, a Comité Pro-Paz staff member.

225 Interview with Natalia.

226 See Lehmann (1991) on feminist popular education.

227 They were also referred to as "bolsas de trabajo" [work groups] in order to soften the denunciatory connotation.

228 Interviews with Ana, Cristina, and the coordinating committee of arpillera groups in eastern Santiago.

229 Razeto et al. (1990) define bolsas as made up principally of workers fired from their companies (particularly nationalized enterprises) for political reasons, in the first months of the regime, mentioning that it was typically trade union leaders and politically active workers who were fired, regardless of their level of training and qualifications. Hardy (1987) suggests that these authors underestimate the number of women bolsa members.

230 Razeto et al. (1990).

231 It was common for Vicaría staff and women from the shantytowns to refer to the Comité Pro-Paz as the Vicaría, even though the Vicaría did not exist until 1976, because the Comité Pro-Paz essentially became the Vicaría.

232 Briant (1987).

233 In Peru, in Blondet's view (2002), between 1989 and 1992, working-class women leaders and their popular organizations (community kitchens, mothers' clubs, and "glass of milk" committees) provided a "safety net" for women living in conditions of poverty and violence in poor neighborhoods and remote communities. In Chile such groups were not a safety net but an essential means of survival.

234 In Haiti, as in Chile, "conscientization programs" helped low-income, rural women change the way they viewed their own worth and power, and contributed to their militancy in demanding personal and social validation (Bell 2002).

235 As happened with the shantytown women, women's participation in neighborhood associations, base communities, the feminist movement, human rights groups, and ecological associations in Brazil and Argentina resulted in their insisting on the right to leave the house in order to participate in these groups (Mainwaring and Viola 1994).

236 Women in Brazil's shantytowns moved into the political sphere to access resources for their families, and this activism led them to a broader, more collective

understanding of motherhood that included the entire community. The emergence of an overt feminist consciousness was less common (Neuhouser 2008). In Chile, the women did not think of their ideas as "feminist," but their belief in women having the right to be active outside the home, their wish to limit husband's attempts to constrain them, and their growing understanding of women's rights do suggest a feminist consciousness.

237 On how they become radicalized in this way, see Adams (2000). Tripp (1990) notes that in Uganda, a sex-segregated organization that on the surface appeared to be formed along traditional cultural lines paralleling a gendered division of labor, was simultaneously working to challenge female subordination, and she states that poor women's struggles over access to resources are not merely attempts to realize their interests in narrowly defined domestic roles, but are also manifestations of gender consciousness and identity. With rank-and-file group members in Chile's shantytowns, however, women's struggles over access to resources were not *manifestations* of gender consciousness, but rather *resulted in* gender consciousness about women's being oppressed. Some group leaders, however, did from the outset see women as oppressed, and aim to empower them.

238 In other Latin American countries, also, women's struggles against poverty challenged dominant understandings of gender in a variety of ways (see Lind 1992 on Ecuador).

239 Numerous analysts of Chile have found the same. Campero (1987: 72) for example, states that women's increased involvement in community activities and contribution as family providers constituted a challenge to the hierarchy of the patriarchal family. Raczynski and Serrano (1992: 14) and Montecinos (1994) state that these changes, together with the high rate of unemployment among male household heads, have been linked to an increase in family instability, separations, and households headed by women.

240 Adams (2000).

241 Similarly, in Rio de Janeiro's favelas, humor was a weapon of resistance, a discourse created by the poor and used against the wealthier classes, giving voice to a group with little access to the public sphere. It provided a vehicle for expressing sentiments that were difficult to communicate publicly or that pointed to areas of discontent in social life. The meanings behind the laughter revealed the cracks in the system (Goldstein 2003). James Scott (1990) suggests that humor is a disguised form of protest and insubordination carried out by subordinate groups, and part of the "hidden transcript" of resistance.

242 One of the consequences of shantytown women's group membership was coming to feel part of a group, and part of the anti-regime community. This mitigates a finding from comparative research on poor people in 23 countries, namely that they experience social ill-being, that is, the feeling of being isolated, left out, looked down upon, alienated, pushed aside, and ignored by the mainstream socio-cultural and political processes. Social ill-being is one of the multiple dimensions of deprivation that poor people face at the community and household levels (Narayan et al. 2000: 133). Where people join groups to solve their problems, the Chilean case suggests, they may experience less acute social ill-being.

243 The same occurred with organized shantytown women under President Fujimori in Peru (Blondet 2002).

244 Interview with Natalia.

245 See Díaz (1985).

246 Cross-country studies have shown that among the urban poor an increasing number of people contribute to the resources of a single household (Beall 2002).

247 Raczynski et al. (1985) provide an excellent description of such survival strategies.

248 Raczynski et al. (1985).

249 Beall (1999) identified a similar strategy among the urban poor of Kumasi, Ghana, who use of petty credit from storekeepers was a way of buying necessities such as food.

250 Raczynski et al. (1985). A cross-country study of how the urban poor cope with poverty (Beall 2004) found much the same; they modulate patterns of consumption in order to adapt to shifts in household income or shocks to the household resource base, such as price rises, loss of subsidies, or a breadwinner's periods of ill health. In Kumasi, Ghana, for example, poor people talked of cutting meals from three to just one a day, and buying smaller bags of rice. In Mombassa, Kenya, the poor saved by walking to work, eating only once a day, gathering fallen items from the ground to sell or eat, withdrawing children from school, postponing medical treatment, and using self-medication.

251 Interview with Babette.

252 Interviews with Bettina and Ana.

253 Interview with San Bruno group; evidence from arpilleras.

254 Raczynski et al. (1985).

255 Raczynski et al. (1985).

256 Interview with Natalia; evidence from arpilleras.

257 Interview with Karina.

258 The same has been observed in other settings, such as Mexico City (González de la Rocha 1994: 13), where "people need to rely on others in their households and their social networks to make ends meet." Other scholars have shown that networks of reciprocal help abound among the urban and rural poor elsewhere in Latin America as well (Lomnitz 1975; Hintze 1989).

259 In shantytowns in Argentina under Peronism, inhabitants also relied on reciprocal networks among neighbors, and on Church charity. There, however, people solved their everyday survival needs through personalized political mediation (similar to clientelism) (Auyero 2001). This was less likely to occur in Chile since many political parties were banned until shortly before the end of the regime. In Argentina people also engaged in underground activities (drug dealing, shoplifting, and petty crime), which were important means of obtaining cash (Auyero 2001).

260 In China, in Solinger's (2004) analysis, unemployed and impoverished workers exhaust themselves with full-time income-seeking, and this quells resistance. This is different from what happened in Chile, where shantytown women' joining groups in search of an income resulted in their becoming involved in protest activities. Along the same lines, Valenzuela (1991) claims that new economic organizations in Chile fast became centers for political organization, and Leiva (1986) suggests that through their ability to develop new types of organization, action, and mobilization, the chronically unemployed and urban poor—men, women, and young people—were at the forefront of the popular struggle challenging authoritarian rule, and transformed themselves from victims into protagonists.

261 Similarly, in Lima's poor neighborhoods under President Fujimori, the organizations women were in were based on principles of collective solidarity (Blondet 2002).

262 Similarly, in Indonesia, in contrast to the male nationalist strategy of frontal attack through armed insurgency, female strategies against the military have taken a more hidden, non-self-promoting form (Siapno 2000: 285).

263 In Haiti under dictatorship, poor women used subterfuge as well. Radical women joined a Duvalierist women's organization because it was the only structure that offered them security as they went into shantytowns to mobilize opposition. In another instance, a woman worked under the sun in the fields with farmers, talking low as she bent to the ground to weed, because that was the only place she could organize without arousing the suspicion of security forces (Bell 2002: 97).

264 Similarly, in Haiti under repressive regimes, vigilance committees seized back control from death squads by organizing defense systems to stop the squads from entering their neighborhoods. Using prearranged signals, lookouts notified neighbors of the entry of suspect people into their areas and arranged escapes for those targeted (Bell 2002: 195).

265 In Haiti, similarly, women built road blockades, which they burned (Bell 2002).

266 See, for example, Ball (2004).

267 Adams (forthcoming).

268 Microfilm data, "Chile, protesta nacional," Princeton University Libraries.

269 This was one of several examples of "infrapolitics" or "under the radar resistance" (Scott 1990), intended not to be detected by the authorities. In Myanmar, students employed a similar strategy, putting a pile of flyers on the top of a bus so that as the bus moved off, they would blow to the ground (Fink 2009).

270 Boletín de Mujeres no. 8.

271 The tone of some of these declarations would seem to disprove Flam's (2004) claim that under repressive regimes, the powerless do not express the anger they feel about relations of domination for fear of negative consequences.

272 Princeton University Libraries, Microfilm, Chilean opposition 1987–1989.

273 Aranda (2003).

274 In other authoritarian contexts, the poor sometimes engage in similarly confrontational tactics. Throughout Haiti, women and men marched through towns to make their demands known, mounted protest campaigns, and shut down towns and regions through strikes (Bell 2002). In Harare, Zimbabwe, a structural adjustment program led to protests, small-scale food riots, more organized industrial action, and full-scale urban riots (Potts 1999). In Iran, there were massive political protests, demonstrations and riots in 1978 and 1979, directed against the Shah's regime and the Pahlavi dynasty (Kazemi 1980).

275 These were not the only protests occurring in Chile. There were also protests by workers pressing for higher wages and changes in labor legislation, and by students protesting high education fees and military intervention in academic life. According to Garretón (2001), the diverse mobilizations between 1973 and 1983 were isolated incidents, erratic, and usually brief. The much larger, almost monthly national protests began in May 1983, organized by the Copper Workers' Confederation.

276 See Adams (2000; 2005; forthcoming).

277 According to Fisher (1993), women whose husbands died or were in jail were the first to organize solidarity groups for political prisoners, and to publicly condemn the human rights abuses committed by the Pinochet government.

278 Schneider (2000).

279 Women have organized as mothers and relatives of victims of repression in many other contexts, including El Salvador, Guatemala, Honduras, Paraguay, Brazil, and Uruguay (Valdés 2000).

280 Agosín (2008).

281 Interview with Ximena, ex-president of the Association.

282 The information in this section comes from an examination of the Association's bulletin, pages from which are housed in the archives of the Princeton University Libraries.

283 See Drogus et al. (2005). In Levine and Mainwaring's (1989) definition, base communities, or CEBs (from their initials in Spanish or Portuguese, "comunidades eclesiales de base") are small groups of 10 to 30 people, found in many Latin American countries but mostly in Brazil. They first emerged in the 1960s in response to the Church's attempt to create more effective linkages to the popular classes. CEBs were most often composed of poor people in a single neighborhood, village, or hamlet, and poor people played a key role in establishing and maintaining them. The meetings involved a religious service that focused on a Bible reading and reflections on the local social reality. The communities became known for pedagogical approaches that emphasized participation, egalitarian ideals, and community. No matter what the social or political agenda might be, in all instances there was great stress on prayer, Bible study, and liturgy. Most of the groups' social and political agendas were quite conventional. Typical activities included sewing, visiting the sick, or "social action," which usually meant collecting money, clothing, or food for those in extreme need. There was often an attempt to found cooperatives, which generally remained limited to very small-scale savings and loan operations, or at most to collective marketing or common purchase arrangements. In Brazil, during the most repressive period of the military regime the CEBs were among the very few popular organizations that developed critical political perspectives, taking on political significance because other channels of political mobilization were closed. Popular class neighborhood associations often sprung from the CEBs and were oriented towards basic urban services such as sewers, electricity, transportation, health posts, and schools. In Chile, there were many organizations in which people developed critical political perspectives (see Chapters 4 and 6), and the base communities were among them (Mainwaring and Viola 1994; Levine and Mainwaring 1989). Levine and Manwaring (1989) show how such groups in Latin America were spaces that "empowered" popular protest.

284 See Valdés et al. (1993) on groups with a feminist orientation.

285 Briant (1987).

286 Briant (1987).

287 Roberts (1995).

288 Interviews with shantytown women, 1995 and 1996.

289 Organizations like homeless committees, groups planning land seizures, unemployed persons' groups, or debtors' clubs were seen as political, and men dominated these, especially in the leadership. Women shied away from what might be construed as political activity (Fisher 1993).

290 Agurto et al. (1985); Valenzuela (1984); Velasco (1986).

291 Campero (1987); Drake (2003); Roberts (1995).

292 In many repressive contexts, the poor form coordinating committees. In Peru in the 1980s, for example, there was an organization that brought together organized women engaged in multiple activities aimed at coping with the economic crisis, and in 1990, when President Fujimori applied structural adjustment, the community kitchens started to band together to form coordinating committees (Valdés 2000). In China, however, there are resistance movements that are for the most part small, local, and isolated from one another, lacking interconnective ideological and organizational bonds, according to Perry (2003).

293 Fisher (1993).

294 In 1986 the first Metropolitan Congress of Pobladores took place in Santiago, with 40 percent of the 400 representatives being women (Leiva 1986). The representatives would have been coordinating committee members from varied groups based in many areas of Santiago.

295 As my interviewees alone mention three arpillera coordinating committees, one health team coordinating committee, one Santiago-based coordinating committee of multiple kinds of popular organization, and at least one national coordinating committee, I suspect this is an underestimate.

296 A cross-country study (Beall 2004) found that the federations of smaller organizations that the urban poor had formed engaged with local government, but in dictatorial contexts this is less likely to happen when the groups that make up the federation are anti-regime, as was the case in Santiago under Pinochet.

297 Arzobispado de Santiago-Vicaría de la Solidaridad (1985).

298 Princeton University's Department of Rare Books and Special Collections, microfilm, Chilean opposition 1987–1989 Box 1.

299 Princeton University's Department of Rare Books and Special Collections, microfilm, Chilean opposition 1987–1989 Box 1.

300 Narayan et al. (2000: 133).

301 See Adams (2003).

302 See Adams (2000).

303 See Adams (2000).

304 Corporación José Domingo Cañas 1367 (2005); Schneider (1995).

305 Some women, however, had other reasons for joining a group, such as escaping loneliness, wanting to be less dependent on their husbands, or seeking the support of other women.

306 Pei (2003).

307 Puryear (1994).

308 Abusharaf (2009: 15) suggests that for shantytown women in Khartoum, the "grave contraventions of women's rights in the context of the violent political disputes in Sudan had the unintended consequence of sharpening women's views about their civil, political, economic, and cultural rights," but the Chilean case suggests that contraventions alone do not lead to awareness; rather it is interacting with others as a result of these contraventions that produces such understandings of rights.

309 Adams (2000).

310 In El Salvador also, the formation of a field of civic organizations greatly expanded the scale of potential political mobilization by connecting previously isolated individuals and groups (Almeida 2008: 8).

311 Adams (2000). A study of China's pro-democracy activists (Pei 2003) found that rights consciousness not only increases the frequency of resistance, but changes the forms of such resistance.

312 Radicalization similar to the women's in Chile occurred in Haiti (Bell 2002), where exchanging personal experiences and analyzing social rights and responsibilities built upon Haitian women's historically strong political awareness, and conscientization and women's sense of empowerment made the difference between a spirit of resistance and one of resignation or defeat.

313 The same occurred as a result of participation in base communities in Brazil and Argentina; leadership capacities were nurtured (Levine and Mainwaring 1989).

314 Adams (2002).

315 See, in addition, Gibbs, Lindner, and Fisher (1986); Withey (1954).

316 See, in addition, Tilly (2006); Bertrand et al. (2001).

317 See, in addition, Krueger and Schkade (2007); Kahneman and Krueger (2006).

318 See, in addition, Chambers (2002).

Photography Credits

Figures 1.1–1.4, 1.6, 1.19, 2.1, 2.2, 4.33, 4.38, 5.6, 5.8, 5.10, 6.14:
> Alvarez, Carlos Morales. 1988. *La Victoria de Chile*. Santiago: Editorial Llama S.A.

Figures 1.5, 4.27: Vicaría de la Solidaridad/Fundación Solidaridad calendar.

Figures 1.7, 1.8, 1.12a, 1.12b, 1.17, 1.22a, 1.22b, 1.23, 2.4, 3.4, 3.9, 3.10a, 3.10b, 3.13, 3.14:
> Budnik, Miguel. 1986. *Los Marginados*. Santiago: HOY.

Figures 1.9, 5.4: Jacqueline Adams

Figures 1.10, 3.5: Photograph by Jacqueline Adams. Arpillera from the collection of Verónica Salas.

Figures 1.11, 2.7, 2.12, 2.14, 3.1, 4.40, 6.19, 6.20:
> Photograph by Jacqueline Adams. Arpillera from the collection of André Jacques and Geneviève Camus.

Figures 1.13, 1.14, 1.21, 1.25, 1.26, 3.3:
> Schkolnik, Mariana. 1986. *Sobrevivir en la población José María Caro y en Lo Hermida*. Santiago: PET.

Figure 1.15: Heitmann, Luis Bravo and Carlos Martínez Corbella (Eds.) 1993. *Chile: 50 Años de vivienda social 1943–1993*. Valparaiso: Universidad de Valparaiso, Facultad de Architectura.

Figures 1.16, 4.36:
> Ramirez, Apolonia. 1988. *Renacer en Conchalí. Sindicato de trabajadores independientes*. Santiago: PET.

Figure 1.18: Ruiz, Maria Olga, Eulogia San Martin B., C.P.H. Tierra Nuestra. 2001. *Las Mujeres en la Historia de la Comuna de La Granja*. Santiago: LOM Ediciones.

Figures 1.20, 4.15–4.18:
> Ramirez, Apolonia. 1986. *Comprando juntos frente al hambre*. Santiago: PET.

Figure 1.24: *Chile Fights*, winter 1985, no. 51, p. 10.

Figure 2.3: Meiselas, Susan (Ed.) 1990. *Chile from Within, 1973–1988*. New York and London: W.W. Norton and Company, p. 47. Photograph by Alejandro Hoppe, 1985.

Figure 2.5: Briant, Jo. 1987. *Chili au quotidien*. Paris: Editions l'Harmattan. The book's author states that the photograph originally appeared in an Amnesty International report of 1986.

Figure 2.6:   *Situacion de los derechos humanos en Chile. Informe mensual*, no. 91–92. Julio-agosto 1989. Comision Chlena de Derechos Humanos.

Figure 2.8:   Oñate, Rody et al. 2005. *Exilio y Retorno*. Santiago: Lom Ediciones, p. 8. Photograph by Marcelo Montecinos.

Figure 2.9:   Oñate, Rody et al. 2005. *Exilio y Retorno*. Santiago: Lom Ediciones, p. 9. Photograph by Marcelo Montecinos, p. 32.

Figure 2.10:   Oñate, Rody et al. 2005. *Exilio y Retorno*. Santiago: Lom Ediciones. Photograph by Marcelo Montecinos, p. 9

Figure 2.11:   Aguilera, Silvia; Paulo Slachevsky; Oscar Wittke (Eds.). 1993. *Memorias en blanco y negro*. Santiago: LOM Ediciones, p. 17. Photograph by AP Wide World Photos.

Figure 2.13:   Postcard created by the Chile Solidarity Campaign, London. The arpillera's probable author is Irma Muller, the mother of a disappeared person.

Figures 2.15, 3.6: Photograph by Jacqueline Adams. Arpillera from the collection of the Casa de la Mujer, Huamachuco.

Figure 2.16:   Rama, Carlos. 1974. *Chile. Mil Dias entre la revolución y el fascismo*. Barcelona: Editorial Planeta, p. 199.

Figures 2.17, 3.7, 4.19, 4.20, 4.30, 4.31, 4.32, 4.34, 4.35, 5.1, 5.2, 5.3, 5.5, 5.13, 5.14, 6.1, 6.2, 6.3, 6.4, 6.5, 6.6, 6.7, 6.8, 6.9, 6.10, 6.11, 6.12, 6.13, 6.21, 6.22, 6.23, 6.24, 6.25, 7.2, 7.4, 7.6, 7.8, 7.9, 7.10:
                 Princeton University Libraries, from collections including "Chile Protesta nacional 1983–1984," "Chilean opposition 1987–1989," "Actividades de movimientos políticos, sociales, y culturales, 1985–86," and "Chilean political party and opposition literature."

Figure 3.2:   Echeverría Bascuñan, Fernando, Jorge Rojas Hernández. 1992. *Añoranzas Sueños Realidades. Dirigentes sindicales hablan de la Transición*. Santiago: Ediciones SUR.

Figure 3.8:   *Chile Fights*, spring 1987, no. 55, p. 11.

Figure 3.11:   Photograph by Jacqueline Adams. Arpillera from the collection of Flu Voionmaa.

Figure 3.12:   Wilson, Sergio. 1985. *El drama de las familias sin casa y los allegados*. Santiago: Fundacion para la accion Vecinal y Comunitaria. AVEC.

Figures 4.1, 4.2, 4.3, 4.4, 4.5, 4.24, 4.25:
                 Photograph from albums in the archive of the Vicaría de la Solidaridad, Santiago, Chile.

Figures 4.6, 4.7, 4.8, 4.9, 4.10, 4.11, 4.12, 4.13, 4.14:
                 Hardy, Clarisa. 1986. *Hambre + Dignidad = Ollas Comunes*. Santiago: PET Coleccion Experiencias Populares.

Figures 4.21, 4.22, 4.23:
                 Photograph by Jacqueline Adams. Arpillera from the collection of Flu Voionmaa.

Figure 4.26:   Change. International Reports: Women and Society. 1981. *Military Ideology and the Dissolution of Democracy. Women in Chile*. Change report no. 4. London: CHANGE International Reports.

Figure 4.28:   Arpillera postcard in the collection of Jacqueline Adams. There is no information on the back about who produced the postcard.

Figure 4.29:   *Chile Fights*, Autumn 1987, no. 58, p. 8.

Figure 4.37:   Hardy, Clarisa with Mariana Schkolnik and Berta Teitelboim. 1989. *Pobreza y Trabajo*. Serie Trababjo y Democracia. Santiago: Programa Economia del Trabajo (PET).

Figure 4.39:   Albuquerque, Mario, Mario Garcés, Pedro Milos, Víctor Hugo Miranda, Marcela Segall et al. 1990. "Reconstrucción del movimiento popular bajo dictadura militar, 1973–1983." *Cuadernos de historia popular*, 11. Serie Historia del Movimiento Obrero, tomo IV. Santiago: Taller Nueva Historia del Centro de Estudios del Trabajo CETRA/CEAL y de ECO Educacion y Comunicaciones. Mayo de 1990. P. 20

Figure 5.7:   Grupo de Trabajo de La Victoria (Chile). 2007 *La Victoria Rescatando su Historia*. Santiago: Editorial ARCIS.

Figure 5.9:   Comite de Defensa de la Cultura chilena. 1990. *Muralismo. Arte en la cultura popular chilena*. St. Gallen: Edition Dia.

Figure 5.11:   *Chile Fights*, spring 1987, no. 55, p. 6.

Figure 5.12   Meiselas, Susan (Ed.) 1990. *Chile from within, 1973–1988*. New York and London: W.W. Norton and Company. Photograph by Hector López, p. 30.

Figure 5.15:   *Chile Fights*, 1984, no. 45.

Figure 6.15:   Comite de Defensa de la Cultura chilena. 1990. *Muralismo. Arte en la cultura popular chilena*. St. Gallen: Edition Dia.

Figure 6.16:   Photograph by Jacqueline Adams. The postcard was produced by the Chile Solidarity Campaign.

Figures 6.17, 6.18:
                  Grupo de Trabajo de La Victoria (Chile). 2007 *La Victoria Rescatando su Historia*. Santiago: Editorial ARCIS.

Figure 7.1:   Meiselas, Susan (Ed.) 1990. *Chile from within, 1973–1988*. New York and London: W.W. Norton and Company. Photograph by Oscar Navarro, p. 32.

Figure 7.3:   *Chile Fights*, Autumn 1987, no. 57, p. 8.

Figure 7.5:   ECO, Taller de Analisis Movimientos sociales y coyuntura. 1989. *Los Limites de la Transicion y los desafios de la democratizacion desde la base*. No. 5, Nov. 89.

Figure 7.7:   CODEPU. *Tortura. Documento de denuncia*. Vol. VII. Primer semestre 1987. Santiago: Comite de Defensa de los Dereshos del Pueblo.

Figures 8.1, 8.2: Photograph by Jacqueline Adams. Arpillera from the collection of Riet Delsing.

Bibliography

Abusharaf, Rogaia Mustafa. *Transforming Displaced Women in Sudan. Politics and the Body in a Squatter Settlement.* Chicago: The University of Chicago Press, 2009.

Adams, Jacqueline. "The Wrongs of Reciprocity: Fieldwork among Chilean Working Class Women." *Journal of Contemporary Ethnography* 27.2 (1998): 219–241.

Adams, Jacqueline. "Movement Socialization in Art Workshops: A Case from Pinochet's Chile." *Sociological Quarterly* 41.4 (2000): 615–638.

Adams, Jacqueline. "The Makings of Political Art." *Qualitative Sociology* 24. 3 (2001): 311–348.

Adams, Jacqueline. "Art in Social Movements: A Case from Pinochet's Chile." *Sociological Forum* 17.1 (2002a): 21–56.

Adams, Jacqueline. "Gender and Movement Decline. Shantytown Women and the Prodemocracy Movement in Pinochet's Chile." *Journal of Contemporary Ethnography* 31.3 (2002b): 285–322.

Adams, Jacqueline. "The Bitter End: Emotions at a Movement's Conclusion." *Sociological Inquiry* 73.1 (2003): 84–113.

Adams, Jacqueline. "When Art Loses its Sting: The Evolution of Protest Art in Authoritarian Contexts." *Sociological Perspectives* 48.4 (2005): 531–558.

Adams, Jacqueline. *Art Against Dictatorship: Fighting Pinochet through the International Selling of Shantytown Art.* Austin: University of Texas Press, forthcoming.

Agosín, Marjorie. *Tapestries of Hope, Threads of Love: The Arpillera Movement in Chile.* Lanham, MD: Rowman & Littlefield Publishers, 2008.

Agurto, Irene, Gonzalo de la Maza, Manuel Canales, Roberto Brodsky, Mario Marcet et al. *Juventud Chilena: Razones y subversions.* Santiago: ECO-FOLICO-SEPADE, 1985.

Alexander, William, ed. *Lost in the Long Transition. Struggles for Social Justice in Neoliberal Chile.* Lanham, MD: Lexington Books, 2009.

Allende Gossens, Salvador. *Nuestro camino al socialismo; la vía chilena.* Buenos Aires: Ediciones Papiro, 1971.

Almeida, Paul. *Waves of Protest: Popular Struggle in El Salvador.* Minneapolis: University of Minnesota Press, 2008.

Alvarez, Jorge. *Los hijos de la erradicación.* Santiago: PREALC, 1988.

Angell, Alan. "Unions and Workers in Chile during the 1980s." *The Struggle for Democracy in Chile, 1982–1990.* Eds. Paul W. Drake and Iván Jaksić. Lincoln: University of Nebraska Press, 1991. 199–210.

Angotti, Tom. "Apocalyptic Anti-Urbanism: Mike Davis and his Planet of Slums." *International Journal of Urban and Regional Research.* 30.4 (2006): 961–967.

Aranda, Ximena. *Memorias de una mujer de clase media chilena.* Santiago: Editorial Sudamericana Señales, 2003.

Arditti, Ruth. *Searching for Life. The Grandmothers of the Plaza de Mayo and the Disappeared Children of Argentina.* Berkeley: University of California Press, 1999.

Arraigada, Genaro. *Pinochet. The Politics of Power.* Boston, MA: Unwin Hyman, 1988.

Arzobispado de Santiago-Vicaría de la Solidaridad. *Documento de Trabajo. Encuentro Pobladores por una vida digna. Diciembre 14 de 1985.* Santiago: Arzobispado de Santiago-Vicaría de la Solidaridad, 1985.

Atuanya, E.I. "Nutrition as an Indicator of Urban Poverty. A Dietary Survey of the Urban Poor in Benin City, Nigeria." *The Urban Poor in Nigeria.* Eds. P. Kofo Makinwa and A.O. Ozo. Ibadan: Evans Brothers, 1987. 109–127.

Auyero, Javier. *Poor People's Politics. Peronist Survival Networks and the Legacy of Evita.* Durham and London: Duke University Press, 2001.

Bale, John and David Drakakis-Smith. *The Third World City.* London and New York: Methuen, 1987.

Ball, Laurie. "Entre la mística y la estigmatización en dictadura y democracia: narraciones orales de la población La Victoria, Chile." *Andrew W. Mellon Undergraduate Working Paper Series*, 1. North Carolina: Duke University, 2004.

Bantebya Kyomuhendo, G. "Decision-Making in Poor Households: The Case of Kampala, Uganda." *Urban Poverty in Africa: From Understanding to Alleviation.* Eds. Sue Jones and Nici Nelson. London: Intermediate Technology Publications, 1999. 113–127.

Barbera, Rosemary. "Internal Exile: Effects on Families and Communities." *Refuge: Canada's Periodical on Refugees* 25.1 (2008): 69–76.

Barker, James. *Always Getting Ready: Upterrlainarluta.* Seattle: University of Washington Press, 1993.

Barrig, Maruja. "Quejas y contentamientos: historia de una política social, los municipios y la organización femenina en Lima." *Movimientos sociales: elementos para una relectura.* Eds. Carmen Rosa Balbi, Eduardo Ballón, Maruja Barrig, Manuel Castillo, Julio Gamero, Teresa Tovar, and Antonio Zapata. Lima: DESCO, 1990. 169–200.

Bateson, Gregory and Margaret Mead. *Balinese Character, a Photographic Analysis.* New York: The New York Academy of Sciences, 1942.

Bayat, Asef. *Street Politics. Poor People's Movement in Iran.* New York: Columbia University Press, 1997.

Beall, Jo. "Surviving in the City: Livelihoods and Linkages of the Urban Poor." *Urban Governance, Voice and Poverty in the Developing World.* Eds. Nick Devas, Philip Amis, Jo Beall, Ursula Grant, Diana Mitlin, Fiona Nunan, and Carol Rakodi. London: Earthscan, 1999. 68–94.

Beall, Jo. "Living in the Present, Investing in the Future: Household Security Among the Urban Poor." *Urban Livelihoods. A People-Centred Approach to Reducing Poverty.* Eds. Carole Rakodi and Tony Lloyd-Jones. London: Earthscan, 2002. 71–87.

Beall, Jo. "Surviving in the City: Livelihoods and Linkages of the Urban Poor." *Urban Governance, Voice and Poverty in the Developing World.* Eds. Nick Devas, Philip Amis, Jo Beall, Ursula Grant, Diana Mitlin, Fiona Nunan, and Carol Rakodi. London: Earthscan, 2004. 68–94.

Becker, Howard. *Doing Things Together*. Evanston, IL: Northwestern University Press, 1986.

Bell, Beverly. *Walking on Fire. Haitian Women's Stories of Survival and Resistance.* Ithaca, NY and London: Cornell University Press, 2002.

Bertrand, Marianne and Sendhil Mullaninathan. "Do People Mean What They Say? Implications for Subjective Survey Data." *American Economic Review* 91.2 (2001): 67–72.

Blondet, Cecilia and Carmen Montero. *Hoy: menu popular; comedores en Lima*. Lima: Instituto de Estudios Peruanos Ediciones, 1995.

Blondet, Cecilia. "The 'Devil's Deal': Women's Political Participation and Authoritarianism in Peru." *Gender Justice, Development, and Rights*. Eds. Maxine Molyneux and Shahra Razavi. Oxford: Oxford University Press, 2002. 277–305.

Boletín de la Mujer, Frente de Mujeres Caro-Ochagavía, issue 8, 1987.

Bolzman, Claudio. *Sociologie de l'exil: une approche dynamique. L'exemple des réfugiés chiliens en Suisse*. Zurich: Seismo, 1996.

Bouvier, Virginia Marie. *Alliance or Compliance: Implications of the Chilean Experience for the Catholic Church in Latin America*. Syracuse, NY: Maxwell School of Citizenship and Public Affairs, Syracuse University, 1983.

Briant, Jo. *Chili au quotidien*. Paris: L'Harmattan, 1987.

Budnik, Miguel. *Los Marginados*. Santiago: HOY, 1986.

Bustamante, Jaime. "Algunos antecedentes estadísticos sobre las O.E.P. según catastro de 1985." *Las organizaciones económicas populares*, 2nd edition. Eds. Luis Razeto et al. Santiago: PET, 1986. 157–174.

Campero, Guillermo. *Entre la sobrevivencia y la acción política. Las organizaciones de pobladores en Santiago*. Santiago: Estudios ILET, 1987.

Cereceda, Luz and Maz Cifuentes. *¿Qué comen los pobres? Habitos alimenticios, estrategias de compra y mecanismos de sobrevivencia*. Santiago: Cuadernos del Instituto de Sociologia, Pontifica Universidad Catolica de Chile, 1987.

Chambers, Robert. "Power, Knowledge, and Policy Influence: Reflections on an Experience." *Knowing Poverty: Critical Reflections on Participatory Research and Policy*. Eds. Karen Brock, Rosemary McGee, and Ria Brouwers. London and Sterling, VA: Earthscan, 2002. 135–165.

Chateau, Jorge and Hernan Pozo. "Los Pobladores en el area metropolitan: situación y características," *Espacio y Poder. Los Pobladores*. Eds. Jorge Chateau, Bernarda Gallardo, Eduardo Morales, Carlos Piña, Hernan Pozo, Sergio Rojas, Daniela Sanchez, and Teresa Valdés. Santiago: FLACSO, 1987. 13–74.

Chen, Xi. "Collective Petitioning and Institutional Conversation." *Popular Protest in China*. Ed. Kevin O'Brien. Cambridge, MA and London: Harvard University Press, 2008. 54–70.

Cheng, Yu-Shek and K.L. Ngok. "The Potential for Civil Unrest in China." *Searching for Peace in Asia Pacific. An Overview of Conflict Prevention and Peacebuilding Activities*. Eds. Annelies Heijmans, Nicola Simmonds, and Hans van de Veen. Boulder, CO and London: Lynne Rienner Publishers, 2004. 166–180.

Chile. Comisión Nacional sobre la Prisión Política y Tortura. *Informe de la Comisión Nacional Sobre la Prisión Política y Tortura*. Santiago de Chile: La Comisión, 2005.

Chinchilla, Norma. "Marxism, Feminism, and the Struggle for Democracy in Latin America." *Materialist Feminism: A Reader in Class, Difference, and Women's Lives.* Ed. Rosemary Hennessy. New York: Routledge, 1997. 214–226.

Chuchryk, Patricia. "Subversive Mothers: The Women's Opposition to the Military Regime in Chile." *Women, the State, and Development.* Eds. Sue Ellen Charlton, Jana Everett, and Kathleen Staudt. Albany, NY: SUNY Press, 1989. 130–151.

Chuchryk, Patricia. "Feminist Anti-Authoritarian Politics: The Role of Women's Organizations in the Chilean Transition to Democracy." *The Women's Movement in Latin America: Feminism and the Transition to Democracy.* Ed. Jane Jaquette. Boulder, CO: Westview Press, 1991. 149–184.

Collier, John. *Visual Anthropology: Photography as Research Method.* New York: Holt, Rinehart, and Winston, 1967.

Comisión Nacional de Verdad y Reconciliación, Chile. *Report of the Chilean National Commission on Truth and Reconciliation.* Trans. Phillip Berryman. Notre Dame, IN: University of Notre Dame Press, 1993.

Constable, Pamela and Arturo Valenzuela. *A Nation of Enemies: Chile under Pinochet.* New York: Norton, 1991.

Corporación José Domingo Cañas 1367. *Tortura en poblaciones del Gran Santiago (1973–1990): colectivo de memoria histórica.* Santiago: Corporación José Domingo Cañas, 2005.

Corradi, Juan, Patricia Weiss Fagen, and Manuel A. Garretón, eds. *Fear at the Edge: State Terror and Resistance in Latin America.* Berkeley: University of California Press, 1992.

Dandavati, Annie. *Engendering Democracy in Chile.* New York: Peter Lang, 2005.

Danforth, Loring. *The Death Rituals of Rural Greece.* Princeton, NJ: Princeton University Press, 1982.

Das, Veena. "Language and the Body: Transactions in the Construction of Pain." *Social Suffering.* Eds. Arthur Kleinman, Veena Das, and Margaret Lock. Berkeley: University of California Press, 1997. 67–92.

Davis, Mike. *Planet of Slums.* London and New York: Verso, 2006.

De la Maza, Gonzalo. "Participation and *Mestizaje* of State-Civil Society in Chile." *Widening Democracy. Citizens and Participatory Schemes in Brazil and Chile.* Eds. Patricio Silva and Herwig Cleuren. Leiden and Boston, MA: Brill, 2009. 249–271.

Díaz, Ximena Eugenia and Hola. *Modos de inserción de la mujer de los sectores populares en el trabajo informal urbano.* Santiago: Centro de Estudios de la Mujer, 1985.

Donoso, Isabel. "Human Rights and Popular Organizations." *Popular Culture in Chile.* Eds. Kenneth Aman and Cristián Parker. Boulder, CO: Westview Press, 1991.

Drake, Paul W. and Iván Jaksić. "Introduction." *The Struggle for Democracy in Chile, 1982–1990.* Eds. Paul W. Drake and Iván Jaksić. Lincoln: University of Nebraska Press, 1991. 1–21.

Drake, Paul. "The Labor Movement in Chile: From Popular Unity to Concertación." *Revista de Ciencia Política* 23 (2003): 148–158.

Drogus, Carol Ann and Hannah Stewart-Gambino. *Activist Faith: Grassroots Women in Democratic Brazil and Chile.* University Park, PA: Pennsylvania State University Press, 2005.

Dubet, François, Eugenio Tironi, Vicente Espinoza, and Eduardo Valenzuela. *Pobladores. Luttes sociales et démocratie au Chili.* Paris: L'Harmattan, 1989.

Duneier, Mitchell. *Sidewalk.* New York: Farrar, Strauss, and Giroux, 1999.

Early, Evelyn. "Nest Eggs of Gold and Beans. Baladi Egyptian Women's Invisible Capital." *Middle Eastern Women and the Invisible Economy.* Ed. R. Lobban, Jr. Gainesville: University Press of Florida, 1998. 132–147.

Ensalaco, Mark. *Chile Under Pinochet: Recovering the Truth.* Philadelphia: University of Pennsylvania Press, 2000.

Escobar, Antonio and Sonia Alvarez. Eds. *The Making of Social Movements in Latin America.* Boulder, CO: Westview, 1992.

Eteng, Inya. "Models in Popular Organization and Participation." *Nigeria: Renewal from the Roots?* Eds. Adabayo Adebeji, Onigu Otite, et al. London and Atlantic Highlands, NJ: Zed Books, 1997. 20–32.

Evrigenis, Ioannis. *Fear of Enemies and Collective Action.* Cambridge: Cambridge University Press, 2008.

Feijoó, María del Carmen. "The Challenge of Constructing Civilian Peace: Women and Democracy in Argentina." *The Women's Movement in Latin America: Feminism and the Transition to Democracy.* Ed. Jane Jaquette. Boston, MA: Unwin Hyman, 1989.

Feijoó, María del Carmen. "Women Confronting the Crisis: Two Case Studies from Greater Buenos Aires." *Emergences. Women's Struggles for Livelihood in Latin America.* Eds. John Friedmann, Rebecca Abers, and Lilian Autler. Los Angeles, CA: UCLA Latin American Center Publications, 1996. 31–46.

Fink, Christina. *Living Silence in Burma. Surviving under Military Rule.* Chiang Mai: Silkworm Books, and London: Zed Books, 2009.

Finn, Janet. "La Victoria: Claiming Memory, History, and Justice in a Santiago Población." *Journal of Community Practice* 13 (2006): 9–31.

Fisher, Jo. *Out of the Shadows. Women, Resistance and Politics in South America.* London: Latin American Bureau, 1993.

Flam, Helena. "Anger in Repressive Regimes: A Footnote to Domination and the Arts of Resistance by James Scott." *European Journal of Social Theory* 7.2 (2004): 171–188.

Foweraker, Joe. "Grassroots Movements and Political Activism in Chile and Brazil." *Widening Democracy. Citizens and Participatory Schemes in Brazil and Chile.* Eds. Patricio Silva and Herwig Cleuren. Leiden and Boston, MA: Brill, 2009. 27–25.

Franceschet, Susan. *Women and Politics in Chile.* Boulder, CO: Lynne Rienner Publishers, 2005.

Franco, Jean. "Killing Priests, Nuns, Women, and Children." *On Signs.* Ed. Marshall Blouskey. Baltimore, MD: Johns Hopkins University Press, 1985. 414–442.

Freedom House. "Freedom in the World 2008: Global Freedom in Retreat." Press release, January 16. www.freedomhouse.org/template.cfm?page=70&release=612. 2008.

Freire, Paulo. *Pedagogy of the Oppressed.* New York: Continuum, 2000.

Gallardo, Bernarda. "El redescubrimiento del character social del hambre: las ollas comunes." *Espacio y poder: Los pobladores.* Eds. Jorge Chateau, Bernarda Gallardo, Eduardo Morales, Carlos Piña, Hernan Pozo, Sergio Rojas, Daniela Sanchez, and Teresa Valdés. Santiago: FLACSO, 1987. 171–202.

Garretón, Manuel Antonio. "Popular Mobilization and the Military Regime in Chile: The Complexities of the Invisible Transition." *Power and Popular Protest. Latin American Social Movements.* Ed. Susan Eckstein. Berkeley: University of California Press, 2001. 259–277.

Gibbs, M., R. Lindner, and A. Fisher. "Reliability of Two Survey Techniques: A Study of Innovation Discovery by Farmers." *Statistician* 35.4 (1986): 429–439.

Gilbert, Alan. "Extreme Thinking about Slums and Slum Dwellers: A Critique," *SAIS Review* 29.1 (2009): 35–48.

Glaser, Barney and Strauss, Anselm. *The Discovery of Grounded Theory: Strategies for Qualitative Research*. Chicago: Aldine Pub. Co., 1967.

Goffman, Erving. *Gender Advertisements*. London and Basingstoke: Macmillan, 1979.

Goldstein, Donna. *Laughter Out of Place*. Berkeley: University of California Press, 2003.

González de la Rocha, Mercedes. *The Resources of Poverty, Women and Survival in a Mexican City.* Oxford: Blackwells, 1994.

Green, Linda. *Fear as a Way of Life: Mayan Widows in Rural Guatemala.* New York: Columbia University Press, 1999.

Green, Linda. "Living in a State of Fear." *Violence in War and Peace.* Eds. Nancy Scheper-Hughes and Philippe Bourgois. Malden, MA: Blackwell Publishing, 2004. 186–195.

Hao, Yan. "Emerging Urban Poverty in China." *Emerging Urban Poverty and Social Safety Net in East Asia.* Ed. Yunling Zhang. Beijing: World Affairs Press, 2005. 311–362.

Hardy, Clarissa. *Hambre + Dignidad = Ollas Comunes.* Santiago: Programa de Economía del Trabajo, 1986.

Hardy, Clarissa. *Organizarse para vivir: Pobreza urbana y organización popular*, Santiago: Programa de Economía del Trabajo, 1987.

Harper, Douglas. *Good Company.* Chicago: University of Chicago Press, 1982.

Harper, Douglas. *Working Knowledge. Skill and Community in a Small Shop.* Berkeley: University of California Press, 1987.

Harper, Douglas. *Changing Works. Visions of a Lost Agriculture.* Chicago and London: University of Chicago Press, 2001.

Harper, Douglas. *The Italian Way: Food and Social Life.* Chicago: University of Chicago Press, 2009.

Herreros Vivar, Jesus. *Escuché sus gritos.* Santiago: Mosquito Editores, 1991.

Hintze, Susana. 1989. *Estrategias alimentarias de sobrevivencia: Un estudio de caso en el Gran Buenos Aires.* Buenos Aires: CEAL, 1991.

Hipsher, Patricia. "Democratic Transitions and Social Movement Outcomes: The Chilean Shantytown Dwellers' Movement in Comparative Perspective." *From Contention to Democracy.* Eds. Marco G. Giugni, Doug McAdam, and Charles Tilly. Lanham, MD: Rowman & Littlefield, 1998. 149–168.

Hoodfar, H. "Women in Cairo's (In)visible Economy." *Middle Eastern Women and the Invisible Economy.* Ed. R. Lobban, Jr. Gainesville: University Press of Florida, 1998.

Hurst, William. "Mass Frames and Worker Protest." *Popular Protest in China.* Ed. Kevin O'Brien. Cambridge, MA and London: Harvard University Press, 2008. 71–87.

Jansana, Loreto. *El pan nuestro: Las organizaciones populares para el consume.* Santiago: PET. Colección Experiencias Populares, 1989.

Jaquette, Jane. *The Women's Movement in Latin America: Feminism and the Transition to Democracy.* Boston, MA: Unwin Hyman, 1989.

Jelin, Elizabeth. *Los nuevos movimientos sociales.* Bueno Aires: Centro Editor de América Latina, 1985.

Jelin, Elizabeth. *Ciudadanía e identidad: Las mujeres en los movimientos sociales latinoamericanos.* Geneva: UNRISD, 1987.

Kahneman, Daniel and Alan Krueger. "Developments in the Measurement of Subjective Well-Being." *Journal of Economic Perspectives* 20.1 (2006): 3–24.

Kaplan, Temma. "Community and Resistance in Women's Political Cultures." *Dialectical Anthropology* 15 (1990): 259–267.

Kazemi, Farhad. *Poverty and Revolution in Iran. The Migrant Poor, Urban Marginality and Politics.* New York: New York University Press, 1980.

Klein, Marcus. "Old Habits in New Clothes, or Clientelism, Patronage and the Unión Demócrata Independiente." *Widening Democracy. Citizens and Participatory Schemes in Brazil and Chile.* Eds. Patricio Silva and Herwig Cleuren. Leiden and Boston, MA: Brill, 2009. 295–314.

Krueger, Alan and David Schkade. "The Reliability of Subjective Well-Being Measures." Working Paper 13027, National Bureau of Economic Research, Cambridge, MA, 2007.

Lee, Ching Kwan. "Pathways of labor insurgency." *Chinese Society, Change, Conflict and Resistance*, 2nd edition. Eds. E. Perry and M. Selden. London and New York: Routledge, 2003.

Lehmann, Carolyn. "Bread and Roses: Women Who Live Poverty." Eds. Kenneth Aman and Cristián Parker. *Popular Culture in Chile.* Boulder, CO: Westview Press, 1991. 113–124.

Leiva, Fernando I. and James Petras. "Chile's Poor in the Struggle for Democracy." *Latin American Perspectives* 13 (1986): 5–25.

Levine, Daniel and Scott Mainwaring. "Religion and Popular Protest in Latin America: Contrasting Experiences." *Power and Popular Protest. Latin American Social Movements.* Ed. Susan Eckstein. Berkeley: University of California Press, 1989. 203–240.

Lind, Amy. "Power, Gender, and Development: Popular Women's Organizations and the Politics of Needs in Ecuador." *The Making of Social Movements in Latin America: Identity, Strategy, and Democracy.* Eds. Arturo and Sonia Alvarez Escobar. Boulder, CO: Westview, 1992.

Lind, Amy. "Gender, Development, and Urban Social Change: Women's Community Action in Global Cities." *World Development* 25.8 (1997): 1205–1224.

Lomnitz, Larissa. *Cómo sobreviven los marginados.* Mexico, D.F.: Siglo XXI, 1975.

Lowden, Pamela. *Moral Opposition to Authoritarian Rule in Chile, 1973–90.* Houndmills: Macmillan Press, 1996.

Lozano, Claudio and Roberto Feletti. "Convertibilidad y desempleo, crisis ocupacional en la Argentina." *Aportes para el estado y la administración gubernamental* 3.5 (1996): 155–188.

Machado, Leda. "The Participation of Women in the Health Movement of Jardim Nordeste, in the Eastern Zone of São Paulo, Brazil: 1976–1985." *Social Movements in Latin America. The Experience of Peasants, Workers, Women, the Urban Poor, and the Middle Sectors.* Ed. Jorge. Domínguez. New York and London: Garland Publishing, 1994. 259–276.

Mainwaring, Scott and Eduardo Viola. "New Social Movements, Political Culture, and Democracy: Brazil and Argentina in the 1980s." *Social Movements in Latin America. The Experience of Peasants, Workers, Women, the Urban Poor, and the Middle Sectors.* Ed. Jorge Domínguez. New York: Garland Publishing, 1994.

Makinwa, P. Kofo and A.O. Ozo, eds. *The Urban Poor in Nigeria*. Ibadan: Evans Brothers, 1987.

Matshalaga, Needy. *The Gender Dimensions of Urban Poverty. The Case of Dzivareskwa*. Cambridge, MA and London: Institute of Development Studies, University of Zimbabwe, 1997.

Meikle, Sheilah. "The Urban Context and Poor People." *Urban Livelihoods. A People-Centred Approach to Reducing Poverty*. Eds. Carole Rakodi and Tony Lloyd-Jones. London and Sterling, VA: Earthscan Publications, 2002. 37–51.

Molyneux, Maxine and Shahra Razavi, eds. *Gender Justice, Development, and Rights*. Oxford: Oxford University Press, 2002.

Montecinos, Veronica. "Neoliberal Economic Reforms and Women in Chile." *Women in the Age of Economic Transformation. Gender Impact of Reforms in Post-Socialist and Developing Countries*. Eds. N. Aslanbeigui, S. Pressman, and G. Summerfield. London and New York: Routledge, 1994. 160–177.

Montecinos, Veronica. "Economic Reforms, Social Policy, and the Family Economy in Chile." *Review of Social Economy* 55 (1997): 224–234.

Morales, Eduardo, Susana Levy, Adolfo Aldunate, and Sergio Rojas, eds. *Erradicados en el regimen militar. Una evaluación de los beneficiarios*. Documento de Trabajo no. 448, Santiago: FLACSO, 1990.

Morales, Eduardo and Sergio Rojas. "Relocalización socio-espacial de la pobreza. Política estatal y presión popular, 1979–1985." *Espacio y Poder. Los Pobladores*. Eds. Jorge Chateau, Bernarda Gallardo, Eduardo Morales, Carlos Piña, Hernan Pozo, Sergio Rojas, Daniela Sanchez, and Teresa Valdés. Santiago: FLACSO, 1987. 75–122.

Moser, Caroline. "Adjustment From Below: Low-Income Women, Time and the Triple Role in Guayaquil, Ecuador." *Women and Adjustment Policies in the Third World*. Eds. Haleh Afshar and Carolyne Dennis. Basingstoke and London: Macmillan, 1992.

Moser, Caroline. *Confronting Crisis: A Comparative Study of Household Responses in Four Poor Urban Communities*. Environmentally Sustainable Development Studies and Monograph Series No. 8. Washington, DC: The World Bank, 1996.

Narayan, Deepa, Robert Chambers, Meera K. Shah, and Patti Petesch, eds. *Voices of the Poor. Crying Out for Change*. Oxford: Oxford University Press, 2000.

Narayan, Deepa, Lant Pritchett, and Soumya Kapoor. *Moving Out of Poverty. Vol. 2. Success from the Bottom Up*. Washington, DC: The International Bank for Reconstruction and Development/The World Bank, 2009.

Navia, Patricio. "Top-Down and Bottom-Up Democracy in Chile under Bachelet." *Widening Democracy. Citizens and Participatory Schemes in Brazil and Chile*. Eds. Patricio Silva and Herwig Cleuren. Leiden and Boston, MA: Brill, 2009. 315–228.

Neuhouser, Kevin. "I am the Man and Woman in This House: Brazilian *Jeito* and the Strategic Framing of Motherhood in a Poor, Urban Community." *Identity Work in Social Movements*. Eds. Jo Reger, Daniel J. Myers, and Rachel L. Einwohner. Minneapolis and London: University of Minnesota Press, 2008.

Olavarría, Margot. "Builders of the City: Pobladores and the Territorialization of Class Identity in Chile." *Lost in the Long Transition. Struggles for Social Justice in Neoliberal Chile*. Ed. William Alexander. Lanham, MD: Lexington Books, 2009. 153–168.

Oppenheim, Lois H. *Politics of Chile: Socialism, Authoritarianism, and Market Democracy*, 3rd edition. Boulder, CO: Westview Press, 2007.

Oxhorn, Philip. "The Popular Sector Response to an Authoritarian Regime. Shantytown Organizations Since the Military Coup." *Latin American Perspectives* 18 (1991): 66–91.

Oxhorn, Philip. *Organizing Civil Society: The Popular Sectors and the Struggle for Democracy in Chile.* University Park, PA: Pennsylvania State University Press, 1995.

Palestro, Sandra. *Mujeres en movimiento 1973–1989.* Santiago: FLACSO, 1991.

Paley, Julia. *Marketing Democracy. Power and Social Movements in Post-Dictatorship Chile.* Berkeley: University of California Press, 2001.

Pei, Minxin. "Rights and Resistance. The Changing Contexts of the Dissident Movement." *Chinese Society, Change, Conflict and Resistance*, 2nd edition. Eds. Elizabeth Perry and Mark Selden. London and New York: Routledge, 2003. 23–46.

Perry, Elizabeth and Mark Selden. "Introduction. Reform and Resistance in Contemporary China." *Chinese Society, Change, Conflict and Resistance*, 2nd edition. Eds. Elizabeth Perry and Mark Selden. London and New York: Routledge, 2003. 1–22.

Policzer, Pablo. "Human Rights Violations Beyond the State." *Journal of Human Rights* 5.2 (2006): 215–233.

Policzer, Pablo. *The Rise and Fall of Repression in Chile.* Notre Dame, IN: University of Notre Dame Press, 2009.

Politzer, Patricia. *Fear in Chile: Lives under Pinochet.* Trans. Diane Wachtell. New York: Pantheon Books, 2001.

Posner, Paul. "Local Democracy and Popular Participation in Chile and Brazil." *Widening Democracy. Citizens and Participatory Schemes in Brazil and Chile.* Eds. Patricio Silva and Herwig Cleuren. Leiden and Boston, MA: Brill, 2009. 47–74.

Potts, Deborah. "The Impact of Structural Adjustment on Welfare and Livelihoods: An Assessment by People in Harare, Zimbabwe." *Urban Poverty in Africa.* Eds. Sue Jones and Nici Nelson. London: Intermediate Technology Publications, 1999. 36–48.

Puryear, Jeffrey. *Thinking Politics: Intellectuals and Democracy in Chile, 1973–1988,* Baltimore, MD: The John Hopkins University Press, 1994.

Qureshi, Lubna. *Nixon, Kissinger, and Allende: U.S. Involvement in the 1973 Coup in Chile.* Lanham, MD: Lexington Books, 2009.

Raczynski, Dagmar and Claudia Serrano. "La Cesantía: impacto sobre la mujer y familia popular." *Colección Estudios Cieplan* 14 (1984): 61–97.

Raczynski, Dagmar and Claudia Serrano. *Vivir la Pobreza. Testimonios de mujeres.* Santiago: CIEPLAN, 1985.

Raczynski, Dagmar and Claudia Serrano. "Abriendo el debate: Descentralización del Estado, mujeres y políticas socials." *Políticas sociales, mujeres y gobierno local.* Eds. Dagmar Raczynski and Claudia Serrano. Santiago: CIEPLAN, 1992.

Raczynski, Dagmar and Pilar Romaguera. "Chile: Poverty, Adjustment and Social Policies in the 1980s." *Confronting the Challenge of Poverty and Inequality in Latin America.* Ed. Nora Lustig. Washington, DC: The Brookings Institution, 1995. 275–333.

Ramirez, Apolonia. Renacer en Conchalí. Sindicato de trabajadores independientes. Santiago: PET, 1988.

Razeto, Luis and Programa de Economía del Trabajo et al. *Las organizaciones económicas populares.* Santiago: PET, 1983.

Razeto, Luis and Programa de Economía del Trabajo et al. *Las organizaciones económicas populares, 1973–1990.* Santiago: PET, 1990.

Richards, Patricia. *Pobladoras, Indígenas, and the State: Conflict Over Women's Rights in Chile*. New Brunswick, NJ: Rutgers University Press, 2004.

Roberts, Kenneth. "From the Barricades to the Ballot Box: Redemocratization and Political Realignment in the Chilean Left." *Politics and Society* 23 (1995): 495–519.

Ruiz-Tagle, Jaime and Roberto Urmeneta. *Los Trabajadores del Programa de Empleo Mínimo*. Santiago: PET and Academia de Humanismo Cristiano, 1984.

Sabatini, Francisco. *Barrio y participación: mujeres pobladoras de Santiago*. Santiago: Ediciones Sur, 1995.

Salman, Ton. *The Diffident Movement. Disintegration, Ingenuity and Resistance of the Chilean Pobladores, 1973–1990*. Amsterdam: Thela Publishers, 1997.

Scheper-Hughes, Nancy. *Death Without Weeping: The Violence of Everyday Life in Brazil*. Berkeley: University of California Press, 1992.

Scheper-Hughes, Nancy and Philippe Bourgois, eds. *Violence in War and Peace. An Anthology*. Malden, MA: Blackwell Publishing, 2004.

Schild, Veronica. "Recasting 'Popular' Movements. Gender and Political Learning in Neighborhood Organizations in Chile." *Latin American Perspectives* 21 (1994): 59–82.

Schkolnik, Mariana and Berta Teitelboim. *Pobreza y Desempleo en Poblaciones. La otra cara del modelo neoliberal*. Santiago: PET, 1988.

Schneider, Cathy. "Mobilization at the Grassroots. Shantytowns and Resistance in Authoritarian Chile." *Latin American Perspectives* 18 (1991): 92–112.

Schneider, Cathy. *Shantytown Protest in Pinochet's Chile*. Philadelphia: Temple University Press, 1995.

Schneider, Cathy. "Violence, Identity and Spaces of Contention in Chile, Argentina and Colombia." *Social Research* 67 (2000): 773–802.

Scott, James. *Weapons of the Weak: Everyday Forms of Peasant Resistance*. New Haven, CT: Yale University Press, 1985.

Scott, James. *Domination and the Arts of Resistance*. New Haven, CT and London: Yale University Press, 1990.

Sepúlveda, Emma. *We, Chile. Personal Testimonies of the Chilean Arpilleristas*. Falls Church, VA: Azul Editions, 1996.

Serrano, Claudia. "Mujeres: Sobreviviencia y cambio cultural." *Chile en el umbral de los noventa*. Ed. Jaime Gazmuri. Santiago: Editorial Planeta Chilena, 1988. 95–112.

Shami, Seteney. "Domesticity Reconfigured: Women in Squatter Areas of Amman." *Organizing Women: Formal and Informal Women's Groups in the Middle East*. Eds. Dawn Chatty and Annika Rabo. Oxford: Berg, 1997: 81–89.

Siapno, Jacqueline. "Gender, Nationalism, and the Ambiguity of Female Agency in Aceh, Indonesia, and East Timor." *Frontline Feminisms. Women, War, and Resistance*. Eds. Marguerite Waller and Jennifer Rycenga. New York: Garland Publishing, 2000. 275–295.

Sigmund, Paul. *The Overthrow of Allende and the Politics of Chile, 1964–1976*, Pittsburgh, PA: University of Pittsburgh Press, 1977.

Sigmund, Paul. "Revolution, Counterrevolution, and the Catholic Church in Chile." *The Annals of the American Academy of Political and Social Science* 483 (1986): 25–35.

Silva, Eduardo. "The Political Economy of Chile's Regime Transition: From Radical to 'Pragmatic' Neo-liberal Policies." *The Struggle for Democracy in Chile, 1982–1990*. Eds. Paul W. Drake and Iván Jaksić. Lincoln: University of Nebraska Press, 1991. 98–127.

Silva, Patricio and Herwig Cleuren. "Assessing Participatory Democracy in Brazil and Chile: an Introduction." *Widening Democracy. Citizens and Participatory Schemes in Brazil and Chile.* Eds. Patricio Silva and Herwig Cleuren. Leiden and Boston, MA: Brill, 2009. 1–23.

Simone, AbdouMalig. "People as Infrastructure: Intersecting Fragments in Johannesburg." *Public Culture* 16.3 (2004): 407–429.

Skidmore, Monique. *Karaoke Fascism. Burma and the Politics of Fear.* Philadelphia: University of Pennsylvania Press, 2004.

Smith, Brian. *The Church and Politics in Chile.* Princeton, NJ: Princeton University Press, 1982.

Solinger, Dorothy. "The Floating Population in the Cities. Markets, Migration, and the Prospects for Citizenship." *China Off Center. Mapping the Margins of the Middle Kingdom.* Eds. Susan Blum and Lionel Jensen. Honolulu: University of Hawai'i Press, 2002. 273–290.

Solinger, Dorothy. "The New Crowd of the Dispossessed. The Shift of the Urban Proletariat from Master to Mendicant." *State and Society in 21st-Century China.* Eds. Hays Gries and Susan Rosen. New York: RoutledgeCurzon, 2004. 50–66.

Sorensen, Kristin. *Media, Memory, and Human Rights in Chile.* New York: Palgrave Macmillan, 2009.

Stokes, Susan. "Politics and Latin America's Urban Poor: Reflections from a Lima Shantytown." *Social Movements in Latin America. The Experience of Peasants, Workers, Women, the Urban Poor, and the Middle Sectors.* Ed. Jorge Domínguez. New York and London: Garland Publishing, 1994. 355–382.

Sur Profesionales. *Hechos Urbanos* 47 (November 1985).

Taller de Lavandería, Taller de Accion cultural. *Lavando la esperanza.* Santiago: Taller de Acción Cultural, 1984.

Tarrow, Sidney. "Prologue: The New Contentious Politics in China: Poor and Blank or Rich and Complex?" *Popular Protest in China.* Ed. Kevin O'Brien. Cambridge, MA and London: Harvard University Press, 2008. 1–10.

Taussig, Michael. *Shamanism, Colonialism, and the Wild Man.* Chicago, IL and London: University of Chicago Press, 1987.

Teitelboim, Berta, ed. *Serie de indicadores económico sociales. Indicadores económicos y sociales, series anuales 1960–1989.* Santiago: Programa de Economía del Trabajo, 1990.

Tilly, Charles. *Why?* Princeton, NJ: Princeton Univeristy Press, 2006.

Tironi, Eugenio. "Pobladores e integración social." *Proposiciones* 14 (1987): 64–84.

Tripp, Aili Mari. *Women and Politics in Uganda.* Madison: University of Wisconsin Press, 2000.

Turner, Terisa and M.O. Oshare. "Women's Uprisings Against the Nigerian Oil Industry in the 1980s." *Arise Ye Mighty People! Gender, Class and Race in Popular Struggles.* Eds. Terisa Turner and Bryan Ferguson. New Jersey: Africa World Press, 1994. 123–160.

United Nations Human Settlements Program (UN-HABITAT). *The Challenge of Slums: Global Report on Human Development.* London and Sterling, VA: Earthscan, 2003.

Valdés, Teresa. *Las mujeres y la dictadura military en Chile.* Santiago: FLACSO, 1987.

Valdés, Teresa. "Being Female and Poor: A Double Oppression." Eds. Kenneth Aman and Cristián Parker. *Popular Culture in Chile.* Boulder, CO: Westview Press, 1991. 97–112.

Valdés, Teresa and Marisa Weinstein. *Mujeres que Sueñan: Las organizaciones de pobladores en Chile: 1973–1989.* Santiago: FLACSO, 1993.

Valdés, Teresa. *De lo social a lo politico. La acción de las mujeres latinoamericanas.* Santiago: LOM Ediciones, 2000.

Valenzuela, Arturo. "The Military in Power: The Consolidation of One-Man Rule." *The Struggle for Democracy in Chile, 1982–1990.* Eds. Paul W. Drake and Iván Jaksić. Lincoln: University of Nebraska Press, 1991. 21–73.

Valenzuela, Eduardo. *La rebelión de los jóvenes: un estudio sobre anomía social.* Santiago: Ediciones SUR, 1984.

Valenzuela, María Elena. "The Evolving Roles of Women under Military Rule." *The Struggle for Democracy in Chile 1982–1990.* Eds. Paul W. Drake and Iván Jaksić. Lincoln: University of Nebraska Press, 1991. 161–187.

Van der Winden, Bob, Alexia Gambito, et al., eds. *A Family of the Musseque: Survival and Development in Postwar Angola.* Oxford: WorldView Publishing, 1996.

Vargas Llosa, Mario. *El lenguaje de la passion.* Madrid: Ediciones El País Grupo Santillana, 2001.

Velasco, B. "Sexualidad y marginación en mujeres jóvenes." *De Juventud: Revista de Estudios e Investigaciones* 20 (1986): 217–223.

Vergara, Pilar. *Políticas hacia la extrema pobreza en Chile 1973–1988,* Santiago: FLACSO, 1990.

Vicaría de la Solidaridad. *Solidaridad* 22 (April 18–29 1986). Santiago: Arzobispado de Santiago.

Vicaría de la Solidaridad. *Vicaría de la Solidaridad: Historia de su trabajo social.* Santiago: Ediciones Paulinas, 1991.

Waller, Marguerite and Jennifer Rycenga. *Frontline Feminisms: Women, War, and Resistance.* New York: Garland Publishing, 2000.

Weinstein, Eugenia and Elizabeth Lira. "La Tortura." *Trauma, duelo y reparación: Una experiencia de trabajo psicosocial en Chile.* Eds. Eugenia Weinstein, Elizabeth Lira, María Eugenia Rojas, et al. Santiago: FASIC and Editorial Interamericana, 1987. 33–94.

Weston, Timothy. "The Iron Man Weeps. Joblessness and Political Legitimacy in the Chinese Rust Belt." Eds. Peter Hays Gries and Stanley Rosen. *State and Society in 21st-Century China.* New York: RoutledgeCurzon, 2004. 67–86.

Withey, Stephen. "Reliability of Recall of Income." *Public Opinion Quarterly* 18.2 (1954): 197–204.

Wright, Thomas C. and Rody Oñate, eds. *Flight from Chile: Voices of Exile.* Trans. Irene B. Hodgson. Albuquerque: University of New Mexico Press, 1998.

Zheng, Wang. "Gender, Employment and Women's Resistance." *Chinese Society, Change, Conflict and Resistance,* 2nd edition. Eds. Elizabeth Perry and Mark Selden. London and New York: Routledge, 2003. 158–182.

Index